EXPLORING
CULTURE & GENDER
THROUGH
FILM

revised preliminary edition

EDITED BY **CHRISTIAN S. HAMMONS**
University of Colorado—Boulder

cognella
academic publishing

Bassim Hamadeh, CEO and Publisher
Michael Simpson, Vice President of Acquisitions
Jamie Giganti, Senior Managing Editor
Miguel Macias, Graphic Designer
Mark Combes, Senior Field Acquisitions Editor
Sean Adams, Project Editor
Luiz Ferreira, Senior Licensing Specialist
Rachel Singer, Interior Designer

First published in the United States of America in 2016 by Cognella, Inc.

Trademark Notice: Product or corporate names may be trademarks or registered trademarks, and are used only for identification and explanation without intent to infringe.

Cover image copyright © Depositphotos/M_Prusaczyk.

Printed in the United States of America

ISBN: 978-1-63189-575-3 (pbk) / 978-1-63189-576-0 (br)

www.cognella.com   800-200-3908

Contents

On the Phenomenon of Bullshit Jobs

BY DAVID GRAEBER

In the year 1930, John Maynard Keynes predicted that technology would have advanced sufficiently by century's end that countries like Great Britain or the United States would achieve a 15-hour work week. There's every reason to believe he was right. In technological terms, we are quite capable of this. And yet it didn't happen. Instead, technology has been marshaled, if anything, to figure out ways to make us all work more. In order to achieve this, jobs have had to be created that are, effectively, pointless. Huge swathes of people, in Europe and North America in particular, spend their entire working lives performing tasks they secretly believe do not really need to be performed. The moral and spiritual damage that comes from this situation is profound. It is a scar across our collective soul. Yet virtually no one talks about it.

Why did Keynes' promised utopia—still being eagerly awaited in the '60s—never materialise? The standard line today is that he didn't figure in the massive increase in consumerism. Given the choice between less hours and more toys and pleasures, we've collectively chosen the latter. This presents a nice morality tale, but even a moment's reflection shows it can't really be true. Yes, we have witnessed the creation of an endless variety of new jobs and industries since the '20s, but very few have anything to do with the production and distribution of sushi, iPhones, or fancy sneakers.

So what are these new jobs, precisely? A recent report comparing employment in the US between 1910 and 2000 gives us a clear picture (and I note, one pretty much exactly echoed in the UK). Over the course of the last century, the number

Figure 1–1.

of workers employed as domestic servants, in industry, and in the farm sector has collapsed dramatically. At the same time, "professional, managerial, clerical, sales, and service workers" tripled, growing "from one-quarter to three-quarters of total employment." In other words, productive jobs have, just as predicted, been largely automated away (even if you count industrial workers globally, including the toiling masses in India and China, such workers are still not nearly so large a percentage of the world population as they used to be).

But rather than allowing a massive reduction of working hours to free the world's population to pursue their own projects, pleasures, visions, and ideas, we have seen the ballooning not even so much of the "service" sector as of the administrative sector, up to and including the creation of whole new industries like financial services or telemarketing, or the unprecedented expansion of sectors like corporate law, academic and health administration, human resources, and public relations. And these numbers do not even reflect on all those people whose job is to provide administrative, technical, or security support for these industries, or for that matter the whole host of ancillary industries (dog-washers, all-night pizza deliverymen) that only exist because everyone else is spending so much of their time working in all the other ones.

These are what I propose to call "bullshit jobs."

It's as if someone were out there making up pointless jobs just for the sake of keeping us all working. And here, precisely, lies the mystery. In capitalism, this is exactly what is not supposed to happen.

Sure, in the old inefficient socialist states like the Soviet Union, where employment was considered both a right and a sacred duty, the system made up as many jobs as they had to (this is why in Soviet department stores it took three clerks to sell a piece of meat). But, of course, this is the very sort of problem market competition is supposed to fix. According to economic theory, at least, the last thing a profit-seeking firm is going to do is shell out money to workers they don't really need to employ. Still, somehow, it happens.

While corporations may engage in ruthless downsizing, the layoffs and speed-ups invariably fall on that class of people who are actually making, moving, fixing and maintaining things; through some strange alchemy no one can quite explain, the number of salaried paper-pushers ultimately seems to expand, and more and more employees find themselves, not unlike Soviet workers actually, working 40 or even 50 hour weeks on paper, but effectively working 15 hours just as Keynes predicted, since the rest of their time is spent organising or attending motivational seminars, updating their facebook profiles or downloading TV box-sets.

The answer clearly isn't economic: it's moral and political. The ruling class has figured out that a happy and productive population with free time on their hands is a mortal danger (think of what started to happen when this even began to be approximated in the '60s). And, on the other hand, the feeling that work is a moral value in itself, and that anyone not willing to submit themselves to some kind of intense work discipline for most of their waking hours deserves nothing, is extraordinarily convenient for them.

Once, when contemplating the apparently endless growth of administrative responsibilities in British academic departments, I came up with one possible vision of hell. Hell is a collection of individuals who are spending the bulk of their time working on a task they don't like and are not especially good at. Say they were hired because they were excellent cabinet-makers, and then discover they are expected to spend a great deal of their time frying fish. Neither does the task really need to be done—at least, there's only a very limited number of fish that need to be fried. Yet somehow, they all become so obsessed with resentment at the thought that some of their co-workers might be spending more time making cabinets, and not doing their fair share of the fish-frying responsibilities, that before long there's endless piles of useless badly cooked fish piling up all over the workshop and it's all that anyone really does.

I think this is actually a pretty accurate description of the moral dynamics of our own economy.

* * * * *

Now, I realise any such argument is going to run into immediate objections: "who are you to say what jobs are really 'necessary'? What's necessary anyway? You're an anthropology professor, what's the 'need' for that?" (And indeed a lot of tabloid readers would take the existence of my job as the very definition of wasteful social expenditure.) And on one level, this is obviously true. There can be no objective measure of social value.

I would not presume to tell someone who is convinced they are making a meaningful contribution to the world that, really, they are not. But what about those people who are themselves convinced their jobs are meaningless? Not long ago I got back in touch with a school friend who I hadn't seen since I was 12. I was amazed to discover that in the interim, he had become first a poet, then the front man in an indie rock band. I'd heard some of his songs on the radio having no idea the singer was someone I actually knew. He was obviously brilliant, innovative, and his work had unquestionably brightened and improved the lives of people all over the world. Yet, after a couple of unsuccessful albums, he'd lost his contract, and plagued with debts and a newborn daughter, ended up, as he put it, "taking the default choice of so many directionless folk: law school." Now he's a corporate lawyer working in a prominent New York firm. He was the first to admit that his job was utterly meaningless, contributed nothing to the world, and, in his own estimation, should not really exist.

There's a lot of questions one could ask here, starting with, what does it say about our society that it seems to generate an extremely limited demand for talented poet-musicians, but an apparently infinite demand for specialists in corporate law? (Answer: if 1% of the population controls most of the disposable wealth, what we call "the market" reflects what they think is useful or important, not anybody else.) But even more, it shows that most people in these jobs are ultimately aware of it. In fact, I'm not sure I've ever met a corporate lawyer who didn't think their job was bullshit. The same goes for almost all the new industries outlined above. There is a whole class of salaried professionals that, should you meet them at parties and admit that you do something that might be considered interesting (an anthropologist, for example), will want to avoid even discussing their line of work entirely. Give them a few drinks, and they will launch into tirades about how pointless and stupid their job really is.

This is a profound psychological violence here. How can one even begin to speak of dignity in labour when one secretly feels one's job should not exist? How can it not create a sense of deep rage and resentment. Yet it is the peculiar genius of our society that its rulers have figured out a way, as in the case of the fish-fryers, to ensure that rage is directed precisely against those who actually do get to do meaningful work. For instance: in our society, there seems a general rule that, the more obviously one's work benefits other people, the less one is likely to be paid for it. Again, an objective measure is hard to find, but one easy way to get a sense is to ask: what would happen were this entire class of people to simply disappear? Say what you like about nurses, garbage collectors, or mechanics, it's obvious that were they to vanish in a puff of smoke, the results would be immediate and catastrophic. A world without teachers or dock-workers would soon be in trouble, and even one without science fiction writers or ska musicians would clearly be a lesser place. It's not entirely clear how humanity would suffer were all private equity CEOs, lobbyists, PR researchers, actuaries, telemarketers, bailiffs or legal consultants to similarly vanish. (Many suspect it might markedly improve.) Yet apart from a handful of well-touted exceptions (doctors), the rule holds surprisingly well.

Even more perverse, there seems to be a broad sense that this is the way things should be. This is one of the secret strengths of right-wing populism. You can see it when tabloids whip up resentment against tube workers for paralysing London during contract disputes: the very fact that tube workers can paralyse London shows that their work is actually necessary, but this seems to be precisely what annoys people. It's even clearer in the US, where Republicans have had remarkable success mobiliz-ing resentment against school teachers, or auto workers (and not, significantly, against the school administrators or auto industry managers who actually cause the problems) for their supposedly bloated wages and benefits. It's as if they are being told "but you get to teach children! Or make cars! You get to have real jobs! And on top of that you have the nerve to also expect middle-class pensions and health care?"

If someone had designed a work regime perfectly suited to maintaining the power of finance capital, it's hard to see how they could have done a better job. Real, productive workers are relentlessly squeezed and exploited. The remainder are divided between a terrorised stratum of the—universally reviled—unemployed and a larger stratum who are basically paid to do nothing, in positions designed to make them identify with the perspectives and sensibilities of the ruling class (managers, administrators, etc)—and particularly its financial avatars—but, at the same time, foster a simmering resentment against anyone whose work has clear and undeniable social value. Clearly, the system was never consciously designed. It emerged from almost a century of trial and error. But it is the only explanation for why, despite our technological capacities, we are not all working 3–4 hour days.

Shakespeare in the Bush

BY LAURA BOHANNA

Just before I left Oxford for the Tiv in West Africa, conversation turned to the season at Stratford. "You Americans," said a friend, "often have difficulty with Shakespeare. He was, after all, a very English poet, and one can easily misinterpret the universal by misunderstanding the particular."

I protested that human nature is pretty much the same the whole world over; at least the general plot and motivation of the greater tragedies would always be clear—everywhere—although some details of custom might have to be explained and difficulties of translation might produce other slight changes. To end an argument we could not conclude, my friend gave me a copy of *Hamlet* to study in the African bush: it would, he hoped, lift my mind above its primitive surroundings, and possibly I might, by prolonged meditation, achieve the grace of correct interpretation.

It was my second field trip to that African tribe, and I thought myself ready to live in one of its remote sections—an area difficult to cross even on foot. I eventually settled on the hillock of a very knowledgeable old man, the head of a homestead of some hundred and forty people, all of whom were either his close relatives or their wives and children. Like the other elders of the vicinity, the old man spent most of his time performing ceremonies seldom seen these days in the more accessible parts of the tribe. I was delighted. Soon there would be three months of enforced isolation and leisure, between the harvest that takes place just before the rising

Laura Bohannan, "Shakespeare in the Bush," *Natural History*, vol. 75, no. 7, pp. 28-33.

of the swamps and the clearing of new farms when the water goes down. Then, I thought, they would have even more time to perform ceremonies and explain them to me.

I was quite mistaken. Most of the ceremonies demanded the presence of elders from several homesteads. As the swamps rose, the old men found it too difficult to walk from one homestead to the next, and the ceremonies gradually ceased. As the swamps rose even higher, all activities but one came to an end. The women brewed beer from maize and millet. Men, women, and children sat on their hillocks and drank it.

People began to drink at dawn. By midmorning the whole homestead was singing, dancing, and drumming. When it rained, people had to sit inside their huts: there they drank and sang or they drank and told stories. In any case, by noon or before, I either had to join the party or retire to my own hut and my books. "One does not discuss serious matters when there is beer. Come, drink with us." Since I lacked their capacity for the thick native beer, I spent more and more time with *Hamlet*. Before the end of the second month, grace descended on me. I was quite sure that *Hamlet* had only one possible interpretation, and that one universally obvious.

Early every morning, in the hope of having some serious talk before the beer party, I used to call on the old man at his reception hut—a circle of posts supporting a thatched roof above a low mud wall to keep out wind and rain. One day I crawled through the low doorway and found most of the men of the homestead sitting huddled in their ragged cloths on stools, low plank beds, and reclining chairs, warming themselves against the chill of the rain around a smoky fire. In the center were three pots of beer. The party had started.

The old man greeted me cordially. "Sit down and drink." I accepted a large calabash full of beer, poured some into a small drinking gourd, and tossed it down. Then I poured some more into the same gourd for the man second in seniority to my host before I handed my calabash over to a young man for further distribution. Important people shouldn't ladle beer themselves.

"It is better like this," the old man said, looking at me approvingly and plucking at the thatch that had caught in my hair. "You should sit and drink with us more often. Your servants tell me that when you are not with us, you sit inside your hut looking at a paper."

The old man was acquainted with four kinds of "papers": tax receipts, bride price receipts, court fee receipts, and letters. The messenger who brought him letters from the chief used them mainly as a badge of office, for he always knew what was in them and told the old man. Personal letters for the few who had relatives in the government or mission stations were kept until someone went to a large market where there was a letter writer and reader. Since my arrival, letters were brought to me to be read. A few men also brought me bride price receipts, privately, with requests to change the figures to a higher sum. I found moral arguments were of no avail, since in-laws are fair game, and the technical hazards of forgery difficult to explain to an illiterate people. I did not wish them to think me silly enough to look at any such papers for days on end, and I hastily explained that my "paper" was one of the "things of long ago" of my country.

"Ah," said the old man. "Tell us." I protested that I was not a storyteller. Storytelling is a skilled art among them; their standards are high, and the audiences critical—and vocal in their criticism. I protested in vain. This morning they wanted to hear a story while they drank. They threatened to tell me no more stories until I told them one of mine. Finally, the old man promised that no one would criticize my style, "for we know you are struggling with our language." "But," put in one of the elders, "you must explain what we do not understand, as we do when we tell you our stories." Realizing that here was my chance to prove *Hamlet* universally intelligible, I agreed.

The old man handed me some more beer to help me on with my storytelling. Men filled their long wooden pipes and knocked coals from the fire to place in the pipe bowls; then, puffing contentedly, they sat back to listen. I began in the proper style, "Not yesterday, not yesterday, but long ago, a thing occurred. One night three men were keeping watch outside the homestead of the great chief, when suddenly they saw the former chief approach them."

"Why was he no longer their chief?"

"He was dead," I explained. "That is why they were troubled and afraid when they saw him."

"Impossible," began one of the elders, handing his pipe on to his neighbor, who interrupted, "Of course it wasn't the dead chief. It was an omen sent by a witch. Go on."

Slightly shaken, I continued. "One of these three was a man who knew things"—the closest translation for scholar, but unfortunately it also meant witch. The second elder looked triumphantly at the first. "So he spoke to the dead chief saying, 'Tell us what we must do so you may rest in your grave,' but the dead chief did not answer. He vanished, and they could see him no more. Then the man who knew things—his name was Horatio—said this event was the affair of the dead chief's son, Hamlet."

There was a general shaking of heads round the circle. "Had the dead chief no living brothers? Or was this son the chief?"

"No," I replied. "That is, he had one living brother who became the chief when the elder brother died."

The old men muttered: such omens were matters for chiefs and elders, not for youngsters; no good could come of going behind a chief's back; clearly Horatio was not a man who knew things.

"Yes, he was," I insisted, shooing a chicken away from my beer. "In our country the son is next to the father. The dead chief's younger brother had become the great chief. He had also married his elder brother's widow only about a month after the funeral."

"He did well," the old man beamed and announced to the others, "I told you that if we knew more about Europeans, we would find they really were very like us. In our country also," he added to me, "the younger brother marries the elder brother's widow and becomes the father of his children. Now, if your uncle, who married your widowed mother, is your father's full brother, then he will be a real father to you. Did Hamlet's father and uncle have one mother?"

His question barely penetrated my mind; I was too upset and thrown too far off-balance by having one of the most important elements of *Hamlet* knocked straight out of the picture. Rather uncertainly I said that I thought they had the same mother, but I wasn't sure—the story didn't say. The old man told me severely that these genealogical details made all the difference and that when I got home I must ask the elders about it. He shouted out the door to one of his younger wives to bring his goatskin bag.

Determined to save what I could of the mother motif, I took a deep breath and began again. "The son Hamlet was very sad because his mother had married again so quickly. There was no need for her to do so, and it is our custom for a widow not to go to her next husband until she has mourned for two years."

"Two years is too long," objected the wife, who had appeared with the old man's battered goatskin bag. "Who will hoe your farms for you while you have no husband?"

"Hamlet," I retorted, without thinking, "was old enough to hoe his mother's farms himself. There was no need for her to remarry." No one looked convinced. I gave up. "His mother and the great chief told Hamlet not to be sad, for the great chief himself would be a father to Hamlet. Furthermore, Hamlet would be the next chief: therefore he must stay to learn the things of a chief. Hamlet agreed to remain, and all the rest went off to drink beer."

While I paused, perplexed at how to render Hamlet's disgusted soliloquy to an audience convinced that Claudius and Gertrude had behaved in the best possible manner, one of the younger men asked me who had married the other wives of the dead chief.

"He had no other wives," I told him.

"But a chief must have many wives! How else can he brew beer and prepare food for all his guests?"

I said firmly that in our country even chiefs had only one wife, that they had servants to do their work, and that they paid them from tax money.

It was better, they returned, for a chief to have many wives and sons who would help him hoe his farms and feed his people; then everyone loved the chief who gave much and took nothing—taxes were a bad thing.

I agreed with the last comment, but for the rest fell back on their favorite way of fobbing off my questions: "That is the way it is done, so that is how we do it."

I decided to skip the soliloquy. Even if Claudius was here thought quite right to marry his brother's widow, there remained the poison motif, and I knew they would disapprove of fratricide. More hopefully I resumed, "That night Hamlet kept watch with the three who had seen his dead father. The dead chief again appeared, and although the others were afraid, Hamlet followed his dead father off to one side. When they were alone, Hamlet's dead father spoke."

"Omens can't talk!" The old man was emphatic.

"Hamlet's dead father wasn't an omen. Seeing him might have been an omen, but he was not." My audience looked as confused as I sounded. "It was Hamlet's dead father. It was a thing we call a 'ghost.'" I had to use the English word, for unlike many of the neighboring tribes, these people didn't believe in the survival after death of any individuating part of the personality.

"What is a 'ghost?' An omen?"

"No, a 'ghost' is someone who is dead but who walks around and can talk, and people can hear him and see him but not touch him."

They objected. "One can touch zombis."

"No, no! It was not a dead body the witches had animated to sacrifice and eat. No one else made Hamlet's dead father walk. He did it himself."

"Dead men can't walk," protested my audience as one man.

I was quite willing to compromise.

"A 'ghost' is the dead man's shadow."

But again they objected. "Dead men cast no shadows."

"They do in my country," I snapped.

The old man quelled the babble of disbelief that arose immediately and told me with that insincere, but courteous, agreement one extends to the fancies of the young, ignorant, and superstitious, "No doubt in your country the dead can also walk without being zombis." From the depths of his bag he produced a withered fragment of kola nut, bit off one end to show it wasn't poisoned, and handed me the rest as a peace offering.

"Anyhow," I resumed, "Hamlet's dead father said that his own brother, the one who became chief, had poisoned him. He wanted Hamlet to avenge him. Hamlet believed this in his heart, for he did not like his father's brother." I took another swallow of beer. "In the country of the great chief, living in the same homestead, for it was a very large one, was an important elder who was often with the chief to advise and help him. His name was Polonius. Hamlet was courting his daughter, but her father and her brother … [I cast hastily about for some tribal analogy] warned her not to let Hamlet visit her when she was alone on her farm, for he would be a great chief and so could not marry her."

"Why not?" asked the wife, who had settled down on the edge of the old man's chair. He frowned at her for asking stupid questions and growled, "They lived in the same homestead."

"That was not the reason," I informed them. "Polonius was a stranger who lived in the homestead because he helped the chief, not because he was a relative."

"Then why couldn't Hamlet marry her?"

"He could have," I explained, "but Polonius didn't think he would. After all, Hamlet was a man of great importance who ought to marry a chief's daughter, for in his country a man could have only one wife. Polonius was afraid that if Hamlet made love to his daughter, then no one else would give a high price for her."

"That might be true," remarked one of the shrewder elders, "but a chief's son would give his mistress's father enough presents and patronage to more than make up the difference. Polonius sounds like a fool to me."

"Many people think he was," I agreed. "Meanwhile Polonius sent his son Laertes off to Paris to learn the things of that country, for it was the homestead of a very great chief indeed. Because he was afraid that Laertes might waste a lot of money on beer and women and gambling, or get into trouble by fighting, he sent one of his servants to Paris secretly, to spy out what Laertes was doing. One day Hamlet came upon Polonius's daughter Ophelia. He behaved so oddly he frightened her. Indeed"—I was fumbling for words to express the dubious quality of Hamlet's madness—"the chief and many others had also noticed that when Hamlet talked one could understand the words but not what they meant. Many people thought that he had become mad." My audience suddenly became much more attentive. "The great chief wanted to know what was wrong with Hamlet, so he sent for two of Hamlet's age mates [school friends would have taken a long explanation] to talk to Hamlet and find out what troubled his heart. Hamlet, seeing that they had been bribed by the chief to betray him, told them nothing. Polonius, however, insisted that Hamlet was mad because he had been forbidden to see Ophelia, whom he loved."

"Why," inquired a bewildered voice, "should anyone bewitch Hamlet on that account?"

"Bewitch him?"

"Yes, only witchcraft can make anyone mad, unless, of course, one sees the beings that lurk in the forest."

I stopped being a storyteller and took out my notebook and demanded to be told more about these two causes of madness. Even while they spoke and I jotted notes, I tried to calculate the effect of this new factor on the plot. Hamlet had not been exposed to the beings that lurk in the forests. Only his relatives in the male line could bewitch him. Barring relatives not mentioned by Shakespeare, it had to be Claudius who was attempting to harm him. And, of course, it was.

For the moment I staved off questions by saying that the great chief also refused to believe that Hamlet was mad for the love of Ophelia and nothing else. "He was sure that something much more important was troubling Hamlet's heart."

"Now Hamlet's age mates," I continued, "had brought with them a famous storyteller. Hamlet decided to have this man tell the chief and all his homestead a story about a man who had poisoned his brother because he desired his brother's wife and wished to be chief himself. Hamlet was sure the great chief could not hear the story without making a sign if he was indeed guilty, and then he would discover whether his dead father had told him the truth."

The old man interrupted, with deep cunning, "Why should a father lie to his son?" he asked.

I hedged: "Hamlet wasn't sure that it really was his dead father." It was impossible to say anything, in that language, about devil-inspired visions.

"You mean," he said, "it actually was an omen, and he knew witches sometimes send false ones. Hamlet was a fool not to go to one skilled in reading omens and divining the truth in the first place. A man-who-sees-the-truth could have told him how his father died, if he really had been poisoned, and if there was witchcraft in it; then Hamlet could have called the elders to settle the matter."

The shrewd elder ventured to disagree. "Because his father's brother was a great chief, one-who-sees-the-truth might therefore have been afraid to tell it. I think it was for that reason that a friend of Hamlet's father—a witch and an elder—sent an omen so his friend's son would know. Was the omen true?"

"Yes," I said, abandoning ghosts and the devil; a witch-sent omen it would have to be. "It was true, for when the storyteller was telling his tale before all the homestead, the great chief rose in fear. Afraid that Hamlet knew his secret he planned to have him killed."

The stage set of the next bit presented some difficulties of translation. I began cautiously. "The great chief told Hamlet's mother to find out from her son what he knew. But because a woman's children are always first in her heart, he had the important elder Polonius hide behind a cloth that hung against the wall of Hamlet's mother's sleeping hut. Hamlet started to scold his mother for what she had done."

There was a shocked murmur from everyone. A man should never scold his mother.

"She called out in fear, and Polonius moved behind the cloth. Shouting, 'A rat!' Hamlet took his machete and slashed through the cloth." I paused for dramatic effect. "He had killed Polonius."

The old men looked at each other in supreme disgust. "That Polonius truly was a fool and a man who knew nothing! What child would not know enough to shout, 'It's me!'" With a pang, I remembered that these people are ardent hunters, always armed with bow, arrow, and machete; at the first rustle in the grass an arrow is aimed and ready, and the hunter shouts "Game!" If no human voice answers immediately, the arrow speeds on its way. Like a good hunter, Hamlet had shouted, "A rat!"

I rushed in to save Polonius's reputation. "Polonius did speak. Hamlet heard him. But he thought it was the chief and wished to kill him to avenge his father. He had meant to kill him earlier that evening...." I broke down, unable to describe to these pagans, who had no belief in individual afterlife, the difference between dying at one's prayers and dying "unhousell'd, disappointed, unaneled."

This time I had shocked my audience seriously. "For a man to raise his hand against his father's brother and the one who has become his father—that is a terrible thing. The elders ought to let such a man be bewitched."

I nibbled at my kola nut in some perplexity, then pointed out that after all the man had killed Hamlet's father.

"No," pronounced the old man, speaking less to me than to the young men sitting behind the elders. "If your father's brother has killed your father, you must appeal to your father's age mates: *they* may avenge him. No man may use violence against his senior relatives." Another thought struck him. "But if his father's brother had indeed been wicked enough to bewitch Hamlet and make him mad that would be a good story indeed, for it would be his fault that Hamlet, being mad, no longer had any sense and thus was ready to kill his father's brother."

There was a murmur of applause. Hamlet was again a good story to them, but it no longer seemed quite the same story to me. As I thought over the coming complications of plot and motive, I lost courage and decided to skim over dangerous ground quickly.

"The great chief," I went on, "was not sorry that Hamlet had killed Polonius. It gave him a reason to send Hamlet away, with his two treacherous age mates, with letters to a chief of a far country, saying that Hamlet should be killed. But Hamlet changed the writing on their papers, so that the chief killed his age mates instead." I encountered a reproachful glare from one of the men whom I had told undetectable forgery was not merely immoral but beyond human skill. I looked the other way.

"Before Hamlet could return, Laertes came back for his father's funeral. The great chief told him Hamlet had killed Polonius. Laertes swore to kill Hamlet because of this, and because his sister Ophelia, hearing her father had been killed by the man she loved, went mad and drowned in the river."

"Have you already forgotten what we told you?" The old man was reproachful. "One cannot take vengeance on a madman; Hamlet killed Polonius in his madness. As for the girl, she not only went mad, she was drowned. Only witches can make people drown. Water itself can't hurt anything. It is merely something one drinks and bathes in."

I began to get cross. "If you don't like the story, I'll stop."

The old man made soothing noises and himself poured me some more beer. "You tell the story well, and we are listening. But it is clear that the elders of your country have never told you what the story really means. No, don't interrupt! We believe you when you say your marriage customs are different, or your clothes and weapons. But people are the same everywhere; therefore, there are always witches and it is we, the elders, who know how witches work. We told you it was the great chief who wished to kill Hamlet, and now your own words have proved us right. Who were Ophelia's male relatives?"

"There were only her father and her brother." Hamlet was clearly out of my hands.

"There must have been many more; this also you must ask of your elders when you get back to your country. From what you tell us, since Polonius was dead, it must have been Laertes who killed Ophelia, although I do not see the reason for it."

We had emptied one pot of beer, and the old men argued the point with slightly tipsy interest. Finally one of them demanded of me, "What did the servant of Polonius say on his return?"

With difficulty I recollected Reynaldo and his mission. "I don't think he did return before Polonius was killed."

"Listen," said the elder, "and I will tell you how it was and how your story will go, then you may tell me if I am right. Polonius knew his son would get into trouble, and so he did. He had many fines to pay for fighting, and debts from gambling. But he had only two ways of getting money quickly. One was to marry off his sister at once, but it is difficult to find a man who will marry a woman desired by the son of a chief. For if the chief's heir commits adultery with your wife, what can you do? Only a fool calls a case against a man who will someday be his judge. Therefore Laertes had to take the second way: he killed his sister by witchcraft, drowning her so he could secretly sell her body to the witches."

I raised an objection. "They found her body and buried it. Indeed Laertes jumped into the grave to see his sister once more—so, you see, the body was truly there. Hamlet, who had just come back, jumped in after him."

"What did I tell you?" The elder appealed to the others. "Laertes was up to no good with his sister's body. Hamlet prevented him, because the chief's heir, like a chief, does not wish any other man to grow rich and powerful. Laertes would be angry, because he would have killed his sister without benefit to himself. In our country he would try to kill Hamlet for that reason. Is this not what happened?"

"More or less," I admitted. "When the great chief found Hamlet was still alive, he encouraged Laertes to try to kill Hamlet and arranged a fight with machetes between them. In the fight both the young men were wounded to death. Hamlet's mother drank the poisoned beer that the chief meant for Hamlet in case he won the fight. When he saw his mother die of poison, Hamlet, dying, managed to kill his father's brother with his machete."

"You see, I was right!" exclaimed the elder.

"That was a very good story," added the old man, "and you told it with very few mistakes." There was just one more error, at the very end. The poison Hamlet's mother drank was obviously meant for the survivor of the fight, whichever it was. If Laertes had won, the great chief would have poisoned him, for no one would know that he arranged Hamlet's death. Then, too, he need not fear Laertes' witchcraft; it takes a strong heart to kill one's only sister by witchcraft.

"Sometime," concluded the old man, gathering his ragged toga about him, "you must tell us some more stories of your country. We, who are elders, will instruct you in their true meaning, so that when you return to your own land your elders will see that you have not been sitting in the bush, but among those who know things and who have taught you wisdom."

Eating Christmas in the Kalahari

BY RICHARD B. LEE

The Ju/'hoan knowledge of Christmas is third-hand. The London Missionary Society brought the holiday to the southern Tswana tribes in the early nineteenth century. Later, native catechists spread the idea far and wide among the Bantu-speaking pastoralists, even in the remotest corners of the Kalahari Desert. The Ju idea of the Christmas story, stripped to its essentials, is "praise the birth of White Man's god-chief"; what keeps their interest in the holiday high is the Tswana-Herero custom of slaughtering an ox for their Ju neighbors as an annual goodwill gesture. Since the 1930s, part of the San's annual round of activities has included a December congregation at the cattle-posts for trading, marriage brokering, and several days of trance-dance feasting at which the local Tswana headman is host.

As a social anthropologist working with the Ju/'hoansi, I found that the Christmas ox custom suited my purposes. I had come to the Kalahari to study the hunting and gathering subsistence economy of the Ju/'hoansi, and to accomplish this it was essential not to provide them with food, share my own food, or interfere in any way with their food-gathering activities. While liberal handouts of tobacco and medical supplies were appreciated, they were scarcely adequate to erase the glaring disparity in wealth between the anthropologist, who maintained a two-month inventory of canned goods, and the Ju, who rarely had a day's supply of food on hand. My approach, while paying off in terms of data, left me open to frequent accusations of stinginess and hard-heartedness. By their lights, I was a miser.

Richard B. Lee, "Eating Christmas in the Kalahari," *Natural History*, vol. 78, no. 10, pp. 14-22, 60-63. Copyright © 1969 by Natural History Magazine, Inc. Reprinted with permission.

The Christmas ox was to be my way of saying thank you for the cooperation of the past year; and since it was to be our last Christmas in the field, I was determined to slaughter the largest, meatiest ox that money could buy, insuring that the feast and trance dance would be a success.

Through December I kept my eyes open at the wells as the cattle were brought down for watering. Several animals were offered, but none had quite the grossness that I had in mind. Then, 10 days before the holiday, a Herero friend led an ox of astonishing size and mass up to our camp. It was solid black, stood five feet high at the shoulder, had a five-foot span of horns, and must have weighed 1200 pounds on the hoof. Food consumption calculations are my specialty, and I quickly figured that bones and viscera aside, there was enough meat—at least four pounds—for every man, woman, and child of the 150 Ju/'hoansi in the vicinity of /Xai/xai who were expected at the feast.

Having found the right animal at last, I paid the Herero £20 ($56) and asked him to keep the beast with his herd until Christmas Day. The next morning word spread among the people that the big solid-black one was the ox chosen by-Tontah for the Christmas feast. That afternoon I received the first delegation. Ben!a, an outspoken 60-year-old mother of five, came to the point slowly.

"Where were you planning to eat Christmas?"

"Right here at /Xai/ xai," I replied.

"Alone or with others?"

"I expect to invite all the people to eat Christmas with me."

"Eat what?"

"I have purchased Yehave's black ox, and I am going to slaughter and cook it."

"That's what we were told at the well but refused to believe it until we heard it from yourself."

"Well, it's the black one," I replied expansively, although wondering what she was driving at.

"Oh, no!" Ben!a groaned, turning to her group. "They were right." Turning back to me she asked, "Do you expect us to eat that bag of bones?"

"Bag of bones! It's the biggest ox at /Xai/ xai."

"Big, yes, but old. And thin. Everybody knows there's no meat on that old ox. What did you expect us to eat off it, the horns?"

Everybody chuckled at Ben!a's one-liner as they walked away, but all I could manage was a weak grin.

That evening it was the turn of the young men. They came to sit at our evening fire. /Gaugo, about my age, spoke to me man-to-man.

"/Tontah, you have always been square with us. What has happened to change your heart? That sack of guts and bones of Yehave's will hardly feed one camp, let alone all the !Kung around /Xai/ xai." And he proceeded to enumerate the seven camps in the /Xai/xai vicinity, family by family. "Perhaps you have forgotten that we are not few, but many. Or are you too blind to tell the difference between a proper cow and an old wreck? That ox is thin to the point of death."

"Look, you guys," I retorted, "that is a beautiful animal, and I'm sure you will eat it with pleasure at Christmas."

"Of course we will eat it; it's food. But it won't fill us up to the point where we will have enough strength to dance. We will eat and go home to bed with stomachs rumbling."

That night as we turned in, I asked my wife Nancy: "What did you think of the black ox?"

"It looked enormous to me. Why?"

"Well, about eight different people have told me I got gypped; that the ox is nothing but bones."

"What's the angle?" Nancy asked. "Did they have a better one to sell?"

"No, they just said that it was going to be a grim Christmas because there won't be enough meat to go around. Maybe I'll get an independent judge to look at the beast in the morning."

Bright and early, Halingisi, a Tswana cattle-owner, appeared at our camp. But before I could ask him to give me his opinion on Yehave's black ox, he gave me the eye signal that indicated a confidential chat. We left the camp and sat down.

"/Tontah, I'm surprised at you; you've lived here for three years and still haven't learned anything about cattle."

"But what else can a person do but choose the biggest, strongest animal one can find?" I retorted.

"Look, just because an animal is big doesn't mean that it has plenty of meat on it. The black one was a beauty when it was younger, but now it is thin to the point of death."

"Well, I've already bought it. What can I do at this stage?"

"Bought it already? I thought you were just considering it. Well, you'll have to kill and serve it, I suppose. But don't expect much of a dance to follow."

My spirits dropped rapidly. I could believe that Ben!a and /Gaugo just might be putting me on about the black ox, but Halingisi seemed to be an impartial critic. I went around that day feeling as though I had bought a lemon of a used car.

In the afternoon it was ≠Tomazho's turn. ≠Tomazho is a fine hunter, a top trance performer, and one of my most reliable informants. He approached the subject of the Christmas cow as part of my continuing education.

"My friend, the way it is with us Ju/'hoansi," he began, "is that we love meat. And even more than that, we love fat. When we hunt we always search for the fat ones, the ones dripping with layers of white fat: fat that turns into a clear, thick oil in the cooking pot, fat that slides down your gullet, fills your stomach and gives you a roaring diarrhea," he rhapsodized.

"So, feeling as we do," he continued, "it gives us pain to be served such a scrawny thing as Yehave's black ox. It is big, yes, and no doubt its giant bones are good for soup, but fat is what we really crave, and so we will eat Christmas this year with a heavy heart."

The prospect of a gloomy Christmas now had me worried, so I asked ≠Tomazho what I could do about it.

"Look for a fat one, a young one … smaller, but fat. Fat enough to make us //gom ('evacuate the bowels'); then we will be happy."

My suspicions were aroused when ≠Tomazho said that he happened to know of a young, fat, barren cow that the owner was willing to part with. Was ≠Tomazho working on commission, I wondered? But

I dispelled this unworthy thought when we approached the Herero owner of the cow in question and found that he had decided not to sell.

The scrawny wreck of a Christmas ox now became the talk of the /Xai/ xai waterhole and was the first news told to the outlying groups as they began to come in from the bush for the feast. What finally convinced me that real trouble might be brewing was the visit from /N!au, an old conservative with a reputation for fierceness. His nickname meant "spear" and referred to an incident 30 years ago in which he had speared a man to death. He had an intense manner; fixing me with his eyes, he said in clipped tones:

"I have only just heard about the black ox today, or else I would have come here earlier. /Tontah, do you honestly think you can serve meat like that to people and avoid a fight?" He paused, letting the implications sink in. "I don't mean fight you, /Tontah; you are a White man. I mean a fight between Ju/'hoansi. There are many fierce ones here, and with such a small quantity of meat to distribute, how can you give everybody a fair share? Someone is sure to accuse another of taking too much or hogging all the choice pieces. Then you will see what happens when some go hungry while others eat."

The possibility of at least, a serious argument struck me as all too real. I had witnessed the tension that surrounds the distribution of meat from a kuku or gemsbok kill, and had documented many arguments that sprang up from a real or imagined slight in meat distribution. The owners of a kill may spend up to two hours arranging and rearranging the piles of meat under the gaze of a circle of recipients before handing them out. And I also knew that the Christmas feast at /Xai/ xai would be bringing together groups that had feuded in the past.

Convinced now of the gravity of the situation, I went in earnest to search for a second cow; but all my inquiries failed to turn one up.

The Christmas feast, was evidently going to be a disaster, and the incessant complaints about the meagerness of the ox had already taken the fun out of it for me. Moreover, I was getting bored with the wisecracks, and after losing my temper a few times, I resolved to serve the beast anyway. If the meat fell short, the hell with it. In the Ju/'hoan idiom, I announced to all who would listen:

"I am a poor man and blind. If I have chosen one that is too old and too thin, we will eat it anyway and see if there is enough meat there to quiet the rumbling of our stomachs."

On hearing this speech, Ben!a offered me a rare word of comfort. "It's thin," she said philosophically, "but the bones will make a good soup."

At dawn Christmas morning, instinct told me to turn over the butchering and cooking to a friend and take off with Nancy and spend Christmas alone in the bush. But curiosity kept me from retreating. I wanted to see what such a scrawny ox looked like on butchering, and if there was going to be a fight, I wanted to catch every word of it. Anthropologists are incurable that way.

The great beast was driven up to our dancing ground, and a shot in the forehead dropped it in its tracks. Then, freshly cut branches were heaped around the fallen carcass to receive the meat. Ten men volunteered to help with the cutting. I asked /Gaugo to make the breast bone cut. This cut, which begins the butchering process for most large game, offers easy access for removal of the viscera. But it also allows the hunter to spot-check the amount of fat on the animal. A fat game animal carries a white layer up to an inch thick on the chest, while in a thin one, the knife will quickly cut to bone. All eyes fixed on his hand as /Gaugo, dwarfed by the great carcass, knelt to the breast. The first cut opened a pool of solid white in the black skin. The second and third cut widened and deepened the creamy white. Still no bone. It was pure fat; it must have been two inches thick.

"Hey /Gau," I burst out, "that ox is loaded with fat. What's this about the ox being too thin to bother eating? Are you out of your mind?"

"Fat?" /Gau shot back, "You call that fat? This wreck is thin, sick, dead!" And he broke out laughing. So did everyone else. They rolled on the ground, paralyzed with laughter. Everybody laughed except me; I was thinking.

I ran back to the tent and burst in just as Nancy was getting up. "Hey, the black ox. It's fat as hell! They were kidding about it being too thin to eat. It was a joke or something. A put-on. Everyone is really delighted with it!"

"Some joke," my wife replied. "It was so funny that you were ready to pack up and leave /Xai/ xai."

If it had indeed been a joke, it had been an extraordinarily convincing one, and tinged, I thought, with more than a touch of malice, as many jokes are. Nevertheless, that it was a joke lifted my spirits considerably, and I returned to the butchering site, where the shape of the ox was rapidly disappearing under the axes and knives of the butchers. The atmosphere had become festive. Grinning broadly, their arms covered with blood well past the elbow, men packed chunks of meat into the big cast-iron cooking pots, 50 pounds to the load, and muttered and chuckled all the while about the thinness and worthlessness of the animal and /Tontah's poor judgment.

We danced and ate that ox for two days and two nights; we cooked and distributed 14 potfuls of meat, and no one went home hungry and no fights broke out.

But the "joke" stayed in my mind. I had a growing feeling that something important had happened in my relationship with the Ju/'hoansi, and that the clue lay in the meaning of the joke. Several days later, when most of the people had dispersed back to the bush camps, I raised the question with Hakekgose, a Tswana man who had grown up among the Ju, married a Ju girl, and who probably knew their culture better than any other non-Ju/'hoan.

"With us Whites," I began, "Christmas is supposed to be the day of friendship and brotherly love. What I can't figure out is why the Ju went to such lengths to criticize and belittle the ox I had bought for the feast. The animal was perfectly good, and their jokes and wisecracks practically ruined the holiday for me."

"So it really did bother you," said Hakekgose. "Well, that's the way they always talk. When I take my rifle and go hunting with them, if I miss, they laugh at me for the rest of the day. But if I hit and bring one down, it's no better. To them, the kill is always too small or too old or too thin; and as we sit down on the kill site to cook and eat the liver, they keep grumbling, even with their mouths full of meat. They say things like, 'Oh this is awful! What a worthless animal! Whatever made me think that this Tswana rascal could hunt!'"

"Is this the way outsiders are treated?" I asked.

"No, it is their custom; they talk that way to each other too. Go and ask them."

/Gaugo had been one of the most enthusiastic in making me feel bad about the merit of the Christmas ox. I sought him out first.

"Why did you tell me the black ox was worthless, when you could see that it was loaded with fat and meat?"

"It is our way," he said, smiling. "We always like to fool people about that. Say there is a Ju/'hoan who has been hunting. He must not come home and announce like a braggart, 'I have killed a big one in the bush!' He must first sit down in silence until I or someone else comes up to his fire and asks, 'What did you see today?' He replies quietly, 'Ah, I'm no good for hunting. I saw nothing at all [pause] just a little tiny one.' Then I smile to myself," /Gaugo continued, "because I know he has killed something big.

"In the morning we make up a party of four or five people to cut up and carry the meat back to the camp. When we arrive at the kill we examine it and cry out, 'You mean to say you have dragged us all the way out here in order to make us cart home your pile of bones? Oh, if I had known it was this thin I wouldn't have come.' Another one pipes up, 'People, to think I gave up a nice day in the shade for this. At home we may be hungry, but at least we have nice cool water to drink.' If the horns are big, someone says, 'Did you think that somehow you were going to boil down the horns for soup?'

"To all this you must respond in kind. 'I agree,' you say, 'this one is not worth the effort; let's just cook the liver for strength and leave the rest for the hyenas. It is not too late to hunt today, and even a duiker or a steenbok would be better than this mess.'

"Then you set to work nevertheless, butcher the animal, carry the meat back to the camp, and everyone eats," /Gaugo concluded.

Things were beginning to make sense. Next, I went to ≠Tomazho. He corroborated /Gaugo's story of the obligatory insults over a kill and added a few details of his own.

"But," I asked, "why insult a man after he has gone to all that trouble to track and kill an animal and when he is going to share the meat with you so that your children will have something to eat?"

"Arrogance," was his cryptic answer.

"Arrogance?"

"Yes, when a young man kills much meat he comes to think of himself as a chief or a big man, and he thinks of the rest of us as his servants or inferiors. We can't accept this, We refuse one who boasts, for someday his pride will make him kill somebody. So we always speak of his meat as worthless. This way we cool his heart and make him gentle."

"But why didn't you tell me this before?" I asked ≠Tomazho with some heat.

"Because you never asked me," said ≠Tomazho, echoing the refrain that has come to haunt every field ethnographer.

The pieces now fell into place. I had known for a long time that in situations of social conflict with Ju/'hoansi I held all the cards. I was the only source of tobacco in a thousand square miles, and I was not incapable of cutting an individual off for non-cooperation. Though my boycott never lasted longer than a few days, it was an indication of my strength. People resented my presence at the waterhole, yet simultaneously dreaded my leaving, In short, I was a perfect target for the charge of arrogance and for the Ju tactic of enforcing humility.

I had been taught an object lesson by the Ju/'hoansi; it had come from an unexpected corner and had hurt me in a vulnerable area. For the big black ox was to be the one totally generous, unstinting act of my year at /Xai/ xai, and I was quite unprepared for the reaction I received.

As I read it, their message was this: There are no totally generous acts. All "acts" have an element of calculation. One black ox slaughtered at Christmas does not wipe out a year of careful manipulation of gifts given to serve your own ends. After all, to kill an animal and share the meat with people is really no more than Ju/'hoansi do for each other every day and with far less fanfare.

In the end, I had to admire how the Ju had played out the farce—collectively straight-faced to the end. Curiously, the episode reminded me of the *Good Soldier Schweik* and his marvelous encounters with authority. Like Schweik, the Ju/'hoansi had retained a thoroughgoing skepticism of good intentions. Was it this independence of spirit, I wondered, that had kept them culturally viable in the face of generations of contact with more powerful societies, both Black and White? The thought that the Ju/'hoansi were alive and well in the Kalahari was strangely comforting. Perhaps, armed with that independence and with their superb knowledge of their environment, they might yet survive the future.

The Uses of 'Ex-centricity'
Cool Reflections from Hot Places

BY JEAN COMAROFF

Inspired by District 9, a sci-fi movie set in South Africa, Jean Comaroff argues for the analytical power of estrangement and defamiliarisation, and the importance of ex-centric perspectives in any quest for critical self-understanding.

In the summer of 2009, movie-goers across the world were captivated by a surprising blockbuster, a relatively low-budget film from the Global South. As a bemused Mike Ryan wrote in *Starpulse Entertainment News*, *District 9*, which on the face of it was just another tired "Man Versus Scary Alien" story, had no business being a great picture, let alone an allegory of our time. This hot item arrived like a blast from somewhere else, from a peripheral place we seldom associate with the cultural cutting-edge. A giant space ship appears over Johannesburg, South Africa. Its sizeable, starving population is brought down to earth with the help of humanitarian sympathizers from across the globe. But the do-gooders lose interest, leaving the impoverished aliens to fend for themselves in an urban slum, exploited by organized crime and threatened by the xenophobia of their human neighbors, who refer to the crustacean-like strangers as "prawns." The drama begins when the state hires a private military corporation to relocate the aliens to a refugee camp beyond the city. Each is served with an eviction notice that seeks signed consent to his or her own dispossession.

Hailed by Lisa Schwartzbaum in *Entertainment Weekly* as "madly original, cheekily political, and altogether exciting", the film has garnered great praise for making a high-tech thriller speak poignantly of some of the paradoxes of our late modern world, a world of porous frontiers and abject refugees, of expansive but inconstant humanitarian sympathy; of anxieties about borders and strangers that grow in proportion to global integration. Sci-fi and action movie nerds have delighted in the film's many references to classics of the genre—from *Alien* and *Blade Runner* to *RoboCop* and *Terminator 2*. More serious minds, on the other hand, might accuse me of invoking something too trivial, too ephemeral for serious intellectual consideration. But I would argue that the film exemplifies an enduring feature of "enlightenment" in its broadest sense: the importance of estrangement from received wisdom and reigning pieties in the way we interrogate the human condition. Estrangement is a necessary component of the production of new, questioning insight into the familiar and the taken-for-granted. It is the cornerstone of critical thinking of all kinds.

> *Estrangement is a necessary component of the production of new, questioning insight into the familiar and the taken-for-granted.*

There have been many champions of alienation as a route to enlightenment. The Russian Formalists referred to it as "defamiliarization"; the dramatist, Bertold Brecht, Frederick Jameson reminds us, called it the "estrangement effect". As an orientation, it draws on a productive paradox at the heart of the concept of alienation itself: a simultaneous quality of dislocation and demystification, the kind of unsettling discrepancy that W.E.B. Du Bois dubbed "double consciousness," and that Edward Said saw as the positive effect of exile. It is this same illuminating displacement that anthropologists pursue in making sense of the meaning of social and cultural phenomena across the lines of radical difference in space and time.

The unsettling impact of *District 9*, then, stems from the fact that it estranges us in a double sense, offering "other worldly" insight of two distinct, but not unrelated kinds. The first is the critical dislocation of the extraterrestrial. The second the instructive disorientation that comes of looking at our own world from what, following Homi Bhabha, I would term an ex-centric location, a place beyond the traditional heartland of Euro-America.

> *the instructive disorientation that comes of looking at our own world from ... an ex-centric location, a place beyond the traditional heartland of Euro-America.*

Figure 4–1. Alien tripod illustration by Alvim Correa, from the 1906 French Edition of H.G. Wells' 'War of the Worlds'. Henrique Alvim Correa, War of the Worlds, 1906. Copyright in the Public Domain.

In its twin ex-centricities, *District 9* invites comparison with that classic work of alien fiction-as-critique, H.G. *Wells' War of the Worlds* (1898), about a Martian invasion of imperial London. In 1953, a movie version would relocate it to Los Angeles, center of a new kind of empire, that of global image production. Well's original aliens prefigured the hapless postcolonial "prawns" in several ways: they, too, had what Wells described as "Gorgon groups of tentacles," with which they gesticulated as they grunted in communication. But Wells was also writing in the shadow of Darwin. His aliens were less abject refugees than superior beings from what he termed a "cooler world." Possessed of highly evolved brains and bodies they viewed humans as an inferior, expendable species. Wells meant his tale not merely as a jolt to what Peter Fitting terms the "complacency of his contemporaries," but also as a commentary on the nature of colonial conquest. In it's opening pages, he notes that the Martian disdain for lowlier, more earth-bound forms of life could be likened to the wars of extermination waged by European invaders on peoples whom they judged racially inferior: the aboriginals of Tasmania, for example. This critique, clothed in extraterrestrial allegory, was one of the earliest, most unflinching denunciations of the violence of British imperialism. Sci-fi at its best, says Darko Suvin, veteran scholar of the genre, is about seeing what is hidden "yet [is] advancing upon us."

War of the Worlds was clairvoyant in another way relevant to my theme here. It was also a story of "first contact," of a consequential first meeting between humans and aliens. At the time of its writing, it invoked European voyages of discovery, and expanding colonial frontiers in Africa and India, where encounters with "others" provided the foil against which a distinctive sense of "Western" civilization took shape. This was also the era in which anthropology, the science of human being in the world, was first gaining recognition. In its founding years, the discipline focused chiefly on the comparative study of other, often radically different cultures, those at the margins of the great European empires. It set out to catalogue the broad range of human social and physical variation, with the aim, as Clifford Geertz would put it in *The Interpretation of Cultures*, of enlarging "the universe of human discourse." But its ex-centric method ensured it another, more subversive role: that of nudging the metropole into critical forms of *self*-discovery. By throwing a skeptical, relativizing light on the axiomatic truths and established institutions of the European heartland, it cast a shadow of doubt upon them, making clear that they were, in fact, particular to their time and place: that they were not the indisputable end-point of all social evolution, of the search for universal truth. In the manner of H.G. Wells, anthropologists gave graphic account of different ways of organizing human society or defining the value and the purposes of life. They challenged us to reflect—as alien visitors might—on our priorities, principles, and precepts, on the organization of our economic and educational systems, on our family lives, our modes of government and our health care.

Like *District 9* and *War of the Worlds*, in short, the ex-centric perspective of anthropology has long prompted us to see ourselves in defamiliarized light. A famous example speaks of another kind of alien in Africa, immortalized in the volume, *Witchcraft, Oracles and Magic among the Azande*, published by Edward Evans-Pritchard in 1937. This work explores the Zande faith in witches, raising questions about the ways in which unquestioned truths—paradigms, if you will—are maintained by communities of believers against the onslaught of doubt and disproof. Witchcraft provides an explanation for why it is that "bad things happen to good people." It attributes misfortune, be it illness or loss of wealth, to the ill-will or jealousy of others. Evans-Pritchard was concerned to explain how ideas so obviously fallacious to the European mind might retain plausibility among an otherwise canny and skeptical African people. The Azande, he insisted, reasoned from evidence in a fully empirical manner. But they did so in such a way as to protect their core assumptions from being refuted—this by a process of "secondary elaboration" that discounted evidence which undermined their entrenched assumptions.

the ex-centric perspective of anthropology has long prompted us to see ourselves in defamiliarized light

Evans-Pritchard's account of the triumph of African witches over disbelief was to have a signal impact on the manner in which philosophers came to think about Western thought itself. One, the Hungarian-British Michael Polanyi—note how many boundary-crossing scholars have themselves been aliens—found the account of Zande reasoning highly suggestive. He saw in it a model for the way in which "tacit awareness," the kind of knowledge that Pierre Bourdieu suggests "goes without saying because it comes without saying," is perpetuated in spite of counter-experience and disproof. His work anticipated Thomas Kuhn's *The Structure of Scientific Revolutions,* often named one of the most influential books of the late Twentieth Century. Kuhn famously posited that, in the everyday practice of "normal science," researchers tend to protect theoretical paradigms in which they have vested their faith by discounting as "mistakes" those data that seem to refute their hypothesis. They engage, in other words, in precisely the same forms of secondary elaboration as do the Zande in justifying the existence of witches.

If the Zande occult unsettled home-truths about the workings of empirical reason, the extra-terrestrials in *District 9* breach boundaries of a different sort. They raise questions about why it is that borders and aliens have become such an overriding preoccupation—not merely in ex-centric places, but everywhere nowadays. The United States, for instance, is famously a nation built by naturalizing strangers. Yet strangers have become an unnatural source of anxiety for Americans. The movie urges us to ask why, in an era that has seen the ever more global flow of goods, images, currency, and knowledge, the migration of human beings should be a matter of hyper-ambivalence; why international frontiers are such sensitive sites of disease about security; why they should be the object of contradictory efforts to ensure their openness, thus to facilitate the free passage of capital and commodities, and their closure, to protect national polities from the loss of scarce jobs and the unrestricted inflow of undesirable people; why, also, the meaning of identity, belonging, and citizenship should pose such urgent challenges in everyday life and in scholarship; why global efforts to protect the rights of refugees and asylum-seekers should exist alongside xenophobia and the abuse of aliens. It urges us to understand why it is that the treatment of strangers emerges as a yardstick of universal human rights and social justice. *District 9*, like anthropology, makes plain that what is happening most evidently in ex-centric places teaches us not about aliens, but about ourselves, about our world, about its contradictions. Those faraway places, in other worlds, pre-figure in many ways what we ourselves are becoming. More than this, the history of the modern world, sometimes stranger than the best science fiction, shows all too often how circumstances can make the most secure of us into aliens.

It urges us to understand why it is that the treatment of strangers emerges as a yardstick of universal human rights and social justice.

The point of ex-centric visions, in conclusion, is to make sense of the present and future of our world by means of the act of critical estrangement. In this respect, travel certainly broadens the mind; the many American students who join "study abroad" programs each year learn a great deal—most of all, about how others view the United States. But estrangement is ultimately an attitude, one that should permit us productively to 'go elsewhere' without actually leaving home: it enables creative doubleconsciousness, both detachment and engagement; it facilitates an ex-centric relationship with the world, both the world of others, and the world which we call our own.

Interpreting Gender and Sexuality

Approaches from Cultural Anthropology

BY ALMA GOTTLIEB

Does an American woman know what it means to be a Japanese woman just because the two are both women? What is a "woman"—is it any person capable of bearing and breastfeeding children, or something more? Something else?

Contemporary Western ideologies often assume the self-evident nature of the terms *woman* and *man, boy* and *girl*. In particular, sex and gender are frequently elided, so that the biological inevitability of the sex organs comes to stand for a perceived inevitability of social roles, expectations, and meanings associated with gender. Yet investigation of people's lives in other places and other times leads us to question this assumption. In this essay we explore how anthropology can help us to reimagine the meanings we often take for granted of seemingly obvious concepts related to *male* and *female.* We will focus on several key issues concerning gender and sexuality as they are conceived in a variety of cultural spaces. We begin by endeavoring to disentangle the two concepts of "gender" and "sexuality," which themselves are so often conflated. To do so, we will problematize the very nature of gender identity. We then explore the issue of power as it relates to constructions of gender and gender identity. We end by considering the cultural construction of sexual desire itself—that seeming bastion of biological urge that, like gender identity, may nevertheless be analyzed through a cultural lens.

GENDER AND IDENTITY

For many people, the most obvious thing to be said about gender is probably that there are two of them. By kindergarten, most schoolchildren know that people come, like the animals in Noah's ark, in pairs—boys and girls—and they easily classify both themselves and everyone else they know into this binary system. Adults do so too, often beginning with the tiniest people: on hearing of a new arrival to this life, the first question that friends and relatives ask is typically, "Is it a boy or a girl?" Having heard the answer, we may easily assume that we understand something of the baby and his or her future. At the immediate consumer level, we know what sort of present to buy for the newborn; at a less conscious level, we may have an idea of how to communicate with the creature. For example, if it's a baby girl, many Westerners are more likely to speak directly even to a newborn; with a baby boy, many Westerners are more likely to gently roughhouse. Put differently, the infant's sexual identity comes easily to stand for what we assume will become—or perhaps what already is—its gender identity. From there, it is a small step to imagine the child's identity overall.

But how much do we really know about someone once we have identified her or his gender? Much as we may assume otherwise, gender is not an inevitable predictor of a given person's life experience For one thing, the experience of gender is not the same from place to place, nor from time to time. Cultural variability reduces considerably the reliability of using gender to foretell the future texture of individual lives. Moreover, one's own experience of gender may change through one's life. Indeed, it is possible that one might experience both genders at different points in the life cycle. Gender identity itself is variable, both in time and in space. This leads us to what is perhaps the most counterintuitive question of all: Do all people everywhere classify each other into two and only two genders? This is an especially unsettling question—some might even think it absurd. After all, isn't the answer self-evident?

Many cultural anthropologists would say that it is not. What we "know"—or, rather, what we think we "know"—is very much shaped by what is available to us in the way of knowledge. Anthropology is constantly challenging the bounds of our knowledge by uncovering new ways of being, thinking, feeling that someone, somewhere, experiences. Just when we think we "know" what it means to be a man, another "man" comes along, say, serving milk and cookies at a children's party, or organizing a fiction readers' book club, or leaving work early to take a sick child to the doctor, or doing any number of other activities with which we may (stereo)typically associate women and not men, and we are forced to reconsider our definitions—however implicit—of "manhood."

Gender identity, then, is not as fixed, determinate, predictable as we may assume. Indeed, it is the supposition of this essay—and of many practitioners of cultural anthropology—that gender identity is so decisively shaped by cultural effort—the mandate of values, the whims of history, the weight of economy, the power of politics—that it may be a task doomed to failure to delineate where "nature" ends and "culture" begins. Our identity is shaped by our gender, yes—but only insofar as we acknowledge that our gender is, in turn, shaped by everything and everyone around us, and how those around us themselves interpret our gender, the expectations they bring with them to understanding our gender.

If all this seems abstract, let us take a real-life situation as an example: the case of women and men who choose work that is unconventional for their gender, as judged by the common norms in their society. In most postindustrial nations, we might think of male secretaries, pediatric nurses, or preschool teachers, or then again, of female firefighters (figure 5–1), executives, or construction workers. All these tend to be professions that require a gendered qualifier before them when describing the unexpected gender reversal. Unless a "female astronaut" is specified. for example, one tends to envision a male when reading about an "astronaut"; by the same token, it would be surprising to hear of a "male astronaut," since the default value of "astronaut," as it were, is male, hence a "male astronaut" is culturally redundant. Female surgeons, male midwives, female engineers—all work against the gendered grain of most contemporary Western societies, challenging gender stereotypes insofar as these individuals embody gender contradictions, defy common expectations. How do such people perceive themselves and their relations with other (gendered) people? How do others perceive them? Do they have a single identity, and if so, is it the one that is implied by their biology, or the identity that is associated with their chosen career?

Figure 5–1. Female firefighter. (Photo by Georganne Rundblad)

To explore these questions, let us examine the case of female bullfighters in the Spanish region of Andalusia. Over the past century, women began to insert themselves in multiple ways into the Spanish bullfighting arena. Some Andalusians—traditionalists who feel comfortable relying on classic gender norms—reject the move wholesale. Among this group are male bullfighters who refuse to fight in the same ring with female bullfighters, parents who discourage their daughters from pursuing a bullfighting career, trainers who refuse to train women bullfighters, and spectators—both men and women—who avoid attending bullfights at which female bullfighters are present. For these Spaniards, the association of bullfighting with masculinity is so strong and single-minded that no challenge to the association will be tolerated.

Yet at the same time, another slice of contemporary Andalusian society is willing to breach convention, expand the bounds of the profession, and permit the possibility of female bullfighters. Among this group there is, of course, the group of women themselves who are training to become bullfighters; their trainers, who may endure criticism or ridicule from their colleagues for training women as bullfighters; and spectators who happily buy tickets to see women fight in the bull ring. Here we see the easy notion of bullfighter-as-embodiment-of-masculinity being contested, and social change—the rush of feminism (whether or not acknowledged as such), with its insistence that women can pursue any profession available to men—changing long-standing notions of professional appropriateness.

The situation is even more complex. In Andalusia, viewers themselves offer a range of opinions and interpretations of the phenomenon of female bullfighters. Some may be sexually aroused by the tight-fitting, bejeweled costume worn by the bullfighters; ironically, this puts the maverick bullfighting woman, who shows both tremendous social courage and tremendous physical courage, in the traditional role of passive sex object, subject to the sexualized male gaze. Other onlookers admire the physical control expressed in an aesthetically pleasing way that female bullfighters demonstrate (qualities these spectators may admire in male bullfighters), playing up the athletes' professionalism and playing down their sexuality. The female bullfighters themselves say they appreciate this latter attitude. Still other spectators maintain that women are doomed to fail at bullfighting because, they allege, women's biology—their fundamental nature or makeup—does not permit them to experience the same bravery and strength that bullfighting demands and that only men by nature fully enjoy. Such fans of the bullfight may feel anything from pity to contempt for women bullfighters.

Examining this range of reactions, we are led to question the long-standing, exclusive association of bullfighting with the masculine. At the same time, we are forced to consider the ways in which the image of a female bullfighter stretches our conventional notions of what it means to be a woman. Can't a female bullfighter be as much a "woman" as is a woman who chooses, say, teaching, nursing, or motherhood as her profession? Yet at the same time that the female bullfighter may opt for the hypermasculinized image in the bullring, she may adopt a more conventionally feminized image outside the ring. And in her late twenties, as many male bullfighters do, she typically renounces the extreme rigors of the bullfight—and may well marry and raise children. In other words, she herself may play with her own insertion into gender identity to the point of experiencing gender identity in the plural. For the contemporary, Spanish, female bullfighter, we might say, gender identity becomes gender identities.

The case of the female bullfighter is, admittedly, a dramatic one. What about the vast majority of people who (at least appear to) lead more ordinary lives, conforming (more or less happily) to conventional gender roles? Recent studies have begun to suggest that the sort of gender flexibility, ambiguity, and controversy characterizing the situation of Spanish female bullfighters may also apply, if more subtly, to others engaged in less public and less controversial professions. For example, the female office secretary who is sexually harassed by one male superior while being treated respectfully and professionally by another surely experiences her gender differently with her two male bosses from hour to hour on a given day. The woman who suffers from PMS does likewise at different points in the month. The male trucker may similarly experience his gender identity in different ways when talking to fellow male truckers, to waitresses, to the odd female trucker, and to his wife on the phone, all at the same truck stop along the highway. Such examples could be multiplied endlessly. They suggest that "identity" itself is not only a multifaceted construction from place to place, but a construction whose contours may change from situation to situation for any one of us.

This brings up a related issue: Is it justifiable to assert that the very difference between male and female is itself a universally acknowledged one? In fact, many non-Western societies have allowed for a gender role that is either a combination of male and female, or that is neither male nor female. In recent years, such an in-between category has sometimes been called a "third gender." The "berdaches" of many Native American communities—men who dress as women and take on some (but not all) typically female roles in society—have long confounded anthropologists trying to classify them via the dual-gendered system that is prevalent in Western thought. Variations on this theme abound in many non-Western societies. Among the Igbo of Nigeria, for example, "female husbands" and "male daughters" are adults who are biologically female but, by playing typically male roles (husbands and sons), rise to high levels of wealth, power, and status in their society.

In urbanized, postindustrial societies, communities of gays and lesbians may similarly play with gender roles in ways that challenge the commonly held notion that gender is determined by biology. Lesbian parents may tell their children that they have two mothers, for example, but one mother may perform more traditionally "maternal" roles in housekeeping and child care, while the other may maintain a greater, more stereotypically "masculine" commitment to her career.

To date, studies of such alternate gender systems have not had much impact on public discussions of the issue beyond the narrow confines of anthropology. Perhaps one of the contributions that anthropology can make is to keep reminding us that it is just when we are most sure of ourselves and our opinions—when we are convinced that our way of doing things, of arranging our society and our lives, is the most commonsensical, the most "natural"—that social roles such as a "third gender" can productively unsettle comfortable assumptions about the "nature" of gender identity.

GENDER AND POWER

Are women and men fundamentally equal or unequal? Do any societies exist whose members have achieved partial or even full gender equality? Are there limits—whether biological or cultural (or both)—to achieving such equality? In recent years, most feminist scholars have asserted that a significant majority of all known societies, both past and present, exhibit at least some degree of patriarchy—the dominance of women by men in socially significant spheres of life—and that many societies exhibit a high level of gender inequality. Nevertheless, feminist scholars assume that male dominance, although widespread, is not inevitable, because its roots lie in cultural practices rather than in any hypothesized biological mandate. Anthropologists are in an especially powerful position to address this enduring issue because of their investigation into the variety of lives as lived around the globe.

Authors have proposed several theories to account for the widespread existence of men's dominance of women. Some have stressed the idea of male dominance as an ideological system to emphasize its symbolic components. Feminist psychologists and psychoanalysts propose child-rearing styles or scenarios as essential to the development of patriarchal attitudes in adulthood. Models derived from Karl Marx's theories have tended to look at the rise of the state and private property as responsible for the fact that in many societies women have fewer legal, economic, and political rights than do men. One variation on this theme suggests that in prestate societies, women's roles as sisters remained critical after marriage; this allowed a married woman to retain a degree of authority vis-à-vis the clan into which she was born, which continued to support her rights within her marriage. But over time, states have tended to erode the authority of the clan system itself. According to this theory, women's roles as (clan) sisters have become eclipsed by the importance of their roles as wives. This shift would have brought about a precipitous decline in women's status overall, accounting for the fact that most contemporary societies exhibit some degree of male dominance at least in the political and economic arenas.

Other authors have cited the restrictions that pregnancy, nursing, and continual care of infants and young toddlers seem to place on women everywhere as the preeminent factors that limit women's access to socially valued resources. Nowadays some middle-class women themselves may view motherhood as a hindrance and may delay or even avoid motherhood so as to further career goals. Yet, ironically, archaeologists have hypothesized that the requirement to carry and care for very young children may have led to the invention of the most significant early technological innovations in human history: the baby sling (freeing women to work and walk while holding a baby) and the hunting net. Moreover, scholars are beginning to question the degree to which the mobility of a given woman may in fact be hampered by pregnancy, nursing, or childcare. The long-standing dominance of many traditional West African markets and farms by women shows the extent to which mothers can maintain active work lives, including critically important economic lives, while retaining a commitment to raising children. In these West African settings, children either accompany their mothers to work or stay behind in villages, where they join in multi-age play groups that are typically supervised by grandparents or other adults remaining in the village.

In contemporary, postindustrial societies, increasing pressure to provide both sufficient maternity and paternity leave for new parents, and comprehensive day care for children of working couples, means that more mothers of babies and toddlers can enter the work force on a full-time basis. Many leaders in a variety of Western nations are now looking for models in the Scandinavian countries, which have been at the forefront of government-supported efforts allowing families to combine successful parenthood and successful work lives.

Indeed, many women around the world are no longer content to remain in "second-class citizen" roles. In recent years, feminism has moved from a small movement of middle-class, Euro-American women to a far more global movement, with international meetings at which women from around the world regularly make their voices heard. Engaging in such consequential activities as lobbying to change unequal inheritance laws that disenfranchise widows in many African countries, Third World feminists are setting their own agendas and reorienting previously dominant paradigms of the relations between gender and privilege. At the same time, in some Western nations, a growing "men's movement" is encouraging men to question both traditional and current gender arrangements with which they may earlier have felt comfortable—or perhaps felt uncomfortable.

Issues relating to power differentials—including both the power to compel or coerce another to follow one's dictates, as well as the power to define and represent another's perceptions of reality—not only mark relations between women and men, they also mark relations among men and among women. Thus it is important to avoid "essentializing" the category of women (or of men) into a single, homogeneous group—not only across societies, but within a given society as well. This is so because the differences that divide women from each other, like those that divide men, are at least as great as the ties that bind them. Ethnic affiliation, class, religion, language, marital status, and age all rupture the seemingly unified or "essential" categories of male and female. Like all other means of defining identities, gender identity is created and recreated by changing circumstances.

Let us consider, for instance, the range of experience that characterizes the lives of women who belong to one apparently homogeneous category: fundamentalist Muslim women in the contemporary era. In Afghanistan, as of this writing, the ruling Islamic Taliban party excludes girls and women from all public spheres and professions, including schools, medical services, and the judiciary. At the same time, in Iran, Egypt, and Turkey, fundamentalist women are creating new brands of Islamic feminism as women reinterpret the Qur'an to claim new rights and freedoms in the spheres of education, work, and family. Although both these groups of women veil themselves, the covering has drastically different effects. In Afghanistan, the veil bars women from the public sphere, whereas in Turkey, Egypt, and Iran, it accords women the comfort to work side by side with men in public without feeling shame or fear.

To complicate matters even more, in Turkey, Egypt, and Iran, the contemporary appearance of veiled working women follows on earlier reforms in the 1920s and 1930s in which women in these three countries were either encouraged or obliged by the state to remove their veils, in a governmental effort to modernize and liberate Muslim women. Ironically, some scholars now claim that this earlier removal of the veil coerced women into conforming to men's positions, and that this in turn eroded women's own social networks, which were traditionally a source of power to them. The contemporary decision to "re-veil" among young Muslim women in Turkey, Egypt, and Iran is thus a significant step filled with multiple, historically layered meanings. It serves at once to affirm a deep devotion to Islam; to critique what these women perceive as depraved Western (especially North American) values and practices; and to provide a visual image that renders acceptable their insertion into the modern workplace. In this case, gender intersects with religion, education, history, and nationalism in complex ways that resist easy associations and predictions.

In the Muslim world, as elsewhere, differences in class and culture are also critical in shaping the experiences of children, both girls and boys. For example, whether among Bedouins in Egypt or Pathans in Pakistan, authoritarian and patriarchal elders in the clan strictly control the day-to-day activities of Muslim boys and girls throughout their youth and adolescence, limiting exposure to activities from soccer to marrying for love, as a means of ensuring continuity of values from generation to generation. Yet elsewhere, elite Muslim men transcend the usual boundaries of both religion and state by jetting in and out of European capitals, where they enjoy the pleasures of wealth, all the while retaining a commitment to Islam. Clearly, class and education radically divide the texture of the lives of men and of women around the globe, even men and women who devoutly espouse the same religious faith. Collectively, these examples of the varied lives of contemporary Muslim people in a variety of cultural spaces compel us to consider the possibility of multiple "masculinities" and multiple "femininities" that lie behind simple notions of male and female.

Moreover, intragender relations are by no means necessarily benign. Differences that divide the members of one gender can produce bitter conflict. A dramatic case of women actively pitted against one another by difference concerns relations among mothers-in-law and daughters-in-law. China provides us with the paradigmatic case. Here, the specific place that one occupies in the life cycle is what determines a woman's experience far more than does the simple fact of her being a "woman." As girls and young brides, Chinese females typically wield no authority in any sphere, but if and when they begin to produce sons, Chinese women slowly but inevitably gain prestige and authority. Acquiring a daughter-in-law to dominate—as she was dominated as a new bride—is the ultimate reward to a mature Chinese woman. Ironically, in this system, women gain power and authority only at one another's expense. In this patriarchal structure, women who are barren, or who produce only daughters, traditionally led tragically restricted and belittled lives; in earlier times, such a fate often led to suicide. Here, one observes both the existence of extensive male privilege and the possibility of female authority, albeit in a restricted context.

As this discussion suggests, the interplay of gender with other features that are critical in a local landscape goes a long way to define both our sense of who we are and other people's senses of who we are. Reducing our identity to gender alone is an unrealistic move that postulates identity as composed essentially of a single factor, when it is far more multiplex than that.

Although feminist anthropologists generally agree that most of the world's societies have exhibited, and continue to exhibit, some degree of domination by men over women, nevertheless scholars have begun recently to document the existence of societies that exhibit a significant measure of gender equality. This is especially the case among some small minority groups living on the fringes of large states. For example, among the Lahu of southwest China, an ideology of gender complementarity dominates virtually all (traditional) spheres of social life. A male and female village chief wield power collectively, and each household is headed by a heterosexual married couple. Men and women perform as much labor collectively as they can. Husbands take over much of their wives' labor load during pregnancy, they serve as midwives during childbirth, and they share with their wives all the tasks of childrearing other than breast-feeding from the first days after the birth (see plate 4). Some Lahu villages have maintained these practices more or less intact even in the face of efforts by the Chinese state to institute socialism—efforts that, in some Lahu villages, have inadvertently undermined the indigenous system of gender relations. This unintended effect is especially ironic, given the ideological commitment to gender equality espoused by the Chinese Communist Party. In such places, the tangle of competing models of (top-down, if unintended) patriarchy and (bottom-up) gender equality challenges us to avoid characterizing the society at large before looking at significant regional variations and contestations.

In general, the way that "gender equality" will look may surprise, taking on features in one place that seem far from what prevails as "equality" in another. As Western feminists struggle to achieve consensus over what an appropriate structure of gender equality might look like in postindustrial societies, feminists elsewhere pose their own answers that challenge us to expand our very definitions of power and equality.

THE CULTURAL CONSTRUCTION OF SEXUAL DESIRE

Anthropologists have a unique ability to argue for the cultural foundations of sexuality as well as of gender identity, having documented an astounding variety of practices and ideologies around the world concerning both sex and gender. If our own sexual practices and our own gender ideologies, whatever those may be, are all demonstrably nonuniversal, what claims can we make for their "naturalness"?

Let us consider a celebrated case in the anthropological literature. Among the Etoro people of Papua New Guinea, every adolescent boy must serve regularly as the "passive" partner in oral sex with his maternal uncle throughout his teen years. This obligatory practice is explained by the Etoro as a method to build up a supply of semen in the young man that will enable him later to prove fertile with a future wife. In this society the biological substance of seminal fluid, far from being seen as the natural outcome of hormonal development, as it is in the scientific model, is instead seen as a constructed creation—one that must be produced actively by the sexual efforts of closely related men. Without such efforts, the Etoro maintain, adult males would never become "real men," and their sterility would prove catastrophic, preventing the society from reproducing itself. Ideas and sexual practices such as this remind us that much as we might find it reasonable to envision sexuality itself as a natural aspect of our identities, it is—like gender identity—as much a cultural as a biological construction.

The model implied in the Etoro practice is, of course, far from the dominant Western model of sexuality, which has a notion of "naturalness" at its very core. Earlier in the century, Sigmund Freud convinced readers of the "naturalness" of sex as an "instinct" or "drive," and of gender roles as outgrowths of the postulated urge. Before Freud, many Westerners endorsed their own folk models of sex as an unavoidable impulse in humans, and many still maintain this position today. Recently, this "naturalness" has been invoked in politicized arenas—for example, in the increasingly public debate about the origins of homosexuality. Thus in the United States, many gays and lesbians insist on a "natural" foundation to their sexual orientation as a reason to grant them equal rights and legal protection, while Christian opponents of gay rights may instead claim that homosexuality is "unnatural." In both arguments, we are far from the Etoro model of sexuality, which instead emphasizes compulsory male homosexuality as a cultural practice that is necessary to create the later possibility of normative heterosexuality.

In many Western societies, a commonly espoused folk model of sexuality insists not only that sexual desire itself is an immutable and/or irrepressible, natural urge, but that it is naturally stronger in men than it is in women. In the United States, men and women alike often attempt to explain the high rape rates prevalent in the nation as the outcome of an unbridled sexual impulse in men that society has not effectively tamed, Sometimes the frequency of rape is accepted as a tragic but inevitable result of the widespread conviction that "boys will be boys."

Yet the existence of an irresistible sexual urge in men concerning women is not a universal perception. For example, Muslims often maintain that women have a greater sexual urge than do men. Indeed, in the views of many Muslims (especially Muslim men), it is precisely to protect women against their own strong desires for sex (which, it is feared, could lead to adultery and other culturally unacceptable transgressions) that the extreme practices of female seclusion (purdah) and female circumcision have come about. By contrast, Dani people of Irian Jaya, Indonesia (West New Guinea), would likely repudiate the common proposition that the urge for sex is a natural one in either men or women. Married Dani men and women alike claim that they refrain from all sexual activity for a period of between four and six years after each child is born to them, and a Western ethnographer who reported this was convinced that no infractions occurred. The contrast is stark when we compare the reported infrequency of sex among the Dani with the frequency of sexual activity in the contemporary United States, where "the average ... couple has intercourse two or three times per week in their twenties and thirties" (though somewhat less frequently as they age; Masters, Johnson, and Kolodny 1986, 326–27).

Even the very private feelings of sexual pleasure that we may experience are themselves shaped—subtly yet decisively—by cultural factors. Let us consider one controversial case: female genital operations performed on some African and Muslim girls. Today, some outspoken leaders are challenging the tradition for myriad reasons—relating not only to medical and ethical issues, but also to sexual pleasure. These critics lambast the practice as destroying any possibility of experiencing sexual pleasure for the women who have undergone the procedure. At the same time, defenders of the practice, including women—in some places, especially women—offer a different scenario. For example, some Pokot women of Kenya report that the pleasure they experience during sex with their husbands is heightened by the fact that their clitoris was ritually removed during their adolescent initiation ritual—a surgico-ceremonial procedure that the girls were told would ensure their fertility. One can surmise that knowing that they are fertile may make these women feel attractive to their husbands, which would in turn produce in them feelings of erotic arousal. Such claims and counterclaims—and the increasingly lively, even explosive internal debate about this issue that is wracking many African and Muslim societies—must surely unsettle any easy dismissal or condemnation we may be prone to espouse regarding a practice that occasions such extreme reactions. At the least, it suggests that the outsider's ability to imagine what circumstances foster private sensations of sexual pleasure in others is limited.

LEGITIMATE SEX, ILLEGITIMATE SEX: VIRGINITY/ADULTERY/INCEST

The social construction of sexuality is not limited to the experience of desire. Every known society also makes clear to its members when it is permissible—or forbidden—simply to have sex, and with whom.

For example, many socially stratified societies that have well-developed distinctions between commoners and elites have required young women (though not young men) to remain sexual virgins before they marry. Nevertheless, the concept of virginity itself is not self-evident: far from being a simple biological fact, the notion has as much of a cultural as a biological foundation. Among the Trobriand Islanders of Papua New Guinea, for instance, the category of "virginity" is extended to adult women whom Westerners would surely not classify as virgins: mothers who have given birth to children that are said to be sired by family spirits rather than by mortal men—even though such women may be married and lead active sexual lives. This ideology is consistent with the matrilineal organization of Trobriand society. In this type of society, women are structurally more critical to the reproduction of the society than are men, who are somewhat peripheral both genealogically and symbolically.

Distant though it may seem to the Westerner, the Trobriand ideology that it is possible for a woman to be impregnated by a god or spirit rather than by a mortal man, is not as "exotic" as it may at first glance appear. How far is it from the Trobriand conception of "virgin birth" to the "virgin birth" that is said to characterize the conception of the major deity that Christians worship around the world? By contrast, other societies do not recognize the category of "virgin" at all. In such settings—Samoa is one example made famous by Margaret Mead's study in the last century—some boys and girls may be permitted to engage in sexual experimentation from a very young age. In such a setting, local sexual practice makes any concept of "virginity" essentially irrelevant.

Even though sex is encouraged or at least permitted early in some societies, nevertheless all societies restrict sexual access to some people. Minimally, a few closely related family members are universally considered taboo as sexual partners. Sex between parent and child is forbidden virtually everywhere, as it is almost everywhere between siblings. Going beyond the "incest taboo," the idea of who is considered an acceptable sex partner and/or an acceptable marriage partner is variable indeed when we look at the gamut of societies cross-culturally. Indeed, just how "incest" is defined is not as easily foreseen as we might imagine. Thus, whereas most Western countries forbid all first cousins and sometimes all second cousins as spouses, many non-Western societies find another distinction far more relevant: cousins who are the children of two sisters or of two brothers are in many societies forbidden as marriage partners, but in many of these same societies, the children of a brother and a sister are not only permitted but are encouraged or even required to marry one another. Here, the definition of "incest" looks different indeed from the shape it typically takes in Western societies, where people tend to insist on the extent of genealogical or genetic difference as the relevant criterion.

At another level, some societies make a clear distinction between an acceptable sex partner as opposed to an acceptable spouse. For one thing, whereas marriage often implies sex, it does not necessarily require it. In some contemporary countries, the case of foreigners who marry natives for citizenship purposes (in the United States, "to get a green card") includes many such sexless marriages. Other circumstances produce complex marriages in contemporary Indonesia. There, gay men generally conceal their homosexual identities; but if they are discovered to have male partners, their sexual habits are usually tolerated so long as the men also marry women, sire children, and lead seemingly conventional—if secretly bisexual—lives. Closer to home for Western readers, many gays and lesbians, including well-known artists, have found it useful to remain in heterosexual marriages as a screen for their homosexuality—though in many of these cases, unlike in Indonesia, their marriages may well be childless and perhaps sexless as well.

In complex societies with significant ethnic and class divisions, the choice suitable marriage partner often includes considerations of social background Marrying (or trying to marry) the "wrong kind of person," or a person from "wrong kind of family"—however that is defined—can result in ostracism from the family or community, or even in suicide. Marriage is frequently a contentious issue for many religious groups, especially minority groups whose members have had difficult relations with the locally dominant religion. Such is the case of Jew in the contemporary United States, for example, where high rates of intermarriage between Jews and Christians frequently cause disputes in Jewish families. Marriages that are considered inappropriate from the perspective of the prospective couple's families have long been the staple of great art, from *Romeo and Juliet* to Spike Lee's film, *Jungle Fever*. Even as contemporary Western couples typically covet the right to choose their own spouses, families may intervene in subtle but decisive ways to shape the marriage decisions their children will one day make—at the least by teaching certain values that will give their children a conceptual grid through which to evaluate possible mate choices.

In many societies, patriarchy further complicates the picture of who marries whom. Typically, in class-stratified societies, men are permitted to marry downward in class, status, education and age, while women are forbidden or at least discouraged from doing so, being allowed or encouraged only to marry upward in class, status, education, or age (a practice that social scientists term "hypergamy"). One important consequence of these rules is that male dominance within the marriage is generally reinforced. This is so because when a man of high standing and/or wealth marries a woman of low standing and/or wealth, his authority over his wife is generally strengthened by his higher general status. By contrast, if a man of low standing marries a woman of high standing (termed "hypogamy"), his authority over his wife might well be undermined by her higher general status, thus challenging the overall patriarchal structure of the society. Surprisingly, women themselves may avoid such marriages, anticipating that they may cause trouble for their potential husbands. Only in unusual circumstances does hypogamy become attractive. For instance, in recent years some well-educated, Euro-American women in their thirties have begun to perceive that they have a shrinking pool of eligible, unmarried men from whom to choose as spouses; as a result, some of these women are opting to marry men who are significantly less educated than they are (hence occupying positions of lesser prestige), although previously these women (and their families) would have ruled out such a marriage.

When different ethnic groups are systematically (and unjustly) accorded variable levels of prestige in a given society, class factors may be further intensified when it comes to choosing a marriage partner. For instance, in the United States, many (racist) Euro-Americans are more perturbed by the thought of a "white" woman marrying a "black" man (hypogamy) than by the thought of a "black" woman marrying a "white" man (hypergamy).

Once married, adults are generally expected to obey relevant laws concerning sexual fidelity to their partners, whatever those laws may be. In many societies, gender and power intersect to produce a "double standard": women are expected to remain sexually faithful to their husbands at the same time that those husbands are permitted to have extramarital sexual liaisons. In recent years, the political scene in the United States has revealed the extensive occurrence of powerful men's extramarital affairs, culminating recently in the near-toppling of Bill Clinton's presidency.

Ironically, women themselves may excuse their husbands' transgressions (as Hillary Clinton did publicly) and in some cases may even refrain from critiquing the existence of the sexual double standard, rationalizing that "it's in men's nature." In parts of Greece, a woman who discovers that her husband is having an adulterous affair typically blames the other woman rather than her husband, whom she likely sees as incapable of controlling his sexual urges. In some societies that subscribe to this sexual double standard, the existence of polygyny (which permits men but not women to remain married to two or more spouses simultaneously) goes hand-in-hand with this ideology. In this case, which characterizes many traditional African societies, "philandering" men may view extramarital liaisons as an attempt to locate a second or third wife, rather than as adultery.

Still, the sexual double standard, while common, is not universal. Elsewhere, far different mores may prevail. In traditional Nuer communities in southern Sudan, for example, certain women were permitted to have multiple lovers while remaining married. Any children such a woman bore would have considered their mother's husband as their legal father, whether or not he was genetically related to them. Elsewhere—as in south India, the Himalayas, and on the Jos Plateau of Nigeria—the practice of "polyandry" permits women to remain married simultaneously to two or more men (who are sometimes brothers). While rare, this marriage system nevertheless demonstrates the non-inevitability of the admittedly far commoner practice of polygyny.

Although transgressing locally upheld rules about sex—whether concerning incest, adultery, or otherwise—may result in punishment, many rules themselves are now being contested. For example, the gay liberation movement, which is increasingly active in non-Western nations as well as in the West, is challenging traditional notions of acceptable sexuality even as its activists are still frequently harassed. The struggle over the commonly accepted definition of legitimate sex continues in arenas as diverse as conference planning and book fairs. For example, many academic organizations have declined to hold their annual meetings in any of the North American states that continue to maintain antisodomy or antihomosexuality laws, and a book fair in southern Africa was wracked by controversy over its decision first to ban and then (by court order) to allow a gay rights group to have a stand at the fair. In such ways, social traditions concerning sexuality are subject to revision, redefinition, and negotiation.

SEXUALITY IN OLD AGE

In urbanized, contemporary, Western societies, sex is typically seen as a monopoly of the young. Advertisements using sex as a lure for consumers to purchase a product almost inevitably hire young actors and actresses to seduce viewers. Even if old people are not secluded in nursing homes (as is common enough in the United States), their sex lives are rarely considered by others. Some societies carry this to an extreme. For example, in contemporary Japan and Taiwan it is considered shameful for even middle-aged, let alone elderly, women to be interested in sex. Routinely sleeping with (some of) their grandchildren is likely to promote long-term celibacy in older Japanese women.

Nevertheless, discomfort with elderly sexuality is not universal. For example, among the !Kung people of southern Africa, women as they age are said to become both more sexually active and more sexually attractive to men. Indeed, it is not uncommon for young !Kung men to have affairs with elderly women, many of whom dress more and more scantily, revealing more and more of their legs, with each passing year. While the idea of geriatric sex may unsettle our stereotypes about the aging process and the appropriate deployment of sexuality, it encourages us to acknowledge the cultural construction of sexual desire itself.

Attitudes about the appropriateness of sexuality through the life cycle are also shaped by the power structure of the society. For example, in a given society, is a widow, especially a young widow, free to remarry? Or, by contrast, is she obliged to remarry a particular man—for example, the brother of her deceased husband, as is (or was) common in some early Western and contemporary, non-Western societies? In India, one sign that women lack autonomy was the traditional rule that prohibited a widow ever to remarry. In classic times, the Indian rule against widows' remarriage even extended to infant girls, who were classified as widows if the infant boys to whom they were betrothed as part of an arranged marriage agreement happened to the as children. As an adult, the highest respect an Indian widow could show her just-deceased husband was to join the funeral pyre with his corpse. Although this practice of *suttee* was outlawed by the British in 1829, it has on occasion been revived in local villages, especially in Rajasthan. These incidents have generated enormous controversy in the Indian press in recent years as Indians (feminists and otherwise) rethink ways of being both Indian and modern. As these examples show, sex, gender, and power continue to be deeply implicated in one another as humans progress through the life cycle.

In this essay we have explored the gamut of possibilities for our lives as gendered and sexual beings. While Western discussions tend to "naturalize" both these components of the human experience as being rooted in biologically immutable structures, cultural anthropologists have long argued that both sex and gender have powerful cultural roots, making it difficult—perhaps impossible—to say where "nature" leaves off and "culture" begins. If anthropology can have any impact on our society as we endeavor to create a more egalitarian set of opportunities for all people regardless of gender, perhaps it is through the realization that gender arrangements and sexual practices alike have an astounding variability as we look around the globe, reminding us that no pattern, however much it may appear to be "natural," is inevitable.

ACKNOWLEDGMENTS

For having given me my start long ago in the scholarly study of gender and sexuality, I remain grateful to my early teachers, Gerda Lerner and Sherry Ortner. For a careful reading of this chapter and many insightful comments, I am thankful to my life partner, Philip Graham. For usefully challenging comments concerning contemporary Muslim experiences, I am grateful to Zohreh Sullivan. For valued advice with a variety of sources used in the preparation of this chapter, I am much obliged to Shyamala Balgopal, Matti Bunzl, Al Kagan, Janet Keller, Jeremy MacClancy, and Beth Stafford. I also thank two anonymous readers of this essay for very helpful suggestions. Finally, many thanks to Bertin Kouadio for much appreciated help in the library.

REFERENCES AND SUGGESTIONS FOR FURTHER READING

Abu-Lughod, Lila. 1993. *Writing Women's Worlds: Bedouin Stories.* Berkeley: University of California Press.

_____, ed. 1998. *Remaking Women: Feminism and Modernity in the Middle East.* Princeton, NJ: Princeton University Press.

Amadiume, Ifi. 1987. *Male Daughters, Female Husbands: Gender and Sex in an African Society.* London: Zed.

Ardener, Shirley, ed. 1993 [1978]. *Defining Females: The Nature of Women in Society.* Oxford: Berg.

Arens, William. 1986. *The Original Sin: Incest and Its Meaning.* Oxford: Oxford University Press.

Ashe, Geoffrey. 1976. *The Virgin.* London: Routledge & Kegan Paul.

Berreman, Gerald D. 1975. "Himalayan Polyandry and the Domestic Cycle." *American Ethnologist* 2, no. 1: 127–39.

Boddy, Janice. 1989. *Wombs and Alien Spirits: Women, Men, and the Zar Cult in Northern Sudan.* Madison: University of Wisconsin Press.

Boserup, Esther. 1970. *Woman 's Role in Economic Development.* New York: St. Martin's Press.

Brumberg, Joan Jacobs. 1992. *The Body Project: An Intimate History of American Girls.* New York: Random House.

Buckley, Thomas, and Alma Gottlieb, eds. 1988. *Blood Magic: The Anthropology of Menstruation.* Berkeley: University of California Press,

Butler, Judith. 1990. *Gender Trouble.* New York: Routledge.

Caudill, William, and David W. Plath. 1966. "Who Sleeps by Whom? Parent-Child Involvement in Urban Japanese Families." *Psychiatry* 29: 344–66.

Chernin, Kim. 1993. *The Obsession: Reflections on the Tyranny of Slenderness.* New York: HarperCollins.

Chodorow, Nancy. 1978. *The Reproduction of Mothering.* New Haven, CT: Yale University Press.

_____. 1989. *Feminism and Psychoanalytic Theory.* New Haven, CT: Yale University Press.

Clark, Gracia. 1994. *Onions Are My Husband: Survival and Accumulation by West African Market Women.* Chicago: University of Chicago Press.

Connell, R. W. 1995. *Masculinities.* Cambridge, U.K.: Polity Press.

Cornwall, Andrea, and Nancy Lindisfarne, eds. 1994. *Dislocating Masculinity: Comparative Ethnographies.* London: Routledge.

Davis-Floyd, Robbie. 1992. *Childbirth as an American Rite of Passage.* Berkeley: University of California Press.

Davis-Floyd, Robbie, and Carolyn F. Sargent, eds. 1997. *Childbirth and Authoritative Knowledge: Cross-Cultural Perspectives.* Berkeley: University of California Press.

Delaney, Carol. 1991. *The Seed and the Soil: Gender and Cosmology in Turkish Village Society.* Berkeley: University of California Press.

del Valle, Teresa, ed. 1993. *Gendered Anthropology.* New York: Routledge.

Dickerson-Putman, Jeanette, and Judith K. Brown. 1998. *Women among Women: Anthropological Perspectives on Female Age Hierarchies.* Urbana: University of Illinois Press.

di Leonardo, Micaela. 1997 [1992]. "White Lies, Black Myths: Rape, Race, and the Black 'Underclass.'" In *The Gender/Sexuality Reader: Culture, History, Political Economy,* ed. Roger N. Lancaster and Micaela di Leonardo, 53–68. New York: Routledge.

Du, Shanshan. In press. *"Chopsticks Only Work in Pairs": Gender Unity and Gender Equality among the Lahu of Southwest China.* New York: Columbia University Press.

Ehrenreich, Barbara, and Deirdre English. 1978. *For Her Own Good: 150 Years of the Experts' Advice to Women.* New York: Doubleday.

Etienne, Mona, and Eleanor Leacock, eds. 1980. *Women and Colonization: Anthropological Perspectives.* New York: J. F. Bergin.

Evans-Pritchard, E. E. 1951. *Kinship and Marriage among the Nuer.* Oxford: Clarendon Press.

Foucault, Michel. 1978 [1976]. *Histoty of Sexuality.* Vol. 1 .*An Introduction.* Trans. Robert Hurley. New York: Pantheon.

_____. 1985 [1984]. *Histoty of Sexuality.* Vol. 2. *The Use of Pleasure.* Trans. Robert Hurley. New York: Pantheon.

"Gay Zimbabweans Win Fight to Open Booth at a Book Fair." 1996. *New York Times,* August 2, A4.

Geertz, Clifford. 1983. "Common Sense as a Cultural System." In *Local Knowledge*, by Clifford Geertz, 73–93. New York: Basic Books.

Gottlieb, Alma. 1988. "American Premenstrual Syndrome: A Mute *Voice." Anthropology Today* 4, no. 6: 10–13.

Gough, Kathleen. 1955. "Female Initiation Rites on the Malabar Coast. *"Journal of the Royal Anthropological Institute* 85: 45–80.

_____. 1959. "The Nayars and the Definition of Marriage." *Journal of the Royal Anthropological Institute* 89: 23–34.

Hastrup, Kirsten. 1993 [1978]. "The Semantics of Biology: Virginity." In *Defining Females: The Nature of Women in Society,* ed. Shirley Ardener, 34–50. Oxford: Berg.

Heider, Karl. 1976. "Dani Sexuality: A Low Energy System." *Man* 11: 188–201.

_____. 1979. *Grand Valley Dani: Peaceful Warriors.* New York: Holt, Rinehart and Winston.

Herdt, Gilbert, ed. 1994. *Third Sex, Third Gender: Beyond Sexual Dimorphism in Culture and History.* New York: Zone Books.

Hirschon, Renée. 1993 [1978]. "Open Body/Closed Space: The Transformation of Female Sexuality." In *Defining Females: The Nature of Women in Society,* ed. Shirley Ardener, 51–72. Oxford: Berg.

Howard, Richard. 1996. *Falling into the Gay World: Manhood, Marriage, and Family in Indonesia.* Ph.D. diss. Department of Anthropology, University of Illinois at Urbana-Champaign.

Johnson, Michelle C. 2000. "Becoming a Muslim, Becoming a Person: Female 'Circumcision,' Religious Identity, and Personhood in Guinea-Bissau." In *Female "Circumcision" in Africa: Culture, Change, and Controversy,* ed. Bettina Shell-Duncan and Ylva Hernlund, 215–33. Boulder, CO: Lynn Rienner.

Kelly, Raymond. 1976. "Witchcraft and Sexual Relations: An Exploration in the Social and Semantic Implications of the Structure of Belief." In *Man and Woman in the New Guinea Highlands,* ed. Paula Brown and Georgeda Buchbinder. Washington, DC: American Anthropological Association, Special Publication no. 8.

Kessler, Evelyn, and Suzanne McKenna. 1978. *Gender: An Ethnomethodological Approach.* New York: John Wiley and Sons.

Kilbride, Philip L. 1994. *Plural Marriage for Our Times: A Reinvented Option?* Westport, CT: Bergin & Garvey.

Kimmel, M. S., and M. A. Messner, eds. 1995. *Men's Lives.* 3d ed. Boston: Allyn and Bacon.

Kratz, Cory. 1994. *Affecting Performance: Meaning, Movement, and Experience in Okiek Women's Initiation.* Washington, DC: Smithsonian Institution Press.

LaFontaine, Jean S. 1985. *Initiation: Ritual Drama and Secret Knowledge across the World.* Harmondsworth, U.K.: Penguin.

Lawrence, Marilyn, ed. 1987. *Fed Up and Hungry: Women, Oppression, and Food.* New York: Peter Bedrick Books.

Leacock, Eleanor Burke. 1972. "Introduction." In *The Origin of the Family, Private Property, and the State,* by Frederick Engels, 7–67. New York: International Publishers.

Lee, Richard B. 1992. "Work, Sexuality, and Aging among !Kung Women." In *In Her Prime: New Views of Middle-Aged Women,* ed. Virginia Kerns and Judith K. Brown, 35–46. 2d ed. Urbana: University of Illinois Press.

Lepowsky, Maria. 1993. *Fruit of the Motherland: Gender in an Egalitarian Society.* New York: Columbia University Press.

Levine, Nancy. 1981. "Perspectives on Love: Morality and Affect in Nyinba Interpersonal Relationships." In *Culture and Morality,* ed. Adrian C. Mayer, 106–25. Oxford: Oxford University Press.

_____. 1988. *The Dynamics of Polyandry: Kinship, Domesticity, and Population on the Tibetan Border.* Chicago: University of Chicago Press.

Levine, Nancy, and Walter H. Sangree. 1980. "Asian and African Systems of Polyandry." *Journal of Comparative Family Studies* 11, no. 3: 385–410.

Lewin, Ellen. 1993. *Lesbian Mothers: Accounts of Gender in American Culture.* Ithaca, NY: Cornell University Press.

Lichter, D. T. 1990. "Delayed Marriage, Marital Homogamy, and the Mate Selection Process among White Women." *Social Science Quarterly* 71, no. 4: 802–11.

Lock, Margaret. 1993. *Encounters with Aging: Mythologies of Menopause in Japan and North America.* Berkeley: University of California Press.

Lu, Hwei-Syin. 1991. *Self-growth, Women's Power, and the Contested Family Order in Taiwan: An Ethnographic Study of Three Contemporary Womens Groups.* Ph.D. diss. Department of Anthropology, University of Illinois at Urbana-Champaign.

Lugo, Alejandro, and Bill Maurer, eds. 2000. *Gender Matters: Rereading Michelle Z. Rosaldo.* Ann Arbor: University of Michigan Press.

Maher, Vanessa, ed. 1992. *The Anthropology of Breast-Feeding: Natural Law or Social Construct.* Oxford: Berg.

Malinowski, Bronislaw. 1929. *The Sexual Life of Savages in North-Western Melanesia: An Ethnographic Account of Courtship, Marriage, and Family Life among the Natives of the Trobriand Islands, British New Guinea.* New York: Harcourt, Brace & World.

Mani, Lata. 1990. "Multiple Mediations: Feminist Scholarship in the Age of Multinational Reception (on the Practice of Suttee, Widow Burning, in India)." *Feminist Review* 35 (summer): 24–41.

Martin, Emily. 1987. *The Woman in the Body: A Cultural Analysis of Reproduction.* Boston: Beacon Press.

_____. 1991. "The Egg and the Sperm: How Science Has Constructed a Romance Based on Stereotypical Male-Female Roles," *Signs* 16, no. 3: 485–501.

Masters, William, Virginia Johnson, and Robert C. Kolodny. 1986. *Masters and Johnson on Sex and Human Loving.* Boston: Little, Brown.

Mathabane, Mark, and Gail Mathabane, 1992. *Love in Black and White: The Triumph of Love over Prejudice and Taboo.* New York: HarperCollins.

Mead, Margaret. 1928. *Coming of Age in Samoa: A Psychological Study in Primitive Youth for Western Civilization.* New York: Blue Ribbon Books.

_____. 1935. *Sex and Temperament in Three Primitive Societies.* New York: Dell.

_____. 1949. *Male and Female: A Study of the Sexes in a Changing World.* New York: William Morrow.

Meggitt, Mervyn J. 1964. "Male-Female Relations in the Highlands of New Guinea." *American Anthropologist* 66, no. 4, part 2: 202–24.

Mikell, Gwendolyn, ed. 1997. *African Feminism: The Politics of Survival in Sub-Saharan Africa.* Philadelphia: University of Pennsylvania Press.

Moran, Mary H. 1990. *Civilized Women: Gender and Prestige in Southeastern Liberia.* Ithaca, NY: Cornell University Press.

Mukhopadhyay, Carol, and P. Higgins. 1988. "Anthropological Studies of Women's Status Revisited: 1977–1987." *Annual Review of Anthropology* 17: 461–95.

Müller, Jean-Claude. 1973. "On Preferential/Prescriptive Marriage and the Function of Kinship Systems: The Rukuba Case (Benue-Plateau State, Nigeria)." *American Anthropologist 75:* 1563–76.

Newton, Esther. 1993. *Cherry Grove, Fire Island: Sixty Years in America 's First Gay and Lesbian Town.* Boston: Beacon Press.

Okonjo, K. 1976. "The Dual-Sex Political System in Operation: Igbo Women and Community Politics in Midwestern Nigeria." In *Women in Africa: Studies in Social and Economic Change,* ed. Nancy J. Hafkin and Edna G. Bay, 45–58. Stanford, CA: Stanford University Press.

Ortner, Sherry. 1996. *Making Gender: The Politics and Erotics of Culture.* Boston: Beacon Press.

Pellow, Deborah. 1977. *Women in Accra: Options for Autonomy.* Algonack, MI: Reference Publications.

Pink, Sarah. 1997. *Women and Bullfighting: Gender, Sex, and the Consumption of Tradition.* Oxford: Berg.

Potash, Betty, ed. 1986. *Widows in African Societies: Choices and Constraints.* Stanford, CA: Stanford University Press.

Rapp, Rayna. 1999. *Testing Women, Testing the Fetus: The Social Impact of Amniocentesis in America.* New York: Roudedge.

Richards, Audrey. 1956. *Chisungu: A Girl's Initiation Ceremony among the Bemba of Zambia.* London: Faber and Faber.

Riley, Denise. 1988. *Am I That Name? Feminism and the Category of "Women" in History.* Minneapolis: University of Minnesota Press.

Rosaldo, Michelle Zimbalist. 1974. "Woman, Culture, and Society: A Theoretical Overview." In *Woman, Culture, and Society,* ed. Michelle Zimbalist Rosaldo and Louise Lamphere, 17–42. Stanford, CA: Stanford University Press.

Rosaldo, Michelle Zimbalist, and Louise Lamphere, eds. 1974. *Woman, Culture, and Society.* Stanford, CA: Stanford University Press.

Roth, Denise. In press. *Managing Motherhood, Managing Risk: Fertility and Danger in West Central Tanzania.* Ann Arbor: University of Michigan Press.

Sacks, Karen. 1982. *Sisters and Wives: The Past and Future of Gender Equality.* 2d ed. Urbana: University of Illinois Press.

Sanday, Peggy. 1990. *Fraternity Gang Rape: Sex, Brotherhood, and Privilege on Campus.* New York: New York University Press.

Sanday, Peggy, and Ruth Goodenough, eds. 1988. *Beyond the Second Sex: New Directions in the Anthropology of Gender.* Philadelphia: University of Pennsylvania Press.

Shostak, Marjorie. 1981. *Nisa: The Life and Words of a !Kung Woman.* Cambridge: Harvard University Press.

Slocum, Sally. 1974. "Woman the Gatherer: Male Bias in Anthropology." In *Toward an Anthropology of Women,* ed. Rayna Rapp Reiter, 36–50. New York: Monthly Review Press.

Steinem, Gloria. 1983. "If Men Could Menstruate." In *Gloria Steinem, Outrageous Acts and Everyday Rebellions.* New York: Holt, Rinehart, and Winston.

Stone, Linda. 1997. *Kinship and Gender: An Introduction.* Boulder: Westview Press/Harper-Collins.

Sudarkasa, Niara [Gloria Marshall]. 1973. *Where Women Work: A Study of Yoruba Women in the Marketplace and in the Home.* Ann Arbor: University of Michigan Museum of Anthropology, Anthropological Papers no. 53.

Sullivan, Zohreh T. 1998. "Eluding the Feminist, Overthrowing the Modern? Transformations in Twentieth-Century Iran." In *Remaking Women: Feminism and Modernity in the Middle East,* ed. Lila Abu-Lughod, 215–42. Princeton, NJ: Princeton University Press.

Tavris, Carol. 1992. *The Mismeasure of Woman.* New York: Simon and Schuster.

Weston, Kath. 1991. *Families We Choose: Lesbians, Gays, Kinship.* New York: Columbia University Press.

_____. 1996. *Render Me, Gender Me: Lesbians Talk Sex, Class, Color, Nation, Studmuffins.* New York: Columbia University Press.

Whitehead, Harriet. 1981. "The Bow and the Burden Strap: A New Look at Institutionalized Homosexuality in Native North America." In *Sexual Meanings: The Cultural Construction of Gender and Sexuality,* ed. Sherry B. Ortner and Harriet Whitehead, 80–115. Cambridge: Cambridge University Press.

Wolf, Margery. 1975. "Women and Suicide in China." In *Women in Chinese Society,* ed. Margery Wolf and Roxane Witke, 114–42. Stanford, CA: Stanford University Press.

Yanagisako, Sylvia J., and Carol Delaney, eds. 1995. *Naturalizing Power: Essays in Feminist Cultural Analysis.* New York: Roudedge.

Zihlman, Adrienne. 1989. "Woman the Gatherer: The Role of Women in Early Hominid Evolution." In *Gender and Anthropology: Critical Reviews for Research and Teaching*, ed. Sandra Morgen, 21–40. Washington, DC: American Anthropological Association.

Defining the Documentary

BY PATRICIA AUFDERHEIDE

NAMING

Documentary film begins in the last years of the nineteenth century with the first films ever projected, and it has many faces. It can be a trip to exotic lands and lifestyles, as was *Nanook of the North* (1922). It can be a visual poem, such as Joris Ivens's *Rain* (1929)—a story about a rainy day, set to a piece of classical music, in which the storm echoes the structure of the music. It can be an artful piece of propaganda. Soviet filmmaker Dziga Vertov, who ardently proclaimed that fiction cinema was poisonous and dying and that documentary was the future, made *Man with a Movie Camera* (1929) as propaganda both for a political regime and for a film style.

What is a documentary? One easy and traditional answer is: not a movie. Or at least not a movie like *Star Wars* is a movie. Except when it *is* a theatrical movie, like *Fahrenheit 9/11* (2004), which broke all box-office records for a documentary. Another easy and common answer could be: a movie that isn't fun, a serious movie, something that tries to teach you something—except when it's something like Stacy Peralta's *Riding Giants* (2004), which gives you a thrill ride on the history of surfing. Many documentaries are cannily designed with the express goal of entertainment. Indeed, most documentary filmmakers consider themselves storytellers, not journalists.

A simple answer might be: a movie about real life. And that is precisely the problem; documentaries are *about* real life; they are not real life. They are not even windows onto real life. They are portraits of real life, using real life as their raw material, constructed by artists and technicians who make myriad decisions about what story to tell to whom, and for what purpose.

You might then say: a movie that does its best to represent real life and that doesn't manipulate it. And yet, there is no way to make a film without manipulating the information. Selection of topic, editing, mixing sound are all manipulations. Broadcast journalist Edward R. Murrow once said, "Anyone who believes that every individual film must represent a 'balanced' picture knows nothing about either balance or pictures."

The problem of deciding how much to manipulate is as old as the form. *Nanook of the North* is considered one of the first great documentaries, but its subjects, the Inuit, assumed roles at film-maker Robert Flaherty's direction, much like actors in a fiction film. Flaherty asked them to do things they no longer did, such as hunt for walrus with a spear, and he showed them as ignorant about things they understood. In the film, "Nanook"—not his real name—bites a gramophone record in cheerful puzzlement, but in fact the man was quite savvy about modern equipment and even helped Flaherty disassemble and reassemble his camera equipment regularly. At the same time, Flaherty built his story from his own experience of years living with the Inuit, who happily participated in his project and gave him plenty of ideas for the plot.

A documentary film tells a story about real life, with claims to truthfulness. How to do that honestly, in good faith, is a never-ending discussion, with many answers. Documentary is defined and redefined over the course of time, both by makers and by viewers. Viewers certainly shape the meaning of any documentary, by combining our own knowledge of and interest in the world with how the filmmaker shows it to us. Audience expectations are also built on prior experience; viewers expect not to be tricked and lied to. We expect to be told things about the real world, things that are true.

We do not demand that these things be portrayed objectively, and they do not have to be the complete truth. The filmmaker may employ poetic license from time to time and refer to reality symboli-cally (an image of the Colosseum representing, say, a European vacation). But we do expect that a documentary will be a fair and honest representation of somebody's experience of reality. This is the contract with the viewer that teacher Michael Rabiger meant in his classic text: "There are no rules in this young art form, only decisions about, where to draw the line and how to remain consistent to the contract you will set up with your audience."

TERMS

The term "documentary" emerged awkwardly out of early practice. When entrepreneurs in the late nineteenth century first began to record moving pictures of real-life events, some called what they were making "documentaries." The term did not stabilize for decades, however. Other people called their films "educationals," "actualities," "interest films," or perhaps referred to their subject matter— "travel films," for example. John Grierson, a Scot, decided to use this new form in the service of the

British government and coined the term "documentary" by applying it to the work of the great American filmmaker Robert Flaherty's *Moana* (1926), which chronicled daily life on a South Seas island. He defined documentary as the "artistic representation of actuality"—a definition that has proven durable probably because it is so very flexible.

Marketing pressures affect what is defined as a documentary. When the philosopher-filmmaker Errol Morris's *The Thin Blue Line* (1988) was released in theaters, public relations professionals downplayed the term "documentary" in the interest of ticket sales. The film is a sophisticated detective story—did Randall Adams commit the crime for which he is sentenced to die in Texas? The film shows the dubious quality of key witnesses' testimony. When the case was reopened and the film entered as evidence, the film's status suddenly became important, and Morris now had to assert that it was, indeed, a documentary.

Conversely, Michael Moore's first feature, *Roger and Me* (1989), a savage indictment of General Motors for precipitating the decline of the steel town of Flint, Michigan, and a masterpiece of black humor, was originally called a documentary. But when journalist Harlan Jacobson showed that Moore had misrepresented the sequence of events, Moore distanced himself from the word "documentary." He argued that this was not a documentary but a movie, an entertainment whose deviations from strict sequencing were incidental to the theme.

In the 1990s, documentaries began to be big business worldwide, and by 2004 the worldwide business in television documentary alone added up to $4.5 billion revenues annually. Reality TV and "docusoaps"—real-life miniseries set in potentially high-drama situations such as driving schools, restaurants, hospitals, and airports—also burgeoned. Theatrical revenues multiplied at the beginning of the twenty-first century. DVD sales, video-on-demand. and rentals of documentaries became big business. Soon documentaries were being made for cell phones, and collaborative documentaries were being produced online. Marketers who had discreetly hidden the fact that their films were documentaries were now proudly calling such works "docs."

WHY IT MATTERS

Naming matters. Names come with expectations; if that were not true, then marketers would not use them as marketing tools. The truthfulness, accuracy, and trustworthiness of documentaries are important to us all because we value them precisely and uniquely for these qualities. When documentarians deceive us, they are not just deceiving viewers but members of the public who might act upon knowledge gleaned from the film. Documentaries are part of the media that help us understand not only our world but our role in it, that shape us as public actors.

The importance of documentaries is thus linked to a notion of the public as a social phenomenon. The philosopher John Dewey argued persuasively that the public—the body so crucial to the health of a democratic society—is not just individuals added up. A public is a group of people who can act together for the public good and so can hold to account the entrenched power of business and government. It is an informal body that can come together in crisis if need be. There are as many publics as there are occasions and issues to call them forth. We can all be members of any particular public, if we have a way to communicate with each other about the shared problems we face. Communication, therefore, is the soul of the public.

As communications scholar James Carey noted, "Reality is a scarce resource." Reality is not *what* is out there but what we *know, understand,* and *share* with each other of what is out there. Media affect the most expensive real estate of all, that which is inside your head. Documentary is an important reality-shaping communication, because of its claims to truth. Documentaries are always grounded in real life, and make a claim to tell us something worth knowing about it.

True, consumer entertainment is an important aspect of the business of filmmaking, even in documentary. Most documentary filmmakers sell their work, either to viewers or to intermediaries such as broadcasters and distributors. They are constrained by their business models. Even though documentary costs much less than fiction film to make, it is still much more expensive to produce than, say, a brochure or a pamphlet. Television and theatrical documentaries usually require investors or institutions such as broadcasters to back them. And as documentaries become ever more popular, more of them are being produced to delight audiences without challenging assumptions. They attract and distract with the best-working tools, including sensationalism, sex, and violence. Theatrical wildlife films such as *March of the Penguins* (2005) are classic examples of consumer entertainment that use all of these techniques to charm and alarm viewers, even though the sensationalism, sex, and violence occur among animals.

Paid persuaders also exploit the reality claims of the genre, often as operatives of government and business. This may produce devastating social results, as did Nazi propaganda such as the viciously anti-Semitic *The Eternal Jew* (1937). Such work may also provoke important positive change. When the Roosevelt administration wanted to sell Americans on expensive new government programs, it commissioned some of the most remarkable visual poems made in the era, those by Pare Lorentz and a talented team. Works such as *The Plow that Broke the Plains* (1936) and *The River* (1938) helped to invest taxpayers in programs that promoted economic stability and growth.

In its short history, however, documentary has often been made by individuals on the edges of mainstream media, working with a public service media organization such as public broadcasting, with commercial broadcasters eager for awards, with nonprofit entities, or with private foundation or public education funds. On the margins of mainstream media, slightly off-kilter from status-quo understandings of reality, many documentarians have struggled to speak truthfully about—and to—power. They have often seen themselves as public actors, speaking not only to audiences but to other members of a public that needs to know in order to act.

Some recent examples demonstrate the range of such activity. Brave New Films's *Wal-Mart: The High Cost of Low Price* (2005) is an impassioned, didactic argument indicting the large retail superstore for such practices as inadequate medical plans for employees and the willful destruction of small businesses. It does not strive for balance in representing Wal-Mart's point of view; it does strive for accuracy in representing the problem. The film was made for action; it was used to organize legislative pushback and social resistance to the company's most exploitative practices. Wal-Mart aggressively countered the film with attack ads, and the filmmakers countercharged Wal-Mart with inaccuracy. Bloggers and even mainstream media picked up the discussion. Brave New Films positioned itself as a voice of the public, filling a perceived gap in the coverage that mainstream media provided on the problem. Viewers of the film, most of whom saw it through DVD-by-mail purchases and as a result of an e-mail campaign, viewed it not as entertainment but as an entertainingly-produced argument about an important public issue.

Michael Moore's *Fahrenheit 9/11,* a sardonic, anti-Iraq war film, addressed the American public directly, as people whose government was acting in the public's name. Right-wing commentators in commercial media attempted to discredit the film by charging that it was indeed propaganda. But Moore is not a minion of the powerful as propagandists are. He was putting forward, as he had every right to, his own view about a shared reality, frankly acknowledging his perspective. Further, he was encouraging viewers to look critically at their government's words and actions. (Potentially weakening this encouragement, however, was his calculated performance of working-class rage, which can lead viewers to see themselves not as social actors but merely as disempowered victims of the powerful.)

Other recent documentaries for public knowledge and action use techniques designed to attract interest across lines of belief. Eugene Jarecki's *Why We Fight* (2005) showcases an argument about the collusion between politicians, big business, and the military to spend the public's money and lives for wars that do not need to be fought. Jarecki deliberately chose Republican subjects, who could transcend partisan politics and speak to the public interest. In Davis Guggenheim's *An Inconvenient Truth* (2006), Al Gore and Davis Guggenheim, in an easy-to-understand presentation, let scientific data speak to the urgency of the issue. The director of the NASA Goddard Institute for Space Studies, Jim Hansen, noted the public value of the work: "Al Gore may have done for global warming what *Silent Spring* did for pesticides. He will be attacked, but the public will have the information needed to distinguish our long-term well-being from short-term special interests."

Styles can be dramatically different, in order to accomplish the end of public engagement. Judith Helfand and Dan Gold's *Blue Vinyl (2002)* employs the personal diary format to personalize a problem. The film follows Helfand as she takes a piece of her parents' home's vinyl siding and discovers the cancer-causing toxicity of vinyl at the beginning and end of its life cycle (it creates dioxin). Helfand becomes a representative of the public—people who need inexpensive siding and also suffer the health consequences of using it. Brazilian José Padilha's *Bus 174* (2002), in retelling a sensational news event in Rio de Janeiro—the hijacking of a bus, a several-hour standoff, and ultimate death of both hijacker and a bus rider, telecast live—brings viewers both into the life of the hijacker and the challenges of the police. By contrasting television footage that had glued viewers to their sets for an entire day along with investigations into the stories leading up to the event, the film reframes the "news" as an example of how endemic and terrible social problems are turned into spectacle. *Three Rooms of Melancholia* (2005), an epic meditation by Finnish filmmaker Pirjo Honkasalo, draws viewers into the Russian war against Chechnya by creating an emotional triptych. In "Longing," her camera caresses the earnest faces of twelve-year-old cadets in St. Petersburg, training to fight Chechens; in the second part, "Breathing," a local social worker visits the sad apartments of Grozny under siege, where daily-life problems become insuperable; the third, "Remembering," takes place in an orphanage just over the border, where Chechnyan young people learn bitterness. Little is said; in contemplative close-up, the faces of puzzlement, pain, and endurance speak volumes. The viewer has become complicit with the camera in knowing.

Whether a filmmaker intends to address the public or not, documentaries may be used in unexpected ways. One of the most infamous propaganda films of all time, *Triumph of the Will* (1935), has had a long life in other, anti-Nazi propaganda and in historical films. Israeli Yo'av Shamir's *Checkpoint* (2003), a scrupulously observed, non-narrated record of the behavior of Israeli troops at Palestinian checkpoints, was intended and was used as a provocation to public discussion of human rights violations. The Israeli Army embraced it as a training film.

Our shared understanding of what a documentary is—built up from our own viewing experience—shifts over time, with business and marketing pressures, technological and formal innovations, and with vigorous debate. The genre of documentary always has two crucial elements that are in tension: representation, and reality. Their makers manipulate and distort reality like all filmmakers, but they still make a claim for making a truthful representation of reality. Throughout the history of documentary film, makers, critics, and viewers have argued about what constitutes trustworthy storytelling about reality. This book introduces you to those arguments over time and in some of its popular subgenres.

FORM

What does a documentary look like? Most people carry inside their heads a rough notion of what a documentary is. For many of them, it is not a pretty picture. "A "regular documentary" often means a film that features sonorous, "voice-of-God" narration, an analytical argument rather than a story with characters, head shots of experts leavened with a few people-on-the-street interviews, stock images that illustrate the narrator's point (often called "b-roll in broadcasting), perhaps a little educational animation, and dignified music. This combination of formal elements is not usually remembered fondly. "It was really interesting, not like a regular documentary," is a common response to a pleasant theatrical experience.

In fact, documentarians have a large range of formal choices in registering for viewers the veracity and importance of what they show them. The formal elements many associate with "regular documentary" are part of a package of choices that became standard practice in the later twentieth century on broadcast television, but there are quite a few more to be had. This chapter provides you with several ways to consider the documentary as a set of decisions about how to represent reality with the tools available to the filmmaker. These tools include *sound* (ambient sound, soundtrack music, special sound effects, dialogue, narration); *images* (material shot on location, historical images captured in photographs, video, or objects); *special effects* in audio and video, including animation; and *pacing* (length of scenes, number of cuts, script or storytelling structure). Filmmakers choose the way they want to structure a story—which characters to develop for viewers, whose stories to focus on, how to resolve the storytelling.

Filmmakers have many choices to make about each of the elements. For instance, a single shot may be framed differently and carry a different meaning depending on the frame: a close-up of a father grieving may say something quite different from a wide shot of the same scene showing the entire room; a decision to let the ambient sound of the funeral dominate the soundtrack will mean something different than a swelling soundtrack.

Since there is nothing natural about the representation of reality in documentary, documentary filmmakers are acutely aware that all their choices shape the meaning they choose. All documentary conventions—that is, habits or clichés in the formal choices of expression—arise from the need to convince viewers of the authenticity of what they are being told. For instance, experts vouch for the truthfulness of analysis; dignified male narrators signify authority for many viewers; classical music connotes seriousness.

Challenges to conventions stake an alternative claim to authenticity. At a time when ambient sound could be collected only with difficulty, conventions of 35mm sound production included authoritatively delivered narration. They also included lighting and even staging, appropriate to the heavy, difficult-to-move equipment. Some documentaries used careful editing between the crafted compositions of each scene, to create the illusion of reality before the viewer's eyes. When filmmakers began experimenting with lighter 16mm equipment after World War II, the conventions that arose differently persuaded viewers of the documentary's truthfulness. Using very long "takes" or scenes made viewers feel that they were watching unvarnished reality; the jerkiness of handheld cameras was testimony to the you-are-there immediacy, and it implied urgency; "ambush" interviews, catching subjects on the fly or by surprise, led viewers to believe that the subject must be hiding something. The choice against narration, which became fashionable in the later 1960s, allowed viewers to believe that they were being allowed to decide for themselves the meaning of what they saw (even though editing choices actually controlled what they saw).

Documentarians employ the same techniques as do fiction filmmakers. Cinematographers, sound technicians, digital designers, musicians, and editors may work in both modes. Documentary work may require lights, and directors may ask their subjects for retakes; documentaries usually require sophisticated editing; documentarians add sound effects and sound tracks.

A shared convention of most documentaries is the narrative structure. They are stories, they have beginnings, middles, and ends; they invest viewers in their characters, they take viewers on emotional journeys. They often refer to classic story structure. When Jon Else made a documentary about J. Robert Oppenheimer, the creator of the first atomic bomb—a scientist who anguished over his responsibilities—Else had his staff read *Hamlet*.

Conventions work well to command attention, facilitate storytelling, and share a maker's perspective with audiences. They become the aesthetic norm—off-the-shelf choices for documentarians, shortcuts to register truthfulness. Conventions also, however, disguise the assumptions that makers bring to the project, and make the presentation of the particular facts and scenes seem both inevitable and complete.

SHOWCASING CONVENTION

How, then, to see formal choices as choices, to see conventions as conventions? You may turn to films whose makers put formal choice front and center as subject matter, and contrast their choices with more routine work.

One of the easiest ways to see conventions is through satire and parody. For example, the great Spanish surrealist artist Luis Buñuel's *Land without Bread (Las Hurdes: Tierra sin Pan,* 1932) begins as a seemingly tedious, pompous excursion into an impoverished corner of Spain. Soon, however, it becomes clear that Buñuel, aided by the commentary written by the surrealist artist Pierre Unik, is using dry, pseudo-scientific conventions to incite bewilderment and outrage, both at the narrator and then at the horrific social conditions of the countryside. The British Broadcasting Company (BBC)'s 1957 *The Spaghetti Story,* a segment in its *Panorama* series, takes viewers to Switzerland to discuss the latest spaghetti harvest (growing on trees) as a joke that also functions as a media literacy lesson. The wry *In Search of the Edge* (1990), purportedly about why the earth is flat, employs a wide range of educational-documentary devices that people associate with "regular documentary"—all with deliberate clumsiness—to demonstrate false logic in scientific arguments and manipulation in filmmaking. Here, experts are given such titles as "university professor" and are shown in front of bookcases signifying scholarship, although they speak nonsense; flashy graphics demonstrate physical impossibilities; the narrator's tone is contemptuous of the notion that the earth is round; a family photo is shown in gradual close-up, Ken Burns-style, only to show the mentioned character with her head turned. The Australian film *Babakiueria* (1988), made by an aboriginal group, satirizes ethnographic film conventions, including the ascribing of mysterious or magical properties to exotic others in narration, the expert witness, the pretentious narrator, and the portrayal of scientific investigation as heroic exploration. In the film, aboriginal scientists investigate what they believe to be a white Australian cultural ritual site, which actually is a barbecue area.

Mockumentaries, or tongue-in-cheek fake documentaries, also offer the chance to see conventions at an angle. Rob Reiner's *This Is Spinal Tap!* (1984), about an imaginary heavy metal band, famously parodied rockumentaries—performance films of rock bands—with their contrast of high-energy stage performance with goofy backstage antics and their populist success narratives. Like later mockumentaries such as *Best in Show* (2000) and *A Mighty Wind* (2003), the humor depended on the audience being able to identify the conventions.

ARTISTIC EXPERIMENT

Another way to see conventions is to analyze films by makers who see themselves primarily as artists—makers manipulating form rather than storytellers using the film medium—as they invent, reinvent, and challenge. Where the market pressures of attracting audiences have led many filmmakers to employ familiar conventions, artists working outside the film and video marketplaces have sought to go beyond them. They are frontline innovators and experimenters.

One highly celebrated example of such artistic countercurrents is the city symphony film. In the 1920s and 1930s, when theaters were showing nature adventures, war newsreels, and exotica, artists producing for galleries in interwar Europe imagined cinema (then a silent medium) as, among other things, a visual poem, one that could unite the experience of different senses. It was a time of exuberant experimentation and international communication. City symphonies participated in the modernist love of the urban, of machinery, and of progress. They absorbed elements from artistic movements such as surrealism and futurism, and they let people see what they usually could not or would not. Among the machines artists loved was the camera itself, which represented a superior "mechanical eye," as Russian documentarian and theorist Dziga Vertov called it. An early example of the city symphony was Paul Strand and Charles Sheeler's *Manhatta* (1921), and the form proliferated on the European continent in the later 1920s.

The city symphony was given its name by the German filmmaker Walther Ruttmann's *Berlin: Symphony of a Great City* (1927), Ruttmann also commissioned a score for the film. The very term "city symphony" unites the brash industrial enterprise of the modern city with the classical musical form that demonstrates the capacity to organize and coordinate many individual expressions into a whole. The film takes the viewer into Berlin on a train and then on a day-long tour of the many urban patterns emerging from the interaction of people and machines, culminating with fireworks. In the film, Ruttmann experimented with Vertov's ideas about the power of documentary to be an "eye" on society in a way that transcended the power of human observation.

Many artists seized upon the city symphony notion as a way of experimenting with the medium. The Brazilian artist Alberto Cavalcanti was inspired by the project Ruttmann was developing and made *Rien que les Heures* (1926), a film about Paris, even before Ruttmann completed his. It features clever special effects in a whirlwind tour of Paris that includes both the highest and lowest classes of society. In the south of France, Vertov's exiled younger brother, Boris Kaufman, and the French artist Jean Vigo, produced a slyly satirical little film, *À Propos de Nice* (1930), showing the beach town as a self-indulgent culture of gambling and sun-and self-worshiping. (Vertov wrote filmmaking instructions to his brother.) In Belgium, Henri Storck made a closely observed film about his own beach town, in *Images d'Ostende* (1930), and the Dutch filmmaker Joris Ivens, who went on to work with Storck, made what became a classic of these films, *Rain.* Vertov, in touch with these developments, created his masterpiece, *Man with a Movie Camera.*

The city symphony form remains an unusual, poetic choice, an exception to the rule of documentary conventions. Godfrey Reggio's 1982 *Koyaanisqatsi* uses lightshow-like techniques along with time-lapse photography (one of the techniques pioneered by city symphony films) to make a histrionic commentary on mankind's devastating effect on the earth. The title refers to a Hopi word meaning "life out of balance." American film scholar Thom Andersen used nearly a century of cinema to look at how Los Angeles has been represented in the movies in *Los Angeles Plays itself* (2003). It sometimes wryly, sometimes bleakly shows the city in the commercial and public imagination.

Other self-described artists have searched for ways to use documentary film as a road to purity of vision and a celebration of the ecstasy of sensation itself. Because their films deliberately eschew conventions such as story line, narrator, and sometimes even discern able objects in the world, they provide another way of understanding what we have come to expect. Kenneth Anger, Jonas Mekas, Carolee Schneeman, Jordan Belson, and Michael Snow all made films that creatively interpreted real life, although they identified themselves as avant-garde artists and not documentarians. One of the best known American avant-garde artists who did think of himself as a documentarian—and a scientist—was Stan Brakhage.

Brakhage wanted viewers to return to an "innocent eye," a purity of experience of vision. He wanted to help people *see,* not only what the eye takes in from the outside but also what the eye creates as a result of memory or bodily energy from the inside. "I really think my films are documentaries. All of them," he said. "They are my attempts to get as accurate a representation of seeing as I possibly can." Most of Brakhage's work was silent and executed in the passionate belief that seeing was a full-body action. Surprisingly, his artistic intuitions and perceptions of how the eye works are supported by scientific research on optics.

Brakhage made hundreds of films; two of the most seen are *Mothlight* (1963) and *The Garden of Earthly Delights* (1981). In both short films, Brakhage encased found natural objects, put them between two pieces of celluloid and then printed the images created. *Mothlight* contained moth wings; *Garden* contained twigs, flowers, seeds, and weeds. The images produced then created an experience for viewers, which referred to the original but was entirely different.

Art films have also experimented with sound. The German experimental filmmaker Hans Richter translated sound rhythms into visual experience in the 1920s and 1930s. The Indian filmmaker Mani Kaul, who grew up artistically in India's subsidized "parallel cinema" (i.e., parallel to commercial cinema) in the 1970s, has worked repeatedly with Indian song traditions, including *Dhrupad* (1982), which mesmerizes with the sound and image of one classical music performance style designed to facilitate spiritual meditation. Such work highlights the way in which we often take sound for granted as a convenient emotional conductor.

In all these works, the conventions of "regular documentary" are largely absent. No narrator tells us what is going on; no experts provide authority; ordinary reality is deliberately distorted so that we will see it differently; soundtracks are used for other purposes than cueing story-linked emotions. Patterns of light and dark, the hypnotic sound of repetitive music, the sight of objects from the natural world projected at many times their size, and other devices shock us out of our visual habits. These experiments have greatly expanded the repertoire of formal approaches for documentary filmmakers.

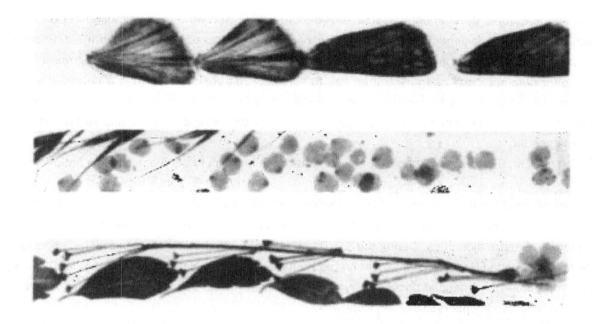

Figure 6–1. In *Mothlight*, experimental documentarian Stan Brakhage pressed moth wings and scraps of twigs and flowers between celluloid strips. Directed by Stan Brakhage, 1963. Source: Stan Brakhage, Mothlight, 1963.

At the same time, these experiments provide a sharp contrast to the most common conventions, those usually used in broadcast television.

ECONOMIC CONTEXT

Conventions are also conditioned by business realities. On television, where viewers make a decision within one or two seconds about whether to watch, producers now strive to make every moment compelling and to signal brand identity not only through identifying logos but through style. They also search for ways to streamline production and reduce costs through style and form. A History Channel executive in the later 1990s memorably explained that channel's then-formula—clips either of stock footage or of small staged scenes or objects interpolated with talking heads and stitched together with narration—to a group of striving producers: "We do it because it's cheap and it works."

Filmmakers have looked to three kinds of funders to pay for their documentaries: *patrons* or *sponsors*, both corporate and governmental; *advertisers,* typically on television and usually at one remove; and *users* or *audiences.* Each source of funding has powerfully affected the choices of filmmakers.

Government sponsors have been critically important to documentary filmmaking. In the British Commonwealth, institutions that promote the making and distribution of documentary film include the BBC, the Australian Broadcasting Corporation, and the Canadian National Film Board. Throughout continental Europe, governments provide subsidies to artists who work on documentaries. German, French, and Dutch documentary work has flourished with this kind of investment. In the developing world, ex-colonial powers sometimes provide stipends for cultural production; national governments may offer resources and often control access to screens. Cultural nationalism is a powerful motive for national governments to provide these subsidies. Programming themes and styles often reflect a concern to express national identity, especially against the unceasing international flow of U.S. popular media.

By contrast, U.S. taxpayer support for documentary has historically been anemic, in a nation where cultural policy has always strongly supported commercial media. U.S. public broadcasting was given a rebirth in the liberal heyday of Lyndon Johnson's Great Society, with committed public funds for the noncommercial, nongovernmental entity to help build capacity of the then-feeble public broadcast stations in most major cities. During the 1970s and 1980s, other cultural organizations, especially the taxpayer-funded National Endowment for the Humanities and the National Endowment for the Arts, also contributed to American documentary. Unconventional styles, themes, and politically sensitive topics often raised conservative ire in Congress.

Another way in which governments have been important to documentary filmmaking is through regulation that encourages certain kinds of production over others. For example, when the British government authorized the existence of private commercial television channels, it also required hefty public interest responsibilities, which translated into ambitious documentary projects funded in hopes of prestige, recognition, and license renewal. British Channel 4 was launched with funds siphoned from advertising revenues of a commercial channel and was given a mandate to feature the work of independent producers, including many documentarians. Chad Raphael has argued that American broadcast network fear of government regulation (networks had been caught rigging quiz shows) led to a period of lavish funding for investigative public affairs documentaries. (Indeed, the decline of government regulation of television in the 1980s resulted in a decline in public affairs documentaries.)

Government regulators play a de facto role in standards-setting and enforcing of conventions. Broadcasters are usually under tight scrutiny by regulators who patrol use of airwaves, which the government typically leases to individual companies with conditions. In a documentary about drug smuggling, *The Connection,* Brian Winston recounted a scandal that erupted in Britain in 1998 over re-created or possibly even fictional footage. The British Independent Television Commission, a regulatory body, fined the television channel that aired the film and set in motion debates about government censorship.

The U.S. Federal Communications Commission (FCC) levied an indecency fine, widely criticized as arbitrary, on a public television station for airing a history program, *The Blues* (2003), because in it a jazz musician uttered a vulgar word. The judgment then made many broadcasters even more cautious in their programming.

The role of private-sector sponsors in the history of documentary has been large, and surely will continue to be. Key works of documentary founder Robert Flaherty were backed by corporate sponsors who hoped to associate their image with his romantic vision. Corporate underwriters and sponsors were also essential to early documentary on television. For instance, the American public affairs program featuring the great journalist Edward R. Murrow, *See It Now* (1951), was funded by Alcoa, which at the time was looking to burnish its reputation after an antitrust suit. Corporate underwriters have been crucial to public service television as well. Nonprofit organizations have also become significant clients for documentary film work on issues they consider important. Sponsors pay to have a film made because they want a particular story told or they want to improve their image. Either way, a filmmaker has limited autonomy but often it is enough to be able to do important work. Sometimes a filmmaker's priorities accord well with an organization's, as well. Advertisers are also sponsors, each of whom pays for a little time or space on a program that can attract viewers to their messages. Advertising favors lightweight, low-budget documentaries that do not challenge the status quo and sensationalist documentaries that can drive up ratings.

Direct sale is the fastest-growing model for documentary support. Theatrical audiences looking for novelty and awe find it in IMAX documentaries, whether on the miracle of flight or the astounding world of tropical insects. Subscribers to cable channels, such as HBO or Canada's Doc Channel, receive a flow of documentary programming the same way they subscribe to magazines. Video on demand also offers documentaries direct to viewers, as do rental services such as Netflix and Blockbuster. Home users are purchasing, often online, DVDs of documentaries that may never have seen the inside of a theater, and they are also downloading films to their video iPods and cell phones; this drives documentarians to identify a "personal audience," as producer Peter Broderick calls it, and to craft work around the interests of this niche or identify a constituency passionate about a particular cause or issue.

A breakthrough example of direct distribution was the Robert Greenwald-produced *Outfoxed* (2004), which lambastes Fox News for its right-wing bias. Launched during the 2004 election season in the United States, this film was offered to viewers via e-mails from the liberal website MoveOn.org. According to organizers, more than 100,000 viewers purchased the DVDs within the month, mostly for use in house parties where several viewers saw it at once. The film also received a limited, simultaneous theatrical run. The example was rapidly imitated and tweaked; soon conservatives were making their own incendiary films and circulating them to their constituencies.

Digital production in a download era bids fair to develop new market models. By 2006 video downloads occupied perhaps half the total traffic on the Internet. Within days, obscure homemade parodies have drawn worldwide audiences larger than many documentaries ever gained in a festival and theatrical run. At the same time, the business model that can support such work still remained to be seen.

ETHICS AND FORM

Ethical issues have been as critical as aesthetic ones in the formal choices of documentarians. American historical filmmaker Jon Else and theorist Bill Nichols among others have called for professional filmmakers themselves to articulate ethical standards.

One ongoing question is that of how much simulation of reality is acceptable. Outright fakery is easy to condemn, although it is common from the origins of film: Thomas Edison's studio produced war footage from the Philippines in New Jersey, and the supposed record of the sinking of the *Maine* in the Havana harbor was actually filmed in a New York bathtub.

Other practices are less ethically clear. Reenactment was a staple of 35mm documentary film production. Given the cumbersome machinery, without lighting and staging, most filmmaking of this kind would have been impossible. Cinema verité purists in the 1960s, using new lighter-weight and more-flexible equipment, scorned such techniques, denigrating them as artificial.

Reenactment burgeoned again, though, in the 1990s. Sometimes, it was because of the low budgets offered by cable programmers that filmmakers struggled to produce compelling storytelling for television audiences used to high production values. Thus, on the History Channel, for example, it became common for a few feet in sandals to represent the march of thousands of Roman warriors, or for a few coins and a vase to represent the wealth of kings in another era. Other times, filmmakers used reenactment to evoke an uncaptured moment. In the Holocaust-memoir film *Tak for Alt* (1999), scenes of a mother making challah and lighting candles were staged to represent the memories of the survivor's childhood. Such use is not confusing to viewers, since they usually can distinguish what is genuine experience from the symbolic representation of it.

Controversy has grown up around filmmaking in which the fake is interwoven with the real, without giving viewers the chance to distinguish. The civil rights history *Mighty Times: Volume 2: The Children's March* (2004), by Robert Hudson and Bobby Houston, intermixed reenactments and archival material, and also used archival material from one place and time to signify another. When it won an Academy Award, the film generated controversy for its intermixing. David McNab's *The Secret Plot to Kill Hitler* (2004) was part of a Discovery Channel experiment in "virtual history," in which actors reenact a moment in history, and the heads of historical figures are borrowed from archival footage. The film admitted this at the outset, but some believed the approach of mixing actors with archival images crossed an ethical line and could potentially confuse people.

Films that throughout use actors and scripts, with creative license, to retell true events are usually called docudramas. Films such as *Gandhi* (1982) or television series such as *Roots* (1977) are docudramas. They look and feel like fiction films, and it is generally understood that they can take some license with details in order to dramatically represent a reality. However, neither viewers nor journalists think falsifying reality is appropriate. A 2006 ABC network docudrama, *The Path to 9/11,* cast actors in roles of real Clinton administration officials, including that of the secretary of state, and had them say and do things that they clearly had not. These falsifications showed the Clinton administration neglecting a terrorist threat. The network deleted some errors at the last minute and then tried to absolve itself by noting that the film was only a docudrama, but outraged viewers and commentators were not mollified by the disclaimer.

Some documentaries mix in fictional elements while still laying claim to being documentaries. This style is growing with the popularity of documentary entertainment. For example, Danish filmmaker Jeppe Rønde's *The Swenkas* (2004) tells a fable about a father-and-son reunion, within documentation of real-life male fashion contests in South Africa. Although it was popular in film festivals in the global North, the film raises questions for its representation of a fictional plot as real life.

Some documentary filmmakers deliberately use fiction as a provocation. British left-wing filmmaker Peter Watkins has made many films using nonactors to reenact historical incidents that reveal structures of power and movements of resistance, from the Battle of Culloden to the Paris Commune. American radical filmmaker Emile de Antonio in his *In the King of Prussia* (1982) restaged a trial of anti-Vietnam War protesters, after reporters were banned from the courtroom. The film starred the actual defendants, including the priestly brothers Philip and Daniel Berrigan, with the Hollywood actor Martin Sheen as the judge. The reenactment not only retold the events but implicitly critiqued the banning of reporters during the trial. The French filmmaker Chris Marker, in his *Sans Soleil* (1982) mixed documentary images and sound with a fictional narration. The result was a provocative inquiry into the meaning of memory and a meditation on filmmaking. In *Perfumed Nightmare* (1977), Philippine filmmaker Kidlat Tahimik recycled documentary footage to tell a fictional story about a Third World innocent who traveled to the West—a tale that was also a critical documentary essay about the interpenetration of West and East. The recycling itself was a commentary on the Philippines' syncretic and eclectic culture.

German artist Harun Farocki has created many complex and self-reflexive film essays where documentary footage is used and wrenching questions of public importance addressed. His essay on the complicity of industrial workers in the Vietnam war, *Nicht löschbares Feuer (The Indistinguishable Fire*, 1969)—the fire referred to napalm—was scripted and staged in a style that attempted Brechtian alienation. American filmmaker Jill Godmilow later remade the film shot-for-shot as *What Farocki Taught* (1998).

Are such hybrids still documentary? Like the mainstream of documentary, they claim to portray real life, telling the viewer something important about it. But to some, these experiments are outside the bounds of documentary, as are mockumentaries. Godmilow herself, within her film, asks the viewer what kind of movie *What Farocki Taught* is. She points out that almost all scenes were reenacted, such as most scenes in the film it mimics had been, and yet the film is an argument about real life. She suggests, partly tongue in cheek, that the viewer regard the film as "agit-prop," recalling the Soviet-era term for "agitation-propaganda" films to incite social change. Her own questioning points to the fuzzy lines around the border of the genre.

Filmmakers' formal choices all make persuasive claims to the viewer about the accuracy, good faith, and reasonableness of the filmmaker. The fact that filmmakers have a wide variety of choices in representing reality is a reminder that there is no transparent representation of reality. No one can solve these ethical dilemmas by eschewing choice in expression, and no formal choices are wrong in themselves. A good-faith relationship between maker and viewer is essential. Filmmakers can facilitate that by being clear to themselves why they are using the techniques that they do, and striving for formal choices that honor the reality they want to share.

Manufacturing Vision

Kino-Eye, *The Man with a Movie Camera*, and the Perceptual Reconstruction of Social Identity

BY DAVID TOMAS

Our eyes, spinning like propellers, take off into the future on the wings of hypothesis.
— Dziga Vertov[1]

This compelling metaphor encapsulates the pioneering Modernist spirit of one of the twentieth century's most radical experiments in creating a working interface between social revolution and cinematic practice. The experiment was developed by the Russian filmmaker Dziga Vertov in the 1920s during the 'golden age' of the Russian Revolution, one of the most fertile periods of cultural upheaval since the Industrial Revolution. Because of its documentary orientation, political engagement, and commitment to formal experimentation, Vertov's work has been a seminal influence on the *cinema verité* movement as well as avant-garde experimental film; it has had a decisive influence on filmmakers of the calibre of Jean-Luc Godard and Chris Marker; and has been the subject of numerous commentaries and analyses.[2] However, there has been no attempt to examine his work and, in particular, his classic 1929 silent film *The Man with a Movie Camera* from an 'anthropological' point of view, that is as the social symbolic product of a particular culture. This is surprising since his work has dual ethnographic value: as a documentary product of the making of a new society as well as the product of a new way of looking (cinema) and seeing (montage editing). If his work differs fundamentally from the work of his great rival Sergei Eisenstein it is precisely in its initial focus on the everyday world of Soviet Russia and in its attempt to critically engage this world in cinematic terms, that is in terms of a technology of representation which was the complex product of the kind of social environment he was examining. Vertov's writings and films can therefore provide a particularly rich source of information on the social construction of vision, not only because they are the fruit of a period of unparalleled change but also because they represent a conscious, indeed reflexive, attempt to socially engineer vision in order that it could function in pace with this change. Moreover, to treat his ideas and film from this point of view leads to a surprising observation since the principal exemplar of this new mode of social engineering—*The Man with a Movie Camera*—appears to have been cast in the form of an age-old panhuman ritual: a rite of passage.

While it can be argued that Vertov's cinematic practice provides an object-lesson in the design of *social* imaging systems on the basis of existing hardware because it directly links cinematic observation to social organization and the production of new cultural/perceptual spaces, one must situate this argument in a broader political context. In Vertov's case, this was of course a determining context, since his work was eventually marginalized in the name of another social agenda. Later politically engaged filmmakers would also find themselves in a similar position.[3] Nevertheless, Vertov's unusual model of collective observation and cinematic manufacture remain, to this day, one of the few coordinated attempts to design a 'social technology of observation'[4] that could account for an expanding media culture while retaining a tactical political and social 'situational reflexivity.'[5]

In the following pages I will present a case for considering film and photography as rites of passage, I will extend this discussion to *The Man* with *a* Movie *Camera,* detail the novel 'social technology of observation' that served as its foundation and, finally, note their relationships to the production of new social identities. During the course of this discussion I will have occasion to comment on some possibilities and questions raised by this approach to Vertov's cinematic theory and practice.

1. PHOTOGRAPHIC AND CINEMATIC RITES OF PASSAGE

Rites of passage have traditionally been understood to be limited to the symbolic mediation of socially problematic and ambiguous biological processes such as birth, puberty, and death. They have also been identified as mediating major seasonal or cosmic transitions or, alternatively, conventional passages between important social stages, for instance, marriage.[6] These rituals have notably excluded technological and industrial processes in general and, in particular, those processes used in engendering and sustaining Western traditions of pictorial representation. However, there are two reasons why one should begin to consider these latter technologies as ritual systems and processes of social/symbolic transformation. First, photography and film are powerful systems of optical, mechanical, and chemical transformation, more accurately *transubstantiation,* that serve as well defined spatio-temporal passages between the worlds of everyday human existence and parallel worlds of pictorial representations having very particular (ie. coded) photochemical compositions and cognitive organizations. The efficiency of these mass-produced systems which are, in turn, able to mass-produce visual images and the ubiquity of their use in the Modern world suggests that they might represent important portals between distinctive collective social states or stages. Second, these systems are, in fact, structured according to three clearly demarcated or differentiated stages of production that replicate, in important ways, the governing tripartite structure and corresponding symbolic logic of a classic rite of passage.

Thus, the first stage, or rite of separation, of an ideal form of photographic or cinematic rite of passage consists of the optical/mechanical procedures and photochemical reactions involved in physically 'taking' photographs and films. The product of this stage (a latent image) is then chemically processed to produce a negative, which corresponds to the second or liminal stage of a photographic or cinematic rite of passage. The negative is an exemplary liminal artifact, a strange and uncanny social object in which light and dark, the binary components of many ocularcentric systems of social/ symbolic classification, the most prominent of which is day/night, are reversed while a subject/image retains its given morphological characteristics. The negative is also rather unusual and unique in that its transparency provides the means for almost infinite reproduction. The third stage of an ideal photographic or cinematic rite of passage, which corresponds to a rite of incorporation in a classic rite of passage, comprises the optical, mechanical and chemical procedures used for processing and printing a positive image. These procedures ensure an orderly transformation or passage from the liminal stage to a final 'positive' social condition *represented* by a final photographic or cinematic print.

However, cinematic prints are part of a larger social system or technology of representation since they are designed to be viewed in the context of special environments called *cinemas.* These environments bear a striking resemblance to traditional liminal sites in their curious exclusionary spatial and social properties. Cinemas are dark enclosed environments in which a group of people view physically non-existent realities projected onto a two-dimensional surface by way of a beam of light. These realities, whose cultural contents are as diverse as their social and political inflections, range from depictions of the monstrous to the mundane. But in all cases they tell us something about the ways in which we live and behave *or* the ways in which others live and behave. In other words, as in the case of a traditional liminal stage, they provide us with special insights into what it means to be human and social beings. The liminality of cinemas is further accentuated by a symbolic exchange between the 'living' and 'dead'—the former virtually presented on screen as moving, talking, interacting figures, while the latter are reproduced in the order and rigidity (almost a form of social rigor mortis) of an audience enveloped in a mausoleatory darkness.

A ritual approach to cinematic technologies and the image cultures they generate is therefore in order not only because such compelling similarities warrant further investigation, but also because this approach would allow one to begin to address the social and cultural dimensions of the *technological* systems that produce photographs and films. In particular, such an approach would allow one to explore these extraordinary products of a Western industrial imagination from the points of view of the overall functions of their systems of manufacture in order to answer such traditional 'anthropological' questions as what kind of social and symbolic transformations are they designed to deal with? How do they achieve these ends? For whom and in terms of whom do they operate?

One can also conceive of a whole series of other questions in connection with the so-called objective technological transparency of film and photography. What does it mean to take photographs and/or films of other cultures? What world(s) are these other peoples really entering when we film them or when they film themselves according to a ritual of technology that articulates Western technological and aesthetic values? While this is not the place to address such issues, Vertov's work on Kino-Eye should sensitize us to the politics—both symbolic and mimetic—implicated in film production and its culture of vision while reminding us once again of the range of human expression that is possible when we begin to challenge inherited ways of looking at and seeing ourselves and others in the name of other visions, other realities.

Vertov's Kino-Eye project is especially significant in this regard because it provides a unique, relatively well documented, attempt to perceptually reconstruct human vision by redefining its social/technological foundations and political orientation. In contrast to other types of film organization, Kino-Eye was dedicated to exploring, in an almost comparative ethnographic fashion, Soviet society at a given point in time. This attempt was, moreover, radical enough to have effectively challenged cinema practice as then understood and its challenge continues to resonate to this day.

2. PREAMBLE TO A KINOMATIC RITE OF PASSAGE: A NOTE ON VERTOV'S POLITICS OF REPRESENTATION

Vertov's revolutionary film practice was founded on a 'nonacted' or documentary model of film production. He argued that an inherent weakness of fictional films was their tendency to separate, too easily, the realms of work and leisure according a governing opposition between methods of analysis (science) and practices of interpretation (art). In contrast, his factually based 'nonacted' film was predicated on a synthesis of art and science, interpretation and analysis. This synthesis was carefully crafted under the auspice of a logic of montage editing to produce a revolutionary poetics powerful enough to induce a critical social consciousness in film audiences. Its power resided in its ability to redefine the parameters of binocular vision and thus challenge and transform an audience's habital modes of perception according to cinematic knowledge (that is knowledge of and knowledge by way of cinema). When considered in the context of the dominant models for early twentieth century film production, this poetics was nothing less than a carefully honed weapon with which to attack the literary and theatrical tendencies which Vertov considered to be destructive counter-revolutionary forces in a young Soviet film culture. Its main objective was to undermine their modes of social production and system of coding which, in the latter case, amounted to an assault on their technological transparency, narrative linearity, and illusionism, the combination of which resulted, in Vertov's opinion, in the spectator's unconscious intoxication.[7]

This poetics was the product of three innovations. First, Vertov shifted the emphasis in film production's social logic from product to process of manufacture. He hoped, by doing so, to draw attention to film as mode of production as opposed to film as mode of entertainment. Second, he argued that it was necessary to recast the notion of process itself in a 'nonacted' or documentary mould. Film production would thus be displaced from the studio to the street—propelled, in other words, into a industrialized culture and thus forced to take account of its new forms of manufacture, social organization, cultural expressions and volatile post-Euclidean perceptual spaces. Moreover, as *The Man with a Movie Camera* illustrated, this shift allowed for the cinematic ingestion of a wide range of social protagonists, including 'cameramen' and editors, as film characters and subjects. Third, Vertov developed a common basis of social/cinematic organization that would link these innovations directly to the most fundamental unit of film production/reproduction: The creation of difference between two frames of a film a) at the level of production in the passage of a film-strip through its film gate (the elementary procedure for recording movement) and b) at the level of reproduction in the passage of a film-strip through the film gate of a projector (the elementary procedure for reproducing movement). The sum total of these innovations embodied, in Vertov's estimation, the spirit as well as the political and social aspirations of the October Revolution.

The Man with a Movie Camera is the most radical statement of Vertov's Kino-Eye method from both the points of view of its observational *and* documentary strategies. It is, moreover, a prototypical cinematic product of a society in transition and a cinematographer who was attempting to come to terms with this transition. At the level of manufacture, it links the activities of a cameraman to those of the editor and finally the audience, and grounds these activities in a wider industrial culture. As a visual artifact, it also represents a perceptual process of manufacture, its product a new social vision. The 'conveyor belt' for these processes is provided by a formal and thematic itinerary which visually interweaves the human activities that define a society in the making with the socio-technological activities that generate and survey its new mode and domain of vision: a social/ cinematic space. Together they (re)constitute themselves in the process of reconstituting a factually grounded day in the fictional life of a Soviet city. The film thus articulates two parallel interconnected rites of passage, the one that embodied and sustained its production as cinematic object, the other that articulates a particular 'dioptric' solution to the problematic of generating an alternative camera-based socialist culture of vision, a problematic posed and solved in terms of an architectonics of collective observation.

3. *THE MAN WITH A MOVIE CAMERA:* A KINOMATIC RITE OF PASSAGE

The Man with a Movie Camera (Cheloveks Kinoapparatom) is a six reel approximately 95 minute film released in 1929 under the auspices of the Ukrainian Film and Photography Administration (VUFKU). As credited on the film, Vertov was the "author-supervisor of the experiment," Elizaveta Svilova, his wife, the editor or montage assistant, and his brother, Mikhail Kaufman, the chief cameraman. Vertov considered the film to be a major statement of the 'Kinoks' principles of non-fiction film making and as the first part of a projected two part study of the language of the cinema which would oppose the world as seen and reproduced by Vertov's new mode of social/cinematic observation/manufacture, christened 'Kino-Eye,' to the world as seen by the imperfect human eye.[8]

At once a brilliant exposition of film production's place in an industrialized society, a masterly display of the formal and rhetorical codes of cinematic representation and a complex polythematic montage of everyday social activities in Soviet Russia, *The Man with a Movie Camera* is Vertov's most direct visual statement of Kino-Eye method[9]—not only "a practical result" but also, and most importantly, "a theoretical manifestation on the screen."[10] Finally, in keeping with its artifactual status as manufactured object, it was also considered a 'film-thing' or 'film-object.'

Recently, the film been described by Annette Michelson as a meta-cinematic celebration of filmmaking as a mode of production and ... a mode of epistemological inquiry" in which a "'world of naked truth' is, in fact, the space upon which epistemological inquiry and the cinematic consciousness converge in dialectical mimesis."[11] This space, whose specific social topography remains undefined in this cogent description of the film's status qua revolutionary film, is, perhaps, best defined by way of a new social/industrial matrix for cinematic communication: a hierarchic division of observational labour that functioned as a technology or process for manufacturing cinematic vision. It is this social technology, a fusion of Vertov's Kino-Eye collective with the cinematic apparatus, that articulates the complex thematic armature consisting of a day in the life of the composite Soviet city depicted in *The Man with a Movie Camera;* and it is this technology that finally provides the visual means for staging a perceptually induced revolutionary transformation in the consciousnesses of both producers and spectator/audience.

However, it does so in a curious manner for such an avowedly revolutionary visual experience, since the film appears to replicate in its overall organization the tripartite form and symbolic structure of a traditional rite of passage. Although there is no evidence to suggest that Vertov was aware of the cultural status and 'anthropological' significance of this type of ritual, he was certainly aware of the existence of similar rituals in his culture,[12] and he did depict socially sensitive events widely subject to rites of passage mediation, such as birth, marriage and death—albeit under the aegis of a new revolutionary social and cultural agenda and cinematic medium of representation.

As a cinematic rite of passage, the first section of the film reflexively introduces the spectator/ audience to its own context of observation: the cinema. The sequence is introduced by the following warning: "Attention viewers: This film represents in itself an experiment in the cinematic communication of visible events; without the aid of intertitles (a film without intertitles); without the aid of a scenario (a film without a script); without the aid of theatre (a film without sets, actors, etc.); this experimental work was made with the intention of creating a truly international ultimate language of cinema on the basis of its total separation from the language of theatre and literature." The warning shatters any expectations about seeing a conventional fictional film while simultaneously sensitizing the audience to the rather unusual 'story' that immediately begins to unfold before their eyes. This 'story' is introduced by a survey of the mechanics of cinema reproduction. Although it is presented under the sign of production, in this case a giant movie camera which serves as the platform for the appearance (introduction) of the cameraman and his camera (the film is always dear as to the priority of this distinction), representation is considered, in this separation sequence, from the point of view of the cinema as opposed to the movie camera: interior of cinema with its empty seats, projector and projectionist, film, chandeliers, seats (animated this time), audience, orchestra and conductor. The audience is thus immediately presented as divided in terms of representation (an audience on the screen) and self-representation (the audience is depicted as preparing to watch a film). This ensures a common identification between 'audiences' while introducing the idea that the film's 'story' might have nothing to do with "the old 'artistic' [ie. narrative] models" of literature or the theatre that were based, as Vertov saw it, on "a literary skeleton plus film-illustrations."[13] In fact, the possibility that the old models, whose narrative unfurling was ultimately determined by a script's point of view, might be operating in this case, is almost immediately negated by the perceptual conjoining of audiences about to watch a 'common' but highly unusual film in which they already have a collaborative role in ensuring its social articulation.

If the film goes on to produce a cinematic dislocation of the audiences's atomistic or individual powers of vision, powers previously governed by a "process of identification and participation,"[14] it nevertheless does so under a contradictory sign: the dialectic of identification and alienation first introduced in a separation sequence. The result is the inauguration of a "crisis of belief," as Michelson has succinctly described it, which will be consumated by the "exposure of the terms and dynamics of cinematic illusion-ism."[15]

The liminal phase of this kinomatic rite of passage, introduced by the numeral '1', is governed by a 'dominant' dioptric symbol, the Camera/Eye, which is periodically foregrounded during the course of the film either in the form of a camera lens or a superimposition of camera lens and human eye.[16] The film articulates its socialist 'vision', in this phase, according to a series of thematic vignettes of, amongst others, paradigmatic rites of passage subjects (birth, marriage, death), a series of social themes (work and leisure) and political issues (the constrast between socialist behaviour and residues of Bourgeois behaviour); and it does so according to a pure film semio-logic based on the unique spatio-temporal possibilities offered by motion picture technology *when used outside of the studio and within the context of the 'real.'* It is, therefore, the Camera/Eye's ability to witness the full range of social life that is celebrated in this liminal phase.

The audience is then reintroduced, through a cinematic rite of perceptual reincorporation or aggregation, to the conditions of cinema representation: with 'itself *qua* audience; with the special context in which the film is being presented; and thus to its status as representation and self-representation. But the situation is somewhat different this time because the audience is also introduced to an anthropomorphized movie camera who, in performing in front of the audience and in taking its bow, seems to be claiming a central role in the staging of this cinematic 'event'—a claim apparently confirmed by the ensuing recapitulation of major themes which are punctuated by copious references to the mechanics of cinema and cinematic representation in a constant montage of audience, screen, cameraman and editor. This montage ensures that film and the audience cross over into each other's domains and are incorporated in a spectacular perceptual *mise en abyme* in which the audience becomes spectator to an audience watching a film which turns out to be *The Man with a Movie Camera,* a connection that had not been made during the opening separation sequence. The film ends with the Camera/Eye staring at the audience, its diaphragm closing into pure light then darkness.

In sum, therefore, *The Man with a Movie Camera* is structured in the form of a rite of passage which connects and mediates two social stages of vision: a prerevolutionary reality, whose dominant model Vertov isolated and defined in terms of the natural or unconscious acceptance of an unproblematized illusionism, and a postrevolutionary cubo-futurist model that took form as a dynamic, dialectical, 'nonacted' cinematic culture predicated on a new logic of perception or method of constructing a film: *montage.* The transformation between the two was clearly mediated by an optically induced crisis of mimetic belief accompanied by a visual celebration of the transformative social powers of Kino-Eye—powers generated by "its own dimensions of time and space" and presented as if completely severed from "the weakness of the human eye."[17] The transformation was presented, moreover, through the medium of a new form of intelligence, in the words of a earlier 1923 manifesto, "the kinok-pilot [Mikhail Kaufman amongst others], who not only controls the camera's movements, but entrusts himself to it during experiments in space."[18] Vertov had anticipated the results of such a transformative union in this manifesto when he argued that as a "result of this concerted action of the liberated and perfected camera and the strategic brain of man directing, observing, and gauging—the presentation of even the most ordinary things will take on an exceptionally fresh and interesting aspect"—a comment that suggests a familiarity with Viktor Shklovsky's theory of defamiliarization or *ostranenie.*[19]

Cinematic defamiliarization was produced, in the case of *The Man with a Movie Camera,* by an array of visual strategies of perceptual distantiation which included references to the film screen as representational surface; the disruption of action sequences through the use of techniques of animation; the use of different film speeds to produce arrested, slow and accelerated motion that call into question the notion of normal film speed and thus the pace of conventional cinematic vision; the disruption of filmic illusion by distinguishing between "illusion experienced" and "illusion revealed" or film and film screen as distinct surfaces of representation; the use of techniques of distortion and abstraction as means of drawing attention to the constructed nature of the image; and finally a consistent attempt to place cinematic understanding, according to these means of perceptual distantiation, on an intellectual as opposed to an emotive footing.[20]

The sum total of these strategies was a cinematically manufactured crisis of habitual ocular perception (that is belief based on the experience of eyesight conditioned by an inherited social and cultural environment whose demise was most prominently symbolized in the film by the optical implosion of the Bolshoi Theatre Building) and the aesthetic pleasure that was based on this habitual perception. This ocular crisis functioned as the motive force for a simultaneous thematic transformation in a given audience's patterns of social identity. As in some classic rites of passage,[21] the audience was introduced to the social and cultural mechanics of their (Socialist) way of life and its normative and ethical frameworks. Thus, in keeping with the 'social' functions of liminal activities where a culture is decomposed along the lines of its dominant symbols and recomposed in new and unusual ways, this new pattern of existence was deployed in a new post-Euclidean cinematic space and based on a cinematic process of socialization whose thematic context was provided by new systems of communication, transportation, manufacture and the patterns of work, including Kino-Eye work, and leisure they engendered.

However, Vertov's ambitions extended well beyond ocularcentric transformations in archaic social/cinematic practices. He was ultimately interested in inaugurating a revolutionary transformation in the total human sensorium. With this aim we pass beyond the immediate experience of *The Man with a Movie Camera* in order to reconsider in detail the function of the kinoks and Kino-Eye in Vertov's model of film production.

4. ON THE RATIONALIZATION OF OBSERVATION AND ITS LINKAGE TO SPECTATORIAL CONSCIOUSNESS: VERTOV ON 'THE WORK OF THE KINO-EYE'

Vertov's strategies of film production were deployed in relation to an inherited scopic regime: Cartesian perspectivalism.[22] He proposed to challenge this regime on its own terms, that is, through the use of a recently invented (1895) technology of observation/reproduction that embodied that regime in its optical system; the film camera. Thus, he argued:

> We ... take as the point of departure the use of the camera as a Kino-eye, more perfect than the human eye, for the exploration of the chaos of visual phenomena that fills space.
>
> The Kino-eye lives and moves in time and space; it gathers and records impressions in a manner wholly different from that of the human eye. The position of our bodies while observing or our perception of a certain number of features of a visual phenomenon in a given instant are by no means obligatory limitations for the camera which, since it is perfected, perceives more and better

> Until now, we have violated the movie camera and forced it to copy the work of our eye. And the better the copy, the better the shooting was thought to be. Starting today we are liberating the camera and making it work in the opposite direction—away from copying.[23]

However, it was not just the film camera's superior powers of observation that converted cinema into a tool of perceptual liberation. Transformation was the product of a complex mode of observation that was itself structured according to a new perceptual logic—montage—derived from a politically reconditioned cubo-futurist aesthetic. While Vertov's artistic generation was first to intuitively understand the role of powerful Modern technologies and industries in mediating contemporary urban existence, the Russian constructivist artists were the first to seek to systematically articulate this understanding in terms of a political agenda that went beyond intellectual critique to embrace total social revolution.

The Man with a Movie Camera is an exemplary experiential product of this understanding precisely because it clearly proposes in the overt linkage of its material, formal, and thematic organizational levels according to an acausal logic of representation (montage) that the technology *and* social organization of cinema directly "mediates," in the words of Judith Mayne, "perception and production;"[24] indeed, that it can also mediate social existence. Thus, what Vertov described as "the *organization of the visible world*"(emphasis in the original)[25] was, in keeping with this understanding, considered to be a *complete* system and process of social manufacture: ultimately a collective *work of editing* that ranged from initial thematic research and primary observation 'in the field' to a final product to be perceptually experienced in a cinema. As Vertov pointed out at the time:

The kinoks distinguish among:

1. *Editing during observation*—orienting the unaided eye at any place, any time.
2. *Editing after observation*—mentally organizing what has been seen, according to characteristic features.
3. *Editing during filming*—orienting the aided eye of the movie camera in the place inspected in step 1. Adjusting for the somewhat changed conditions of filming.
4. *Editing after filming*—roughly organizing the footage according to characteristic features. Looking for the montage fragments that are lacking.
5. *Gauging by sight (hunting for montage fragments)*—instantaneous orienting in any visual environment so as to capture the essential link shots. Exceptional attentiveness. A military rule: gauging by sight, speed, attack.
6. *The final editing*—revealing minor, concealed themes together with the major ones. Reorganizing all the footage into the best sequence. Bringing out the core of the film-object. Coordinating similar elements, and finally, numerically calculating the montage groupings.[26]

It is clear from this passage that Kino-Eye was ideally composed of a hierarchic division of labour that functioned as a *technology of observation*—a kind of collective imaging system that had the capability to simultaneously observe a multitude of different social spaces. Moreover, this technology was also a *process of manufacture* socially defined in terms of editing stages and aesthetically defined in terms of montage stages. Thus, a clear practical logic linked social labour from the individual kinok-observers to kinok-cameramen, kinok-constructors [designers], kinok-editors (women and men), kinok laboratory assistants[27] to the final cinematic experience (its final stage of manufacture and observation—a new visual consciousness in an audience).

The concept of Kino-Eye film production was therefore not only predicated on lightweight and mobile camera technology, a concern with a 'culture of materials'—"the materiality of the [film] object and ... its architectonics,"[28] it was articulated in terms of a powerful social technology of observation/manufacture that ranged from the beginning to the end of production. Although one would imagine that, ideally, there were no privileged points of view or observers in this collective mode of observation/manufacture, its hierarchic organization implied, in keeping with Vertov's military model, coordination by a 'leader' whose job was to ensure observational coherence according to an overall thematic goal.[29]

Traces of this technology of observation and process of manufacture are clearly visible in *The Man with a Movie Camera*. The film's thematic flow is governed by a cameraman (Kaufman) who is seen pursuing 'themes' and an editor (Svilova) who is seen classifying and working thematic components into a final product. Collective authority tends therefore to be foregrounded in terms of these activities as opposed to an individually defined directorial authority. The foregrounding of collective authority is also evident insofar as the division of editorial labour is dominated by an observational logic whose presence in the film is more than symbolized by the Camera/Eye.

In Kino-Eye terms, a kinomatic rite of passage would involve the Camera/Eye, and its operator(s) (the kinoks-cameraman), and an audience in a continuous vertically extended intersystem of manufactured perceptual transformation whose axis was precisely the Camera/Eye. As "masters of vision, the organizers of visible life, armed with the omnipresent kino-eye,"[30] the kinoks would—after having gone through a process of resocialization marked by a shift of observational context from studio to the street—be in a position to be continually educated by 'life:' "that whirlpool of colliding visible phenomena, where everything is real."[31] In other words, far from being independent of the 'real,' as in the case of personnel involved in filming fictional films, camera/persons would become at once visible and invisible, submissive and sensitive to its sociopolitical vississitudes and cultural contradictions. It was this process of reeducation, grounded as it was in the reality of the everyday and subtly orchestrated by a system of observation, that ensured that the collective consciousness of Kino-Eye and, by extension, the audience would no longer fall prey to "the director's megaphone"[32] and to all that it symbolized for Vertov.

If Vertov's concept of Kino-Eye is clearly reflected in *The Man with the Movie Camera's* perceptual/thematic intergration, his espousal of the title 'author-supervisor' is a further, if oblique, acknowledgement of its collective authority. Thus, if, as Michelson suggests, *The Man with a Movie Camera* is a film that marks "a threshold in the development of consciousness" whereby the 'cameraman' was transformed "through the systematic subversion of the certitudes of illusion ... from a Magician into an Epistemologist,"[33] it is perhaps more accurate to suggest that the Kino-Eye model of cinematic production ensured that the cameraman, editor, and audience were collectively accorded a new epistemological identity in its name, the result of a coming of collective age by way of an uncompromising cinematic rite of passage.

5. BEYOND POETIC DOCUMENTARY: ORCHESTRATING VISION ACCORDING TO A POST-OCULARCENTRIC CULTURE OF REPRESENTATION

Vertov considered himself a "film poet" who 'wrote' "on film" and who produced "poetic documentary film."[34] Poetry, for Vertov, was cinematic truth rooted in the invisible. In other words, poetic documentary film was the product of strategic "comparisons" of social behavior which aimed "to decipher reality" by way of a particular social technology of observation/manufacture that worked on pieces of film "from the beginning to the end of production."[35] This process was governed, as we have seen, by a dialectical form of thought ("most easily translated by montage"[36]) which would allow for the exploitation of the inherent difference between two adjacent film frames—a difference defined, in the final analysis, in terms of *intervals* but nevertheless experienced at all the levels of observation/manufacture.[37] As Vertov pointed out at the time,

> To find the most convenient itinerary for the eyes of the spectator in the midst of all these mutual reactions, of these mutual attractions, of these mutual repulsions of images among themselves, to reduce this whole multiplicity of intervals (of movements from one image to the other) to a simple spectacular equation: to a spectacular formula expressing in the best possible manner the essential theme of the cine-thing, such is the most difficult and important task of the author of montage.[38]

If montage functioned as the dialectical semio-logic articulating Kino-Eye's social technology of observation/manufacture and its tripartite ritual structure, Vertov's theory of intervals was its thematic complement in the sense that it made perceptual sense of the visual connections that articulated particular thematic vignettes. From the point at which documents were to be related to a chosen theme ("montage evaluation"), through the stage of "montage synthesis" of the human eye ("montage of personal observation or of reports by the information-gatherers and scouts of the film") involving the "plan of shots," the "result of the selection and classification of the observations of the 'human eye'" conceived in relation to the "peculiarities of the 'machine-eye' of Kino-Eye", to the period of "general montage" when the visual equation is worked out, one can understand the *production of truth* to pivot on the interval, "upon a movement between the pieces," minimally expressed in the difference between two successive frames;" upon the proportions of these pieces between themselves, upon the transitions from one visual impulse to the one following it"[39] and upon the reflexively generated at the thematic level by means of the 'meaning ties' or formal linkages established by the visual rhythm created by orchestrating the intervals.[40]

The interval would thus serve to link montage technique directly to the mechanical and photochemical foundations of the film process: to the photochemical creation of difference in the movement of two frames through the film-gate of a camera, and the reproduction of that difference in the movement of a film through the film-gate of a projector. A theory of the interval would, in other words, ensure a linkage and engagement between the evolving thematic geography of the film and a spectator's maturing consciousness by way of a specific perceptual itinerary plotted, as in the case of the *The Man with a Movie Camera*, under the aegis of the Camera/Eye.

In the process of reconstructing meaning, the audience, as both subjects and objects articulated in the context of a kinomatic rite of passage, would no longer find themselves excluded from the process of observation/manufacture that constructed this cinematic experience. At the beginning of the rite of incorporation sequence of *The Man with a Movie Camera* the audience is introduced to the 'real' author of the film: an anthropomorphic Camera/Eye. Thus, in the course of the film, consciousness has thus been gradually redefined from a human to a panhuman consciousness: its final form—an animated camera and tripod symbolizing the convergence of a new collective consciousness whose 'representation' or identity pattern is not the dense factually based thematic interpretation Kino-Eye had forged in relation to a contemporary Soviet reality in this film, but rather Kino-Eye's simple and refined observational logic, a logic that managed to articulate, as never before, a newly evolving social space in terms of previously unmapped cinematic space. Had this blueprint for a kinomatic rite of passage found social sanction with post-revolutionary authorities, Vertov's dream of an open ended socialist vision might have found broader collective expression. Instead, Vertov's film was ignored—its revolutionary impulse to be subsequently legitimated within the context of an avant-garde aesthetic tradition of a capitalist social system Vertov had fought hard against.

6. KINO-EYE'S LOGICAL EXCESS: VERTOV ON THE TOTAL COLLECTIVIZATION OF THE HUMAN SENSORIUM

In retrospect, it is evident that the kinoks were not, in fact, considered to be individual persons but rather basic elements in observational modules composed of two integrated components (film camera and kinok intelligence) that together comprised a minimal social unit in an technology of observation whose collective cinematic intelligence was compounded through physical and emotional bonding into a perfect bio-cinematic consciousness. In terms of our current understanding of this linking of machine and human organism these elements combined to form a prototype *cyborg* consciousness:

a kinomatically integrated 'brain' and consciously reflexive observational technology. It was this consciousness—whose dominant symbol is the Camera/Eye—which operated on the audience during the course of *The Man with a Movie Camera*.

However, Vertov proposed that the Kino-Eye mode of organizing observation/manufacture be also extended *horizontally* in order to link together other technologies of the human senses with the aim of transforming human thought itself:

> The theoretical and practical work of the *kinoks-radioks* … have run ahead of their technical possibilities and for along time have been awaiting a technical basis the advent of which will be late, in relation to Kino-Eye; they await the Sound-Cine and Television. Recent technical acquisitions in this area lend powerful arms to the partisans and workers of *documentary sound cinegraphy* in their struggle for a revolution in the cinema, for the abolition of play, for an October of Kino-Eye.
>
> From the montage of visual facts recorded on film (Kino-Eye) we pass to the montage of visual and acoustic facts transmitted by radio (Radio-Eye).
>
> We shall go from there to the simultaneous montage of visual-acoustic-tactile-olfactory facts, etc.
>
> We shall then reach the stage where we will surprise and record *human thoughts*, and, finally, we shall reach to the greatest experiments of direct organization of thoughts (and consequently of actions) of all mankind. Such are the technical perspectives of Kino-Eye, born of the October Revolution.[41]

This passage, from a lecture delivered in the same year *The Man with a Movie Camera* was released, presents a vision of a highly rationalized cultural politics of representation. As the individual biological eye became increasingly collectivized in relation to the other senses and its powers were increasingly dissipated through sensorial integration there would be a progressive diminution in its undisputed ability to govern the dominant social spaces of culture. Vertov suggests that this democratization of the senses by way of an expanded sensorial intersystem, or Culture of Representation, would ultimately engender a comprehensive post-ocularcentric culture.

The model Vertov outlined in this 1929 lecture was thus an extension of Kino-Eye in the sense that it expanded the latter's organization model for observational diffusion. At this final stage in his poetic blueprint for socialist reconstruction of the human sensorium it was, however, no longer a question of organizing people into a given technology of observation so much as organizing new patterns of identity emerging from a range of 'intelligent' sensorially integrated human/machine interfaces.

"Kino-eye is learning" Vertov replied to a question by the poet Vladimir Mayakovsky concerning its progress in 1934.[42] That reply best sums up Vertov's attitude to his project: Kino-Eye learns, which means that the Kinoks and the audience are collectively introduced to new identities which would ideally continue to be generated along a continuum of technologies of representation until the October Revolution would consumate itself in a grand sensorial excess.

7. CONCLUSION

There are a number of lessons to be extracted from Vertov's revolutionary but abortive experiment. First, there is the curious phenomenon of an ultramodern visual experience—*The Man with a Movie Camera's*—being structured in terms of a panhuman ritual. Could this represent a profound intuition concerning the human capacity to negotiate radical change or does it illustrate the limits of Vertov's vision? There is of course no clear answer to this question other than to suggest that this mode of negotiating major social transitions deserves further investigation in the context of other technologies and in particular in connection with new technologies such as virtual reality.[43] This does not, of course, preclude the investigation of other ways of negotiating change but just what form they might take is beyond this paper's speculative range.

Second, there is the question of Vertov's kinomatic practice and its relevance to contemporary cinematic practice. It is evident that Vertov still has much to teach us about the relationship of theory and practice, the politics of representation, vision and its connections to social change, and the necessity of exploring different organizational models for technologies of observation (notwithstanding his utopian call for a global sensibility which, in hindsight, rings ominously in the late-twentieth century ear). One might correctly point out that filmmakers such as Godard and Jean Pierre Gorin have already attempted without much success to build on Vertov's legacy. However, if the failure of these attempts demonstrates the political constraints under which all artists and political activists operate at any one point in time, they also make it very clear that without these challenges and continual attempts at redirecting social expectations and restructuring cultural experience we are in grave danger of succumbing, at the very least, to a kind of blind technological amnesia. It is therefore worth bearing in mind Vertov's arguments and demonstrations concerning the social foundations of imaging systems (while adopting a critical stance in regard to his dream for a collectivization of human consciousness). *The Man with a Movie Camera* is exemplary in this connection, for it clearly presents its particular vision as a product of a theoretical and practical conjunction of a given imaging system (the movie camera) and a social technology of observation/manufacture. In other words, it is a model technology that not only creates and controls space but is *in itself* an organization of space, an inner space of critical social consciousness.

Third, there is Vertov's suggestion that technologies of representation be considered relationally—sociologically—within a given mediascape. And that they be defined in terms of a complex intersystem of technologies of observation and related image cultures whose impact on the human sensorium can be measured according to alterations in its sense ratios. Walter Benjamin and a number of contemporary theorists, notably Marshall McLuhan and Paul Virilio, have made similar observations. Benjamin, for example, noted the impact of media on the relationship between the human senses as did McLuhan almost thirty years later.[44] Recently Virilio has devoted considerable energy to describing the logistics of military perception and its penetration throughout our social fabric.[45] Clearly, Vertov's work on the Kino-Eye predates the work of these theorists and goes beyond them in the sense of working or attempting to work his theory through cinematic practice as in the case of his espousal of a military model for Kino-Eye or his call for a collectivization of the human sensorium. There is, however, another direction in Vertov's work which might provide a more fruitful contribution to contemporary debate on media: his suggestion that a critical poetics is only possible at the cultural intersection of observational technologies which manufacture the 'real' (clearly in Vertov's estimation, a floating signifier of the historical artifact 'representation') and that it can only take form through an active and critical engagement with the comparative differences generated by fundamental contradictions inhering in particular cultural formations. For Vertov, it was this conjunction of the two which gave political sense to social consciousness and identity. Perhaps it is this aspect of Vertov's legacy that will prove to be the most enduring since it motivates and gives conscious form to an open and situationally reflexive poetics.

While production has given way to consumption as a cultural dominant and new technologies such as virtual reality threaten to redefine our sensorial landscape and indeed the very basis of our identities as human beings, Vertov's practice remains, to this day, a useful touchstone in the search for ways to foster new modes of looking, new ways of seeing ourselves and others.

ENDNOTES

An earlier version of this paper was presented at the 'Film as Ethnography' conference, University of Manchester in September 1990.

1. Dziga Vertov, 'We: Variant of a Manifesto,' in Annette Michelson (ed.), *Kino-Eye: The Writings of Dziga Vertov,* Kevin O'Brien (trans.), (London and Sydney: Pluto Press, 1984) p.9.

2. On the avant-garde see Peter Wollen, 'The Two Avant-Gardes,' *Studio International* Vol 190, No. 978, (1975), pp. 171–175. For a discussion of Vertov's influence on Godard see Kent E. Carroll, 'Film and Revolution: Interview with the Dziga-Vertov Group,' in Royal S. Brown (ed.) *Focus on Godard* (Englewood Cliffs: Prentice Hall, 1972) pp. 50–64. For a discussion of the social and political background to Vertov's work and its relationship to postrevolutionary Russian culture see Annette Michelson, Introduction, *Kino-Eye,* op. cit., pp. xv-lxi and Stephen Crofts and Olivia Rose, 'An Essay Towards *Man with a Movie Camera,*' *Screen* Vol. 18, No. 1, (1977) pp. 9–58. An extensive formal analysis of *The Man with a Movie Camera* can be found in Vlada Petric *Constructivism in Film: The Man with the Movie Camera, A Cinematic Analysis* (Cambridge: Cambridge University Press, 1987).

3. See, for example, Godard's comments in Kent E. Carroll, 'Film and Revolution: Interview with the Dziga-Vertov Group,' ibid.

4. My use of the phrase 'social technologies of observation' is derived, in part, from Teresa de Lauretis's influential definition of gender as a social technology. Thus, according to de Lauretis, gender can be

considered "both as representation and as self-representation … the product of various social technologies, such as cinema, and of institutionalized discourses, epistemologies, and critical practices, as well as practices of daily life." *Technologies of Gender: Essays on Theory, Film, and Fiction* (Bloomington and Indianapolis: Indiana University Press, 1987) p. 2.

5. I have borrowed the term 'situational reflexivity' from *Femamatic* (L. Hissey, A. Hearn, L. McLarty), 'Alice Does or Situational Reflexivity: Toward a Theory of Active Female Spectators' (unpublished manuscript, 1990) because it encapsulates the radical spirit, if not the gendered letter, of Vertov's Modernist cinematic practice. In Femamatic's words (pp. 11–12): "The term 'situational' refers to the immediate social context of subjects … those intersecting elements of … subjectivities: race, class, gender, sexual preference, age, etc. It also incorporates the specific context of viewing and the particular text in question. The situation is both materially and discursively constituted. In short, the situation involves our momentary sense of 'self' and the representation of that 'self' to us through discourse. The situation is never static: its status is always changing and temporally defined…. The notion of reflexivity adds to the immediacy and temporality of situation a reflective dimension which permits the apprehension of common experiences of oppression. This, in turn, points not only to the possibility, but to the very necessity, of making normative claims."

6. For classic discussions of rites of passage, see Arnold Van Gennep, *The Rites of Passage*, M. B. Vizedom and G. L. Caffee (trans.), (Chicago: University of Chicago Press, 1960); and Victor Turner, 'Betwixt and Between: The Liminal Period in *Rites de Passage*,' in V. Turner, *The Forest of Symbols; Aspects of Ndembu Ritual*, (Ithaca and London, Cornell University Press, 1977) pp. 93–111. For an analysis of the photographic process as a rite of passage see David Tomas, 'Toward an Anthropology of Sight: Ritual Performance and the Photographic Process,' *Semiotica*, vol. 68 no. 3/4, (1988), pp. 245–270.

7. Vertov, 'Kino-Eye,' in *Kino-Eye*, op. cit., p. 63: Musical, theatrical, and film-theatrical representations act, above all, on the viewer's or listener's subconscious, completely circumventing his protesting consciousness.

8. cf. Vertov, 'From Kino-Eye to Radio-Eye,' *Kirto-Eye*, op. cit., p. 87:

     Kino-eye = kino-seeing (I see through the camera) + Kino-writing (I write on film with the camera) + kino-organization (I edit).

     The kino-eye method is the scientifically experimental method of exploring the visible world —

     a. based on the systematic recording on film of facts from life;

     b. based on the systematic organization of the documentary material recorded on film.

     Thus, kino-eye is not only the name of a group of film workers. Not only the name of a film… And not merely some so-called artistic trend (left or right). Kino-eye is an ever-growing movement for influence through facts as opposed to influence through fiction, no matter how strong the imprint of fiction.

9. For a description of the film's rhetorically based cinematic language see Annette Michelsion, 'The Man with the Movie Camera:' From Magician to Epistemologist,' *Anforum* Vol. 10, no. 7 (1972), pp. 66–67, 69.

10. Vertov, 'The Man with a Movie Camera,' in *Kino-Eye*, op. cit., p. 83.

11. Annette Michelson, 'The Kinetic Icon in the Work of Mourning: Prolegomena to the Analysis of a Textual System' *October* 52 (1990) p. 19; Michelson, op. cit., note 7, p. 63.

12. Michelson, op. cit., note 10.

13. Vertov, 'Kinoks: A Revolution,' in *Kirto-Eye*, op. cit., pp. 13, 12.

14. Michelson op. cit., note 7. p. 69.

15. ibid.

16. For a discussion of dominant symbols see Victor Turner, 'Symbols in Ndembu Ritual,' op. cit., note 11, pp. 30–32.

17. Vertov, 'Kinoks: A Revolution,' in *Kino-Eye*, op. cit., p. 16. In Vertov's words (p. 19):

    The mechanical eye, the camera, rejecting the human eye as crib sheet, groaps its way through the chaos of visual events, letting itself be drawn or repelled by movement, probing, as it goes, the path of its own movement. It experiments, distending time, dissecting movement, or, in contrary fashion, absorbing time within itself, swallowing years, thus schematizing processes of long duration inaccessible to the normal eye.

18. ibid., p. 19

19. ibid. For the standard discussion of ostranenie or defamiliarization see Victor Shklovsky, 'Art as Technique,' in *Russian Formalist Criticism: Four Essays*, Lee T. Lemon and Marion J. Reis (trans.), (Lincoln: University of Nebraska Press, 1965), pp. 3–24.

20. Michelson, op. cit., note 7., pp. 69–70.

21. cf. Turner, op. cit., note 11, pp. 99–110.

22. Martin Jay, 'Scopic Regimes of Modernity' in Hal Foster (ed.), *Vision and Visuality*, (Seattle, Bay Press, 1988), p. 5

23. Vertov, 'Kinoks: A Revolution,' in *Kino-Eye*, op. cit., pp. 14–16.

24. Judith Mayne, 'Kino-Truthand Kino-Praxis: Vertov's Man with a Movie Camera,' *Cine-Tracts*, vol. 1, no 2, (1977), p. 88.

25. Vertov, 'Kino-Eye,' in *Kino-Eye*, op. cit., p. 72.

26. ibid.

27. ibid., p. 75.

28. Michelson, op. cit., note 7, p 65.

29. Vertov, 'Kino-Eye,' in *Kino-Eye*, op. cit., p. 69. There is a parallel to be explored here between Vertov's project and the militarization of perception as described by Paul Virilio in *War and Cinema: The Logistics of Perception*, Patrick Camiller (trans.), (London: Verso, 1989). However, this is the subject of another paper.

30. Vertov, 'Kinoks: A Revolution,' in *Kino-Eye*, op. cit., p. 20.

31. ibid., 'Notebooks, Diaries,' p. 167.

32. ibid.

33. Michelson, op. cit., note 7., p. 72

34. Vertov, 'Notebooks, Diaries,' in *Kino-Eye*, op. cit. pp. 199, 183.

35. Vertov, 'Notebooks, Diaries,' in *Kino-Eye*, op. cit., 197 and '"Kinoks-Revolution,"' op. cit., note 34, pp. 90, 103.

36. Luda Schnitzer, Jean Schnitzer, and Marcel Martin (eds.), *Cinema in Revolution*, (London: Secker &c Warburg, 1973) p. 85.

37. Vertov, '"Kinoks-Revolution,"' op. cit., note 34, p. 104:

"The school of Kino-Eye requires that the cine-thing be built upon 'intervals,' that is, upon a movement between the pieces, the frames; upon the proportions of these pieces between themselves, upon the transitions from one visual impulse to the one following it."

38. ibid., pp. 104–105-

39. ibid., pp. 103, 104.

40. cf. Vertov, 'From Kino-Eye to Radio-Eye,' in *Kino-Eye*, op. cit., pp. 90–91:

41. The "movement between shots"—the transitions from one visual stimulus or "visual 'interval'" were negotiated by way of a "sum of various correlations," amongst which were:

    1. the correlation of planes (close-up, long shot, etc.);

    2. the correlation of foreshortenings;

    3. the correlation of movements within the frame;

    4. the correlation of light and shadow;

    5. the correlation of recording speeds.

    Vertov goes on to note: "besides the movement between shots (the 'interval'), one takes into account the visual relation between adjacent shots and of each individual shot to all others engaged in the 'montage battle' that is beginning" in order "to find amid all these mutual reactions, these mutual attractions and replusions of shots, the most expedient 'itinerary' for the eye of the viewer, to reduce this multitude of 'intervals.' ... to a simple visual equation ... expressing the basic theme of the film-object."

41. Dziga Vertov '"Kinoks-Revolution," Selections' in Harry M. Geduld (ed.), *Filmmakers on Film Making* (Bloomington and London: Indiana University Press, 1967) pp. 101–102.

42. Vertov, 'Notebooks, Diaries,' in Kino-Eye, op. cit., p. 180.

43. See, for example, my 'Old Rituals for New Space: *Rites de Passage* and William Gibson's Cultural Model of Cyberspace.' In Michael Benedikt (ed.) *Cyberspace; First Steps* (Cambridge Mass.: M.I.T. Press, 1991) pp. 31–47.

44. Walter Benjamin, 'The Work of Art in the Age of Mechanical Reproduction,' in Hannah Arendt (ed.) *Illuminations* (New York: Schocken Books, 1976), pp. 222; Marshall McLuhan, *Understanding Media: The Extensions of Man* (New York: A Mentor Book, 1964) p. 61.

45. Virilio, op. cit., Note 29.

Myths, Racism and Opportunism
Film and TV Representations of the San

BY KEYAN G. TOMASELLI

The central dynamic between film-makers and subject-communities is one of power. Questions of accountability with regard to production and distribution practices are rarely dealt with in ethnographic films, or in publications about them.[1] In this chapter I will examine the origins and effects of critical responses to films and television programmes about the San, specifically those films which some American academics within the Anti-Apartheid Movement argue are part of the problem leading to their destruction.

WHAT'S IN A NAME?

The San of Namibia and Botswana have been labelled with a variety of 'scientifically-derived' names, most being external impositions which sooner or later take on pejorative connotations. Wiley *et al* (1982, p. xix) in commenting on John Marshall's *The Hunters* (1958), objected to the label, 'Bushman', as 'a racist, pejorative term used by those who sought to dehumanize them as a prelude to their removal from the land and slaughter'. In defying Edwin Wilmsen's (1989, pp. 26–32) critique, Rob Gordon insists that Paul Myburgh's use of 'Bushmen' in *People of the Great Sandface* (1985) is correct since 'San' is derived from 'Sab', meaning robber. 'Bushmen' stems from Dutch, meaning bandit or outlaw. Gordon (1990a, p. 30) argues that 'San' is mystificatory, and that 'Bushmen' is a 'lumpen-category' once used by colonial authorities for resisters to colonial rule. He concludes: 'perhaps it is time to make Bushmen (and banditry) respectable again'.

While none of the films discussed in this chapter make banditry or begging respectable, the squabbles amongst anthropologists and historians about naming have serious political consequences. One is to foreground the apparent 'scientific' nature of anthropology and, in so doing, to suppress the unspoken subjectivities of anthropologists and/or film-makers. More immediately, however, the debate opened a space for political opportunism on the part of the South African authorities. The South West African Department of Tourism and Conservation, the South African Defence Force and other state departments played certain paradigms against others in film and other media in their abortive attempts to establish a 'Bushmen' reserve in Namibia, and to dispossess the !Kung, and other groups of their previously inhabited territories and waterholes. The disagreement over 'naming' thus empowers 'scientific' discourse over the everyday collective nouns used by people to describe themselves. 'Science', certainly positivist science, is ahistorical and easily mobilised for ideological and political purposes. The 'Bushmen' have never considered themselves a single entity or society (Marshall and Ritchie 1984); this has been the prerogative of anthropologists, film-makers and state authorities whose misleading scientific categories told them otherwise. Most films about the San have thus been located within this incorrect assumption, one that coincides with the direction the South African government tried to impose vis-à-vis a 'Bushmen homeland'. Jamie Uys's *The Gods Must be Crazy* (1980) is the most well-known example, having earned more than 100 million US$ worldwide.

CINEMA, SOCIAL SCIENCE AND THE SAN

The unprecedented international success of *The Gods Must be Crazy* (hereafter *Gods I*) cracked open a debate within American social science and media studies on the way white South Africans have represented 'Bushmen' on film and television (Volkman 1988; Gordon 1990a, 1990b; Tomaselli 1990; Blythe 1986; Lee 1985). In *Gods I* a coke bottle thrown from a plane disrupts the harmony of an isolated band of 'Bushmen' as they begin to fight over it. Xi's quest in the film, set in the Kalahari Desert, is to return the botde to the Gods. Xi's trek takes him through the lives of a clumsy white botanist and the woman he is trying to impress, a 'coloured' jack-of-all-trades, and marauding black terrorists. He is imprisoned by the strange white society for killing and eating a goat. As in Jaques Tati's *Monseur Hulot's Holiday* (1953), Xi's relationship to the people around him hardly impinges on his consciousness, and he returns to his band unchanged in the face of his novel and traumatic experiences.

Critiques of *Gods I*, and Uys's earlier *Beautiful People* (1974), a Disneyfied comedy about animals in the Kalahari which includes a vignette of 'Bushmen' imitating them (see Blythe 1986), range from historically sensitive explanations of the Afrikaner psyche (Davis 1985) to reductive equations of Uys's films with official apartheid propaganda (Gilliam 1984; Lee 1985) which single-mindedly seize their viewers in vice-like racist pronouncements. The argument that directors 'position' their viewers in an uncritical relation to their films arose from British Screen Theory' which dominated critical media studies during the 1970s and early 1980s. In this now discredited paradigm, scholars assumed that their decoding of a film's dominant messages coincided with the way all viewers understood—or should have understood—them. This assumption underlies the dominant academic response to Uys's films, and makes no distinction between documentary and other film genres, or the way audiences, in fact, make sense of films.

Critics foregrounded certain elements of Uys's films but simultaneously suppressed the broader historically and culturally discursive contexts from which Uys and his films emerged. Richard Lee (1985), for example, mistakenly classified *Gods I* alongside two earlier, supposedly South African-produced, racist films, which although shot on location in South Africa, were produced by foreigners. These were the British-made *The Wild Geese* (1977), about mercenaries rescuing an old and sick black African leader from tribal conflict somewhere in Central Africa, and the American-produced *Zulu* (1966), on their defeat by the British at Rorke's Drift in Natal in 1879. Having reminded readers of white South African racism on the basis of these foreign-made films, he concluded that *Gods I* was part of this 'official' apartheid conspiracy, notwithstanding its much more disarming style. All this conclusion shows is that British and American perceptions of black Africans are part of an international discourse on race and racism, to which *Gods 1* is connected.

The preferred North American analytical frameworks lack four necessary dimensions in their application to films made in South Africa. Firstly, the complex relations between film-makers and the production of ideology tend to be reduced to vulgar analyses of the mechanistic relations assumed to exist between film-makers and the apartheid state. Secondly, the technological, ideological and subjective processes which shape discursive cinematic practices in particular historical conjunctures in different societies need elaboration. The third dimension relates to how and why different audiences interpret the same films differently. As will become clear, the application of solely ethnographic criteria to an analysis of the two *Gods* films and *People of the Great Sandface*, suppresses crucial autobiographical, psychoanalytic and symbolic information residing in the texts of these films. And, fourth, as Alan Rosenthal (1989/90, p. 59) cautions with regard to Toby Volkman's (1988) critique of *Gods I*, audiences approach comedy and fantasy differently to documentary. They do not necessarily interpret everything they see literally.

Uys is portrayed by his critics as a cynical and ruthless opportunist who deliberately and maliciously distorts the image of 'Bushmen' for the political purposes of the South African government. Fundamental ideological questions are lost in the welter of accusations made against him by an incensed anthropological community as they bore witness to the destruction of the San in Namibia, which was under South African control until 1989. A seemingly bewildered Uys, however, continues to play out his innocence and anti-academic rhetoric in media interviews and press releases. His remarks about the *Gods* films constandy invoke white myths about the 'Bushmen' as a happy, culturally innocent and isolated group of hunter-gatherers, whose social equilibrium can only remain in balance with nature when alien influences like the coke bottle are purged. These myths, however, remain at their most destructive in his publicity kits, as they are presented as anthropological facts. In his publicity for *The Gods Must Be Crazy II* (1989) for example, Uys reasserted that the 'Bushmen' still live in their pure, pristine condition of remote primitive affluence, in exactly the way that he fictionalised their existence in the two *Gods* films.

Uys's slapstick comedies, through drawing on ethnographic and documentary codes, are very different to Paul Myburgh's documentary, *People of the Great Sandface* (1985). Myburgh (1989) claims to have lived with the Gwikwe and other bands in the Kalahari Desert on and off for ten years. His inspiration for this film was catalysed, he states, by his studies of anthropology, and the films of explorer Robert Flaherty and British documentarist John Grierson, both of whom made their respective contributions during the 1930s. *Sandface* resembles the Flaherty films in its 'man-against-environment' theme, the struggle of Myburgh's 'last band' of 'wild Bushmen' being against thirst and the temptation of a water tap in a Botswanan government settlement. The film also recalls Grierson's intent of dignifying working and marginalised people. *Sandface* similarly tries to redress the image of a group so often made fun of in comedic narrative cinema and tourist images. In *Sandface*, the lives of the isolated remnants of a Gwikwe band are documented through four metaphorical seasons, not unlike the time-scales used by Flaherty in his films. The desert substitutes for Flaherty's Arctic wastes (*Nanook of the North,* 1922), or the rocks and sea of the Isle of Aran (*Man of Aran,* 1934).

Despite its fundamental differences to the *Gods* films, *Sandface* too, has been labelled a 'fraud' and argued to perpetuate the 'killer-myth' of 'the wild Bushman' (Gordon 1990, p. 30a). In Namibia, the San are dying faster than they are reproducing themselves in squatter settlements (Volkman 1986, p. 27) and, in Botswana, where Myburgh made his film, they have suffered similar pressures of dispossession, resettlement and the negative effects of tourism (Hitchcock and Brandenburgh 1990).

HISTORY DENIED

Wiley *et al.* charge that *The Hunters* is a denial of history, as does Gordon (1990a, p. 31) of *Sandface*. Neither film referred to the social linkages between the San and their hostile white and black neighbours who chased them into the Kalahari over many hundreds of years. But, then, neither did many of the social anthropologists who originally studied them (eg., Lee and DeVore 1968; Thomas 1959; Silberbauer 1981). The dominant anthropological paradigm until the late 1970s was that the San were remnants of the stone age living in a state of 'pristine primitiveness'. As Gordon (1990b, pp. 3–5) argues, *Gods I* (though to a lesser extent, *Sandface*), rode to box-office success both in South Africa and the United States as 'part of a larger current in contemporary scholarly discourse' which ignored modern influences and tried to reinforce the myth of Bushmen living in splendid isolation, uncontaminated purity and primitive affluence (see Wilmsen and Denbow 1990). Jacqueline Solway and Richard Lee (1990) mention *Gods I* in this paradigmatic context, borrowing an image from the film in formulating the 'Coke Bottle in the Kalahari Syndrome' whereby:

modernity falls mysteriously from the sky, setting in motion an inevitable spiral of cultural disintegration that can only be checked by the removal of the foreign element. This is clearly a caricature, but it reveals the common and unstated perception of foraging societies as so delicately balanced and fragile that they cannot accommodate innovation and change ... The 'Coke Bottle in the Kalahari' imagery also bears a subtext, the rueful recognition of the unlimited capacity of 'advanced societies' to consume everything in their path. (p. 109–10)

Treating *Gods I* as ethnographic data of the dominant 'consuming' society which represents the San in media, as do Solway and Lee, offers more constructive leads than simply dismissing it as 'propaganda' or 'Kalahari ... caricature' (Wilmsen and Denbow 1990, p. 493). The latter part of Solway and Lee's statement accounts for Gordon's recurringly published lament that the 'Bushmen' have become the most highly scientifically (and commercially) commodified 'disappearing' group anywhere in the world, and is a reference to the myth so effectively commercialised by Uys in his two *Gods* films. Any society under the extraordinary gaze of international lenses is going to experience stress as their very 'disappearance' becomes consommé for television and film audiences elsewhere. Where whole societies once fell under the gaze of a few European explorers, their disorganised and tatty remnants are now 'authentically' redressed and packaged between TV advertising slots, which themselves, in South Africa for example, use myths about the Bushmen to 'demonstrate' that a Japanese four-wheel drive vehicle can go 'where the Bushmen go', perhaps even outperforming them in the desert. In this vein, Renato Rosaldo (1989, p. 17) links *Gods I* to the idea of 'imperialism with nostalgia', a trajectory incorporating films like *Heat and Dust*, *A Passage to India* and *Out of Africa*, as well as *Zulu* and *Wild Geese*. The colonial societies seen in these films appear decorous and orderly, as if constructed in accordance with the norms of classic ethnography. The narratives of these films, however, barely hint at these societies' impending collapse.

EXPEDITIONARY DISCOURSE

Western fascination with exploring the 'unknown' has long focused on expeditions to exotic places inhabited by people seen to be primitive neolithic relics: the peoples of Papua New Guinea, the Amazon Basin, Pygmies in Central Africa and the Inuit peoples of North America, have all been part of the popular Western imagination from at least Victorian times.

Early accounts of how whites searched the Kalahari for glimpses of 'wild Bushmen' form the bulk of many filmic and written accounts from the 1890s, continuing almost to the close of the twentieth century. This expeditionary metaphor was first articulated in *The Denver African Expedition* (1926), made by the Universities of Denver and Cape Town. It encoded a 'zoo ethos' and a method of luring 'the elusive little yellow men' into the open. Time and shifting academic perceptions about societies and ways of studying them humanised the expeditionary discourse into 'endearing' diminutive metaphors rather than overtly racist themes. Elizabeth Marshall Thomas (1959, p. 7), for example, wrote about how the San would hide 'like foxes in the grass' to avoid 'strangers', notably the Marshall expeditions of 1950–53. Other studies reflected the 'expeditionary' social discourse of exotic tribes with regard to the ways of the 'First' and/or 'harmless people': for example, Lourens Van der Post's *Lost World of the Kalahari* (1954) and its literary sequel, *The Heart of the Hunter* (1961), and his TV series *Testament to the Bushmen* (1982). John Marshall's *The Hunters* (1956) and National Geographic's *Bushmen of the Kalahari* (1974), also fall into this discourse. To paraphrase James Clifford (1988, p. 167), these journeys make sense as a 'coming to consciousness', of encountering and coming to know the 'Other'. Uys, for example, especially talks about, *and* images, the San in four of his films in this way. In *Gods I*, the clumsy girl-shy botanist comes to understand Xi, though Xi is traumatized in his encounter with modernity with its incomprehensible white laws and punitive institutions.

Marshall only admitted setting up scenes, especially the 'kills', in *The Hunters* (1956), almost 38 years after the film's release. This was done to perpetuate the myth of 'wild Bushmen' (Gordon 1990a, p. 32). An irony, then, is that the arch-villain, Jamie Uys, in his naivete, cut through academically legitimised myths, by offering a perverse allegory in *Gods I* of the disruptive effects of Western civilisation and modernity on a fictional Bushmen clan. But this was interpreted as 'racist' by American commentators whose own analyses and edited films until the late 1970s had, paradoxically, eliminated most traces of alien contamination, and who themselves contributed to the myth of modernity versus the traditional (see Volkman 1988, p. 242; Howell 1988, p. 7; Gordon 1990a; and Wilmsen 1989).

To what extent, then, is the attack on Uys an indication of guilt atonement by those who contributed to the unilinear model of human material development? The roots of Anglo-Saxon anthropology in colonialism and racism remain a sore point in the discipline. While some schools of modern anthropology would seem to have finally divested themselves of these taints, certain residual insecurities remain. These, I believe, are to be found firstly, in the nature of embarrassment with early racism in American cinema and its unique tradition of blackface actors, and of the *Amos and Andy* genre; secondly, in questions of 'objectivity' claimed by social science and the essentially positivistic nature of much of the anthropological enterprise; and thirdly, in the supportive relationship of certain early schools of anthropology to the theory of apartheid itself.

Social science has often proved itself incapable of preventing historical processes destructive of particular groups of people. Often, the best it could do was to publish and make films on 'vanishing' and 'disappearing' peoples. Indeed, social science has often held itself outside history and process altogether, basking in its seeming ideological innocence and claims of neutrality. Alternatively, it was harnessed by governments for their political ends, as was the case with Afrikaner *volkekunde* (ethnology—see Sharp 1979) and conservative cultural theory (Muller and Tomaselli 1990), which unconsciously underlies Uys's isolate model and purist ethnic representation of the San. In his terms, the San are indeed 'a kind of narrow and opaque window to the Pleistocene' (Yellen 1984, p. 54), a perspective which was of use to apartheid planners.

Sandface is not concerned with *finding* wild Bushmen, although Myburgh (1989, p. 27) claims that the Gwikwe *was* the last nomadic clan to exist in Botswana. This is another myth, asserts Gordon, on which entrepreneurs throughout the twentieth century have made money. *Sandface*, in fact, does not operate within the paternalistic discourse of the 'expedition', although Myburgh's interview gives the impression of his 'coming to consciousness' while making the film. He claims to have so thoroughly immersed himself into Gwikwe culture that he believed himself 'beyond the point where (his) subjectivity could have been a limitation to the truth' (Myburgh 1989, p. 29). The 'expeditionary' metaphor in *Sandface* works at a different level, concealed in Myburgh's mostly third person narration. *Sandface* is really Myburgh's own self-exploration, an ethno-biography in attempting to re-discover a coherent unity and culture so thoroughly evacuated by postmodern societies (Tomaselli *et al.* 1991). As such, it is Myburgh rather than the Gwikwe who may be unable, like Monsieur Hulot, to 'come to consciousness'.

When Myburgh talks about 'wild Bushmen', however, he is articulating the anthropological paradigm of his student days, irrespective of his rejection of textbook commentaries on the San. This contradiction is evidenced all through *People of the Great Sandface* through his dependence on largely conventional Western documentary film codes, a sense of progression and closure, and direct address narration which speaks 'for' the Gwikwe seen in the film.

CREW-SUBJECT RELATIONS

While desperately seeking a 'connectedness' (even if mythological), anthropologists and film-makers tend to create discourses about 'their' subject-communities which have more to do with their own positions in dominant societies than with actual situations on the ground. Self-validations of 'closed discourses' are often derived from taken-for-granted assumptions about class and social science. Uys, Myburgh, Van der Post and Marshall exhibit four different kinds of connectedness, each premised on particular ideologies, assumptions, myths and practices.

Van der Post's motivations for filming and writing about the San were basically two-fold: first was 'atonement' for the massacre of the last Bushman rock artist and his clan perpetrated by his grandfather, and the influence of his part-Bushman nanny, Klara, on his childhood (Van der Post 1986). Van der Post (1961, p. xv–xvi) hoped his books would 'incite a campaign' to benefit the 'Bushmen'. It is not clear, however, how he expected this to happen. Second, Van der Post was searching for origins. The 'First People' provided a vehicle for this recuperation of Southern Africa's original culture and its social harmony. *In A Mantis Carol*, for example, Hans Taaibosch is a bridge between the Western and San cultures, between the pre-modern and the modem: 'Hans Taaibosch was not only himself but also a mirror in which there was also a reflection of ourselves' (Van der Post 1975, p. 154).

Myburgh (1989, p. 26) was drawn by the 'wind' in his head (see also Marshall Thomas, p. 24), a desire to interpellate himself as a 'Bushman'. Myburgh felt that he had 'to become a Bushman, a Gwikwe in order to speak for the Gwikwe'. This attempt at taking on another identity resulted in Myburgh smudging his interpellation with a thesaurus of white myths which overdetermined his attempts at fully integrating himself into a San subjectivity—at least in the way he presented his film. As such, the film is really an auto-biography which often connects and empathizes with what Myburgh perceived as 'Bushman' culture, but which just as often also dismisses it (Tomaselli *et al.* 1991). Like Van der Post, Myburgh was searching for his origins, a sense of self, a First Culture. Myburgh's *Sandface*, however, cannot be so dismissively re-titled 'People of the Great White Lie' just because his historically naive narration repeats some of the numerous white myths about the 'Bushmen' excavated by Gordon (1990a). Myburgh has more in common with Van der Post than he realizes as both sought to discover the 'mind' of the San, and not necessarily offer data-filled 'scientific' ethnographies, although *Sandface* does tend to meander between the two forms of encounter.

Van der Post's Jungian analysis stresses the 'collective unconscious': the 'Bushman' as 'our dreaming selves' (Barnard 1989, p. 110). This unconscious 'longing' is perhaps analogous to Myburgh's (1989, p. 26) more earthy metaphor of 'wind': 'when I first went into the Kalahari the feeling of the "wind" inside my head was the same feeling as the "wind" outside my head. I felt like I had come home. Home is an intangible qualitative place, that feeling of familiarity within'. Although Myburgh is physically absent from the visual track, his subjectivity percolates through every frame; but the interpellation—'wind'—of a 'bridging' Hans Taaibosch—largely eludes him. Myburgh's empathy with his 'band' is evident, but the mysticism of the 'Bushman mind' and the joining of the premodern and modernist 'winds' is under-developed in the film.

Marshall's initial intention might have been expeditionary in intent. The hundreds of reels of film shot by himself and his family between 1950 and 1953[2] suggest an expeditionary atmosphere as the white 'bwanas' dressed in safari suits and pith helmets traverse an inhospitable terrain in their Dodge Power Wagons to direct filming proceedings. The film documentation of this phase and *The Hunters*, cut from the Marshall Expedition footage of the early 1950s, locates the young John Marshall as an adventurer and an explorer of the exotic. An epi-stemological rupture, however, occurred after Marshall returned to the United States where he then studied anthropology. Anthropology through film followed, with the !Kung San series, filmed during his adventurer phase of the early 1950s.

This footage was edited very differently to that used in *The Hunters*, and was accompanied by anthropological study guides. But with the demise of the San in the 1970s under apartheid, he inter-pellated himself as a family member, a rescuer. Marshall was the only film-maker to address materially the plight of the !Kung groups with which he worked. He established the Ju/Wa Bushman Foundation in 1981 to facilitate the survival of the Ju/Wasi through agriculture. He published ethnographies of the San, concentrating on how to improve their material conditions, rather than concerning himself with 'mind', or a search for origins and self *The Hunter's* narration does, however, encode a respect and poetic tone and something of the mysticism of a Van der Post. The narration is in the third person, but Marshall nevertheless shows an intimacy with his subjects, interpreting their behaviour and what they are thinking, doing and saying. Apart from this film, and *N!ai: Story of a !Kung Woman* (1980), Marshall has made very few films on the San, the 800,000 feet of 16 mm shot on the various Marshall Expeditions since 1950 notwithstanding.

For Uys, a basic narrative structure of repetition with difference, used successfully as the core of most of his twenty-five feature films, mobilised the mythical discourse about Bushmen to which both explorers and anthropologists had contributed. These mostly made fun of Boer-Briton taboos and the humorous way these played out in the white South African Afrikaner-English inter-cultural context. Metaphorically, then, *Gods I* may *not* be about Bushmen or Uys's idealist projection of bantustans as claimed by his American critics, but about the Eden myth and the way Afrikaners imagine an ideal state for themselves separate from alien influences (Tomaseili 1990). Only Uys seems to have no sense of further responsibility, whether financial or moral, towards the 'Bushmen'. His payment of a meagre R2,000 to his star actor, N!Xau, for *Gods I* and R5,000 for *Gods II* plus R200 a month *(Vrye Weekblad,* 17 November 1989) underscores an exploitative streak of the worst kind. This is, no doubt, rational-ised in his discredited claim that the 'Bushmen' are still hunter-gatherers living the life described by anthropologists of the 1950s—too much money might 'spoil' this exemplar of primeval life.

ETHNOGRAPHIC MOTIVES

Contemporary academic interest in the San has been sustained partly because of their accessibility to observation even while 'disappearing'. However, the prominence given to the San in the late 1980s is a direct product of the world's antipathy towards apartheid, as well as a major, often traumatic, introspection, caused by Wilmsen's (1989; Wilmsen and Denbow 1990) savage critiques of scholars like Lee and DeVore. This interest heightened as the San were caught up in the South African military onslaught against Angola. While the emphasis is well placed, it runs the risk of focusing on apartheid as the single factor threatening the survival of the San, while neglecting other causes.

While anthropologists like Gordon, Volkman, Lee and Wilmsen and film-makers like Marshall have done everything they can to discredit myths and stereotypes about the San, they should not be sur-prised at the way the myths motor on, given their original anthropological stimulus. Paradigms might 'shift' in science, but they don't always evacuate popular discourses or genres of representation. Given the noise of accusation and counter-accusation in *Current Anthropology* (1990) and *CVA Review* (1990–1), the student might be forgiven for wondering just what it is that separates myth from fact.

Even if Gordon's sarcastically dismissive account of Myburgh and his film is valid, there are other ways of reading and making sense of *Sandface*. This is through nomadic aesthetics offered by Teshome Gabriel (1988), where the overriding quest is for water. If Myburgh's (1989, p. 27) claim that he 'lived with the Bushmen according to their own ancient manner', is correct, then unlike anthropologists and film-makers who brought trucks stocked with food, water and other comforts of modernity, Myburgh thirsted and hungered along with his adoptive clan. Whether or not he deliberately constituted his band and reconstructed a nomadic existence is not, then, the main issue in terms of cinematic ethno-biography (though the criticism remains in terms of his ethnographic claims). The 'thirst' that Myburgh speaks of must then, in terms of this analysis, also be a metaphorical one. It is a thirst for deep memories of the past which are thought to offer a key to opening the meanings of the present. Or, as Van der Post's biographer expresses it, 'past experiences interact with present circumstances, until the exploration of the interior wilderness of Africa becomes also the exploration of the interior wilderness of the heart of man' (Carpenter 1969, p. 82). In terms of Gabriel's (1988, p. 75) theory of nomadic aesthetics, what Myburgh presents are images belonging to the past. Though representing remembrances, 'they carry simultaneously possibilities and promises, because they also belong to the future'. This intent, however, was partially subverted through Myburgh's reliance on closure, emphasis on individuals rather than collective relations, and acceptance of official history (Time and history have taken a heavy toll on their numbers'), which undermine the openness of nomadic aesthetics.

FILM AND TV: ARCHETYPAL WINDOWS

Media theorists have battled against the perception by most film and video makers that their cameras are windows looking on 'real life'. Anthropologists charged that *Sandface* and the *Gods* movies did not offer accurate representations of the way things are—that they were lies. This \isual positivism collapses the distinction between two forms of coded reality: the representations of everyday life, and their *re-representation* on screen. The problem for the film viewer is how to distinguish between the mental text elicited by the re-presentation on screen, the representation as it occurred or was enacted, and the pro-filmic event itself (what actually existed prior to the making of the film). Failure to see these distinctions will result in the film being read in terms of a single criterion—ethnographic—thus missing other levels of encoding (e.g. psychoanalytical) in which the key to interpretation exists.

Since both Myburgh and Van der Post (in *Testament to the Bushmen*) are searching for origins, for the 'mind' of the Bushmen, for 'original (South African) culture' they 'speak for' their subjects, telling us what they are doing, thinking and saying. Their objective is not ethnography, even San survival, as both imply that this 'people' had already disappeared. Van der Post tells us that this occurred before he even started to write about the Bushmen; while Myburgh states that his was the last 'wild' band to exist, moving to a settlement during the filming itself. Van der Post and Myburgh are searching for universal subjectivities, a way to the future, an essential South Africanism that first colonialism, and then apartheid, destroyed. They are less concerned with providing ethnographic detail and validity. Neither are they addressing the material needs of the San as does Marshall in his fund-raising film, *Pull Ourselves Up or Die Out* (1984), which complements an appeal pamphlet distributed through Cultural Survival.

No film, however, is neutral when threatened people are its subjects. Uys's *Gods I*, for example, was considered a dangerous film by anti-apartheid anthropologists for two main reasons. Firstly, there was Uys's perpetuation of stereotypes about the San, which exonerated the brutality of European colonialism and apartheid from complicity in their demise. Secondly, the film was *used* by apartheid planners to argue the case for a game park in which international safari tourists could view and live with 'Bushmen' in their 'original' state. This park would freeze the San in terms of the apartheid mythical construct so effectively popularised by *Gods I*.

The game park idea had its roots in *volkekunde* (ethnology) as developed by Afrikaner Nationalist ethnologists. *Volkekunde* offers a static, genetically determined sense of 'ethnos' which locates particular 'races' in specific 'homelands'. The interrelation of place and inherited social identity also has another origin. This source can be traced back to the proposition that eighteeth-and nineteenth-century discoverers/explorers/expeditionary enterprises mapped out the unknown world, both physically and cognitively. The same people who discovered and named lakes and mountains also discovered and named 'tribes' and peoples and decided that where they were found is where and how they had always lived. It is not surprising, then, that journals like *National Geographic* see their province as exploring both geography and anthropology, since studying environments and peoples are seen as two sides of the same project.

It is in this vein that the idea of a national park for the Bushmen in Namibia should be seen. It was envisaged that the San could not survive outside 'their' environment. Prevention of the 'biological crime' of permitting 'such a peculiar race to die out' (Reitz 1948, p. 17), required that their habitat be protected. This line of thinking underscores the notion that a symbiotic relationship exists between people and their environment, and to destroy the one means to destroy the die other. The problem arises when the idea is opportunistically used to promote sectarian political ends and reinforce the notion of tribalism in other contexts.

Gordon (1984) charged that this plan would 'conserve (the Bushmen) to extinction'. Referring to the effect of *Gods I* on apartheid thinking and the game reserve idea with regard to the San in Namibia, he concludes that 'Some films can kill' (Gordon 1990c, p. 1). The game reserve plan, however, was shelved in 1989 following a world outcry and lobbying by Marshall.

THEORISING CREW–COMMUNITY ENCOUNTERS

If cinema has contributed to the demise of the Bushmen, then new strategies should have been developed to counter this. Instead of making ever more mass-distributed movies about their plight, one response could have facilitated the techniques developed by anthropologists more attuned to the politics of survival. Great strides have been made in providing video channels for disadvantaged and repressed communities, even transforming the relations of production, as facilitated by Eric Michaels with Aboriginals in Australia. See, for example, O'Regan (1990), Terence Turner (1990) with the Kayapo in Brazil, and Marshall's fund-raising interventionist films like *Pull Ourselves Up or Die Out*.

When the camera and technical processes remain in the hands of the anthropologists, problems occur concerning the nature of the relationships that develop, crew assumptions about the composition, cohesion and nature of the 'community', issues of form, and questions of power. If anthropologists are to guide constructive processes resulting from their encounter with communities, they need to theorise the nature of that encounter and to acknowledge the power structures and relationships that develop. This is done by Marshall in *N!ai: Story of a !Kung Woman* (1980) with his vignette on Uys's concluding shots of *Gods 1*. But this reflexivity about another film is lacking from his own films, although a Documentary Educational Resources (DER) catalogue states: 'Ironically, some of N!ai's problems stem from the wealth she has acquired through her work with the Marshall film crew, as well as work from numerous other white photographers and film-makers who have found her beautiful' (Marshall Cabezas and Nierenberg 1990, p. 14). N!ai's photogenic demeanour has become the community's nemesis: they are just as dependent upon her as is she on white film crews.

The Study Guides produced by DER make no mention of how any of Marshall's films were made nor of the nature of the crews' encounters with the Ju/wasi and other bands filmed. The films are presented as though they were innocent: the archetypal windows to the San, although Timothy and Patsy Asch have helpfully written on how to use the Marshall films to teach anthropology. The lack of epistemological writing on methods of production alerts us to a fundamental issue: who initiates videos or films and why?

Films about people are specific discourses embedded in broader, constantly changing social processes and ways of encountering others, whether or not these are acknowledged in the films themselves. Marketing success is intertwined with dominant discourses which determine what kind of representations are most vulnerable to commercial exploitation. *The Hunters*, for example, cinematically anchored the evolutionary theory of isolate human material development that was the accepted teaching model within social science in the 1950s. Though superseded in contemporary anthropology, this model is now an accessory to contemporary popular Western belief in the superiority of modern over pre-modern societies. This is basic to the success of the *Gods* films for, even though Uys makes fun of runaway technology through the use of comedic devices first developed by Buster Keaton, the technology can be made to save the day. *Testament to the Bushmen*, like *Sandface*, straddles the pre-modern/modern trajectory in an initially anthropologically convincing way. These productions recall the more pristine times, but herald 'disappearance'. They empathize with, rather than make fun of, the San's encounters with others.

Sandface tells us something about Myburgh and his search for self, but does not explain much anthropologically. Perhaps this is the problem with most films about the San. By not writing about their filming experiences, film-makers exclude a whole level of ethnographic detail that needs to be known in order to make sense of particular films and the relationships that develop between crews and their subjects during particular conjunctures. In the interview in *CVA Review*, Myburgh exposes himself in a way that few have had the courage to do. This interview provides additional data from which to make sense of *Sandface*, of Myburgh himself, and ultimately of Western perceptions of and encounters with, and attempts to merge with, or bridge between, or mirror, the Other.

CONCLUSION: THE NOMADIC LENS

What I have tried to offer is an argument which explains the subjectivities of four film-makers and how these identities hailed them in different directions, though all remain adamant on the ethnographic accuracy of their respective statements about the San. To recast the 'Coke Bottle in the Kalahari Syndrome', perhaps it is academia which suffers from the syndrome as a result of problems within social science itself. Let us not forget that anthropologists had themselves ignored evidence of modernising influences amongst the San. They objected to Uys raising questions of modernity in *Gods I* partly because he embedded his narrative in a paradigm which denied these influences and which they had earlier legitimised. The ultimate comment may be that Marshall's *N!ai: Story of a !Kung Woman* (1980), the first edited ethnographic film to admit modernity amongst the San, was made at the same time and place as *Gods I*, and includes a scene on the making of Uys's film. The two films intersected each other, each a comment on different paradigmatic moments and ways of representing the San. These films may well articulate two sides of the same coin, the one side now legitimated at the expense of the other.

Film-makers either impose inappropriate aesthetics on 'their' nomads, or they can try to reveal an aesthetic intrinsic to the people being filmed. The cinematic apparatus imposes an aesthetic permitted by the technical properties built into the recording technology. But this aesthetic can be adapted in the course of its travels into stories and places beyond the conceptual boundaries and ideological frames imposed by the dominant media. And herein lies the contradiction:

> A travelling aesthetic requires travelling theory and criticism; yet theory and criticism are canonized, and thus become a way of fixing rather than liberating their objects. Nomadic practice thus creates havoc for such an orientation. Intrinsic to the nomadic mode of expression is an ever-constant shifting of form and content and the relationship among them and audience. (Gabriel 1988, p. 74–5)

Myburgh's film has traces of a nomadic aesthetic but he fails to draw it out. *Testament to the Bushmen* suppresses the visuality of the nomadic aesthetic under conventional documentary conventions. The *Gods* films encode the nomadic as a psychic wilderness which exists in the Afrikaner mind only. Only in *The Hunters* does Marshall have any sense of the nomadic—the problem for him thereafter is a question of material San survival.

ENDNOTES

I am greatly indebted to Ruth Tomaselli, Ken Harrow and Patrick Dionne for their critical comments and help in the preparation of this chapter, and to the Human Sciences Research Council, Fulbright, the Smithsonian Institution and the African Studies Center, Michigan State University, for resources to undertake the research.

1. Exceptions are O'Regan (1990) on Eric Michaels; Michaels (1986, 1987); *Media Development* ('Video for the People') 36(4) 1989 and Turner (1990). Most published commentators on questions of accountability would not, however, regard themselves as anthropologists, but as communication scholars.
2. Held in the Human Studies Film Archive, Smithsonian Institution, Washington DC.

REFERENCES

Books and articles

Asch, T. and Asch, P. (nd), 'Images that Represent Ideas: The Use of Films on the !Kung to Teach Anthropology' in Biesele, M., Gordon, R. and Lee, R. (eds.), *The Past and Future of !Kung Ethnography*, Helmust Buske Verlag, Hamburg.

Barnard, A. (1989), 'The lost world of Laurens van der Post', *Current Anthropology*, XXX, pp. 104–13.

Blythe, M. (1986), 'A Review: *The Gods Must be Crazy*', *UCLA African Studies Center Newsletter*, Spring, pp. 17–21.

Carpenter, F. (1969), *Laurens van der Post*, Twayne, New York.

Clifford, J. (1988), *Predicament of Culture*, Harvard University Press, Cambridge.

Davis, P. (1985), 'The Gods Must be Crazy', *Cineaste*, XIV, pp. 51–3. Also published as 'The Missionary Position: An Analysis of Jamie Uys' *The Gods Must be Crazy*', *Pacific Coast Africanist Newsletter*, IX, (1985), pp, 7–11; and Tomaseili, K.G. and Henne-belle, G. (eds.) (1986), *Le cinéma sud-africaine est-il tombé sur la téte?*, CinemAction, Paris. Literally translated, this title is a pun on *The Gods Must be Crazy*: 'Has South African Cinema Fallen on its Head?'

Gilliam, A. (1984), 'The Gods Must be Crazy', *Interracial Books for Children*, XV, p. 34,

Gabriel, T. (1988), 'Thoughts on Nomadic Aesthetics and the Black Independent Cinema: Traces of a Journey' in Cham, M. and Watkins, C.A. (eds.), *Blackframes: Critical Perspectives on Black Independent Cinema*, MIT, pp. 62–79.

Gordon, R. (1984), 'Conserving Bushmen to extinction'. Paper presented at First World Conference on Culture Parks. Published as 'Conserving Bushmen to extinction: the metaphysics of bushmen hating and empire building', *Survival International Review* (1985), XLIV, pp. 22–42.

Gordon, R. (1990a), 'People of the Great Sandface: People of the Great white Lie', *CVA Review* (Spring), pp. 30–4.

Gordon, R. (1990b), *The Bushman Myth and The Making of the Namibian Underclass*, Mimeo (forthcoming in Westview Press).

Gordon, R. (1990c), 'The prospects for anthropological tourism in Bushmanland', *Cultural Survival Quarterly*, XIV, pp. 1–3.

Hitchcock, R. and Brandenburgh, R. (1990), 'Tourism, Conservation, and Culture in the Kalahari Desert, Botswana', *Cultural Survival Quarterly*, XIV, pp. 20–4.

Howell, N. (1988), 'The Tasaday and the !Kung: reassessing isolated hunter-gatherers', Paper delivered at 53rd Meeting of the Society for American Archaeology, Phoenix Arizona, April.

Lee, R.B. (1985), '*The Gods Must Be Crazy*—but the producers know exactly what they are doing', *Southern Africa Report*, June, pp. 19–20.

Lee, R. and DeVore, I. (1968), *Man the Hunter*, Aldine, Chicago.

Marshall, J. and Ritchie, C. (1984), *Where are the Ju/wasi of Nyae Nyae? Changes in Bushmen Society 1958-1981*, Centre for African Studies, University of Cape Town.

Marshall Cabezas, S. and Nierenberg, J.(1990), *Films and Videos From DER*, DER (Documentary Educational Resources) Watertown, Mass.

Michaels, E. (1987), *For a Cultural Future: Frances Jupurrurla Makes TV,* Artspace, Art and Criticism Series, Sydney.

Michaels, E. (1986), 'The impact of television, videos, and satellites in Aboriginal communities' in Foran, B. and Walker, B. (eds.), *Science and Technology for Aboriginal Development,* Project report No 3 (Canberra, CSIRO).

Muller, J. and Tomaseili, K.G. (1990), 'Becoming appropriately modern: towards a genealogy of cultural studies in South Africa' in Mouton, J. (ed.), *Knowledge and Method in the Social Sciences*, Human Sciences Research Council, Pretoria, pp. 287–305.

Myburgh, J.P. (1989), 'Paul Myburgh talks on People of the Great Sandface: An interview with Keyan Tomaselli', *CVA Review*, (Fall), pp. 26–31.

O'Regan, T. (ed.) (1990), 'Communication and tradition: Essays after Eric Michaels', *Continuum: An Australian Journal of Media Theory,* III.

Reitz, D. quoted in Boydell, T. (1948), *My Luck's Still In,* Stewart, Cape Town.

Rosaldo, R. (1989), 'Imperialist nostalgia', *Representations*, XXVI, pp. 107–21.

Rosenthal, A. (1989/90), 'Review of *Image Ethics*', *Film Quarterly,* XLIII, p. 59.

Rosenthal, A. (1988), *New Challenges for Documentary,* California University Press, Berkeley.

Silberbauer, G. (1981), *Hunter and Habitat in the Central Kalahari Desert,* Cambridge University Press, Cambridge.

Sharp, J.S. (1979), 'Two separate developments: anthropology in South Africa,' *RAIN,* XXXV, pp. 4–5. Solway, J.S and Lee, R.B. (1990), 'Foragers, genuine or spurious? Situating the Kalahari

San in history', *Current Anthropology, XXXI.*

Thomas Marshall, E. (1959), *The Harmless People,* Vintage, New York.

Tomaselli, K.G. (1990) 'Annoying anthropologists: Jamie Uys's films on 'Bushmen' and animals', *SVA Review* (Spring), pp. 75–80.

Tomaselli, K.G., Gabriel, T., Masilela, N. and Williams, A. (1991), 'A dialogue on autobiography in *People of the Great Sandface. '*Mimeo.

Turner, T. (1990), 'Visual media, cultural politics, and anthropological practice: some implications of recent uses of film and video among the Kayapo of Brazil', *CVA Review* (Spring), pp. 8–12.

Van der Post L. (With Pottiez, J-M) (1986*),A Walk With a White Bushman,* Hogarth Press, London.

Van der Post, L. (1975), A *Mantis Carol,* Island Press, Covelo, Calif.

Van der Post, L. (1961), *The Heart of the Hunter,* Penguin, Harmondsworth.

Volkman, T.A. (1986), 'The hunter-gatherer myth in Southern Africa: preserving nature or culture?', *Cultural Survival Quarterly*, X, pp. 25–32.

Volkman, T.A. (1988), 'Out of Africa: *The Gods Must Be Crazy*' in Gross, L., Katz, J.S. and Ruby, J. (eds.), *Image Ethics: The Moral Rights of Subjects in Photographs, Film and TV,* Oxford, New York, pp. 237–47.

Wilmsen, E.N. (1989), *Land Filled With Flies: A Political Economy of the Kalahari,* Chicago University Press, Chicago.

Wilmsen, E.N. and Denbow, J.R. (1990), 'Paradigmatic history of San-speaking peoples and current attempts at revision', *Current Anthropology,* XXXI, pp. 489–524.

Wiley, D., Cancel, R., Pflugrad, D., Elkiss, T. H. and Campbell, A. (1982*), Africa on Film and Videotape 1960–1981: A Compendium of Reviews,* African Studies Center, Michigan State University, East Lansing.

Yellen, J. (1984), 'The integration of herding into prehistoric hunting and gathering economies' in Hall, M. and Avery, G. (eds.), *Frontiers: Southern African Archaeology Today.* Cambridge University Press, Cambridge.

Films

Asch, T. and N. Chagnon (1975), *The Ax Fight,* Documentary Educational Rescources, Watertown, Mass. Colour, 30 mins.

Cradle, E. and J. Grant (1926), *Denver African Expedition,* Universities of Denver and Cape Town, and the South African Museum. Black and white, *c.* 5 hours.

Enfield, C. (1966), *Zulu,* JE Levine Films New York. Colour, 135 mins.

Flaherty, R. (1922), *Nanook of the North,* Révillon Frères, Paris. Black and white, 70 mins.

_____ (1934), *Man of Aran,* Gainsborough Pictures. Black and white, 76 mins.

Ivory, J. (1982), *Heat and Dust,* Merchant Ivory Productions UK. Colour, 130 mins.

Lean, D. (1984), *A Passage to India.* EMI, UK. Colour, 163 mins.

Marshall, J. (1956), *The Hunters.* Harvard Film Study Center. Colour, 73 mins.

_____ (1980), *N!Ai, the Story of a !Kung Woman.* Documentary Educational Resources, Watertown, Mass. Colour, 59 mins.

_____ (1984), *Pull Ourselves Up or Die Out,* Documentary Educational Resources, Watertown, U-Matic, colour, 20 mins.

_____ (1986), *!Kung San: Traditional Life,* Documentary Educational Resources, Watertown, Mass. Video, colour, 26 mins.

McGlaglan, A. (1977), *The Wild Geese,* Euon Lloyd Productions, London. Colour, 134 mins.

Myburgh, P. (1985), *People of the Great Sandface.* Anglia Television, 'Survival' Series. Colour, 120 mins.

Pollack, S. (1986), *Out of Africa,* Technovision. Colour, 150 mins.

Tati, J. (1953*), Monsieur Hulot's Holiday,* Cady. Black and white, 91 mins.

Uys, J. (1974), *Beautiful People*, Mimosa Films, Bloemfontein. Colour, 90 mins.

_____ (1980), *The Gods Must Be Crazy*, Mimosa Films, Botswana. Colour, 109 mins.

_____ (1989), *The Gods Must Be Crazy II*, Mimosa Films, Botswana. Colour.

Van der Post, L. (1959), *Lost World of the Kalahari*, South Africa. Black and white.

_____ (1982), *Testament to the Bushmen.* Bellinger-Bermeister, South Africa. 6 × 30 mins.

Wolper, D. (1974), *Bushmen of the Kalahari.* National Geographic Society, Washington, DC. Colour, 52 mins.

Doing Fieldwork among the Yąnomamö[1]

BY NAPOLEON A. CHAGNON

VIGNETTE

The Yąnomamö are thinly scattered over a vast and verdant tropical forest, living in small villages that are separated by many miles of unoccupied land. They have no writing, but they have a rich and complex language. Their clothing is more decorative than protective. Well-dressed men sport nothing more than a few cotton strings around their wrists, ankles, and waists. They tie the foreskins of their penises to the waiststring. Women dress about the same. Much of their daily life revolves around gardening, hunting, collecting wild foods, collecting firewood, fetching water, visiting with each other, gossiping, and making the few material possessions they own: baskets, hammocks, bows, arrows, and colorful pigments with which they paint their bodies. Life is relatively easy in the sense that they can 'earn a living' with about three hours' work per day. Most of what they eat they cultivate in their gardens, and most of that is plantains—a kind of cooking banana that is usually eaten green, either roasted on the coals or boiled in pots (Figure 9–1) Their meat comes from a large variety of game animals, hunted daily by the men. It is usually roasted on coals or smoked, and is always well done. Their villages are round and open—and very public. One can hear, see, and smell almost everything that goes on anywhere in the village. Privacy is rare, but sexual discreetness is possible in the garden or at night while others sleep. The villages can be as small as 40 to 50 people or as large as 300 people, but in all cases there are many more children and babies than there are adults. This is true of most primitive populations and of our own demographic past. Life expectancy is short.

Figure 9–1. Bahimi, wife of Bisaasi-teri headman, harvesting plantains, a cooking banana that comprises a large fraction of Yąnomamö diet.

The Ya̧nomamö fall into the category of Tropical Forest Indians called 'foot people'. They avoid large rivers and live in interfluvial plains of the major rivers. They have neighbors to the north, Carib-speaking Ye'kwana, who are true 'river people': They make elegant, large dugout canoes and travel extensively along the major waterways. For the Ya̧nomamö amö, a large stream is an obstacle and can be crossed only in the dry season. Thus, they have traditionally avoided larger rivers and, because of this, contact with outsiders who usually come by river.

They enjoy taking trips when the jungle abounds with seasonally ripe wild fruits and vegetables. Then, the large village—the shabono—is abandoned for a few weeks and everyone camps out for from one to several days away from the village and garden. On these trips, they make temporary huts from poles, vines, and leaves, each family making a separate hut.

Two major seasons dominate their annual cycle: the wet season, which inundates the low-lying jungle, making travel difficult, and the dry season—the time of visiting other villages to feast, trade, and politic with allies. The dry season is also the time when raiders can travel and strike silently at their unsuspecting enemies. The Ya̧nomamö are still conducting intervillage warfare, a phenomenon that affects all aspects of their social organization, settlement pattern, and daily routines. It is not simply 'ritualistic' war: At least one-fourth of all adult males die violently in the area I lived in.

Social life is organized around those same principles utilized by all tribesmen: kinship relationships, descent from ancestors, marriage exchanges between kinship/descent groups, and the transient charisma of distinguished headmen who attempt to keep order in the village and whose responsibility it is to determine the village's relationships with those in other villages. Their positions are largely the result of kinship and marriage patterns; they come from the largest kinship groups within the village. They can, by their personal wit, wisdom, and charisma, become autocrats, but most of them are largely 'greaters' among equals. They, too, must clear gardens, plant crops, collect wild foods, and hunt. They are simultaneously peacemakers and valiant warriors. Peacemaking often requires the threat or actual use of force, and most headmen have an acquired reputation for being waiteri: fierce.

The social dynamics within villages are involved with giving and receiving marriageable girls. Marriages are arranged by older kin, usually men, who are brothers, uncles, and the father. It is a political process, for girls are promised in marriage while they are young, and the men who do this attempt to create alliances with other men via marriage exchanges. There is a shortage of women due in part to a sex-ratio imbalance in the younger age categories, but also complicated by the fact that some men have multiple wives. Most fighting within the village stems from sexual affairs or failure to deliver a promised woman—or out-and-out seizure of a married woman by some other man. This can lead to internal fighting and conflict of such an intensity that villages split up and fission, each group then becoming a new village and, often, enemies to each other.

But their conflicts are not blind, uncontrolled violence. They have a series of graded forms of violence that ranges from chest-pounding and club-fighting duels to out-and-out shooting to kill. This gives them a good deal of flexibility in settling disputes without immediate resort to lethal violence. In addition, they have developed patterns of alliance and friendship that serve to limit violence—trading and feasting with others in order to become friends (Figure 9–2). These alliances can, and often do,

Figure 9–2. Kạobawä, headman of Upper Bisaasi-teri, trading with his Shamatari allies for arrows, baskets, hammocks, and dogs.

result in intervillage exchanges of marriageable women, which leads to additional amity between villages. No good thing lasts forever, and most alliances crumble. Old friends become hostile and, occasionally, treacherous. Each village must therefore be keenly aware that its neighbors are fickle and must behave accordingly. The thin line between friendship and animosity must be traversed by the village leaders, whose political acumen and strategies are both admirable and complex.

Each village, then, is a replica of all others in a broad sense. But each village is part of a larger political, demographic, and ecological process, and it is difficult to attempt to understand the village without knowing something of the larger forces that affect it and its particular history with all its neighbors.

COLLECTING THE DATA IN THE FIELD

I have now spent over 60 months with Yạnomamö, during which time I gradually learned their language and, up to a point, submerged myself in their culture and way of life.[2] As my research progressed, the thing that impressed me most was the importance that aggression played in shaping their culture. I had the opportunity to witness a good many incidents that expressed individual vindictiveness on the one hand and collective bellicosity on the other hand. These ranged in seriousness from the ordinary incidents of wife beating and chest pounding to dueling and organized raids by parties that set out with the intention of ambushing and killing men from enemy villages. One of the villages was raided approximately twenty-five times during my first 15 months of fieldwork—six times by the group among whom I was living. And, the history of every village I investigated, from 1964 to 1991, was intimately bound up in patterns of warfare with neighbors that shaped its politics and determined where it was found at any point in time and how it dealt with its current neighbors.

The fact that the Ya̧nomamö have lived in a chronic state of warfare is reflected in their mythology, ceremonies, settlement pattern, political behavior, and marriage practices. Accordingly, I have organized this case study in such a way that students can appreciate the effects of warfare on Ya̧nomamö culture in general and on their social organization and political relationships in particular (Figure 9–3).

Figure 9–3. Visitors dancing as a group around the *shabono* during a formal feast.

I collected the data under somewhat trying circumstances, some of which I will describe to give a rough idea of what is generally meant when anthropologists speak of 'culture shock' and 'fieldwork.' It should be borne in mind, however, that each field situation is in many respects unique, so that the problems I encountered do not necessarily exhaust the range of possible problems other anthropologists have confronted in other areas. There are a few problems, however, that seem to be nearly universal among anthropological fieldworkers, particularly those having to do with eating, bathing, sleeping, lack of privacy, loneliness, or discovering that the people you are living with have a lower opinion of you than you have of them—or you yourself are not as culturally or emotionally 'flexible' as you assumed.

The Yąnomamö can be difficult people to live with at times, but I have spoken to colleagues who have had difficulties living in the communities they studied. These things vary from society to society, and probably from one anthropologist to the next. I have also done limited fieldwork among the Yąnomamö's northern neighbors, the Carib-speaking Ye'kwana Indians. By contrast to many experiences I had among the Yanomamö, the Ye'kwana were very pleasant and charming, all of them anxious to help me and honor bound to show any visitor the numerous courtesies of their system of etiquette, In short, they approached the image of 'primitive man' that I had conjured up in my mind before doing fieldwork, a kind of 'Rousseauian' view, and it was sheer pleasure to work with them. Other anthropologists have also noted sharp contrasts in the people they study from one field situation to another. One of the most startling examples of this is in the work of Colin Turnbull, who first studied the Ituri Pygmies (1965, 1983) and found them delightful to live with, but then studied the Ik (1972) of the desolate outcroppings of the Kenya/Uganda/Sudan border region, a people he had difficulty coping with intellectually, emotionally, and physically. While it is possible that the anthropologist's reactions to a particular people are personal and idiosyncratic, it nevertheless remains true that there are enormous differences between whole peoples, differences that affect the anthropologist in often dramatic ways.

Hence, what I say about some of my experiences is probably equally true of the experiences of many other fieldworkers. I describe some of them here for the benefit of future anthropologists—because I think I could have profited by reading about the pitfalls and field problems of my own teachers. At the very least I might have been able to avoid some of my more stupid errors. In this regard there is a growing body of excellent descriptive work on field research. Students who plan to make a career in anthropology should consult these works, which cover a wide range of field situations in the ethnographic present.[3]

The Longest Day: The First One

My first day in the field illustrated to me what my teachers meant when they spoke of 'culture shock.' I had traveled in a small, aluminum rowboat propelled by a large outboard motor for two and a half days. This took me from the territorial capital, a small town on the Orinoco River, deep into Yąnomamö country. On the morning of the third day we reached a small mission settlement, the field 'headquarters' of a group of Americans who were working in two Yąnomamö villages. The missionaries had come out of these villages to hold their annual conference on the progress of their mission work and were conducting their meetings when I arrived. We picked up a passenger at the mission station, James P. Barker, the first non-Yąnomamö to make a sustained, permanent contact with the tribe (in 1950). He had just returned from a year's furlough in the United States, where I had earlier visited him before leaving for Venezuela. He agreed to accompany me to the village I had selected for my base of operations to introduce me to the Indians. This village was also his own home base, but he had not been there for over a year and did not plan to join me for another three months. Mr. Barker had been living with this particular group about five years.

We arrived at the village, Bisaasi-teri, about 2:00 P.M. and docked the boat along the muddy bank at the terminus of the path used by Yąnomamö to fetch their drinking water. It was hot and muggy, and my clothing was soaked with perspiration. It clung uncomfortably to my body, as it did thereafter for the remainder of the work. The small biting gnats, *bareto*, were out in astronomical numbers, for it was the beginning of the dry season. My face and hands were swollen from the venom of their numerous stings. In just a few moments I was to meet my first Yąnomamö, my first primitive man. What would he be like? I had visions of entering the village and seeing 125 social facts running about altruistically calling each other kinship terms and sharing food, each waiting and anxious to have me collect his genealogy. I would wear them out in turn. Would they like me? This was important to me; I wanted them to be so fond of me that they would adopt me into their kinship system and way of life. I had heard that successful anthropologists always get adopted by their people. I had learned during my seven years of anthropological training at the University of Michigan that kinship was equivalent to society in primitive tribes and that it was a moral way of life, 'moral' being something 'good' and 'desirable.' I was determined to work my way into their moral system of kinship and become a member of their society—to be 'accepted' by them.

How Did They Accept You?

My heart began to pound as we approached the village and heard the buzz of activity within the circular compound. Mr. Barker commented that he was anxious to see if any changes had taken place while he was away and wondered how many of them had died during his absence. I nervously felt my back pocket to make sure that my notebook was still there and felt personally more secure when I touched it.

The entrance to the village was covered over with brush and dry palm leaves. We pushed them aside to expose the low opening to the village. The excitement of meeting my first Yąnomamö was almost unbearable as I duck-waddled through the low passage into the village clearing.

I looked up and gasped when I saw a dozen burly, naked, sweaty, hideous men staring at us down the shafts of their drawn arrows! Immense wads of green tobacco were stuck between their lower teeth and lips making them look even more hideous, and strands of dark-green slime dripped or hung from their nostrils—strands so long that they clung to their pectoral muscles or drizzled down their chins. We arrived at the village while the men were blowing a hallucinogenic drug up their noses. One of the side effects of the drug is a runny nose. The mucus is always saturated with the green powder and they usually let it run freely from their nostrils (Figure 9–4). My next discovery was that there were a dozen or so vicious, underfed dogs snapping at my legs, circling me as if I were to be their next meal. I just stood there holding my notebook, helpless and pathetic. Then the stench of the decaying vegetation and filth hit me and I almost got sick. I was horrified. What kind of welcome was this for the person who came here to live with you and learn your way of life, to become friends with you? They put their weapons down when they recognized Barker and returned to their chanting, keeping a nervous eye on the village entrances.

We had arrived just after a serious fight. Seven women had been abducted the day before by a neighboring group, and the local men and their guests had just that morning recovered five of them in

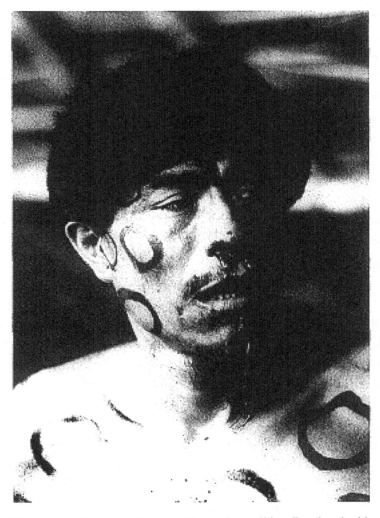

Figure 9–4. Yąnomamö man with monkey-tail headband and with ebene, a hallucinogenic snuff, drizzling from his nostrils.

a brutal club fight that nearly ended in a shooting war. The abductors, angry because they had lost five of their seven new captives, vowed to raid the Bisaasi-teri. When we arrived and entered the village unexpectedly, the Indians feared that we were the raiders. On several occasions during the next two hours the men in the village jumped to their feet, armed themselves, nocked their arrows and waited nervously for the noise outside the village to be identified. My enthusiasm for collecting ethnographic facts diminished in proportion to the number of times such an alarm was raised. In fact, I was relieved when Barker suggested that we sleep across the river for the evening. It would be safer over there.

As we walked down the path to the boat, I pondered the wisdom of having decided to spend a year and a half with these people before I had even seen what they were like. I am not ashamed to admit that had there been a diplomatic way out, I would have ended my fieldwork then and there. I did not look forward to the next day—and months—when I would be left alone with the Ya̧nomamö; I did not speak a word of their language, and they were decidedly different from what I had imagined them to be. The whole situation was depressing, and I wondered why I ever decided to switch from physics and engineering in the first place. I had not eaten all day, I was soaking wet from perspiration, the *bareto* were biting me, and I was covered with red pigment, the result of a dozen or so complete examinations I had been given by as many very pushy Ya̧nomamö men. These examinations capped an otherwise grim day. The men would blow their noses into their hands, flick as much of the mucus off that would separate in a snap of the wrist, wipe the residue into their hair, and then carefully examine my face, arms, legs, hair, and the contents of my pockets. I asked Barker how to say, 'Your hands are dirty'; my comments were met by the Ya̧nomamö in the following way: They would 'clean' their hands by spitting a quantity of slimy tobacco juice into them, rub them together, grin, and then proceed with the examination.

Mr. Barker and I crossed the river and slung our hammocks. When he pulled his hammock out of a rubber bag, a heavy, disagreeable odor of mildewed cotton and stale wood smoke came with it. 'Even the missionaries are filthy,' I thought to myself. Within two weeks, everything I owned smelled the same way, and I lived with that odor for the remainder of the fieldwork. My own habits of personal cleanliness declined to such levels that I didn't even mind being examined by the Ya̧nomamö, as I was not much cleaner than they were after I had adjusted to the circumstances. It is difficult to blow your nose gracefully when you are stark naked and the invention of handkerchiefs is millennia away.

Life in the Jungle: Oatmeal, Peanut Butter, and Bugs

It isn't easy to plop down in the Amazon Basin for a year and get immediately into the anthropological swing of things. You have been told about horrible diseases, snakes, jaguars, electric eels, little spiny fish that will swim up your urine into your penis, quicksand, and getting lost. Some of the dangers are real, but your imagination makes them more real and threatening than many of them really are. What my teachers never bothered to advise me about, however, was the mundane, unexciting, and trivial stuff—like eating, defecating, sleeping, or keeping clean. These turned out to be the bane of my existence during the first several months of field research. I set up my household in Barker's abandoned mud hut, a few yards from the village of Bisaasi-teri, and immediately set to work building my own mud/thatch hut with the help of the Yąnomamö. Meanwhile, I had to eat and try to do my 'field research.' I soon discovered that it was an enormously time-consuming task to maintain my own body in the manner to which it had grown accustomed in the relatively antiseptic environment of the northern United States. Either I could be relatively well fed and relatively comfortable in a fresh change of clothes and do very little fieldwork, or I could do considerably more fieldwork and be less well fed and less comfortable.

It is appalling how complicated it can be to make oatmeal in the jungle. First, I had to make two trips to the river to haul the water, Next, I had to prime my kerosene stove with alcohol to get it burning, a tricky procedure when you are trying to mix powdered milk and fill a coffee pot at the same time. The alcohol prime always burned out before I could turn the kerosene on, and I would have to start all over. Or, I would turn the kerosene on, optimistically hoping that the Coleman element was still hot enough to vaporize the fuel, and start a small fire in my palm-thatched hut as the liquid kerosene squirted all over the table and walls and then ignited. Many amused Yąnomamö onlookers quickly learned the English phrase 'Oh, shit!', and, once they discovered that the phrase offended and irritated the missionaries, they used it as often as they could in their presence. I usually had to start over with the alcohol. Then I had to boil the oatmeal and pick the bugs out of it. All my supplies, of course, were carefully stored in rat-proof, moisture-proof, and insect-proof containers, not one of which ever served its purpose adequately. Just taking things out of the multiplicity of containers and repacking them afterward was a minor project in itself. By the time I had hauled the water to cook with, unpacked my food, prepared the oatmeal, milk, and coffee, heated water for dishes, washed and dried the dishes, repacked the food in the containers, stored the containers in locked trunks, and cleaned up my mess, the ceremony of preparing breakfast had brought me almost up to lunch time!

Eating three meals a day was simply out of the question. I solved the problem by eating a single meal that could be prepared in a single container, or, at most, in two containers, washed my dishes only when there were no clean ones left, using cold river water, and wore each change of clothing at least a week to cut down on my laundry problem—a courageous undertaking in the tropics. I reeked like a jockstrap that had been left to mildew in the bottom of some dark gym locker. I also became less concerned about sharing my provisions with the rats, insects, Yąnomamö, and the elements, thereby eliminating the need for my complicated storage process. I was able to last most of the day on *café con leche*, heavily sugared espresso coffee diluted about five to one with hot milk. I would prepare this in the evening and store it in a large thermos. Frequently, my single meal was no more complicated than a can of sardines and a package of soggy crackers. But at least two or three times a week I would do something 'special' and sophisticated, like make a batch of oatmeal or boil rice and add a can of tuna fish or tomato paste to it. I even saved time by devising a water system that obviated the trips to the river. I had a few sheets of tin roofing brought in and made a rain water trap; I caught the water on the tin surface, funneled it into an empty gasoline drum, and then ran a plastic hose from the drum to my hut. When the drum was exhausted in the dry season, I would get a few Yąnomamö boys to fill it with buckets of water from the river, 'paying' them with crackers, of which they grew all too fond all too soon.

I ate much less when I traveled with the Y̧anomamö to visit other villages. Most of the time my travel diet consisted of roasted or boiled green plantains (cooking bananas) that I obtained from the Y̧anomamö, but I always carried a few cans of sardines with me in case I got lost or stayed away longer than I had planned. I found peanut butter and crackers a very nourishing 'trail' meal, and a simple one to prepare. It was nutritious and portable, and only one tool was required to make the meal: a hunting knife that could be cleaned by wiping the blade on a convenient leaf. More importantly, it was one of the few foods the Y̧anomamö would let me eat in relative peace. It looked suspiciously like animal feces to them, an impression I encouraged. I referred to the peanut butter as the feces of babies or 'cattle'. They found this disgusting and repugnant. They did not know what 'cattle' were, but were increasingly aware that I ate several canned products of such an animal. Tin cans were thought of as containers made of 'machete skins', but how the cows got inside was always a mystery to them. I went out of my way to describe my foods in such a way as to make them sound unpalatable to them, for it gave me some peace of mind while I ate: They wouldn't beg for a share of something that was too horrible to contemplate. Fieldworkers develop strange defense mechanisms and strategies, and this was one of my own forms of adaptation to the fieldwork. On another occasion I was eating a can of frankfurters and growing very weary of the demands from one of the onlookers for a share in my meal. When he finally asked what I was eating, I replied: 'Beef.' He then asked: 'Shȩki!4 What part of the animal are you eating?' To which I replied, 'Guess.' He muttered a contemptuous epithet, but stopped asking for a share. He got back at me later, as we shall see.

Meals were a problem in a way that had nothing to do with the inconvenience of preparing them. Food sharing is important to the Y̧anomamö in the context of displaying friendship. 'I am hungry!' is almost a form of greeting with them. I could not possibly have brought enough food with me to feed the entire village, yet they seemed to overlook this logistic fact as they begged for my food. What became fixed in their minds was the fact that I did not share my food with whomsoever was present—usually a small crowd—at each and every meal. Nor could I easily enter their system of reciprocity with respect to food. Every time one of them 'gave' me something 'freely', he would dog me for months to 'pay him back', not necessarily with food but with knives, fishhooks, axes, and so on. Thus, if I accepted a plantain from someone in a different village while I was on a visit, he would most likely visit me in the future and demand a machete as payment for the time that he 'fed' me. I usually reacted to these kinds of demands by giving a banana, the customary reciprocity in their culture—food for food—but this would be a disappointment for the individual who had nursed visions of that single plantain growing into a machete over time. Many years after beginning my fieldwork I was approached by one of the prominent men who demanded a machete for a piece of meat he claimed he had given me five or six years earlier.

Despite the fact that most of them knew I would not share my food with them at their request, some of them always showed up at my hut during mealtime. I gradually resigned myself to this and learned to ignore their persistent demands while I ate. Some of them would get angry because I failed to give in, but most of them accepted it as just a peculiarity of the subhuman foreigner who had come to live among them. If or when I did accede to a request for a share of my food, my hut quickly filled with Yąnomamö, each demanding their share of the food that I had just given to one of them. Their begging for food was not provoked by hunger, but by a desire to try something new and to attempt to establish a coercive relationship in which I would accede to a demand. If one received something, all others would immediately have to test the system to see if they, too, could coerce me.

A few of them went out of their way to make my meals downright unpleasant—to spite me for not sharing, especially if it was a food that they had tried before and liked, or a food that was part of their own cuisine. For example, I was eating a cracker with peanut butter and honey one day. The Yąnomamö will do almost anything for honey, one of the most prized delicacies in their own diet. One of my cynical onlookers—the fellow who had earlier watched me eating frankfurters—immediately recognized the honey and knew that I would not share the tiny precious bottle. It would be futile to even ask. Instead, he glared at me and queried icily, 'Shąki! What kind of animal semen are you pouring onto your food and eating?' His question had the desired effect and my meal ended.

Finally, there was the problem of being lonely and separated from your own kind, especially your family. I tried to overcome this by seeking personal friendships among the Yąnomamö. This usually complicated the matter because all my 'friends' simply used my confidence to gain privileged access to my hut and my cache of steel tools and trade goods—and looted me when I wasn't looking. I would be bitterly disappointed that my erstwhile friend thought no more of me than to finesse our personal relationship exclusively with the intention of getting at my locked up possessions, and my depression would hit new lows every time I discovered this. The loss of the possessions bothered me much less than the shock that I was, as far as most of them were concerned, nothing more than a source of desirable items. No holds were barred in relieving me of these, since I was considered something subhuman, a non-Yąnomamö.

The hardest thing to learn to live with was the incessant, passioned, and often aggressive demands they would make. It would become so unbearable at times that I would have to lock myself in my hut periodically just to escape from it. Privacy is one of our culture's most satisfying achievements, one you never think about until you suddenly have none. It is like not appreciating how good your left thumb feels until someone hits it with a hammer. But I did not want privacy for its own sake; rather, I simply had to get away from the begging. Day and night for almost the entire time I lived with the Yąnomamö I was plagued by such demands as: 'Give me a knife, I am poor!'; 'If you don't take me with you on your next trip to Widokaiya-teri, I'll chop a hole in your canoe!'; 'Take us hunting up the Mavaca River with your shotgun or we won't help you!'; 'Give me some matches so I can trade with the Reyaboböwei-teri, and be quick about it or I'll hit you!'; 'Share your food with me, or I'll burn your hut!'; "Give me a flashlight so I can hunt at night!'; 'Give me all your medicine, I itch all over!'; 'Give me an ax or I'll break into your hut when you are away and steal all of them!' And so I was bombarded by such demands day after day, month after month, until I could not bear to see a Yąnomamö at times.

It was not as difficult to become calloused to the incessant begging as it was to ignore the sense of urgency, the impassioned tone of voice and whining, or the intimidation and aggression with which many of the demands were made. It was likewise difficult to adjust to the fact that the Yą̧nomamö refused to accept 'No' for an answer until or unless it seethed with passion and intimidation—which it did after a few months. So persistent and characteristic is the begging that the early 'semi-official' maps made by the Venezuelan Malaria Control Service *(Malarialogía)* designated the site of their first permanent field station, next to the village of Bisaasi-teri, as *Yababuhii:* 'Gimme.' I had to become like the Yą̧nomamö to be able to get along with them on their terms: somewhat sly, aggressive, intimidating, and pushy.

It became indelibly clear to me shortly after I arrived there that had I failed to adjust in this fashion I would have lost six months of supplies to them in a single day or would have spent most of my time ferrying them around in my canoe or taking them on long hunting trips. As it was, I did spend a considerable amount of time doing these things and did succumb often to their outrageous demands for axes and machetes, at least at first, for things changed as I became more fluent in their language and learned how to defend myself socially as well as verbally. More importantly, had I failed to demonstrate that I could not be pushed around beyond a certain point, I would have been the subject of far more ridicule, theft, and practical jokes than was the actual case. In short, I had to acquire a certain proficiency in their style of interpersonal politics and to learn how to imply subtly that certain potentially undesirable, but unspecified, consequences might follow if they did such and such to me. They do this to each other incessantly in order to establish precisely the point at which they cannot goad or intimidate an individual any further without precipitating some kind of retaliation. As soon as I realized this and gradually acquired the self-confidence to adopt this strategy, it became clear that much of the intimidation was calculated to determine my flash point or my 'last ditch' position—and I got along much better with them. Indeed, I even regained some lost ground. It was sort of like a political, interpersonal game that everyone had to play, but one in which each individual sooner or later had to give evidence that his bluffs and implied threats could be backed up with a sanction. I suspect that the frequency of wife beating is a component in this syndrome, since men can display their *waiteri* (ferocity) and 'show' others that they are capable of great violence. Beating a wife with a club is one way of displaying ferocity, one that does not expose the man to much danger—unless the wife has concerned, aggressive brothers in the village who will come to her aid. Apparently an important thing in wife beating is that the man has displayed his presumed potential for violence and the intended message is that other men ought to treat him with circumspection, caution, and even deference.

After six months, the level of Yą̧nomamö demand was tolerable in Bisaasi-teri, the village I used for my base of operations. We had adjusted somewhat to each other and knew what to expect with regard to demands for food, trade goods, and favors. Had I elected to remain in just one Yą̧nomamö village for the entire duration of my first 15 months of fieldwork, the experience would have been far more enjoyable than it actually was. However, as I began to understand the social and political dynamics of this village, it became patently obvious that I would have to travel to many other villages to determine the demographic bases and political histories that lay behind what I could understand in the village of Bisaasi-teri. I began making regular trips to some dozen neighboring Yą̧nomamö villages as my language fluency improved. I collected local genealogies there, or rechecked and cross-checked those I had collected elsewhere. Hence, the intensity of begging was relatively constant and relatively high for the duration of my fieldwork, for I had to establish my personal position in each village I visited and revisited.

For the most part, my own 'fierceness' took the form of shouting back at the Yąnomamö as loudly and as passionately as they shouted at me, especially at first, when I did not know much of the language. As I became more fluent and learned more about their political tactics, I became more sophisticated in the art of bluffing and brinksmanship. For example, I paid one young man a machete (then worth about $2.50) to cut a palm tree and help me make boards from the wood. I used these to fashion a flooring in the bottom of my dugout canoe to keep my possessions out of the water that always seeped into the canoe and sloshed around. That afternoon I was working with one of my informants in the village. The long-awaited mission supply boat arrived and most of the Yąnomamö ran out of the village to see the supplies and try to beg items from the crew. I continued to work in the village for another hour or so and then went down to the river to visit with the men on the supply boat. When I reached the river I noticed, with anger and frustration, that the Yąnomamö had chopped up all my new floor boards to use as crude paddles to get their own canoes across the river to the supply boat.[5] I knew that if I ignored this abuse I would have invited the Yąnomamö to take even greater liberties with my possessions in the future. I got into my canoe, crossed the river, and docked amidst their flimsy, leaky craft. I shouted loudly to them, attracting their attention. They were somewhat sheepish, but all had mischievous grins on their impish faces. A few of them came down to the canoe, where I proceeded with a spirited lecture that revealed my anger at their audacity and license. I explained that I had just that morning paid one of them a machete for bringing me the palmwood, how hard I had worked to shape each board and place it in the canoe, how carefully and painstakingly I had tied each one in with vines, how much I had perspired, how many *bareto* bites I had suffered, and so on. Then, with exaggerated drama and finality, I withdrew my hunting knife as their grins disappeared and cut each one of their canoes loose and set it into the strong current of the Orinoco River where it was immediately swept up and carried downstream. I left without looking back and huffed over to the other side of the river to resume my work.

They managed to borrow another canoe and, after some effort, recovered their dugouts. Later, the headman of the village told me, with an approving chuckle, that I had done the correct thing. Everyone in the village, except, of course, the culprits, supported and defended my actions—and my status increased as a consequence.

Whenever I defended myself in such ways I got along much better with the Yąnomamö and gradually acquired the respect of many of them. A good deal of their demeanor toward me was directed with the forethought of establishing the point at which I would draw the line and react defensively. Many of them, years later, reminisced about the early days of my fieldwork when I was timid and *mohode* ('stupid') and a little afraid of them, those golden days when it was easy to bully me into giving my goods away for almost nothing.

Theft was the most persistent situation that required some sort of defensive action. I simply could not keep everything I owned locked in trunks, and the Ya̧nomamö came into my hut and left at will. I eventually developed a very effective strategy for recovering almost all the stolen items: I would simply ask a child who took the item and then I would confiscate that person's hammock when he was not around, giving a spirited lecture to all who could hear on the antisociality of thievery as I stalked off in a faked rage with the thief's hammock slung over my shoulder. Nobody ever attempted to stop me from doing this, and almost all of them told me that my technique for recovering my possessions was ingenious. By nightfall the thief would appear at my hut with the stolen item or send it over with someone else to make an exchange to recover his hammock. He would be heckled by his covillagers for having been caught and for being embarrassed into returning my item for his hammock. The explanation was usually, 'I just borrowed your ax! I wouldn't think of stealing it!'

Collecting Ya̧nomamö Genealogies and Reproductive Histories

My purpose for living among the Ya̧nomamö was to systematically collect certain kinds of information on genealogy, reproduction, marriage practices, kinship, settlement patterns, migrations, and politics. Much of the fundamental data was genealogical—who was the parent of whom, tracing these connections as far back in time as Ya̧nomamö knowledge and memory permitted. Since 'primitive' society is organized largely by kinship relationships, figuring out the social organization of the Ya̧nomamö essentially meant collecting extensive data on genealogies, marriage, and reproduction. This turned out to be a staggering and very frustrating problem. I could not have deliberately picked a more difficult people to work with in this regard. They have very stringent name taboos and eschew mentioning the names of prominent living people was well as all deceased friends and relatives. They attempt to name people in such a way that when the person dies and they can no longer use his or her name, the loss of the word in their language is not inconvenient. Hence, they name people for specific and minute parts of things, such as 'toenail of sloth,' 'whisker of howler monkey,' and so on, thereby being able to retain the words 'toenail' or 'whisker' but somewhat handicapped in referring to these anatomical parts of sloths and monkeys respectively. The taboo is maintained even for the living, for one mark of prestige is the courtesy others show you by not using your name publicly. This is particularly true for men, who are much more competitive for status than women in this culture, and it is fascinating to watch boys grow into young men, demanding to be called either by a kinship term in public, or by a teknonymous reference such as 'brother of Himotoma' (see Glossary). The more effective they are at getting others to avoid using their names, the more public acknowledgment there is that they are of high esteem and social standing. Helena Valero, a Brazilian woman who was captured as a child by a Ya̧nomamö raiding party, was married for many years to a Ya̧nomamö headman before she discovered what his name was (Biocca, 1970; Valero, 1984). The sanctions behind the taboo are more complex than just this, for they involve a combination of fear, respect, admiration, political deference, and honor.

At first I tried to use kinship terms alone to collect genealogies, but Ya̧nomamö kinship terms, like the kinship terms in all systems, are ambiguous at some point because they include so many possible relatives (as the term 'uncle' does in our own kinship system). Again, their system of kin classification merges many relatives that we 'separate' by using different terms: They call both their actual father and their father's brother by a single term, whereas we call one 'father' and the other 'uncle.' I was forced, therefore, to resort to personal names to collect unambiguous genealogies or 'pedigrees'. They quickly grasped what I was up to and that I was determined to learn everyone's 'true name', which amounted to an invasion of their system of prestige and etiquette, if not a flagrant violation of it. They reacted to this in a brilliant but devastating manner: They invented false names for everybody in the village and systematically learned them, freely revealing to me the 'true' identities of everyone. I smugly thought I had cracked the system and enthusiastically constructed elaborate genealogies over a period of some five months. They enjoyed watching me learn their names and kinship relationships. I naively assumed that I would get the 'truth' to each question and the best information by working in public. This set the stage for converting my serious project into an amusing hoax of the grandest proportions. Each 'informant' would try to outdo his peers by inventing a name even more preposterous or ridiculous than what I had been given by someone earlier, the explanations for discrepancies being 'Well, he has two names and this is the other one.' They even fabricated devilishly improbable genealogical relationships, such as someone being married to his grandmother, or worse yet, to his mother-in-law, a grotesque and horrifying prospect to the Yąnomamö. I would collect the desired names and relationships by having my informant whisper the name of the person softly into my ear, noting that he or she was the parent of such and such or the child of such and such, and so on. Everyone who was observing my work would then insist that I repeat the name aloud, roaring in hysterical laughter as I clumsily pronounced the name, sometimes laughing until tears streamed down their faces. The 'named' person would usually react with annoyance and hiss some untranslatable epithet at me, which served to reassure me that I had the 'true' name. I conscientiously checked and rechecked the names and relationships with multiple informants, pleased to see the inconsistencies disappear as my genealogy sheets filled with those desirable little triangles and circles, thousands of them.

My anthropological bubble was burst when I visited a village about 10 hours' walk to the southwest of Bisaasi-teri some five months after I had begun collecting genealogies on the Bisaasi-teri. I was chatting with the local headman of this village and happened to casually drop the name of the wife of the Bisaasi-teri headman. A stunned silence followed, and then a villagewide roar of uncontrollable laughter, choking, gasping, and howling followed. It seems that I thought the Bisaasi-teri headman was married to a woman named "hairy cunt." It also seems that the Bisaasi-teri headman was called 'long dong' and his brother 'eagle shit.' The Bisaasi-teri headman had a son called "asshole" and a daughter called 'fart breath.' And so on. Blood welled up to my temples as I realized that I had nothing but nonsense to show for my five months of dedicated genealogical effort, and I had to throw away almost all the information I had collected on this the most basic set of data I had come there to get. I understood at that point why the Bisaasi-teri laughed so hard when they made me repeat the names of their covillagers, and why the 'named' person would react with anger and annoyance as I pronounced his 'name' aloud.

I was forced to change research strategy—to make an understatement to describe this serious situation. The first thing I did was to begin working in private with my informants to eliminate the horseplay and distraction that attended public sessions. Once I did this, my informants, who did not know what others were telling me, began to agree with each other and I managed to begin learning the 'real' names, starting first with children and gradually moving to adult women and then, cautiously, to adult men, a sequence that reflected the relative degree of intransigence at revealing names of people. As I built up a core of accurate genealogies and relationships—a core that all independent informants had verified repetitiously—I could 'test' any new informant by soliciting his or her opinion and knowledge about these 'core' people whose names and relationships I was confident were accurate. I was, in this fashion, able to immediately weed out the mischievous informants who persisted in trying to deceive me. Still, I had great difficulty getting the names of dead kinsmen, the only accurate way to extend genealogies back in time. Even my best informants continued to falsify names of the deceased, especially closely related deceased. The falsifications at this point were not serious and turned out to be readily corrected as my interviewing methods improved (see below). Most of the deceptions were of the sort where the informant would give me the name of a living man as the father of some child whose actual father was dead, a response that enabled the informant to avoid using the name of a deceased kinsman or friend.

The quality of a genealogy depends in part on the number of generations it embraces, and the name taboo prevented me from making any substantial progress in learning about the deceased ancestors of the present population. Without this information, I could not, for example, document marriage patterns and interfamilial alliances through time. I had to rely on older informants for this information, but these were the most reluctant informants of all for this data. As I became more proficient in the language and more skilled at detecting fabrications, my informants became better at deception. One old man was particularly cunning and persuasive, following a sort of Mark Twain policy that the most effective lie is a sincere lie. He specialized in making a ceremony out of false names for dead ancestors. He would look around nervously to make sure nobody was listening outside my hut, enjoin me never to mention the name again, become very anxious and spooky, and grab me by the head to whisper a secret name into my ear. I was always elated after a session with him, because I managed to add several generations of ancestors for particular members of the village. Others steadfastly refused to give me such information. To show my gratitude, I paid him quadruple the rate that I had been paying the others. When word got around that I had increased the pay for genealogical and demographic information, volunteers began pouring into my hut to 'work' for me, assuring me of their changed ways and keen desire to divest themselves of the 'truth'.

BEYOND THE BISAASI-TERI AND INTO THE REMOTE VILLAGES

As my work progressed with Ka͇obawä, Rerebawä, and many other informants, a very important scientific problem began to emerge, one that could be solved only by going to visit many distant Yąnomamö villages to collect genealogies, demographic data, and local histories from the people there. But the fieldwork required to solve the scientific question led to some exciting and even dangerous adventures, for it meant contacting totally unknown Yąnomamö—people who had never before seen foreigners. The 'first contact' with a primitive society is a phenomenon that is less and less likely to happen, for the world is shrinking and 'unknown' tribes or villages are now very rare. In fact, our generation is probably the last that will have the opportunity to know what it is like to make first contact. For this reason, I include a description of what one such situation was like, put into the context of the scientific reasons for going into the unknown Yąnomamö area.

The Scientific Problem That Emerged

It became increasingly clear that each Yąnomamö village was a 'recent' colony or splinter group of some larger village, and a fascinating set of patterns—and problems—began to emerge. I could see that there were cause effect relationships among a number of variables. These included village size, genealogical composition of villages, age and sex distributions, ecological and geographic variables, and marriage ties or 'alliances' between 'families'. Moreover, it became abundantly clear that inter-village warfare was an indelible force that affected village size and village distribution—how large villages got to be before they would 'fission' and divide into two groups, and where the newly created groups would move as they avoided their old enemies, attempted to get away from those they had just separated from, or sought new allies in distant places. The simple discovery of the pattern had a marked influence on my fieldwork: It meant that I would have to travel to many villages in order to document the genealogical aspects of the pattern, take detailed censuses, collect local versions of 'historical truth' from all parties concerned, and map as best I could the locations of existing villages and locations of sites that they had abandoned in the recent past, sometimes penetrating new, virgin, unknown forest as pioneers on the expanding front of their population. What was exciting about this was the formal and ecological similarity that it suggested during the early centuries of the discovery of agriculture, and how our own ancestors in Eurasia and Africa spread agriculture into new lands, lands formerly inhabited by hunters and gatherers, or lands that had never been occupied.

Getting to some of these new villages turned out to be a staggering problem for a number of reasons. First, I was living in Bisaasi-teri, and old wars and current animosities prevented me from easily recruiting trustworthy guides who were politically able to visit some of the distant villages, or if able, willing to. Second, I had to deal with the political pressures put on any of my guides by the older men in the village, who would have much preferred to have me dispense all my goods and gifts in *their* village and not take them inland to other Yạnomamö. Some of the older men went to great lengths to sabotage my plans to visit other villages, putting pressure on my guides to back out or to cause me to turn back once started. Third, some of the villages were at a great distance away and their precise locations to my guides unknown: They were uncontacted villages many days by trail away, and usually bitter, mortal enemies of the Bisaasi-teri among whom I lived—and with whom I was somewhat identified by Yạnomamö in all surrounding villages. My first year's research, which unraveled many details of previous wars, killings and treachery, convinced me that the Bisaasi-teri were justified in holding very caustic, hostile attitudes toward some of their distant neighbors, particularly members of villages that they collectively referred to as 'the Shamatari.' The Shamatari, to the Bisaasi-teri, were a congeries of many interrelated villages to the south, some of which had a long history of bitter warfare with the Bisaasi-teri. All the Shamatari villages were related to each other and had come into existence as larger villages fissioned into smaller ones, grew, fissioned again, and occupied new lands, moving in a general direction from northeast to southwest. Two of the closest 'Shamatari' villages lay immediately to the south of the Bisaasi-teri, and I visited both of them on foot my first year in the field—a 10-hour walk to the closest one, a two-day walk to the more distant one. These two groups were on somewhat friendly terms with the Bisaasi-teri, and a number of intermarriages had recently taken place between them. They were Kạobawä's allies, but a good deal of mutual suspicion and occasional expressions of contempt also marked their relationships.

Far to the south and southeast of these two Shamatari villages lay other Shamatari villages, mortal enemies to the Bisaasi-teri. It became clear to me, as my genealogical, demographic, and settlement pattern histories accumulated, that I would have to visit them. They had never before seen outsiders and the Bisaasi-teri chronically advised me about their treachery and viciousness, particularly Kạobawä and Rerebawä, who genuinely had my personal safety at heart.

The group of Shamatari I wanted to reach on my initial foray into this region was known to the Bisaasi-teri as 'Sibarariwä's' village, Sibarariwä being the headman of the village and a man who was hated by all Bisaasi-teri for engineering a treachery that led to the deaths of many Bisaasi-teri, including Kạobawä's's father (see Prologue). Sibarariwä was *waiteri* and had a reputation for aggressiveness in many villages, even in villages whose members had never met him or members of his village.

The first attempt I made to contact Sibarariwä's village was in 1966, near the end of my first field trip. It was unsuccessful primarily because my young guides, three in number, forced me to turn back. Two were from Bisaasi-teri and the third was from one of the friendly Shamatari villages, Mọmaribọwei-teri, a 10-hour walk away. We ascended the Mavaca River for about two days, chopping our way through large trees and tons of brush that clogged the river and made canoe passage very difficult. The river had not been ascended that far up in many years, perhaps 75 years if the historical sources reveal any clues (Rice, 1921). The last adventurers ran into hostile Yạnomamö, and some died at their hands (Rice, 1921). Apparently my young guides banked on the assumption that the hardships would discourage me and I would give up. Much to their consternation, I refused to turn back and, on the third day's travel, we began running into fresh signs that Shamatari hunters or travelers had recently crossed the Mavaca. We found their flimsy foot bridges made of poles and vines. These signs began to worry my guides as we ran into more and more of them. By that night they were adamantly opposed to going any further and even refused to sleep at the place where I had pulled in the canoe: it turned out to be right on a recently traveled trail, a trail that my young guides concluded was used only by raiders. Angered, I had no choice but to go back downstream to a location more suitable to them. We left for home, Bisaasi-teri, the next morning, and on reaching it, I was pressed for the payment I originally promised to my guides. I was reluctant to pay them because they forced me to turn back, and when I asked them why they agreed to guide me in the first place, they responded: 'For the machetes you. promised to us! We *never* thought we would get to the Shamatari!'

It was too late that year to make another attempt. On my next field trip I tried again to reach Sibarariwä's village. This time I chose my guides more carefully, or at least that was my plan. I picked an older man whose name translates into 'Piranha.' He was from a village far to the north and had married into Kạobawä's village recently. Thus, he had no personal reasons to either fear the Shamatari or be despised by them, but he *was* from Kạobawä's village at this point and that might be taken with hostility by the Shamatari. The other guide I picked was just a kid, a boy named Karina. I had met him briefly the year before, when he and his mother straggled into the village of Mọmaribọwei-teri, the Shamatari village 10 hours' walk south of Kạobawä's. He and his mother had been abducted by Sibarariwä's group some 10 years earlier, so Karina had grown up, to the extent he was grown at all, in Sibarariwä's village and knew all the current residents. He had been terrified at the sight of me—his first glimpse of a non-Yạnomamö—the year before (Figure 9–5), but several visits to Kạobawä's village exposed him to the missionaries there and he gradually lost his fear of foreigners. Still, he was only about 12 or 13 years old. This, actually, was an advantage in one respect: He was still innocent enough to give me the accurate names and shallow genealogies of all the residents of Sibarariwä's village before I had even reached it.

The first attempt in 1968 ended when I discovered that all my 'gasoline' had been stolen and re-placed with water, a common problem in the Upper Orinoco where gasoline is scarce, has to be hauled in by an eight-day river trip, and filched by all who come in contact with it at every step of the way, including the very people you paid to bring it to you. We had gotten far up the Mavaca when I switched to one of my reserve gasoline tanks and the motor died—the tanks were full of plain water. We thus had to return to Bisaasi-teri where my gasoline supplies were stored and where I could dismantle my motor and spend the night cleaning it.

We set off again the next morning with fresh gasoline supplies and again were high up the Mavaca when I switched to one of my reserve tanks. This time it wasn't water, but it wasn't gasoline either. It was kerosene. Back down the Mavaca again, clean the engine again, and set off again. By this time—four or five days after starting the first trip—my guides were growing impatient and weary. My older guide failed to show up at dawn as agreed, and Karina, the 12-year-old, was feeling ill and didn't want to go. I pursuaded Karina that he would feel better in a day and he decided to come with me again.

He was my only guide at this point. I sat in my canoe, tired and depressed, wondering if I should try to make it with just a 12-year-old guide. It was a murky, dismal dawn. I hadn't slept more than a few hours each night, for I had to dismantle and reassemble my outboard motor each time we floated back home, a task I had to do at night to save time to assure my waning guides that we would make progress. As I sat there, half ready to throw in the towel, a young man, Bäkotawä, appeared at the river to take an early bath. He was the young man that Rerebawä had challenged to the club fight over the possession of Rerebawä's wife's younger sister. He knew that my other guide had backed out and that I was down to just one. I asked him if he were willing to go with me to Sibarariwä's village. He thought about it for a moment. 'I'm a Bisaasi-teri, and they might kill me,' he said, adding '… but I could tell them that I'm really a Patanowä-teri and they wouldn't know the difference.' I turned to Karina, who lay wimpering in the canoe in the most comfortable 'bed' I could arrange, using my pack and gasoline tanks as props. 'Would you vouch for him if he said he was a Patanowä-teri?' I asked. He grunted, unenthusiastically, that he'd go along with the deception and agreed that it was better than being a Bisaasi-teri. At that, we agreed that

Figure 9–5. Karina, my young guide when I first met him—a year before be led me into Shamatari country.

Bäkotawä would be my second guide. He rushed off to the *shabono* (village) to collect his hammock and a few items to trade, and returned a few minutes later, ready for the great adventure into unknown lands where his older kin feared to tread. I brought along a second shotgun that I said he could 'use' (he didn't know which end to put the cartridges in), and this pleased him immensely, not to mention bolstering his confidence.

We thus set off for the headwaters of the Mavaca in my large wooden dugout canoe, on top of which I carried a smaller, lighter aluminum boat for negotiating the high Mavaca where the big boat could not get through. My plan was to go as far in the bigger, heavier boat as we could, dropping off gasoline and other stores along the way for the trip back.

The dry season was at its peak and the rivers were very low, so low that we only made it about a day and a half upstream in the larger canoe before reaching an insurmountable obstacle: two very large trees had fallen across the river and were half submerged. They were there before, but the water was high enough that I managed to get the canoe across them. But the river had dropped since then. They were too thick to chop through with axes, and too much of the trunks was above the water to permit the three of us to horse the heavy dugout over. We thus had to leave the big canoe at that point, transfer everything to the smaller aluminum boat, and set off, badly overloaded, for the headwaters of the Mavaca. Karina was feeling normal again. He began goading Bäkotawä, asking rhetorically, 'What would they do if they knew you were really a Bisaasi-teri? Maybe I might slip and tell them that you are Bisaasi-teri.' Bäkotawä grew silent, then moody, then visibly nervous. On the third day, Karina rose up to his knees, began looking intently at the river banks on both sides, and then exclaimed: 'I know this place! We're getting close to Sibarariwä's village! Their trail to Iwähikoroba-teri is just a short way off the river, over there!' as he pointed to the east bank of the tangled, narrow river, a stream so small at this point that it would have been difficult to turn our boat around without lifting it most of the way. We proceeded a few hours further upstream, slowly, because the river was both shallow and narrow, but mostly because it was now choked with deadfalls and branches through which we had to constantly chop our way.

We pulled over about midday and dragged the boat up a bank after unloading the supplies. We would walk inland from this point, for the river was now too narrow to proceed any further. We were in a hilly region and could catch glimpses of relatively high peaks, all covered with dense vegetation and punctuated with scraggy outcroppings of rocks. We were in the headwaters of the Mavaca, and beyond the stark ridge ahead of us lay the almost legendary Shukumöna kä u, the River of Parakeets and homeland of the Shamatari—and lair of the legendary Sibarariwä and his warriors.[8]

I divided the supplies into those we would take inland with us and those we would leave behind for the return trip. As I did, I was alarmed at the relatively small amount of food we had at that point. In my concern over gasoline and sputtering motors, I had failed to restock the food after each aborted trip. There was enough for several days, but if we failed to contact the Shamatari, we would have to ration ourselves carefully.

Karina said the village was to the southeast, indicating the distance as Yanomamö always do, by pointing to where the sun would be if we left now and where it would be when we reached the village. It was about a 4-or 5-hour walk by his description, and it meant that we would reach the village just before dark—not a good thing to do on a first contact. Even the Yanomamö like to have as much daylight as they can get when they visit a strange village. That way, you have time to make friends and assess the situation. We set off with our back packs at about 2:00 P.M. and soon began running into fresh signs of human activity—footprints made a day before, husks of palm fruits, discarded items of no value, broken twigs where someone cleared the trail as he proceeded along it, and so on. My heart began to pound, for clearly we were close to Sibarariwä's village.

A ferocious rain, the onset of the rainy season, hit us about an hour after we began walking, and we had to huddle together under a small nylon tarp I always carried for such occasions. We lost about an hour because of the rain and decided that we should camp for the night: We would reach the village too late in the day to 'make friends'. We ate some boiled rice and strung our hammocks in an abandoned temporary hut made by some Shamatari hunter months earlier. As dusk settled, Karina began teasing Bäkotawä about the nastiness of Sibarariwä's group, reminding him mischievously that he was really a Bisaasi-teri, not a Patanowä-teri. Bäkotawä lay sullenly and unhappily in his hammock, and I had to scold Karina for his ill-natured humor. At dawn we got up and began packing. Bäkotawä quietly informed me that he was going no further and intended to return to the canoe; he honestly and frankly admitted, *"Ya kirii."* (I am frightened.)

I gave him a share of the food and a quick lesson in how to load and fire the shotgun, providing him with a box of 25 cartridges. I told him we would be gone about 'three days' (indicating the duration by three fingers) before we would rejoin him at the canoe. He assured me that whereas he was frightened here, he would be safe and confident at the canoe and he would make his camp there, waiting for our return. Karina and I set off to the southeast. Bäkotawä disappeared silently into the shadowy forest, heading north, back toward the canoe. Karina and I walked for several hours, continuing to run into fresh signs of Yąnomamö travelers. We found footprints that had been made just that morning, last night's rainwater still oozing into the depressions. A banana peeling here, a discarded bunch of palm fruits there. We were now very close. Karina grabbed my arm and whispered excitedly: "The village is just beyond the top of this hill!" We crept to the ridge and looked down into the valley below, where a gigantic, well-kept banana plantation surrounded an extremely large, circular *shabono,* the largest one I had ever seen up to then. We were there. Karina peered intently and then urged me to follow. In a few minutes we were in the garden, and shortly after we could see the back side of the *shabono* roof, the village structure, and the clearing. But something was wrong: no noise. No babies crying, no men chanting to the hekura spirits, no smoke, no dogs barking, and no buzzing of voices. The shabono was *broke*—empty.

Deserted, but only recently deserted. Karina went to investigate the garden, returning with a pile of ripe plantains a few minutes later and with the information that someone had been in the garden that very morning to harvest plantains. He guessed that Sibarariwä's group was camped out, but camped close enough to the garden that they could return easily to harvest food. He guessed that they would be further upstream, at a place they often camped at this time of the year because certain wild fruits were in season there. We decided to leave our packs behind, in the abandoned village, and strike off to find them. The sun was high, and we would have all afternoon to look for them.

By this point I was down to my hammock, sneakers, shotgun, and a red loincloth I had borrowed from one of the Bisaasi-teri men—I had given all my new loincloths away. I wanted to look as inconspicuous as possible when I contacted these people, and wearing a loincloth instead of clothing would help. Karina brought only his bow, several arrows, and a large wad of now-aging tobacco tucked behind his lower lip—and his own loincloth. As we walked, we ran into fresher and more abundant signs of Sibarariwä's group, and I knew that we would soon run into them. As dusk began to settle we smelled smoke and, a few minutes later, saw a lazy cloud of bluish smoke drifting through the grey forest and rising slowly to the tree tops. Then we heard the chatter of many voices and babies crying. We had found their camp at last.

We approached quietly and cautiously, stopping at a small stream just short of the campsite to 'beautify' ourselves. Karina scolded me and urged me to clean up—my legs were all muddy and my loincloth dangled haphazardly between my scratched knees. I made myself as 'presentable' as I could, washing the mud and perspiration off, straightening my loincloth, and tying my sneakers. We had no feathers or red *nara* paint to add final touches. Karina handed me his bow and arrows and took up my shotgun, commenting, as he headed for the camp: 'They might be frightened by your shotgun, so I'll take it. You carry my bow and arrows and wait for me to tell you to come in. They'll really be scared to see a *nabä* (non-Yąnomamö)!' He disappeared into the jungle, whistled a signal to alert people that a visitor was coming in. A chorus of cheers, whistles, and welcoming hoots rebounded through the darkening jungle as they welcomed him in.

I suddenly realized the absurdity of my situation and the magnitude of what I was doing. Here I stood, in the middle of an unexplored, unmapped jungle, a few hundred feet from a previously uncontacted group of Yąnomamö with a reputation for enormous ferocity and treachery, led there by a 12-year-old kid, and it was getting dark. My only marks of being human were my red loincloth, my muddy and tom sneakers, my hammock, and a bow with three skinny arrows.

An ominous hush fell over the forest ahead: Karina had obviously told them that I was waiting outside, and they were now pondering what to do. Uncomfortable recollections flashed through my head, and I recalled some of the tales that Kąobawä had recited to me about the Shamatari. I reflected on his intensely serious warnings that it would be hazardous to try to find them. They would pretend to be friendly, he explained, but when my guard was down they would fall on me with bowstaves and clubs and kill me. Perhaps they would do it on the spot, but they might wait until I had taken up a hammock, as visitors are supposed to do, and lay there defenseless. Perhaps they would do it at night, as I slept, or just before dawn. Silence. Anxiety. My temples pounded. I wanted to run. I could hear the hushed buzzing of voices and people moving around in the jungle, spreading out: Some of them were leaving the camp. Were they surrounding me? Could I trust Karina? Was someone now staring at me down the long shaft of his war arrow?

Karina suddenly appeared on the trail and motioned for me to come—to present myself. I tried to give the expected visitor's announcement, but I had trouble puckering my dry lips and only a pathetic hiss of meaningless air came forth as I tried to whistle. I walked by Karina and noticed his curious look. I could not decide if it were the same look he had when he told Bäkotawä he would vouch that he was a Patanowä-teri, but it was too late now to consider weighty implications and too late to do anything about them.

I was greeted by a host of growling, screaming men, naked and undecorated, who pranced nervously around me, menacingly pointing their long, bamboo-tipped war arrows at my face, nocked in the strings of their powerful bows. I stood my ground, motionless and as poised as I could be, trying desperately to keep my legs from trembling, trying to look dignified, defiant, and fearless. After what seemed like an eternity, one of them gruffly told me to follow him to one of the temporary huts. As we walked toward it, I could see young men scrambling to clear off the ground and straighten a *nara*-stained cotton hammock—intended for my temporary use. They worked quickly and nervously, and scattered as I approached. Karina placed my shotgun at the backpost and I reclined in the hammock, striking the visitor's pose—one hand over my mouth, staring at the space above me and swaying gently, pretending I was on display in Macy's front window with a noontime crowd peering in.

Eventually a few of the bolder men came closer, hissing commands to the others to "get some food prepared, quickly!" They began whispering excitedly to each other, describing my most minute and most private visible parts. 'Look at how hairy his legs are! Look at all that ugly hair on his chest! Look how pale he looks! Isn't he strange looking, and did you see how 'long' he was when he was standing there? I wonder if he has a regular penis? What are those skins he has tied to his feet?' Their curiosity gradually became overwhelming. The bolder ones came in closer, duck-waddling right at me. A hand came forward and cautiously and ever so delicately touched my leg. The hand retracted quickly with a hiss of amazement from its owner—'Aaahhh!' A chorus of admiring tongue clicks followed from the less bold, and then more touches and hisses, and soon many hands were touching me all over, pulling on my hairs, and they smelled my spoor repeatedly in their red-stained cupped hands, clicking their tongues and marveling that someone so different was so similar. Just a bit longer, hairier, and lighter than they were. Then I spoke to them, and again they marveled: I spoke a 'crooked' version of Ya̧nomamö, like the Bisaasi-teri do, but they understood me.

Soon we were jabbering and visiting like long-lost friends. They scolded me for not having come sooner, for they had known about me for years and had wanted to meet me. The Reyaboböwei-teri had told them about me and had passed on what they themselves had known directly from meeting me personally, and what they had learned from the Mo̧mariböwei-teri or the Bisaasi-teri second-hand. The Ya̧nomamö language is very precise about what is known firsthand and what has come from second, hearsay, sources. I was flabbergasted at the detail and accuracy of what they knew about me. They knew I had a wife and two children, and the sexes and approximate ages of my children. They could repeat with incredible accuracy conversations I had had with Ya̧nomamö in many different villages. One of them even wanted to see a scar on my left elbow. When I asked what he meant, he described in intimate detail a bad fall I had taken several years earlier on a trip to Reyaboböwei-teri when I slipped on a wet rock and landed on my elbow, which bled profusely. He even quite accurately repeated the string of Ya̧nomamö vulgarities I uttered at the time, and my complaint to my guides that their goddamned trails foolishly went up and down steep hills when they could more efficiently go around them! For people who had never before seen a non-Ya̧nomamö, they certainly knew a great deal about at least one of them![7]

I stayed with them for several days, but Karina had revealed that I had a small treasure of trade goods at my boat and they were anxious to go there to examine them. They were also disappointed that Bäkotawä did not come to the village, for 'they wouldn't have harmed him but would have befriended him.' After systematically checking the genealogical data that Karina had given me about the current families and visiting with them at length, I reluctantly decided to take them to my boat and the cache of gifts I had left there.

It had taken Karina and me at least six hours of walking to get from the boat to this place, but since they were anxious to see the boat and the trade goods, they made very rapid time guiding me back to where I had left the river. We ran most of the way. They carried only their weapons. No food and no hammocks. I didn't know what they planned to do for sleeping or eating, since we left for the boat near midday. I guess I assumed that they planned to spend the night in their abandoned *shabono*, which they could probably have reached by dark even if they spent an hour at the boat with me.

We came upon the spot where we had separated from Bakotawa. Soon after that we came upon two expended shotgun shells, then soon after that, two more, then two more, and so on. It appeared as though Bäkotawä had fired the gun every few minutes as he retreated to the boat, and it was obvious that he was out of ammunition by the time he reached it.

We crossed the last rise before reaching the spot where I had left the boat and supplies and, much to my horror, I discovered that the boat, motor, gasoline, food, tarps, and trade goods were all gone. Bäkotawä had panicked and had taken off, leaving me stranded with people he was sure would kill all of us.

I was in a decidely unenviable position at that point, for nobody except a few Yąnomamö knew where I was. I couldn't walk out, for that would have taken at least two weeks in the best of conditions, and

Figure 9–6. Woman in a bark canoe. These canoes are occasionally made by the Yąnomamö for a single trip downstream or for fording rivers. After a few days they sag, leak, and deteriorate beyond use.

it had been raining regularly since I arrived. The river was rising fast, and that meant that the land between me and Bisaasi-teri was beginning to flood. We spent a miserable wet night huddling under my small tarp thinking about the problem. I decided that the only feasible way to get out would be by river.

My first scheme was to build a raft, similar to the log palisades the Ya̧nomamö make around their villages. I had one machete with me and we set about cutting numerous trees and vines for the raft. At the end of the day we assembled it in the river, and when I stepped onto it, it promptly sank.

The next day we went into Plan II—building a 'trough' of the sort that the Ya̧nomamö characteristically use when they have ceremonial feasts. They make a bark trough and fill it full of plantain soup, but the same trough is occasionally used by them, when reinforced with a few ribs, as a temporary canoe that is suitable only for floating downstream (Figure 9–6). It is a kind of 'throw-away' canoe, useful in the kind of circumstance I was presently in. This plan was laid to rest when they told me that no suitable trees could be found in the immediate area to make such a trough. They suggested that since I was a foreigner and since foreigners make canoes, why didn't I just make myself a canoe? I explained that it wasn't quite that simple. Canoe-making is a complex enterprise, and I was from one of those foreign villages where we had to 'trade' with others for our canoes—we had 'forgotten' how to make them, as they had 'forgotten' how to make clay pots in some villages. They insisted that it

Figure 9–7. The canoe I made to descend the Mavaca River—with Karina, who clutches one of our hand-hewn paddles.

was easy to remember lost arts. I said that it took axes to make canoes. They said they had axes at the village. They would not take "No" for an answer, and sent young men running off to the village to fetch the axes. They returned in record time, after dark, with two of the most miserable 'axes' I have ever seen. They had been worn down by years, perhaps decades, of heavy use and were about one third the size they had been when they were first manufactured. But their confidence inspired me, so we set about looking for the largest, pithiest tree we could find—one that could be easily hollowed out for a single voyage. We found one, cut in, and began hollowing it out. It took all day. It looked like a long, fat cigar with a square notch cut into it. We dragged it to the river. I knew it would roll over as soon as any weight were put into it, so I designed an outrigger system that served also as a pair of seats where the two poles were lashed to the gunwales. I then lashed a pithy long pole parallel to the axis of the canoe (Figure 9–7). We spent much of another day whittling canoe paddles—three of them. One for Karina, one for me, and one for a spare. They had given me a large number of bows and arrows in exchange for the knives that I had carried in my pack. We loaded these into the outrigger and then climbed in, very gently. We sank. We unloaded the bows and arrows and all nonnecessary items from my pack. I kept only my notes, hammock, food, camera, and a small transistor radio for monitoring Mission broadcasts. With our burden thus reduced, we climbed in again, and to my delight, the water rose only to about half an inch from the gunwales: We could float and stay afloat if we kept perfectly balanced. But the Yąnomamö are 'foot' Indians, not 'river' Indians, and Karina was perhaps the classic example of what that meant. If the Yąnomamö had decided to be river Indians, they might be extinct. We probably swamped and sank 30 or 40 times in the first two days, despite my passionate explanations that it was hazardous to lean too far to the right or the left when paddling. Karina ignored my heated injunctions and, as he leaned too far one way or the other, paralysis invariably seized him and he stoically maintained his posture as we inevitably went under and had to dogpaddle the 'canoe' to the bank to bail it out and start over again.

It still amazes me that we managed to make it all the way back down to the spot where we had earlier left the large canoe, and amazes me even more that Bäkotawä had left the large canoe there as he passed by, for he had stopped at every place and collected my stores of gasoline in his voyage downstream.

Eventually, we made it back to Bisaasi-teri, much to the genuine relief of Kąobawä and Rerebawä, who had assumed the worst ... that Sibarariwä's group had killed me. Bäkotawä had gotten back several days before we did, and his fears provoked much anxiety in the village. I knew it would have been 'unprofessional' to hunt Bäkotawä down when I returned, for my mind was full of very hideous and vindictive plans for his future. In anthropological jargon, I wasn't in a very relativistic mood. We eventually had our predicted confrontation, the details of which I have discussed elsewhere (Chagnon, 1974). He is alive and well yet today, we greet each other pleasantly, but he doesn't go on trips with me anymore.

That is what it is sometimes like to meet an uncontacted tribe of South American Indians. Other experiences I have had were much more dangerous. On one occasion my hosts very nearly succeeded in killing me as I slept (Chagnon, 1974: Chapter V). More recently, in 1990 and 1991, I also contacted Yą̧nomamö villages that had never been visited before, but these experiences were much less dramatic because the people there had heard a great deal about 'foreigners' and, in most cases, at least some men of these villages had walked out to places where there were missionaries and had seen what foreigners look like (Brooke, 1990; 1991). While excited that they finally got to see me, they knew in advance what I probably looked like. The results of these trips have led to significant new insights into Yą̧nomamö culture and political history.

ENDNOTES

1. The word Yą̧nomamö is nasalized through its entire length, indicated by the diacritical mark '̧.' When this mark appears on any Yą̧nomamö word, the whole word is nasalized. The vowel 'ö' represents a sound that does not occur in the English language. It is similar to the umlaut 'ö' in the German language or the 'oe' equivalent, as in the poet Goethe's name. Unfortunately, many presses and typesetters simply eliminate diacritical marks, and this has led to multiple spellings of the word Yą̧nomamö—and multiple mispronunciations. Some anthropologists have chosen to introduce a slightly different spelling of the word Yą̧nomamö since I began writing about them, such as Yą̧nomamö, leading to additional misspellings as their diacriticals are characteristically eliminated by presses, and to the *incorrect* pronunciation 'Yanomameee.' Vowels indicated as 'ä' are pronounced as the 'uh' sound in the word 'duck'. Thus, the name Ka̧obawä would be pronounced 'cow-ba-wuh,' but entirely nasalized.

2. I spent a total of 60 months among the Yą̧nomamö between 1964 and 1991. The first edition of this case study was based on the first 15 months I spent among them in Venezuela. I have, at the time of this writing, made 20 field trips to the Yą̧nomamö and this edition reflects the new information and understandings I have acquired over the years. I plan to return regularly to continue what has now turned into a life-long study.

3. See Spindler (1970) for a general discussion of field research by anthropologists who have worked in other cultures. Nancy Howell has recently written a very useful book (1990) on some of the medical, personal, and environmental hazards of doing field research, which includes a selected bibliography on other fieldwork problems.

4. They could not pronounce "Chagnon." It sounded to them like their name for a pesky bee, shą̧ki, and that is what they called me: pesky, noisome bee.

5. The Yą̧nomamö in this region acquired canoes very recently. The missionaries would purchase them from the Ye'kwana Indians to the north for money, and then trade them to the Yą̧nomamö in exchange for labor, produce, or 'informant' work in translating. It should be emphasized that those Yą̧nomamö who lived on navigable portions of the Upper Orinoco River moved there recently from the deep forest in order to have contact with the missionaries and acquire the trade goods the missionaries (and their supply system) brought.

6. At this time in my fieldwork the Shukumöna Kä u, i.e., the Siapa River, was not even correctly shown on official maps of Venezuela. Its true location and course was not 'officially' established until 1972 when aerial radar maps of the region were developed. Most maps, prior to that, incorrectly showed the headwaters of the Mavaca River as the Siapa River.

7. In 1972 several of my colleagues from the University of Michigan Medical School made a trip to the Brazilian Yąnomamö to continue the biomedical research we had jointly pursued between 1966 and 1972. One of them casually mentioned my Yąnomamö name, Shąki, in front of a Yąnomamö. The Yąnomamö immediately and excitedly demanded to know where I was and if I were going to visit them. This Yąnomamö village was many miles away from any Yąnomamö village I had ever visited.

The Controversy and the Broader Issues at Stake

BY ROBERT BOROFSKY

At first glance, the Yanomami controversy might be perceived as being focused on a narrow subject. It centers on the accusations made by the investigative journalist Patrick Tierney against James Neel, a world-famous geneticist, and Napoleon Chagnon, a prominent anthropologist, regarding their fieldwork among the Yanomami, a group of Amazonian Indians, But it. would be a mistake to see the Yanomami controversy as limited to these three individuals and this one tribe.

First, the accusations Tierney made against Neel and Chagnon in his book *Darkness in El Dorado* (2000) generated a media storm that spread around the world. People knew about the accusations in New York, New Zealand, and New Guinea. Tierney accused Neel and Chagnon of unethical behavior among the Yanomami that at times bordered on the criminal. Many perceived the problem as being larger than the mistakes of two famous scientists. They wondered if anthropology and perhaps science itself had gone astray in. allowing such behavior to take place.

Second, and critical for the themes of this book, the way the controversy played out offers an important lens through which to examine the entire discipline of anthropology. We see not only how anthropologists idealize themselves in describing their work to others. We also see the actual practice of anthropology—up close and clear. We are led to explore questions central to the discipline.

Readers should keep this point in mind as they read *Yanomami; The Fierce Controversy and What We Can Learn from It.* The controversy goes beyond what

Neel and Chagnon stand accused of. It extends beyond the media storm generated by Tierney's accusations and the accusations that others, in turn., made against him. The controversy draws us into examining issues at the heart of modern anthropology. As we will see, there are lessons for the learning here for everyone, whatever their specialty, whatever their status within the discipline. Let me begin by providing certain background information. For clarity's sake, I order the material as a set of commonly asked questions.

WHO ARE THE YANOMAMI AND WHY ARE THEY IMPORTANT IN ANTHROPOLOGY?

Through the work of Chagnon and others, the Yanomami have become one of the best-known, if not the best-known, Amazonian Indian groups in the world. People in diverse locales on diverse continents know of them. 'They have become a symbol in the West of what life is like beyond the pale of "civilization." They are portrayed in hooks and films, not necessarily correctly, as one of the world's last remaining prototypically primitive groups.

The Yanomami are also one of the foundational societies of the anthropological corpus. They are referred, to in most introductory textbooks. Anthropology has become increasingly fragmented over the past several, decades, with anthropologists studying a wide array of societies. The Yanomami—along with, the Trobriand Islanders, the Navajo, and the Nuer—constitute shared points of reference for the discipline in these fragmented times. The Yanomami are one of the groups almost every anthropology student learns about during his or her course of study.

The Yanomami tend to be called by three names in the literature: Yanomami, Yanomamö, and Yanomama. The names all refer to the same group of people. Different subgroups are labeled (and label themselves) with different terms; there is no broadly accepted indigenous term for the whole group. There is a politics of presentation regarding which of these three terms one uses. Yanomamö is the term Chagnon gave the collective group, and those who refer to the group as Yanomamö generally tend to be supporters of Chagnon's work. Those who prefer Yanomami or Yanomama tend to take a more neutral or anti-Chagnon stance. I use Yanomami in this book because of its wide usage and greater neutrality. (When citing Chagnon in describing the group, I use Yanomamö to remain consistent with his usage.) Readers can substitute whichever term they wish.

Chagnon wrote Yanomamö: 'The Fierce People (1968) at a critical time in the discipline's development. American universities expanded significantly in the 1960s and 1970s, and, related to this, so did the discipline of anthropology, Prior to the 1950s, American anthropology had focused on the native peoples of North America and was only seriously turning, in the 1950s and 1960s, to other areas of the world. The Holt, Rinehart and Winston, series in which Chagnon published Yanomamö emphasized a broadening of the anthropological corpus. The series offered new works for new times. The foreword to Yanomamö states that the case studies in the series "are designed to bring students, in beginning and intermediate courses ... insights into the richness and complexity of human, life as it is lived in different ways and in different places" (1968.-vii).

I presume, though I have no way of knowing for certain, that at one time or another the majority of anthropologists have read Chagnon's book. At least one, and perhaps several, generations of American anthropologists have been raised on it.

The Yanomami are a tribe of roughly twenty thousand Amazonian. Indians living in 200 to 250 villages along the border between Venezuela and Brazil "The fact that the Yanomamö live in a state of chronic warfare," Chagnon writes, "is reflected in their mythology, values, settlement pattern, political behavior and marriage practices" (1968:3). He continues: "Although their technology is primitive, it permits them to exploit their jungle habitat: sufficiently well to provide them with the wherewithal of physical comfort. The nature of their economy— slash-and-burn agriculture—coupled with the fact that they have chronic warfare, results in a distinctive settlement pattern and system of alliances that permits groups of people to exploit a. given area over a relatively long period of time.... The Yanomamö explain the nature of man's ferocity ... in myth and legend, articulating themselves intellectually with the observable, real world" (1968:52–53), Chagnon notes that members of one patrilineage tend to intermarry with members of another, building ties of solidarity between the lineages through time. The local descent group—the patrilineal segment residing in a particular village—does not collectively share corporate rights over land. Rather it shares corporate rights over the exchange of women (1968:69), whose marriages are used to build alliances. Chagnon observes, "The fact that the Yanomamö rely heavily on cultivated food has led to specific obligations between members of allied villages: ... The essence of political life ... is to develop stable alliances with neighboring villages so as to create a social network that potentially allows a local group to rely for long periods of time on the gardens of neighboring villages" when they are driven from their own by enemy raids (1968:44). While stressing the violent nature of Yanomamö life, Chagnon indicates that there are graduated levels of violence with only the final one—raiding other villages—equivalent to what we would call "war."

It is Chagnon's description of the Yanomami. as "in a state of chronic warfare" that is most in dispute. The French anthropologist Jacques Lizot, in *Tales of the Yanomami,* writes: "I would like my book to help revise the exaggerated representation that has been given of Yanomami violence. The Yanomami are warriors; they can be brutal and cruel, but they can also be delicate, sensitive, and loving. Violence is only sporadic; it never dominates social life for any length of time, and long peaceful moments can separate two explosions. When one is acquainted with the societies of the North American plains or the societies of the Chaco in South America, one cannot say that Yanomami culture is organized around warfare as Chagnon does" (1985:xiv–xv).

Chagnon. depicts the Yanomami as "the last major primitive tribe left in the Amazon Basin, and the last such people *anywhere on earth*" (1992b:xiii). We need to note, however, that the Yanomami have been in direct or indirect contact with westerners for centuries (see Ferguson 1995:77–98). They are not a primitive isolate lost in time. Ferguson writes: "The Yanomami have long depended on iron and steel tools. All ethnographically described. Yanomami had begun using metal tools long before any anthropologist, arrived" (1995:23).

In providing this brief overview, I have focused on Chagnon's *Yanomamö* because it is the most widely known account. But there are other recognized ethnographers who have written about the Yanomami who might be cited as well: notably, Bruce Albert, Marcus Colchester, Ken Good, Ray Hames, Jacques Lizot, Alcida Ramos, Les Sponsel, and Ken Taylor.

WHO ARE THE CONTROVERSY'S MAIN CHARACTERS?

The three individuals who have played the most important roles in the controversy and whose names are repeatedly referred to in discussions of it are James Neel, Napoleon Chagnon, and Patrick Tierney.

The late **James Neel** has been called by many the father of modern human genetics. He served on the University of Michigan's faculty for more than forty years, becoming one of its most distinguished members. He was elected to the National Academy of Sciences as well, as to the American Academy of Arts and Sciences and was awarded the National Medal of Science and the Smithsonian Institution Medal. Neel is perceived, as the first scientist to recognize the genetic basis for sickle cell anemia. He conducted research on the aftereffects of atomic radiation with survivors of the Hiroshima and Nagasaki bombings of World War II in Japan. He also suggested not only that there was a genetic basis for several modern diseases such as diabetes and hypertension hut that such propensities resulted from an evolutionary adaptation to environments where salt and calories were less than abundant. He died in 2000, some months before the publication of Tierney's *Darkness in El Dorado*.

Neel became interested in Amazonian Indians because of his research relating population genetics to principles of natural, selection—whether certain genetic structures contained particular evolutionary adaptive advantages. Realizing that detailed studies of "civilized populations" would, prove less instructive for examining early human genetic adaptations than "tribal populations," having the Amazon region fairly accessible, and knowing that Amerindians had entered the Americas fairly recently (he believed, between fifteen and forty thousand years ago), Neel sought out relatively undisrupted groups in the Amazon for study. He wrote in his autobiography: "I realized we would probably never assemble from studies of existing tribal populations the numbers of observations necessary to relate specific genes to specific selective advantages, but at least we could take steps to define the range of population structures within which the evolutionary forces shaping humans had to operate" (1994:119). And in the journal *Science* Neel indicates that his studies were based on the assumption that Amazonian Indians were "much closer in their breeding structure to [early] hunter-gatherers than to modern man; thus they permit cautious inferences about human breeding structure prior to large-scale and complex agriculture" (1970:815). Initially, Neel studied the Shavante, another Amazonian Indian group. But in 1966 he turned to the Yanomami and worked with them until roughly 1976.

Two additional points need to be noted. First, Neel worked closely with Napoleon Chagnon during this period and, in the early years, helped fund Chagnon's research through his own research grants (which came partly from the Atomic Energy Commission). He viewed Chagnon as "indispensable" to his program: Napoleon Chagnon "had sought me out in Ann Arbor ... having heard of our developing program. By virtue of'the contacts I had already made, I could facilitate his entry into the field; he, for his part, in addition to pursuing his own interests, could put together the village pedigrees so basic to our work" (1994:134). Neel, indicates in his autobiography that he encouraged Chagnon to work among the Yanomami.

Second, a devastating measles epidemic broke out "coincident with," to use' Neel's phrasing, his arrival in the field, in 1968. Neel indicated he had brought two thousand doses of measles vaccine and had planned to hand these over to missionaries in. the region. But faced with the epidemic, Neel and. his team vaccinated many Yanomami as well. Here is how Neel described his actions: "Much of our carefully designed protocol for that expedition was quickly scrapped as we dashed from village to village, organizing the missionaries, ourselves doing our share of immunizations but also treatment when we reached villages to which measles had preceded us. We always carried a gross, almost ridiculous excess of antibiotics—now we needed everything we had, and radioed for more" (1994:162). To what degree this description accurately reflects Neel's actions during the epidemic is one of the critical questions in the controversy. Tierney accused Neel, of worsening the measles epidemic through his actions; others have suggested Neel could have done more than he did to save Yanomami lives during the epidemic.

Napoleon Chagnon, a retired professor of anthropology at the University of California, Santa Barbara, is one of the best-known members of the discipline. His writings, particularly his introductory ethnography *Yanomamö: The Fierce People* and the films associated with it have made his name familiar to millions upon millions of college students since the 1960s. It is not too far-fetched to suggest that Chagnon helped make the Yanomami famous as a tribe around the world and the Yanomami, in turn, have been the basis for Chagnon's own fame.

As is perhaps fitting given the evolutionary orientation of the University of Michigan's Anthropology Department at the time he received his doctorate (1966), Chagnon has emphasized an adaptive/evolutionary perspective in his writings. In the first edition of *Yanomamö,* for example, he stressed that one needed to see Yanomamö social life as an adaptation not only to the physical environment but also to the social and political environment—including chronic warfare.

Readers should, keep in mind several points regarding Napoleon Chagnon as they proceed further into the politics surrounding the controversy.

First, Chagnon is a good, writer. His chapter "Doing Fieldwork among the Yanomamö" has become a classic in the social sciences. It portrays in. vivid terms his early fieldwork experiences in a way that captures the imagination of readers within and beyond anthropology. His basic ethnography of the Yanomami, *Yanomamö,* has sold perhaps three million copies—far more than any other ethnographic work in recent times.

Second, Chagnon is a dedicated field-worker, Unlike most anthropologists of his or the present generation, Chagnon has—admirably in my view—striven to go back to the Yanomami year after year to study them through time. He has made at least twenty-five visits since beginning his fieldwork among them in 1964, has resided among the Yanomami for over sixty-three months, and has visited more than sixty of their villages. Few anthropologists can make such a claim, especially for a group in a remote region that is far from the creature comforts of their own homes. The problem is that when the Venezuelan and Brazilian governments restricted his field access, Chagnon engaged in various efforts, some of them violations of Venezuelan law, to continue studying the Yanomami.

Third, Chagnon is controversial. His adaptive/evolutionary approach runs counter to the dominant trend in cultural anthropology, which focuses on how cultural contexts shape human behavior. He is more concerned with the biological underpinnings of human behavior. In trying to make sense of Yanomami conflicts over women, Chagnon states (as quoted in an article about him in *Scientific American):* "I basically had to create … my own theory of society." The article continues; "Chagnon's Darwinian perspective on culture jibed with Harvard University scientist E. O. Wilson's 1975 treatise on animal behavior, *Sociobiology* Chagnon—who tends to refer to his detractors as Marxists and lef-twingers—thus became identified with that school of thought, which also made him unpopular among social scientists who believe that culture alone shapes human behavior" (Wong, 2001:2). Chagnon writes, "For better or worse, there is a definite bias in cultural anthropology favoring descriptions of tribal peoples that characterize them as hapless, hopeless, harmless, homeless, and helpless…. The Yanomamö are definitely not that kind of people, and it seemed reasonable to me to point that out, to try to capture the image of them that they themselves held. They frequently and sincerely told me … 'We are really fierce; Yanomamö are fierce people'" (1992b:xv).

As previously noted, this depiction of the Yanomami as the "fierce people" has been challenged by other Yanomami specialists. There is a political context to this. During the debates over whether or not to set aside a large reserve in Brazil for the Yanomami in the 1980s and early 1990s—one was finally established in 1992—various Brazilian, politicians used the depiction of the Yanomami as violent to suggest that they needed to be split up into several small reserves to reduce conflict among them. (The plan, not coincidentally, would have allowed for more gold mining in the region.) What upset many Yanomami specialists was that Chagnon spoke out against this misuse of his work by Brazilian politicians only in the English-speaking press, never in the Portuguese-speaking press of Brazil, where it would have done the most good.

Fourth, Chagnon has been far more forthcoming regarding the details of his fieldwork than have most anthropologists. He is quite open, for instance, about . the manipulative techniques he adopted to gather information when informants lied to him, as well as about the lies he himself told to keep Yanomami from asking for his food. He openly admits that the Yanomami made death threats against him. few anthropologists have been as candid about their fieldwork experiences as Chagnon, and. fewer still at the time he wrote about them. Most anthropologists depict their fieldwork in fairly rosy terms, whether or not they actually experienced it that way. The problem for Chagnon is that certain of the fieldwork details he is so forthcoming about violate the American Anthropological Association's code of ethics.

Patrick Tierney is a freelance investigative journalist based in Pittsburgh. He obtained an under-graduate degree in Latin American studies from the University of California at Los Angeles. Those who interact with him on a personal level describe him as gentle and soft-spoken.

Tierney's first book, *The Highest Altar: The Story of Human Sacrifice,* was published in 1989. Clarebooks.co.uk Online Used Books describes it thus: "In 1983 Patrick Tierney went to .Peru on an assignment to cover the autopsy of a well preserved five-hundred year old mummy. It was discovered that the child had been buried alive, the victim of human sacrifice.... [Tierney] went on to discover that this ancient ritual is apparently still being practiced and tells of his attempts to track down these stories in order to discover the motives behind sacrifice, the motives of the shamans and brujos who perform it." The book is now out of print. But according to Tierney's biographical information, it has been the subject of a National Geographic documentary.

Tierney spent eleven years researching and writing *Darkness in El Dorado.* He started out investigating the disruptive impact gold mining and gold miners were having on the Amazonian region, including on the Yanomami. At some point in this research he turned his attention to the scientists and journalists who have worked among the Yanomami. His gives an account of his research in an article in the *Pittsburgh Post-Gazette:*

> I originally went there [to the Amazon] just documenting the mayhem that was going on ... and trying to understand what was happening and perhaps alert people as to what can be done to help them. But as that evolved, my own participation changed.... It just didn't seem to be an adequate response to document people's deaths in the middle of these kinds of circumstances.... (The story about Neel and Chagnon] wasn't the story I was looking for initially, but it's what I came up with.... And what seemed to me to be the real story is that these people (the Yanomami] have been used to fulfill fantasies, scientific paradigms and preconceptions. And they've been used in ways that have been extremely harmful to them. (Srikameswaran 2000)

Tierney makes a considerable effort to give *Darkness in El Dorado* the trappings of academic scholarship. The book contains more than. 1,510 footnotes; the bibliography contains more than 250 books. The question, however, is whether Tierney's years of research and voluminous citations add up to a credible work. Several anthropologists suggest that his supporting data are stronger for his case against Chagnon than for his case against Neel. Regarding his claim that Neel helped make the 1968 measles epidemic worse through his actions, the overwhelming consensus is that Tierney is wrong.

To understand the media storm surrounding *Darkness in El Dorado,* readers should take note of how Tierney's publisher publicized it. A statement inside the book's dust jacket (in the hardcover edition) reads in ail capitals: "One of the most harrowing books about anthropology to appear in decades. *Darkness in El Dorado* is a brilliant work of investigation that chronicles the history of Western exploitation of the Yanomami Indians." And a CNN.com "Book News" report, dated October 2, 2000, notes, the "publisher W. W. Norton ... is billing the book as 'an explosive account of how ruthless journalists, self-serving anthropologists, and. obsessed scientists placed one of the Amazon basin's oldest tribes on the cusp of extinction.'"

In addition to James Neel, Napoleon Chagnon, and Patrick Tierney, there are three minor characters and one religious group that should be noted here because they are sometimes referred to in the controversy.

Marcel Roche is a Venezuelan doctor. As part of his goiter research, he administered to Yanomami small doses of radioactive iodine in 1958, 1962, arid 1968 to measure their iodine metabolism. Apparently none of the Yanomami tested suffered from goiter problems, nor have Yanomami. in general suffered from the disease. The Yanomami were simply used as a control study to enhance Roche's understanding of the disease. Most people agree that Roche never asked for what is today termed informed consent—permission from subjects to conduct research on. them.

Jacques Lizot is a prominent French, anthropologist who lived among the Yanomami for more than twenty years. He is highly critical of Chagnon's writings. Two points tend to be repeatedly asserted about Lizot's time in the field: that he was a strong public defender of Yanomami rights and that he had homosexual relations with a number of Yanomami boys. Related to these sexual relations, Tierney writes: "Lizot probably distributed more clothes and shotguns than any other individual among the Yanomami" (2000:141). And: "Whatever homosexual practices the Yanomami had prior to Lizot's arrival, shotgun-driven prostitution is nothing to brag about in their culture" (2000:137). Lizot has written two books on the Yanomami: *The Yanomami in the Face of Ethnocide* (1976) and *Tales of the Yanomami: Daily Life in the Venezuelan Forest* (1985).

Ken Good was a doctoral student of Chagnon's who had a falling-out with him after they spent time together in the field. (He ultimately got his doctorate working with Marvin Harris, a critic of Chagnon.) Good spent twelve years among the Yanomami and married a Yanomami (Yarirna), from whom he is now divorced. He has written about his experiences in *Into the Heart: One Man's Pursuit of Love and Knowledge among the* Yanomama (1991), Building on what Lizot wrote, Good observes, "Chagnon made ... [the Yanomama (or Yanomami)] out to be warring, fighting, belligerent people.... That may be his image of the Yanomama; it's certainly not mine" (1991:175).

The Catholic **Salesian missionaries** have had a prominent presence in Yano-mami territory lor decades. Early in the twentieth century, Venezuela legally granted the Salesian missionaries responsibility for educating the indigenous inhabitants of the Amazonas region (which includes the Yanomami). That responsibility continues today. Both Chagnon and Lizot have come into conflict with the Salesians, While they have had positive things to say about the missionaries, both have been highly critical as well. One outside observer labeled Chagnon's conflict with the Salesians a "turf war" over who would control research among the Yanomami (Salamone 1996:4). (Chagnon views the Salesians as partly to blame for his being officially barred from studying the Yanomami in Venezuela.)

WHAT EXACTLY IS THE YANOMAMI CONTROVERSY?

Answering this question draws us into examining not only the accusations Tierney made against Neel and Chagnon in *Darkness in El Dorado* but a number of other issues as well. Let me start with Tierney's accusations and then move on to the additional issues.

The Accusations

Tierney made a number of accusations against a number of people in *Darkness in El Dorado*. But the central ones—and the ones latched onto by the media—involved Neel and Chagnon.

Tierney makes two basic accusations against Neel: (1) that Neel helped make the measles epidemic worse, rather than better, through the actions he took to fight the epidemic and (2) that Neel could have done more than he did to help the Yanomami at this time. Because the first of these accusations in effect charged a distinguished scientist with facilitating the deaths of Yanomami, it received the most media attention. This accusation has been dismissed by most people; the second is very much with us.

Tierney makes seven basic accusations against Chagnon: (1) He indicates that Chagnon misrepresented key dynamics of Yanomami society, particularly their level of violence. The Yanomami were not "the fierce people" depicted by Chagnon, They were significantly less bellicose, in fact, than many Amazonian groups. (2) What warfare Chagnon noticed during his research, Tierney asserts, Chagnon himself helped cause through his enormous distribution of goods, which stimulated warfare among the Yanomami as perhaps never before. (3) Tierney accuses Chagnon of staging the films he helped produce, films that won many cinematic awards and helped make *Yanomamö: The Fierce People* a best seller. The films were not what they appeared to be—live behavior skillfully caught by the camera—but rather staged productions in which Yanomami followed preestablished scripts. (4) Tierney accuses Chagnon of fabricating the data used in Chagnon's most famous article, which appeared in *Science* in 1988. The article asserted that Yanomami men who murdered tended to have more wives and more children—or, phrased another way, that violence was an. evolutionary adaptive principle. (5) Tierney asserts that Chagnon acted unethically in collecting the genealogies needed for Chagnon's and Neel's research. The Yanomani have a taboo against naming deceased relatives. When asked about deceased relatives, Yanomami would invent names, essentially making a shambles of Chagnon's genealogical data. Tierney claims that Chagnon used unethical techniques to get around this difficulty. (6) Tierney asserts that Chagnon's self-depiction as being the first outsider to make contact with several Yanomami. villages is untrue. Long before Chagnon arrived, Helena Valero, an outsider who was kidnapped by the Yanomami in 1932 and who lived among them for fifty years, had visited, all. the villages Chagnon claimed to have contacted. And (7) Tierney accuses Chagnon of violating Venezuelan law while participating in a plan with two prominent Venezuelans to establish a private Yanomami reserve that, would have been controlled by the three of them. This is termed the FUNDAFACI (Foundation to Aid Peasant and Indigenous Families) project. For Chagnon, the project represented a way around the restrictions placed on his visiting the Yanomami by the Venezuelan government.

The publicity generated by Tierney's *Darkness in El Dorado* became part of the controversy. Here is a sampling of what the media said. ABCnews.com reported: "Another red-hot scientific scandal. This time anthropologists and geneticists are getting a noisy wake-up call. A book written by journalist Patrick Tierney, titled *Darkness in El Dorado* ... raises a stink so high that the space station astronauts will get a whiff of it" (Regush 2000). *Time* asked: "What Have We Done to Them?... A new book charges scientists with abusing the famous Yanomami. tribe, stirring fierce debate in academia" (Roosevelt 2000). *USA Today* noted that the "face of anthropology stands riddled with charges that its practitioners engaged in genocide, criminality and scientific misconduct" (Vergano 2000). *Business Week* added: "Tierney makes a persuasive argument that anthropologists for several decades engaged in unethical practices" (Smith 2000). The *New Yorker* spread across its cover: "What happened in the jungle? Patrick Tierney reports from South America on the anthropologist who may have gone too far" (October 9, 2000: cover overleaf).

How did anthropologists respond to the media reports? The *New York Times* wrote: A "new book about anthropologists ... has set off a storm in the profession, reviving scholarly animosities, endangering personal reputations and, some parties say, threatening to undermine confidence in legitimate practices of. anthropology" (Wilford and Romero 2000), The *Chronicle of Higher Education* reported: "Some anthropologists fear that their discipline faces a scandal because of the imminent publication of a book charging several prominent researchers with egregious misbehavior in their work with Amazon tribes.... Scholars axe worried that the allegations will make it hard for all cultural anthropologists who do fieldwork to persuade their subjects and the public that they are responsible, objective, and trustworthy" (Miller 2,000b).

As time went on, other accusations were piled on. top of the ones listed, above.

Regarding Neel, there were two. First, critics suggested that he had never gotten informed consent for his medical research among the Yanomami. (Informed consent, touched on above, involves getting formal permission from subjects to conduct research on them and is required today in all. medical research.) Even if standards of informed consent during the 1960s differed from those existing today, several critics asked if Neel couldn't have done more to inform the Yanomami about the details of his research. This constitutes a critical issue because many Yanomami today claim that they had. been led to expect additional medical assistance that drew on the results of Neel's research among them. This assistance has not been forthcoming. Second, with the publication of Tierney's book many Yanomami came to realize that the blood collected during Neel's research was still being preserved in American laboratories. They felt they had never been informed, that this would occur. While some Yanomami want to be suitably paid for their deceased relatives' blood, others want it destroyed, viewing it as a sacrilege to preserve the blood of dead Yanomami, What the Yanomami concur on is that they want to reopen negotiations regarding the blood and are willing to contest continued use of it until a. suitable agreement is reached.

Regarding Chagnon, three accusations came to the fore. First, various anthropologists in Brazil and the United States brought up an old question of why Chagnon had never openly opposed misuse of his work in the Brazilian press. It seemed a violation of the American Anthropological Association's ethical injunction to do no harm. Second, some anthropologists brought up Chagnon's earlier criticism of Davi Kopenawa, a prominent Yanomami activist who played a key role in the effort to establish a Yanomami reserve in Brazil. They asked if it was right that an anthropologist should undermine the work of an indigenous activist seeking to protect his people. And third, there was the question of how Chagnon should distribute the more than $1 million he made in royalties from his best-selling book *Yanomamö*. Chagnon at one time had set up a fund to assist the Yanomami, but there is no record of the fund ever doing anything to help them. Many asked, shouldn't Chagnon share some of this money with the Yanomami who assisted in the research? Clearly, Chagnon could not have written the book without their help.

As the controversy continued, Tierney was subjected to criticism as well. Several supporters of Neel and. Chagnon suggested that *Darkness in El Dorado* was full of inaccuracies. They described many of the footnotes used to back up statements in the main text as distortions of the original sources. Some critics suggested Tierney's book was little more than a malicious, irresponsible attack on two prominent scientists.

With all the attention focused on the Yanomami. controversy, we might ask whether the Yanomami have benefited in some way from the controversy that has swirled around them. To date, the answer is essentially no. Despite all the publicity and all the good intentions expressed by anthropological organizations and anthropologists, the Yanomami essentially still live under the same tenuous health conditions as before. This is a scandal in itselt it suggests that the Yanomami seem, for many anthropologists, to be primarily tools for intellectual argument and academic advancement.

American Anthropology's Response

One might think these issues quite sufficient to create debate in anthropology departments around the world. But there is more. There are also important questions regarding the way American anthropology has responded to the controversy.

For example, why did no American organization ever investigate the accusations surrounding Chagnon before the publication of Tierney's *Darkness in El Dorado* in 2000, although the accusations had been circulating for years and were supported, in. part, by Chagnon's own writings? Rather than investigating these accusations, most members of the discipline seemed content to ignore them. In fact, thousands of anthropologists continued to use Chagnon's ethnography *Yanomamö* in their classes, even though it was clear that the field practices he described in it violated the American Anthropological Association's code of ethics. Whatever Chagnon's ethical lapses, he remained a hero to many in the discipline. We might ask why so many chose to ignore, rather than investigate, the accusations against him.

We might also voice concern over the way the American Anthropological Association (AAA), American anthropology's largest organization, initially responded to the publicity generated by the publication of Tierney's book. The AAA organized an "open forum" with a number of panelists at its 2000 annual meeting. But as readers will see in chapter 3, most of the panelists were biased against Tierney. In criticizing him, they focused on Tierney's accusation against Neel that had already been disproved. Tierney's accusations against Chagnon were not really addressed.

Readers will have a chance to evaluate for 'themselves where they stand on the controversy's issues. But my impression—if I may inject it at this point—is that the leaders of the American Anthropological Association initially addressed the controversy more as a problem in public relations than as a problem of professional ethics: they were more concerned with protecting the discipline's image than with dealing directly with the issues Tierney had raised.

To its credit, the association set up a. task force to inquire further into the matter. But when the El Dorado Task Force's preliminary report was made public, it appeared to be following the same tack as the panelists at the open forum. The preliminary report caused an uproar among those who wanted to call Chagnon to account. In an effort to calm the troubled waters generated by the report, the Task Force requested public comment on it. The more than 170 responses posted at the association's Web site—most of them from students—caused the Task Force to change course. The comments drew the 'Task Force into seriously assessing, in its final report, Chagnon's various deeds and misdeeds. It was the first time the association had seriously done so.

Whatever one's view of the Task Force's final report—and opinions differ—it is important to acknowledge the role students played in this phase of the controversy. Never before in the discipline's history, I believe, had students participated with such impact in such a prominent disciplinary debate. That participation is the reason I am dedicating this book to these students. At a critical, time, they stood up, got involved, and made a difference in the discipline's politics.

To summarize, the controversy is not simply about the accusations Tierney made against Neel, and Chagnon or the accusations various other people have made against Neel, Chagnon, and Tierney. It is also about how American anthropology has responded to these accusations. There is room for cynicism regarding how the controversy has played out in the discipline. But there is also room for hope, given how students helped draw the association's Task Force into directly assessing accusations against a former member.

The Larger Questions

At a still higher level, beyond the accusations and counteraccusations and beyond American anthropology's responses to them, there is yet another set of issues anthropologists and anthropologists-in-the-making need to confront regarding the controversy. These are the generally unspoken questions that lie at the heart of the discipline and that help to explain why American anthropology has been hesitant to confront the controversy head-on. These are the big questions we need to ask but often are afraid to because they put into doubt what we have come to accept as foundational and firm in anthropology.

The first is the *inequality of power* between anthropologists and their informants. Since anthropologists tend, to come from countries that are more economically developed and militarily powerful than those they study, it is reasonable to ask, what ethical standards should govern how the more powerful use the intellectual and biological resources of the less powerful? Phrased another way, how does anthropology move beyond colonial practices built up when anthropologists mostly studied the subjugated peoples of imperial powers? What today constitutes a fair and just relationship among the parties concerned? Related to the inequality of power are the issues of informed consent, "doing no harm," and just compensation.

Today the first of these, *informed consent*, is required by almost all funding agencies supporting medical and social research. But how do anthropologists acquire permission from the people being studied? How does one explain a prefect to a group of people (or inform them) and gain, their approval (or consent) when. the project involves unfamiliar concepts and practices? Also relevant is the question of the duration *of* such consent. Is it a one-time thing, or do researchers need to gain it again as they find new ways to use and make money from the-initial research that was never envisioned in the initial consent agreement?

The second is the anthropological injunction (embodied in the American Anthropological Association's code of ethics) *to do no harm* to those whom anthropologists study. What this means in practice—what specific actions this directive commits an anthropologist to—remains unclear. Remember that Chagnon, who essentially admitted in his own writings to violating this ethic, was lionized by many within the discipline.

We might, moreover, wonder why the focus is on doing no harm rather than on the third issue, offering *just compensation* to those who assisted in. one's research. Anthropologists tend to present generous gifts to informants. But are such gifts sufficient compensation, given that anthropologists take the informants' information hack to their universities and use it to build financially satisfying careers that often far exceed what their informants can expect in their own lives? Should these informants, who are living in less-privileged circumstances, be given the assistance to create better lives for themselves as well?

There are no easy answers here, and. readers should not expect anthropology, by itself, to right the world's inequities. But these issues should be openly addressed. We need to consider how anthropology as a discipline might reach across the political and economic divides that separate researchers from informants and justly compensate those who help anthropologists build professional careers.

Most anthropologists care deeply about the people they work with. But they get caught up in broader power structures that keep the discipline from moving/beyond the colonizing practices of times past. The persistence of such practices today is a part of the Yanomami controversy.

This point leads to another, the issue of *professional integrity.* Is the American Anthropological Association's code of ethics simply a set of nice-sounding abstractions—window dressing to impress those beyond the discipline—or are anthropologists held accountable to the code in some way? What responsibilities does the code entail for individual anthropologists? What does it entail for the discipline as an organized profession? Some might prefer to deal with such questions in terms of abstract pronouncements (of *shoulds* and *should nots*), but the fact is that anthropologists cannot simply claim to be moral and expect others in nonacademic settings to trust them on that basis, especially given, the discipline's record to date. Again, there are no easy answers. But we all. need consider how to move anthropology beyond talking about morality to practicing a morality that embodies the best ideals of the discipline and that ensures a positive reception, for us in places where our reputations precede us.

We need to also consider *the* way *anthropologists tend to argue past one another* in controversies such as this. Is anthropology simply a matter of vexation and debate—a form of entertainment tor intellectual aficionados of the obscure—or is something approaching a consensus possible in a heated matter where the discipline's own behaviors are called into question? Are controversies such as this ever resolvable? Or do people simply give up arguing after a while and go on to something new?

For anthropology, Chagnon is the central, character. The discipline embraced him and his work for years, making *Yanomamö* the best-selling ethnography in the past half-century. Understandably, partisans of Chagnon—and there are many in the discipline—tend to focus their criticism of Tierney on his account of Neel, reasoning that if Tierney's case is weakened in one area it is weakened in others. That is why the "Referendum on *Darkness in El Dorado*" (sponsored by Chagnon partisans and passed in November 2003 by the American Anthropological Association) focused on Tierney's fallacious claim that Neel helped make the measles epidemic worse. While Chagnon was a participant in Neel's project, he played a minor role in Neel's measles immunization campaign. Chagnon partisans downplay his violations of the association's ethical code and Venezuelan law. Partisans of Tierney, on the other hand, tend to pass over the charges against Neel and focus on Tierney's accusations against Chagnon, where they feel their case is stronger. One can often tell a person's position in the controversy simply by noting the topic he or she wishes to discuss.

As a result of these tactics, there have been few sustained, back-and-forth discussions between opposing partisans regarding the accusations surrounding Neel and Chagnon. Most of the time opposing partisans talk past one another. The only two sustained conversations I know of are in part 2 of this book and the final report of the AAA's El Dorado Task Force, which, is summarized in chapter 11.

In summary, beyond the accusations surrounding Neel, Chagnon, and Tierney, there are critical—indeed, from my perspective, far more critical—issues that need to be addressed in the controversy: those involving relations with informants as well as professional integrity and. competence. Given how central these issues are to anthropology, readers can understand, perhaps, why many in the discipline have sought to sidestep the controversy. Confronting these issues will be hard. But the discipline needs to address them if it is to outgrow its image as an agent of colonizing powers and be both welcomed and understood outside the halls of academia.

WHAT IS RIGHT ABOUT CONTROVERSIES SUCH AS THIS?

I have referred above to the problems controversies such as this can create. They may generate negative publicity for the discipline, making the broader public less willing to support it. They may also foster disciplinary divides as anthropologists passionately argue past one another without resolution. Let me turn now to what is right about these controversies and why they are important, indeed essential, for the discipline's cumulative development.

First, controversies such as this provide a basis for conversations across the specialized research worlds anthropologists now participate in. They enable people grounded in different regions and absorbed by different problems to talk about issues that interest—and in this case affect—them all. In Victor Turner's phrasing, controversies such as this offer a temporary "communitas," a temporary moment of community that transcends the structural boundaries that traditionally separate anthropologists from one another. Turner suggests that such "antistructural" moments allow people to perceive the problematic nature of the structures that shape their everyday lives. We see that here. The Yanomami controversy allows us to reflect on the discipline's dynamics in a special way.

Second, controversies such as this are essential for building a cumulative discipline. There has been, a sea change in the way anthropologists think about their research since Napoleon Chagnon began his Yanomamö fieldwork in 1964. At that time, there was a general disciplinary sense that anthropologists—in seeking to be scientific—were concerned with "just the facts;" as Detective Joe Friday famously put it in the 1950s television program *Dragnet* Anthropologists saw their job as collecting facts and letting the facts speak for themselves.

Today, there is a greater appreciation that gathering "just the facts" is not a simple process. During the past two decades, the discipline has worked its way through what has been termed "a crisis of representation," an "uncertainty about adequate means of describing social reality" (Marcus and. Fischer 1986:8). "No longer is it credible," Fischer asserts, "for a single author to pose as an omniscient source on complex cultural settings" (in Barfield 1997:370). While this perspective has been warmly embraced by a substantial portion of the discipline, it has mostly involved—at the case-study level—authors challenging their own authority in ways that, at times, might be perceived as self-serving.

In examining opposing viewpoints as we do in this controversy, readers have a chance to move beyond such accounts to a deeper, fuller sense of how anthropologists, in fact, construct ethnographies. There are, no doubt, self-serving elements in Chagnon's and Tierney's accounts. But we can ferret many of these out by comparing one account with another and comparing both with other accounts written by different anthropologists who have also worked among the Yanomami.

What is now increasingly evident to most members of the profession—and perhaps should have been in the 1960s—is that anthropology needs different accounts of the same subject to gam greater objectivity, to gain a better sense of the social processes described by anthropologists.

Multiple accounts allow us to step behind the screen of anthropological authority—something like seeing the Wizard of Oz in person rather than from behind a screen—and perceive the underlying dynamics at work.

In the search for objectivity, we cannot put our faith in a single account, regardless of the status of the person who produced it. There is always the problem of self-serving rhetoric. *Objectivity does not lie in the assertions of authorities. It lies in the open, public analysis of divergent perspectives.*

What is essential to developing cumulative knowledge—rather than continually increasing the amount of uncertain knowledge, as frequently occurs today—is that anthropological results be publicly called into question. The results must be challenged, the researchers involved must respond, and the broader community must work its way toward consensus on the issue. The problem, of course, is that as long as the material remains obscure—known only by this or that expert—there can never be a real collective resolution of differences.

The hope held out, is that we can collectively listen to the arguments and counterarguments of experts as they debate. And as in a trial, where the jury does not know all the relevant details beforehand but learns them as various experts with opposing views present them, we can come to a set of shared conclusions.

Hills, Valleys, and States
An Introduction to Zomia

BY JAMES C. SCOTT

I open with three diagnostic expressions of frustration. The first two are from would-be conquering administrators, determined to subdue a recalcitrant landscape and its fugitive, resistant inhabitants. The third, from a different continent, is from a would-be conqueror of souls, in some despair at the irreligion and heterodoxy that the landscape appears to encourage:

> Making maps is hard, but mapping Guizhou province especially so.... The land in southern Guizhou has fragmented and confused boundaries.... A department or a county may be split into several subsections, in many instances separated by other departments or counties.... There are also regions of no man's land where the Miao live intermixed with the Chinese....
>
> Southern Guizhou has a multitude of mountain peaks. They are jumbled together, without any plains or marshes to space them out, or rivers or water courses to put limits to them. They are vexingly numerous and ill-disciplined.... Very few people dwell among them, and generally the peaks do not have names. Their configurations are difficult to discern clearly, ridges and summits seeming to be the same. Those who give an account of the arterial pattern of the mountains are thus obliged to speak at length. In some cases, to describe a few kilometers of ramifications needs a pile of documentation, and dealing with the main line of a day's march takes a sequence of chapters.

As to the confusion of the local patois, in the space of fifty kilometers a river may have fifty names and an encampment covering a kilometer and a half may have three designations. Such is the unreliability of the nomenclature.[1]

The hilly and jungly tracts were those in which the dacoits held out longest. Such were [sic] the country between Minbu and Thayetmyo and the terai [swampy lowland belt] at the foot of the Shan Hills and the Arakan and Chin Hills. Here pursuit was impossible. The tracts are narrow and tortuous and admirably suited for ambuscades. Except by the regular paths there were hardly any means of approach; the jungle malaria was fatal to our troops; a column could only penetrate the jungle and move on. The villages are small and far between; they are generally compact and surrounded by dense, impenetrable jungle. The paths were either just broad enough for a cart, or very narrow, and, where they led through the jungle were overhung with brambles and thorny creepers. A good deal of the dry grass is burned in March, but as soon as the rains recommence the whole once more becomes impassable.[2]

The surface has been minutely trenched by winding streams. So numerous are the creeks that the topographical map of a single representative county of 373 square miles indicated 339 named streams, that is, nine streams for each ten square miles. The valleys are for the most part "V"-shaped, with rarely more level space along the banks of a stream for a cabin and perhaps a garden patch.... The isolation occasioned by methods of travel so slow and difficult is intensified by several circumstances. For one thing, the routes are round-about. Travel is either down one branch along a creek and up another branch, or up a stream to a divide and down another stream on the further side of the ridge. This being the case, married women living within ten miles of their parents have passed a dozen years without going back to see them.[3]

Behind each lament lies a particular project of rule: Han rule under the Qing, British rule within the Empire, and finally, the rule of orthodox Protestant Christianity in Appalachia. All would style themselves, unselfconsciously, as bearers of order, progress, enlightenment, and civilization. All wished to extend the advantages of administrative discipline, associated with the state or organized religion, to areas previously ungoverned.

How might we best understand the fraught dialectical relations between such projects of rule and their agents, on the one hand, and zones of relative autonomy and their inhabitants, on the other? This relationship is particularly salient in mainland Southeast Asia, where it demarcates the greatest social cleavage that shapes much of the region's history: that between hill peoples and valley peoples or between upstream (*hulu* in the Malay world) and downstream (*hilir*) peoples.[4] In tracing this dialectic with some care, I believe it also traces a path to a novel historical understanding of the global process of state formation in the valleys and the peopling of the hills.

The encounter between expansionary states and self-governing peoples is hardly confined to Southeast Asia. It is echoed in the cultural and administrative process of "internal colonialism" that characterizes the formation of most modern Western nation-states; in the imperial projects of the Romans, the Hapsburgs, the Ottomans, the Han, and the British; in the subjugation of indigenous peoples in "white-settler" colonies such as the United States, Canada, South Africa, Australia, and Algeria; in the dialectic between sedentary, town-dwelling Arabs and nomadic pastoralists that have characterized much of Middle Eastern history.[5] The precise shape of the encounters is, to be sure, unique to each case. Nevertheless, the ubiquity of the encounter between self-governing and state-governed peoples—variously styled as the raw and the cooked, the wild and the tamed, the hill/forest people and the valley/cleared-land people, upstream and downstream, the barbarian and the civilized, the backward and the modern, the free and the bound, the people without history and the people with history—provides us with many possibilities for comparative triangulation. We shall take advantage of these opportunities where we can.

A WORLD OF PERIPHERIES

In the written record—that is to say, from the beginning of grain-based, agrarian civilizations—the encounter we are examining can fairly be said to preoccupy rulers. But if we stand back and widen the historical lens still further, seeing the encounter in human rather than state-civilization terms, it is astonishing how recent and rapid the encounter has been. *Homo sapiens sapiens* has been around for something like two hundred thousand years, and only about sixty thousand, at the outside, in Southeast Asia. There the region's first small concentrations of sedentary populations appear not earlier than the first millennium before the common era (ce) and represent a mere smudge in the historical landscape—localized, tenuous, and evanescent. Until shortly before the common era, the very last 1 percent of human history, the social landscape consisted of elementary, self-governing, kinship units that might, occasionally, cooperate in hunting, feasting, skirmishing, trading, and peace-making. It did not contain anything one could call a state.[6] In other words, living in the absence of state structures has been the standard human condition.

The founding of agrarian states, then, was the contingent event that created a distinction, hence a dialectic, between a settled, state-governed population and a frontier penumbra of less governed or virtually autonomous peoples. Until at least the early nineteenth century, the difficulties of transportation, the state of military technology, and, above all, demographic realities placed sharp limits on the reach of even the most ambitious states. Operating in a population density of only 5.5 persons per square kilometer in 1600 (compared with roughly 35 for India and China), a ruler's subjects in Southeast Asia had relatively easy access to a vast, land-rich frontier.[7] That frontier operated as a rough and ready homeostatic device; the more a state pressed its subjects, the fewer subjects it had. The frontier underwrote popular freedom. Richard O'Connor captures this dialectic nicely: "Once states appeared, adaptive conditions changed yet again—at least for farmers. At that moment, mobility allowed farmers to escape the impositions of states and their wars. I call this tertiary dispersion.

The other two revolutions—agriculture and complex society—were secure but the state's domination of its peasantry was not, and so we find a strategy of 'collecting people ... and establishing villages.' "[8]

THE LAST ENCLOSURE

Only the modern state, in both its colonial and its independent guises, has had the resources to realize a project of rule that was a mere glint in the eye of its precolonial ancestor: namely to bring nonstate spaces and people to heel. This project in its broadest sense represents the last great enclosure movement in Southeast Asia. It has been pursued—albeit clumsily and with setbacks—consistently for at least the past century. Governments, whether colonial or independent, communist or neoliberal, populist or authoritarian, have embraced it fully. The headlong pursuit of this end by regimes otherwise starkly different suggests that such projects of administrative, economic, and cultural standardization are hard-wired into the architecture of the modern state itself.

Seen from the state center, this enclosure movement is, in part, an effort to integrate and monetize the people, lands, and resources of the periphery so that they become, to use the French term, *rentable*—auditable contributors to the gross national product and to foreign exchange. In truth, peripheral peoples had always been firmly linked economically to the lowlands and to world trade. In some cases, they appear to have provided most of the products valued in international commerce. Nevertheless, the attempt to fully incorporate them has been culturally styled as development, economic progress, literacy, and social integration. In practice, it has meant something else. The objective has been less to make them productive than to ensure that their economic activity was legible, taxable, assessable, and confiscatable or, failing that, to replace it with forms of production that were. Everywhere they could, states have obliged mobile, swidden cultivators to settle in permanent villages. They have tried to replace open common-property land tenure with closed common property: collective farms or, more especially, the individual freehold property of liberal economies. They have seized timber and mineral resources for the national patrimony. They have encouraged, whenever possible, cash, monocropping, plantation-style agriculture in place of the more biodiverse forms of cultivation that prevailed earlier. The term *enclosure* seems entirely appropriate for this process, mimicking as it does the English enclosures that, in the century after 1761, swallowed half of England's common arable land in favor of large-scale, private, commercial production.

The novel and revolutionary aspect of this great enclosure movement is apparent if we open our historical lens to its widest aperture. The very earliest states in China and Egypt—and later, Chandra-Gupta India, classical Greece, and republican Rome—were, in demographic terms, insignificant. They occupied a minuscule portion of the world's landscape, and their subjects were no more than a rounding error in the world's population figures. In mainland Southeast Asia, where the first states appear only around the middle of the first millennium of the common era, their mark on the landscape and its peoples is relatively trivial when compared with their oversized place in the history books. Small, moated, and walled centers together with their tributary villages, these little nodes of hierarchy and power were both unstable and geographically confined. To an eye not yet hypnotized by archeological remains and state-centric histories, the landscape would have seemed virtually all periphery and no centers. Nearly all the population and territory were outside their ambit.

Diminutive though these state centers were, they possessed a singular strategic and military advantage in their capacity to concentrate manpower and foodstuffs in one place. Irrigated rice agriculture on permanent fields was the key.[9] As a new political form, the padi state was an ingathering of previously stateless peoples. Some subjects were no doubt attracted to the possibilities for trade, wealth, and status available at the court centers, while others, almost certainly the majority, were captives and slaves seized in warfare or purchased from slave-raiders. The vast "barbarian" periphery of these small states was a vital resource in at least two respects. First, it was the source of hundreds of important trade goods and forest products necessary to the prosperity of the padi state. And second, it was the source of the most important trade good in circulation: the human captives who formed the working capital of any successful state. What we know of the classical states such as Egypt, Greece, and Rome, as well as the early Khmer, Thai, and Burmese states, suggests that most of their subjects were formally unfree: slaves, captives, and their descendants.

The enormous ungoverned periphery surrounding these minute states also represented a challenge and a threat. It was home to fugitive, mobile populations whose modes of subsistence—foraging, hunting, shifting cultivation, fishing, and pastoralism—were fundamentally intractable to state appropriation. The very diversity, fluidity, and mobility of their livelihoods meant that for an agrarian state adapted to sedentary agriculture, this ungoverned landscape and its people were fiscally sterile. Unless they wished to trade, their production was inaccessible for yet another reason. Whereas the early states were nearly everywhere the creature of arable plains and plateaus, much of the more numerous ungoverned population lived, from a state perspective, in geographically difficult terrain: mountains, marshland, swamps, arid steppes, and deserts. Even if, as was rarely the case, their products were in principle appropriable, they were effectively out of range owing to dispersal and the difficulties of transportation. The two zones were ecologically complementary and therefore natural trading partners, but such trade could rarely be coerced; it took the form of voluntary exchange.

For early state elites, the periphery—seen frequently as the realm of "barbarian tribes"—was also a potential threat. Rarely—but memorably, in the case of the Mongols and the Huns and Osman and his conquering band—a militarized pastoral people might overrun the state and destroy it or rule in its place. More commonly, nonstate peoples found it convenient to raid the settlements of sedentary farming communities subject to the state, sometimes exacting systematic tribute from them in the manner of states. Just as states encouraged sedentary agriculture for its "easy pickings," so, too, did raiders find it attractive as a site of appropriation.

The main, long-run threat of the ungoverned periphery, however, was that it represented a constant temptation, a constant alternative to life within the state. Founders of a new state often seized arable land from its previous occupants, who might then either be incorporated or choose to move away. Those who fled became, one might say, the first refugees from state power, joining others outside the state's reach. When and if the state's reach expanded, still others faced the same dilemma.

At a time when the state seems pervasive and inescapable, it is easy to forget that for much of history, living within or outside the state—or in an intermediate zone—was a choice, one that might be revised as the circumstances warranted. A wealthy and peaceful state center might attract a growing population that found its advantages rewarding. This, of course, fits the standard civilizational narrative of rude barbarians mesmerized by the prosperity made possible by the king's peace and justice—a narrative shared by most of the world's salvational religions, not to mention Thomas Hobbes.

This narrative ignores two capital facts. First, as we have noted, it appears that much, if not most, of the population of the early states was unfree; they were subjects under duress. The second fact, most inconvenient for the standard narrative of civilization, is that it was very common for state subjects to run away. Living within the state meant, virtually by definition, taxes, conscription, corvée labor, and, for most, a condition of servitude; these conditions were at the core of the state's strategic and military advantages. When these burdens became overwhelming, subjects moved with alacrity to the periphery or to another state. Under premodern conditions, the crowding of population, domesticated animals, and the heavy reliance on a single grain had consequences for both human and crop health that made famines and epidemics more likely. And finally, the early states were warmaking machines as well, producing hemorrhages of subjects fleeing conscription, invasion, and plunder. Thus the early state extruded populations as readily as it absorbed them, and when, as was often the case, it collapsed altogether as the result of war, drought, epidemic, or civil strife over succession, its populations were disgorged. States were, by no means, a once-and-for-all creation. Innumerable archeological finds of state centers that briefly flourished and were then eclipsed by warfare, epidemics, famine, or ecological collapse depict a long history of state formation and collapse rather than permanence. For long periods people moved in and out of states, and "stateness" was, itself, often cyclical and reversible.[10]

This pattern of state-making and state-unmaking produced, over time, a periphery that was composed as much of refugees as of peoples who had never been state subjects. Much of the periphery of states became a zone of refuge or "shatter zone," where the human shards of state formation and rivalry accumulated willy nilly, creating regions of bewildering ethnic and linguistic complexity. State expansion and collapse often had a ratchet effect as well, with fleeing subjects driving other peoples ahead of them seeking safety and new territory. Much of the Southeast Asian massif is, in effect, a shatter zone. The reputation of the southwestern Chinese province of Yunnan as a "museum of human races" reflects this history of migration. Shatter zones are found wherever the expansion of states, empires, slave-trading, and wars, as well as natural disasters, have driven large numbers of people to seek refuge in out-of-the-way places: in Amazonia, in highland Latin America (with the notable exception of the Andes, with their arable highland plateaus and states), in that corridor of highland Africa safe from slave-raiding, in the Balkans and the Caucasus. The diagnostic characteristics of shatter zones are their relative geographical inaccessibility and the enormous diversity of tongues and cultures.

Note that this account of the periphery is sharply at odds with the official story most civilizations tell about themselves. According to that tale, a backward, naïve, and perhaps barbaric people are gradually incorporated into an advanced, superior, and more prosperous society and culture. If, instead, many of these ungoverned barbarians had, at one time or another, elected, as a political choice, to take their distance from the state, a new element of political agency enters the picture. Many, perhaps most, inhabitants of the ungoverned margins are not remnants of an earlier social formation, left behind, or, as some lowland folk accounts in Southeast Asia have it, "our living ancestors." The situation of populations that have deliberately placed themselves at the state's periphery has occasionally been termed, infelicitously, secondary primitivism. Their subsistence routines, their social organization, their physical dispersal, and many elements of their culture, far from being the archaic traits of a people left behind, are purposefully crafted both to thwart incorporation into nearby states and to minimize the likelihood that statelike concentrations of power will arise among them. State evasion and state prevention permeate their practices and, often, their ideology as well. They are, in other words, a "state effect." They are "barbarians by design." They continue to conduct a brisk and mutually advantageous trade with lowland centers while steering clear of being politically captured.

Once we entertain the possibility that the "barbarians" are not just "there" as a residue but may well have chosen their location, their subsistence practices, and their social structure to maintain their autonomy, the standard civilizational story of social evolution collapses utterly. The temporal, civilizational series—from foraging to swiddening (or to pastoralism), to sedentary grain cultivation, to irrigated wet-rice farming—and its near-twin, the series from roving forest bands to small clearings, to hamlets, to villages, to towns, to court centers: these are the underpinning of the valley state's sense of superiority. What if the presumptive "stages" of these series were, in fact, an array of social options, each of which represented a distinctive positioning vis-à-vis the state? And what if, over considerable periods of time, many groups have moved strategically among these options toward more presumptively "primitive" forms in order to keep the state at arm's length? On this view, the civilizational discourse of the valley states—and not a few earlier theorists of social evolution—is not much more than a self-inflating way of confounding the status of state-subject with civilization and that of self-governing peoples with primitivism.

The logic of the argument made throughout this book would essentially reverse this logic. Most, if not all, the characteristics that appear to stigmatize hill peoples—their location at the margins, their physical mobility, their swidden agriculture, their flexible social structure, their religious heterodoxy, their egalitarianism, and even the nonliterate, oral cultures—far from being the mark of primitives left behind by civilization, are better seen on a long view as adaptations designed to evade both state capture and state formation. They are, in other words, political adaptations of nonstate peoples to a world of states that are, at once, attractive and threatening.

CREATING SUBJECTS

Avoiding the state was, until the past few centuries, a real option. A thousand years ago most people lived outside state structures, under loose-knit empires or in situations of fragmented sovereignty.[11] Today it is an option that is fast vanishing. To appreciate how the room for maneuver has been drastically curtailed in the past millennium, a radically schematic and simplified fast- forward history of the balance of power between stateless peoples and states may be helpful.

The permanent association of the state and sedentary agriculture is at the center of this story.[12] Fixed-field grain agriculture has been promoted by the state and has been, historically, the foundation of its power. In turn, sedentary agriculture leads to property rights in land, the patriarchal family enterprise, and an emphasis, also encouraged by the state, on large families. Grain farming is, in this respect, inherently expansionary, generating, when not checked by disease or famine, a surplus population, which is obliged to move and colonize new lands. By any long-run perspective, then, it is grain agriculture that is "nomadic" and aggressive, constantly reproducing copies of itself, while, as Hugh Brody aptly notes, foragers and hunters, relying on a single area and demographically far more stable, seem by comparison "profoundly settled."[13]

The massive expansion of European power, via colonialism and white-settler colonies, represented a vast expansion of sedentary agriculture. In the "neo-Europes" such as North America, Australia, Argentina, and New Zealand, Europeans reproduced, as far as possible, the agriculture with which they were familiar. In colonies with preexisting states based on sedentary agriculture, the Europeans replaced the indigenous overlords as sovereigns, collecting taxes and encouraging agriculture as had their predecessors, but more effectively. All other subsistence patterns, except when they provided valuable trade goods (for example, furs), were, fiscally speaking, considered sterile. Thus foragers, hunters, shifting-cultivators, and pastoralists were bypassed and ignored or driven from potentially arable farmland into territories considered wastelands. Nevertheless, as late as the end of the eighteenth century, though they were no longer a majority of the world's population, nonstate peoples still occupied the greater part of the world's land mass—forest lands, rugged mountains, steppes, deserts, polar regions, marshes, and inaccessibly remote zones. Such regions were still a potential refuge for those who had reason to flee the state.

These stateless peoples were not, by and large, easily drawn into the fiscally legible economy of wage labor and sedentary agriculture. On this definition, "civilization" held little attraction for them when they could have all the advantages of trade without the drudgery, subordination, and immobility of state subjects. The widespread resistance of stateless peoples led directly to what might be called the golden age of slavery along the littoral of the Atlantic and Indian Oceans and in Southeast Asia.[14] From the perspective adopted here, populations were forcibly removed en masse from settings where their production and labor were illegible and inappropriable and were relocated in colonies and plantations where they could be made to grow cash crops (tea, cotton, sugar, indigo, coffee) which might contribute to the profits of landowners and the fiscal power of the state.[15] This first step of enclosure required forms of capture and bondage designed to relocate them from nonstate spaces where they were generally more autonomous (and healthy!) to places where their labor could be appropriated.

The final two stages of this massive enclosure movement belong, in the case of Europe, to the nineteenth century and, in the case of Southeast Asia, largely to the late twentieth century. They mark such a radical shift in the relationship between states and their peripheries that they fall largely outside the story I tell here. In this last period, "enclosure" has meant not so much shifting people from stateless zones to areas of state control but rather colonizing the periphery itself and transforming it into a fully governed, fiscally fertile zone. Its immanent logic, unlikely ever to be fully realized, is the complete elimination of nonstate spaces. This truly imperial project, made possible only by distance-demolishing technologies (all-weather roads, bridges, railroads, airplanes, modern weapons, telegraph, telephone, and now modern information technologies including global positioning systems), is so novel and its dynamics so different that my analysis here makes no further sense in Southeast Asia for the period after, say, 1950. Modern conceptions of national sovereignty and the resource needs of mature capitalism have brought that final enclosure into view.

The hegemony, in this past century, of the nation-state as the standard and nearly exclusive unit of sovereignty has proven profoundly inimical to nonstate peoples. State power, in this conception, is the state's monopoly of coercive force that must, in principle, be fully projected to the very edge of its territory, where it meets, again in principle, another sovereign power projecting its command to its own adjacent frontier. Gone, in principle, are the large areas of no sovereignty or mutually canceling weak sovereignties. Gone too, of course, are peoples under no particular sovereignty. As a practical matter, most nation-states have tried, insofar as they had the means, to give substance to this vision, establishing armed border posts, moving loyal populations to the frontier and relocating or driving away "disloyal" populations, clearing frontier lands for sedentary agriculture, building roads to the borders, and registering hitherto fugitive peoples.

On the heels of this notion of sovereignty came the realization that these neglected and seemingly useless territories to which stateless peoples had been relegated were suddenly of great value to the economies of mature capitalism.[16] They contained valuable resources—oil, iron ore, copper, lead, timber, uranium, bauxite, the rare metals essential to the aerospace and electronics industries, hydroelectric sites, bioprospecting and conservation areas—that might in many cases be the linchpin of state revenue. Places that long ago might have been desirable for their deposits of silver, gold, and gems, not to mention slaves, became the object of a new gold rush. All the more reason to project state power to the nethermost reaches of these ungoverned regions and bring their inhabitants under firm control.

Occupying and controlling the margins of the state implied a cultural policy as well. Much of the periphery along national borders of mainland Southeast Asia is inhabited by peoples linguistically and culturally distinct from the populations that dominate the state cores. Alarmingly, they spill promiscuously across national frontiers, generating multiple identities and possible foci of irredentism or secession. Weak valley states have permitted, or rather tolerated, a certain degree of autonomy when they had little choice. Where they could, however, all states in the region have tried to bring such peoples under their routine administration, to encourage and, more rarely, to insist upon linguistic, cultural, and religious alignment with the majority population at the state core. This meant, in Thailand, encouraging, say, the Lahu to become Thai-speaking, literate, Buddhist subjects of the monarchy. In Burma it meant encouraging, say, the Karen to become Burmese-speaking Buddhists loyal to the military junta.[17]

Parallel to policies of economic, administrative, and cultural absorption has been the policy, driven by both demographic pressure and self-conscious design, of engulfment. Huge numbers of land-hungry majorities from the plains have moved, or been moved, to the hills. There, they replicate valley settlement patterns and sedentary agriculture, and, over time, they demo graphically dominate the dispersed, less numerous hill peoples. The combination of forced settlement and engulfment is nicely illustrated by a series of Vietnamese mobilization campaigns in the 1950s and 1960s: "Campaign to Sedentarize the Nomads," "Campaign for Fixed Cultivation and Fixed Residence," "Storm the Hills Campaign," and "Clear the Hills by Torchlight Campaign."[18]

Culturally, this reduction and standardization of relatively autonomous, self-governing communities is a process of long historical lineage. It is an integral theme of the historical consciousness of each of the large mainland Southeast Asian states. In the Vietnamese official national narrative, the "march to the south"—to the Mekong and the trans-Bassac Deltas—inaccurate though it is as a description of the historical process, vies with the wars of national liberation for pride of place.[19] Burmese and Thai history are no less marked by the movement of population from their more northern historical cores of Mandalay, Ayutthaya, and what is now Hanoi into the Irrawaddy, Chao Praya, and Mekong river deltas, respectively. The great cosmopolitan, maritime cities of Saigon (now Ho Chi Minh City), Rangoon, and Bangkok that grew to serve this onetime frontier, delta, hinterland have come, demographically, to dominate the earlier inland capitals.

Internal colonialism, broadly understood, aptly describes this process. It involved the absorption, displacement, and/or extermination of the previous inhabitants. It involved a botanical colonization in which the landscape was transformed—by deforestation, drainage, irrigation, and levees—to accommodate crops, settlement patterns, and systems of administration familiar to the state and to the colonists. One way of appreciating the effect of this colonization is to view it as a massive reduction of vernaculars of all kinds: of vernacular languages, minority peoples, vernacular cultivation techniques, vernacular land tenure systems, vernacular hunting, gathering, and forestry techniques, vernacular religion, and so on. The attempt to bring the periphery into line is read by representatives of the sponsoring state as providing civilization and progress—where progress is, in turn, read as the intrusive propagation of the linguistic, agricultural, and religious practices of the dominant ethnic group: the Han, the Kinh, the Burman, the Thai.[20]

The remaining self-governing peoples and spaces of mainland Southeast Asia are much diminished. We shall, for the most part, concentrate on the so-called hill peoples (often mistakenly called tribes) of mainland Southeast Asia, particularly Burma. While I will clarify what I mean by the awkward term *nonstate spaces*, it is not simply a synonym for hills or for higher altitudes. States, being associated with concentrated grain production, typically arise where there is a substantial expanse of arable land. In mainland Southeast Asia, this agro-ecology is generally at low elevations, allowing us to speak of "valley states" and "hill peoples." Where, as in the Andes, most easily cultivable land under traditional conditions is located at high elevations, it is the other way around. The states were in the hills and nonstate spaces were downhill in the humid lowlands. Thus the key variable is not so much elevation per se as the possibility for concentrated grain production. *Nonstate space*, by contrast, points to locations where, owing largely to geographical obstacles, the state has particular difficulty in establishing and maintaining its authority. A Ming emperor had something like this in mind when he described the southwest provinces of his kingdom: "The roads are long and dangerous, the mountains and rivers present great obstacles, and the customs and practices differ."[21] But swamps, marshes, mangrove coasts, deserts, volcanic margins, and even the open sea, like the ever growing and changing deltas of Southeast Asia's great rivers, all function in much the same way. Thus it is difficult or inaccessible terrain, regardless of elevation, that presents great obstacles to state control. As we shall see at great length, such places have often served as havens of refuge for peoples resisting or fleeing the state.

THE GREAT MOUNTAIN KINGDOM; OR, "ZOMIA"; OR, THE MARCHES OF MAINLAND SOUTHEAST ASIA

One of the largest remaining nonstate spaces in the world, if not *the* largest, is the vast expanse of uplands, variously termed the Southeast Asian *massif* and, more recently, Zomia.[22] This great mountain realm on the marches of mainland Southeast Asia, China, India, and Bangladesh sprawls across roughly 2.5 million square kilometers—an area roughly the size of Europe. As one of the first scholars to identify the massif and its peoples as a single object of study, Jean Michaud has traced its extent: "From north to south, it includes southern and western Sichuan, all of Guizhou and Yunnan, western and northern Guangxi, western Guangdong, most of northern Burma with an adjacent segment of extreme [north]eastern India, the north and west of Thailand, practically all of Laos above the Mekong Valley, northern and central Vietnam along the Annam Cordillera, and the north and eastern fringes of Cambodia."[23]

Rough calculations would put Zomia minority populations alone at around eighty million to one hundred million.[24] Its peoples are fragmented into hundreds of ethnic identities and at least five language families that defy any simple classification.

Lying at altitudes from two hundred or three hundred meters above sea level to more than four thousand meters, Zomia could be thought of as a Southeast Asian Appalachia, were it not for the fact that it sprawls across eight nation-states. A better analogy would be Switzerland, a mountain kingdom at the periphery of Germany, France, and Italy that itself became a nation-state. Borrowing Ernest Gellner's felicitous phrase referring to the Berbers of the High Atlas Mountains, this huge hilly zone might be seen as a "pervasive Switzerland without cuckoo clocks."[25] Far from being a hilly nation, however, this upland belt lies on the marches, far from the main population centers of the nations it traverses.[26] Zomia is marginal in almost every respect. It lies at a great distance from the main centers of economic activity; it bestrides a contact zone between eight nation-states and several religious traditions and cosmologies.[27]

Figure 11–1. Mainland Southeast Asia

Scholarship organized historically around the classical states and their cultural cores and, more recently, around the nation-state is singularly ill-equipped to examine this upland belt as a whole. Willem van Schendel is one of a handful of pioneers who have argued that these cumulative nation-state "shards" merit consideration as a distinctive region. He has gone so far as to give it the dignity of a name of its own: Zomia, a term for highlander common to several related Tibeto-Burman languages spoken in the India-Bangladesh-Burma border area.[28] More precisely, *Zo* is a relational term meaning "remote" and hence carries the connotation of living in the hills; *Mi* means "people." As is the case elsewhere in Southeast Asia *Mi-zo* or *Zo-mi* designated a remote hill people, while at the same time the ethnic label applies to a geographical niche.[29] Although van Schendel proposes a bold expansion of Zomia's boundaries to Afghanistan and beyond, I will confine my use of the term to the hilly areas eastward, beginning with the Naga and Mizo hills in northern India and Bangladesh's Chittagong Hill Tracts.

Zomia, at first glance, would seem an unlikely candidate for consideration as a distinctive region. The premise for calling a geographical area a region is typically that it shares important cultural features that mark it off from adjacent areas. In this fashion, Fernand Braudel was able to show that the coastal societies around the Mediterranean Sea constituted a region, owing to their long and intense commercial and cultural connections.[30] Despite political and religious chasms between, say, Venice and Istanbul, they were integral parts of a recognizable world of exchange and mutual influence. Anthony Reid has made a similar, and in many respects, more powerful claim for the Sunda Shelf littoral in maritime Southeast Asia, where trade and migration were, if anything, easier than in the Mediterranean.[31] The principle behind region-making in each case is that, for the premodern world, water, especially if it is calm, joins people, whereas mountains, especially if they are high and rugged, divide people. As late as 1740 it took no more time to sail from Southampton to the Cape of Good Hope than to travel by stagecoach from London to Edinburgh.

On these grounds, hilly Zomia would seem to be a "negative" region. Variety, more than uniformity, is its trademark. In the space of a hundred kilometers in the hills one can find more cultural variation—in language, dress, settlement pattern, ethnic identification, economic activity, and religious practices—than one would ever find in the lowland river valleys. Zomia may not quite attain the prodigious cultural variety of deeply fissured New Guinea, but its complex ethnic and linguistic mosaic has presented a bewildering puzzle for ethnographers and historians, not to mention would-be rulers. Scholarly work on the area has been as fragmented and isolated as the terrain itself seemed to be.[32]

I will argue not only that Zomia qualifies as a region in the strong sense of the term, but also that it is impossible to provide a satisfactory account of the valley states without understanding the central role played by Zomia in their formation and collapse. The dialectic or coevolution of hill and valley, as antagonistic but deeply connected spaces, is, I believe, the essential point of departure for making sense of historical change in Southeast Asia.

Most of what the hills share as physical and social spaces marks them off fairly sharply from the more populous lowland centers. The population of the hills is far more dispersed and culturally diverse than that of the valleys. It is as if the difficulties of terrain and relative isolation have, over many

Figure 11–2. "Zomia," on the mainland Southeast Asian massif

centuries, encouraged a kind of "speciation" of languages, dialects, dress, and cultural practices. The relative availability of forest resources and open, if steep, land has also allowed far more diverse subsistence practices than in the valleys, where wet-rice monocropping often prevails. Swiddening (or slash-and-burn agriculture), which requires more land and requires clearing new fields and occasionally shifting settlement sites, is far more common in the hills.

As a general rule, social structure in the hills is both more flexible and more egalitarian than in the hierarchical, codified valley societies. Hybrid identities, movement, and the social fluidity that characterizes many frontier societies are common. Early colonial officials, taking an inventory of their new possessions in the hills, were confused to encounter hamlets with several "peoples" living side by side: hill people who spoke three or four languages and both individuals and groups whose ethnic identity had shifted, sometimes within a single generation. Aspiring to Linnaean specificity in the classification of peoples as well as flora, territorial administrators were constantly frustrated by the bewildering flux of peoples who refused to stay put. There was, however, one principle of location that brought some order to this apparent anarchy of identity, and that was its relation to altitude.[33] As Edmund Leach originally suggested, once one looks at Zomia not from a high-altitude balloon but, rather, horizontally, in terms of lateral slices through the topography, a certain order emerges.[34] In any given landscape, particular groups often settled within a narrow range of altitudes to exploit the agro-economic possibilities of that particular niche. Thus, for example, the Hmong have tended to settle at very high altitudes (between one thousand and eighteen hundred meters) and to plant maize, opium, and millet that will thrive at that elevation. If from a high-altitude balloon or on a map they appear to be a random scattering of small blotches, this is because they have occupied the mountaintops and left the midslopes and intervening valleys to other groups.

Specialization by altitude and niche within the hills leads to scattering. And yet long-distance travel, marriage alliances, similar subsistence patterns, and cultural continuity help foster coherent identities across considerable distances. The "Akha" along the Yunnan-Thai border and the "Hani" in the upper reaches of the Red River in northern Vietnam are recognizably the same culture, though separated by more than a thousand kilometers. They typically have more in common with each another than either group has with valley people a mere thirty or forty miles away. Zomia is thus knitted together as a region not by a political unity, which it utterly lacks, but by comparable patterns of diverse hill agriculture, dispersal and mobility, and rough egalitarianism, which, not incidentally, includes a relatively higher status for women than in the valleys.[35]

The signal, distinguishing trait of Zomia, vis-à-vis the lowland regions it borders, is that it is relatively stateless. Historically, of course, there have been states in the hills where a substantial fertile plateau and/or a key node in the overland trade routes made it possible. Nan Chao, Kengtung, Nan, and Lan-na were among the best known.[36] They are the exceptions that prove the rule. While state-making projects have abounded in the hills, it is fair to say that few have come to fruition. Those would-be kingdoms that did manage to defy the odds did so only for a relatively brief, crisis-strewn period.

Such episodes aside, the hills, unlike the valleys, have paid neither taxes to monarchs nor regular tithes to a permanent religious establishment. They have constituted a relatively free, stateless population of foragers and hill farmers. Zomia's situation at the frontiers of lowland state centers has contributed to its relative isolation and the autonomy that such isolation favors. Lying athwart state borders where multiple competing sovereignties abut one another has itself afforded its peoples certain advantages for smuggling, contraband, opium production, and the "small border powers" that negotiate a tenuous, high-wire act of quasi-independence.[37]

A stronger and, I believe, more accurate political description is that the hill populations of Zomia have actively resisted incorporation into the framework of the classical state, the colonial state, and the independent nation-state. Beyond merely taking advantage of their geographical isolation from centers of state power, much of Zomia has "resisted the projects of nation-building and state-making of the states to which it belonged."[38] This resistance came especially to light after the creation of independent states after World War II, when Zomia became the site of secessionist movements, indigenous rights struggles, millennial rebellions, regionalist agitation, and armed opposition to lowland states. But it is a resistance with deeper roots. In the precolonial period, the resistance can be seen in a cultural refusal of lowland patterns and in the flight of lowlanders seeking refuge in the hills.

During the colonial era, the autonomy of the hills, politically and culturally, was underwritten by the Europeans for whom a separately administered hill zone was a makeweight against the lowland majorities resentful of colonial rule. One effect of this classic divide-and-rule policy is that, with a few exceptions, hill peoples typically played little or no role—or an antagonistic one—in the anticolonial movements. They remained, at best, marginal to the nationalist narrative or, at worst, were seen as a fifth column threatening that independence. It is partly for such reasons that the postcolonial lowland states have sought fully to exercise authority in the hills: by military occupation, by campaigns against shifting cultivation, by forced settlements, by promoting the migration of lowlanders to the hills, by efforts at religious conversion, by space-conquering roads, bridges, and telephone lines, and by development schemes that project government administration and lowland cultural styles into the hills.

The hills, however, are not simply a space of political resistance but also a zone of cultural refusal. If it were merely a matter of political authority, one might expect the hill society to resemble valley society culturally except for their altitude and the dispersed settlement that the terrain favors. But the hill populations do not generally resemble the valley centers culturally, religiously, or linguistically. This cultural chasm between the mountains and the plains has been claimed as something of a historical constant in Europe as well, until quite recently. Fernand Braudel acknowledged the political autonomy of the hills when he approvingly quoted Baron de Tott to the effect that "the steepest places have always been the asylum of liberty." But he carried the argument much further, asserting the existence of an unbridgeable cultural gap between plains and mountains. He wrote: "The mountains are as a rule a world apart from civilizations which are an urban and lowland achievement. Their history is to have none, to remain always on the fringes of the great waves of civilization, even the longest and most persistent, which may spread over great distances in the horizontal plane but are powerless to move vertically when faced with an obstacle of several hundred meters."[39] Braudel was, in turn, only echoing a much older view captured by the great fourteenth-century Arab philosopher Ibn Khaldun, who noted that "Arabs can gain control only over flat territory" and do not pursue tribes that hide in the mountains.[40] Compare Braudel's bold assertion that civilizations can't climb hills to a nearly identical assertion made by Oliver Wolters, quoting Paul Wheatley, about precolonial Southeast Asia: "Many people lived in the distant highlands and were beyond the reach of the centers where records survive. The *mandalas* [court centers of civilization and power] were a phenomenon of the lowlands and even there, geographical conditions encouraged under-government. Paul Wheatley puts it well when he notes that 'the Sanskritic tongue was stilled to silence at 500 meters.'"[41]

Scholars of Southeast Asia have been struck again and again by the sharp limits the terrain, particularly altitude, has placed on cultural or political influence. Paul Mus, writing of Vietnam and echoing Wheatley, noted of the spread of the Vietnamese and their culture that "this ethnic adventure stopped at the foot of the high country's buttresses."[42] Owen Lattimore, best known for his studies of China's northern frontier, also remarked that Indian and Chinese civilizations, like those cited by Braudel, traveled well across the plains but ran out of breath when they encountered rugged hills: "This kind of stratification extends far beyond China itself into the Indochinese peninsula, Thailand and Burma with the influence of the ancient high civilizations reaching far out over the lower levels where concentrated agriculture and big cities are to be found, but not up into the higher altitudes."[43]

Though Zomia is exceptionally diverse linguistically, the languages spoken in the hills are, as a rule, distinct from those spoken in the plains. Kinship structures, at least formally, also distinguish the hills from the lowlands. This is in part what Edmund Leach had in mind when he characterized hill society as following a "Chinese model" while lowland society followed an "Indian" or Sanskritic model.[44]

Hill societies are, as a rule, systematically different from valley societies. Hill people tend to be animists, or, in the twentieth century, Christians, who do not follow the "great tradition" salvation religions of lowland peoples (Buddhism and Islam in particular). Where, as occasionally happens, they do come to embrace the "world religion" of their valley neighbors, they are likely to do so with a degree of heterodoxy and millenarian fervor that valley elites find more threatening than reassuring. Hill societies do produce a surplus, but they do not use that surplus to support kings and monks. The absence of large, permanent, surplus-absorbing religious and political establishments makes for a sociological pyramid in the hills that is rather flat and local when compared with that of valley societies. Distinctions of status and wealth abound in the hills, as in the valleys. The difference is that in the valleys they tend to be supralocal and enduring, while in the hills they are both unstable and geographically confined.

This characterization obscures a great deal of variation in the political structure of hill societies. The variation is not by any means simply a function of "ethnicity," although some hill peoples, such as the Lahu, Khmu, and Akha, seem strongly egalitarian and decentralized. It is just as common, however, to encounter groups that defy such generalizations. Among Karen, Kachin, Chin, Hmong, Yao/Mien, and Wa, for example, there seem to be both relatively hierarchical subgroups and relatively decentral-ized, egalitarian subgroups. What is most striking and important is that the degree of hierarchy and centralization is not constant over time. The variation, so far as I can make out, depends largely on a kind of imitative state-making. That is, it is either a kind of short-term war alliance or a sort of "booty-capitalism" for slave-raiding and extracting tribute from lowland communities. Where hill groups are in a tributary relationship with a valley kingdom—which does not imply political incorporation or, necessarily, inferiority—it may be an expedient to control a lucrative trade route or to safeguard privileged access to valuable markets. Their political structures are, with extremely rare exceptions, imitative in the sense that while they may have the trappings and rhetoric of monarchy, they lack the substance: a taxpaying subject population or direct control over their constituent units, let alone a standing army. Hill polities are, almost invariably, redistributive, competitive feasting systems held together by the benefits they are able to disburse. When they occasionally appear to be relatively centralized, they resemble what Barfield has called the "shadow-empires" of nomadic pastoralists, a predatory periphery designed to monopolize trading and raiding advantages at the edge of an empire. They are also typically parasitic in the sense that when their host-empires collapse, so do they.[45]

ZONES OF REFUGE

There is strong evidence that Zomia is not simply a region of resistance to valley states, but a region of refuge as well. By "refuge,"[46] I mean to imply that much of the population in the hills has, for more than a millennium and a half, come there to evade the manifold afflictions of state-making projects in the valleys. Far from being "left behind" by the progress of civilization in the valleys, they have, over long periods of time, chosen to place themselves out of the reach of the state. Jean Michaud notes, in this connection, that what he calls nomadism in the hills can be "an escape or survival strategy" and sees the unprecedented series of massive rebellions in the latter half of the nineteenth century in central and southwest China as having pushed the millions of refugees streaming south into the more remote highlands. He is sympathetic to the view adopted here that Zomia is best seen historically as a region of refuge from states, most especially the Han state. "It is probably fair to say," he concludes, "that the highland populations who migrated from China to the … highlands over the past five centuries were, at least in part, pushed from their homelands by aggression from more powerful neighbors, including especially Han expansion."[47]

Detailed and unambiguous documentary evidence of the conflicts generated by Han expansion and the migratory flights it provoked is abundant from the early Ming Dynasty (1368) onward, becoming even more abundant under the Qing. Earlier documentation is harder to come by and more ambiguous, owing to the great fluidity of ethnic and political labels. The general pattern, however, seems to be as follows: as the reach of the Chinese state grew, peoples at the point of expansion were either absorbed (becoming, in time, Han) or moved away, often after a failed revolt. Those who left became, at least for a time, distinct societies that could be said to have "self-marginalized" by migration.[48] As the process was repeated again and again, culturally complex zones of refuge sprang up in the hinterlands of the state. "The history of the various non-state peoples of this region" can, Fiskesjö believes, be written as the bifurcation between those who had long been in the hills (for example, the Wa people) and those who sought refuge there: "Among those who left [the zone of Chinese state power], we find many Tibeto-Burman ethnolinguistic formations (Lahu, Hani, Akha, etc.) as well as Miao or Hmong speakers, and other peoples ... described as 'hill tribes out of China' with a 'heritage of defeat' that has led many of them during the past few centuries, into the northern parts of the modern states of Thailand, Burma, Laos, and Vietnam where many of them are still regarded as newcomers."[49]

There, in regions beyond the states' immediate writ and, thus, at some remove from taxes, corvée labor, conscription, and the more than occasional epidemics and crop failures associated with population concentration and monocropping, such groups found relative freedom and safety. There, they practiced what I will call escape agriculture: forms of cultivation designed to thwart state appropriation. Even their social structure could fairly be called escape social structure inasmuch as it was designed to aid dispersal and autonomy and to ward off political subordination.

The tremendous linguistic and ethnic fluidity in the hills is itself a crucial social resource for adapting to changing constellations of power, inasmuch as it facilitates remarkable feats of identity shape-shifting. Zomians are not as a rule only linguistically and ethnically amphibious; they are, in their strong inclination to follow charismatic figures who arise among them, capable of nearly instantaneous social change, abandoning their fields and houses to join or form a new community at the behest of a trusted prophet. Their capacity to "turn on a dime" represents the ultimate in escape social structure. Illiteracy in the hills can, more speculatively, be interpreted in the same fashion. Virtually all hill peoples have legends claiming that they once had writing and either lost it or that it was stolen from them. Given the considerable advantages in plasticity of oral over written histories and genealogies, it is at least conceivable to see the loss of literacy and of written texts as a more or less deliberate adaptation to statelessness.

The argument, in short, is that the history of hill peoples is best understood as a history not of archaic remnants but of "runaways" from state- making processes in the lowlands: a largely "maroon" society, providing that we take a very long historical view. Many of the agricultural and social practices of hill peoples can be best understood as techniques to make good this evasion, while maintaining the economic advantages of the lowland connection.

The concentration of people and production at a single location required some form of unfree labor when population was sparse, as it was in Southeast Asia. All Southeast Asian states were slaving states, without exception, some of them until well into the twentieth century. Wars in precolonial Southeast Asia were less about territory than about the seizure of as many captives as possible who were then resettled at the core of the winner's territory. They were not distinctive in this respect. After all, in Periclean Athens, the population of slaves outnumbered full citizens by five to one.

The effect of all state-making projects of this kind was to create a shatter zone or flight zone to which those wishing to evade or to escape bondage fled. These regions of refuge constituted a direct "state effect." Zomia simply happens to be, owing largely to the precocious early expansion of the Chinese state, one of the most extensive and oldest zones of refuge. Such regions are, however, inevitable by-products of coercive state-making and are found on every continent. A few of them will figure as comparative cases in what follows, but here I want to enumerate several examples to suggest how common they are.

The forced-labor characteristic of Spanish colonization in the New World provoked the widespread flight of native peoples out of range, often to hilly or arid places where they could live unmolested.[50]

Such areas were marked by great linguistic and ethnic diversity and occasionally by a simplification of social structure and subsistence routines—foraging, shifting cultivation—to increase mobility. The process was repeated in the Spanish Philippines, where, it is claimed, the cordillera of northern Luzon was populated almost entirely by lowland Filipinos fleeing Malay slave raids and the Spanish *reducciones*.[51] As peoples adapted to hill ecology, a process of ethnogenesis followed, after which highland Filipinos were later misrepresented as the descendants of separate, prehistoric migrations to the island.

The Cossacks on Russia's many frontiers represent another striking example of the process. They were, at the outset, nothing more and nothing less than runaway serfs from all over European Russia who accumulated at the frontier.[52] They became, depending on their location, different Cossack "hosts": the Don (for the Don River basin) Cossacks, the Azov (Sea) Cossacks, and so on. There at the frontier, copying the horseback habits of their Tatar neighbors and sharing a common open-land pasture, they became "a people," later used by the tsars, the Ottomans, and the Poles as cavalry. The history of the Roma and Sinti (Gypsies) in late-seventeenth-century Europe provides a further striking example.[53] Along with other stigmatized itinerant peoples, they were subject to two forms of penal labor: galley slavery in the Mediterranean basin and, in the northeast, forced conscription as soldiers or military porters in Prussia-Brandenburg. As a result they accumulated in a narrow band of territory that came to be known as the "outlaw corridor," the one location between the catchment areas of these twin, mortal dangers.

Inasmuch as the captivity and bondage associated with early state- making generate, in their wake, flight and zones of refuge, slavery as a labor system produced many "Zomias" large and small. It is possible, in this context, to delineate an upland, remote zone of West Africa that was relatively safe from the five hundred-year-long worldwide slave-raiding and trade that caught tens of millions of in its toils.[54] This zone of refuge grew in population despite the difficulties of the terrain and the necessity for new subsistence routines. Many of those who failed to evade the slave raids in Africa, once transplanted to the New World, promptly escaped and created fugitive slave (maroon) settlements wherever slavery was practiced: the famous highland "cockpit" of Jamaica; Palmares in Brazil, a maroon community of some twenty thousand inhabitants; and Surinam, the largest maroon population in the hemisphere, are only three illustrations. Were we to include smaller scale "refugia" such as marshes, swamps, and deltas, the list would multiply many-fold. To mention only a few, the great marsh on the lower Euphrates (drained under Saddam Hussein's rule) was for two thousand years a refuge from state control. So, on a smaller scale, were the storied Great Dismal Swamp on the North Carolina-Virginia border, the Pripet Marshes in Poland, now on the Belarus-Ukraine border, and the Pontian Marshes near Rome (drained finally by Mussolini) known as zones of refuge from the state. The list of such refugia is at least as long as the list of coercive labor schemes that inevitably spawn them.

Hill societies in mainland Southeast Asia, then, for all their riotous heterogeneity, have certain characteristics in common, and most of these characteristics distinguish them sharply from their valley neighbors. They encode a pattern of historic flight and hence a position of opposition if not resistance. If it is this historical, structural relation that we hope to illuminate, then it makes no sense whatever to confine ourselves to a nation-state framework. For much of the period we wish to examine there was no nation-state and, when it did come into being late in the game, many hill people continued to conduct their cross-border lives as if the state didn't exist. The concept of "Zomia" marks an attempt to explore a new genre of "area" studies, in which the justification for designating the area has nothing to do with national boundaries (for example, Laos) or strategic conceptions (for example, Southeast Asia) but is rather based on certain ecological regularities and structural relationships that do not hesitate to cross national frontiers. If we have our way, the example of "Zomia studies" will inspire others to follow this experiment elsewhere and improve on it.

THE SYMBIOTIC HISTORY OF HILLS AND VALLEYS

Histories of the classical lowland court-states, taken in isolation, risk being unintelligible or vastly misleading. Lowland states (mandala or modern) have always existed in symbiosis with hill society.[55] By *symbiosis,* I mean to invoke the biological metaphor of two organisms living together in more or less intimate association—in this case, social organisms. The term does not specify, nor do I wish to do so here, whether this mutual dependence is antagonistic, or even parasitic, or whether it is mutually beneficial, "synergistic."

It is not possible to write a coherent history of the hills that is not in constant dialogue with lowland centers; nor is it possible to write a coherent history of lowland centers that ignores its hilly periphery. By and large, most students of hill societies have been sensitive to this dialectic, stressing the deep history of symbolic, economic, and human traffic between the two societies. The same typically cannot be said of work—even the most distinguished—on lowland centers.[56] The pattern is hardly surprising. Treatment of lowland cultures and societies as self-contained entities (for example, "Thai civilization," "Chinese culture") replicates the unreflective structure of scholarship and, in doing so, adopts the hermetic view of culture that lowland elites themselves wish to project. The fact is that hill and valley societies have to be read against each other to make any sense. I attempt just such a reading here.

Writing an account of valley population centers without including the hills would be like writing a history of colonial New England and the Middle Atlantic States without considering the American frontier. It would be like writing a history of antebellum slavery in the United States while leaving out the freedmen and the lure of freedom in Canada. In each case, an external frontier conditioned, bounded, and in many respects constituted what was possible at the center. Accounts of lowland states that miss this dimension do not merely "leave out" the hills; they ignore a set of boundary conditions and exchanges that make the center what it is.

The constant movement back and forth between the valleys and the hills—its causes, its patterns, its consequences—will preoccupy us. Many valley people are, as it were, "ex-hill people," and many hill people are "ex-valley people." Nor did movement in one direction or the other preclude subsequent moves. Depending on the circumstances, groups have disengaged themselves from a state and then, later, sought to affiliate themselves (or been seized by!) the same or another state. A century or two later, they might again be found outside that state's grasp, perhaps because they had moved away or perhaps because the state in question had itself collapsed. Such shifts were often accompanied by a shift in ethnic identity, broadly understood. I will argue for a radically "constructionist" understanding of the so-called hill tribes of mainland Southeast Asia. They are best understood, at least as a first approximation, as a fugitive population that has come to the hills over the past two millennia. This flight was not only from the Burman, Tai, and Siamese states but also, and most especially, from the Han Empire during the expansionary phases of the Tang, Yuan, Ming, and Qing dynasties, when its forces and settlers pressed into southwest China. In the hills they might have moved several times subsequently, pressed by other, stronger fugitives or threatened by a new state expansion, or in search of new land and autonomy. Their location and many of their economic and cultural practices could again fairly be termed a state effect. This picture is radically at odds with older prevailing assumptions of a primeval population in the hills abandoned by those who moved downhill and developed civilizations.

By the same token, the valley centers of wet-rice cultivation may profitably be seen as constituting a hill effect in the following ways. The valley states are, of course, new structures historically speaking, dating back to roughly the middle of the first millennium CE. They were formed from an earlier ingathering of diverse peoples, some of whom may have adopted fixed-field agriculture, but who were, by definition, not previously part of an established state.[57] The very earliest mandala states were less engines of military conquest than cultural spaces available to all those who wished to conform to their religious, linguistic, and cultural formats, whatever their origin.[58] Perhaps because such identities were newly confected from many cultural shards, the resulting valley self-representations were at pains to distinguish their culture from populations outside the state. Thus if hill society could be termed a state effect, valley culture could be seen as a hill effect.

Most of the terms that we would translate as *crude*, *unrefined*, *barbaric*, and, in the Chinese case, *raw* refer directly to those who live in the hills and forests. "Forest dweller" or "hill person" is shorthand for "uncivilized." Thus, despite a centuries-old, brisk traffic in people, goods, and culture across the very permeable membrane between the hills and valleys, it is striking how stark and durable the cultural divide remains in lived experience. Valley and hill peoples generally have an essentialist understanding of the differences between them that appears to be at odds with the historical evidence over the long run.

How can we make sense of this paradox? Perhaps the first step is to emphasize that the relationship between valley states and hill society is not just symbiotic but also both contemporaneous and quasi-oppositional. In older understandings of hill "tribes," not to mention popular folklore today, they are considered to be the historical remnants of an earlier stage of human history: what we were like before we discovered wet-rice agriculture, learned to write, developed the arts of civilization, and adopted Buddhism. While this "just-so" story treats valley cultures as later, and higher, achievements of civilization, raised from the muck of tribalism, as it were, it grossly distorts the historical record. Valley states and hill peoples are, instead, constituted in each other's shadow, both reciprocal and contemporaneous. Hill societies have always been in touch with imperial states in the valleys directly or via maritime trade routes. Valley states, by the same token, have always been in touch with the nonstate periphery—what Deleuze and Guattari call "the local mechanisms of bands, margins, minorities, which continue to affirm the rights of segmentary societies in opposition to the organs of state power." Such states are, in fact, "inconceivable independent of that relationship."[59]

Precisely the same case has been made about the relationship between itinerant peoples—including pastoral nomads—and states. Thus Pierre Clastres argues persuasively that the so-called primitive Amerindian societies of South America were not ancient societies that had failed to invent settled agriculture or state forms but rather previously sedentary cultivators who abandoned agriculture and fixed villages in response to the effects of the Conquest: both disease-induced demographic collapse and colonial forced labor.[60] Their movement and subsistence techniques were designed to ward off incorporation into the state. On the steppes of Central Asia the most ancient nomads, Griaznov has shown, were former sedentary cultivators who similarly left cultivation behind for political and demographic reasons.[61] Lattimore reached the same conclusion, insisting that pastoral nomadism arose after farming and drew in sedentary cultivators at the edge of the grasslands who "had detached themselves from farming communities."[62] Far from being successive stages in social evolution, such states and nomadic peoples are twins, born more or less at the same time and joined in a sometimes rancorous but unavoidable embrace.

This pattern of paired symbiosis and opposition is a staple of Middle Eastern history and anthropology. In the Maghreb it takes the form of structural opposition between Arabs and Berbers. Ernest Gellner's classic *Saints of the Atlas* captures the dynamic I have in mind. Gellner, too, emphasized that the political autonomy and tribalism of the Berber population in the High Atlas is "not a tribalism 'prior to government' but a political and partial rejection of a particular government combined with some acceptance of a wider culture and its ethic."[63] Sharing elements of a larger culture and a faith in Islam, such tribal opposition is explicitly political and deliberately so. Until very recently, Gellner claims, Moroccan history could be written in terms of the opposition between the land of *makhazen* (the pale) and the land of *siba* (beyond the pale). *Siba* could be defined as "institutional dissidence," though it has sometimes been translated as "anarchy." In practice, *siba* means "ungoverned," a zone of political autonomy and independence, while *makhazen* means "governed," subordinated to the state. Political autonomy was, Gellner insists, a choice, not a given.

To those groups that have self-consciously elected to move or to stay beyond the pale, Gellner applies the term *marginal tribalism* to emphasize that their marginality is a political stance:

> Such tribesmen know the possibility ... of being incorporated in a more centralized state.... Indeed, they may have deliberately rejected and violently resisted the alternative. The tribes of the High Atlas are of this kind. Until the advent of the modern state, they were dissident and self-consciously so.... "Marginal" tribalism ... [is] the type of tribal society which exists at the edge of non-tribal societies. It arises from the fact that the inconveniences of submission make it attractive to withdraw from political authority and the balance of power,

the nature of the mountainous or desert terrain make it feasible. Such tribalism is politically marginal. It knows what it rejects.

In the Maghreb, as in Zomia, the distinction between a zone of state rule and a marginal, autonomous zone was geographical and ecological as well as political. There is a "rough tie-up between high-ground, Berber speech and political dissidence," such that "gorges and mountains were a clear dividing line between the land of the government (*bled el-makhazen*) and the land of dissidence (*bled-es-siba*)."[64]

The Berber case is instructive for two reasons. First, Gellner makes it abundantly clear that the demarcation line between Arab and Berber is not, essentially, one of civilization, let alone religion. Instead, it is a political line distinguishing the subjects of a state from those outside its control. Assuming, as Gellner does, historical movement back and forth across this divide, what becomes intriguing is that a distinction in political status is ethnically coded as if it were a fundamental difference in kinds of people and not a political choice. It means that all those who had reason to flee state power, for whatever reason, were, in a sense, tribalizing themselves. Ethnicity and tribe began, by definition, where sovereignty and taxes ended. The ethnic zone was feared and stigmatized by state rhetoric precisely because it was beyond its grasp and therefore an example of defiance and an ever-present temptation to those who might wish to evade the state.

Gellner's analysis of Berber-Arab relations is also noteworthy as a long overdue corrective to what might be called "the view from the valley" or "the view from the state center." On that view the "barbarian periphery" is a diminishing remnant, drawn sooner or later and at varying speeds into the light of Arab civilization. In Southeast Asia and the Maghreb this view gains credibility because, in the past century, the ungoverned periphery has increasingly been occupied by the modern nation-state. Up until then, however, the view from the valley—the idea of a luminous and magnetic center aligning and drawing in peripheral peoples like so many iron filings—is, at the very least, half wrong. Up until then a life outside the state was both more available and more attractive. Oscillation rather than one-way traffic was the rule. If the account elaborated here emphasizes state avoidance, it is not because that is the whole truth. Rather, it is the largely untold story that has unfortunately had no legitimate place in the hegemonic narrative of civilization, despite its historical importance.

This model of symbiosis and opposition, of political choice and geographical facilitation, is, roughly speaking, applicable to the historical relationship between hill peoples and valley states in mainland Southeast Asia. In Southeast Asia, as in the Maghreb, the distinction between the "governed" and the "ungoverned" is an apparent social fact, but it is even more firmly installed in linguistic usage and popular consciousness. Depending on the particular cultural context, the connotations of the pairs "cooked" and "raw," "tame" and "wild," "valley people" and "hill people" carry the same weight as *makhazen* and *siba*—that is to say, "governed" and "ungoverned.' The linkage between being civilized and being a subject of the state is so taken for granted that the terms *subject peoples* on the one hand or *self-governing peoples* on the other capture the essential difference.

The classical states of Southeast Asia were, as in the Middle East, ringed by relatively free communities: by nonstate spaces and peoples. Such autonomous peoples lived not only in the hills but also in the marshes, swamps, mangrove coasts, and labyrinthine waterways of estuarial regions. This marginal population represented, at one and the same time, an indispensable trading partner of valley kingdoms, a zone of refuge from state power, a zone of relative equality and physical mobility, a source of slaves and subjects for valley states, and an ecocultural identity that was nearly a mirror image of lowland identities. Thus, while our attention here is trained on the uplands of Zomia, we are, more generally, concerned with the relationship between state spaces and extrastate spaces. The focus on Zomia as a vast interstate massif, in particular, arises simply because of its importance as the most significant complex catchment zone for refugees from state-making projects in the valleys. The inhabitants of this zone have come, or remained, here largely because it lies beyond the reach of the state. Here, the geographical expression *Southeast Asia*, as conventionally understood as stopping at the borders of Southeast Asian nations, is again an impediment to our understanding. Over the past two millennia, Zomia has been peopled by countless migrations of populations from well beyond its borders—many of them onetime sedentary cultivators. They have fled west and southward from Han, and occasionally Tibetan, rule (the Tai, the Yao/Mien, the Hmong/Miao, the Lahu, and the Akha/Hani) or northward from Thai and Burman rule. Their geographic location is a political, cultural, and, often, military decision.

I argue further that hill peoples cannot be understood in isolation, say, as tribes, but only relationally and positionally vis-à-vis valley kingdoms. Ethnic distinctions and identity in the hills are not only quite variable over time but also usually encode a group's relative position vis-à-vis state authority. There are, I would hazard, hardly "tribes" at all, except in this limited relational sense of the word. The subsistence practices, the choice of crops to grow, are, by the same token, selected largely with an eye to how they facilitate or thwart state appropriation. Finally, as noted earlier, even the social structures and residence patterns in the hills may be usefully viewed as political choices vis-à-vis state power. Certain egalitarian social structures reflect, I believe, a Southeast Asian variant of Berber practice: "Divide that ye be not ruled."[65] Far from being sociological and cultural givens, lineage practices, genealogical reckoning, local leadership patterns, household structures, and perhaps even the degrees of literacy have been calibrated to prevent (and in rare cases to facilitate) incorporation in the state.[66] A bold case along these lines is subject to many qualifications and exceptions. I venture it, nevertheless, not simply to be provocative but because it seems so much more in keeping with the evidence than the older traditions of relatively self-contained hill tribes left behind by civilization and progress.

TOWARD AN ANARCHIST HISTORY OF MAINLAND SOUTHEAST ASIA

What blocks a clear view of the peoples of mainland Southeast Asia for most of their history is the state: classical, colonial, and independent. While a state-centric view of, say, the past fifty years might be justified, it represents a gross distortion of earlier periods. The earlier the period, the greater the distortion. For most of its history, Southeast Asia has been marked by the relative absence even of valley states. Where they arose, they tended to be remarkably short-lived, comparatively weak outside a small and variable radius of the court center, and generally unable systematically to extract resources (including manpower) from a substantial population. Indeed, *interregna,* far from being uncommon, were more protracted than *regna,* and, before the colonial period, a welter of petty principalities allowed much of the population to shift their residences and loyalties to their advantage or to move to a zone of no sovereignty or of mutually canceling sovereignties.

Where and when they did exist, the states of mainland Southeast Asia lurched from solicitous measures designed to attract subjects to those designed to capture them and extract as much grain and labor as possible. Manpower was the key. Even in those cases where the bulk of the crown's revenue derived from trade, that revenue was ultimately dependent on the state's ability to mobilize the manpower to hold and defend an advantageous position along trade routes.[67] The state was tyrannical, but episodically so. Physical flight, the bedrock of popular freedom, was the principal check on state power. As we shall see in some detail, subjects who were sorely tried by conscription, forced labor, and taxes would typically move away to the hills or to a neighboring kingdom rather than revolt. Given the vagaries of war, succession struggles, crop failures, and monarchical delusions of grandeur, such crises of state-building were unpredictable but, sooner or later, inevitable.

Earlier debates over the writing of Southeast Asian history were about how the history of states should be written—not about whether states should have been the center of attention in the first place. Thus scholars criticized Georges Coedès's *Indianized States of Southeast Asia* for missing the purposeful importation and adaptation of Indian cosmology in the court centers of Southeast Asia.[68] To the distortions of Indian-centric histories were added, later, Eurocentric colonial histories in which the local societies were observed from "the deck of a ship, the ramparts of the fortress, the high gallery of the trading house."[69] The call was subsequently issued for an "autonomous" history of Southeast Asia that might avoid both distortions.[70] And yet until very recently indeed, virtually all the responses to that call have themselves been histories, however learned and original, of the Southeast Asian *state.*

Why this should be so, why the histories of states should have so persistently insinuated themselves in the place that might have been occupied by a history of *peoples,* merits reflection. The reason, in a nutshell, I believe, is that state centers, even the tenuous and evanescent Indic-style classical states, are the political units that leave the most concentrated volume of physical evidence. The same is the case for sedentary agricultural settlements, characteristic of state centers. While they are not necessarily any more complex than foraging or swiddening societies, they are far denser—in the case of irrigated rice, one hundred times denser—than foraging societies, and hence they leave far more concentrated rubble in the form of middens, artifacts, building materials, and architectural ruins.[71] The larger the pile of rubble you leave behind, the larger your place in the historical record! The more dispersed, mobile, egalitarian societies regardless of their sophistication and trading networks, and despite being often more populous, are relatively invisible in the historical record because they spread their debris more widely.[72]

The same logic applies with a vengeance once it comes to the written record. Much of what we know about the classical states of Southeast Asia comes from the stone inscriptions and, later, paper trails they left behind in the form of land grants, memorials, tax and corvée records, religious donations, and court chronicles.[73] The thicker the paper trail you leave behind, the larger your place in the historical record. With the written record, the distortions also multiply. The traditional words in Burmese and Thai for history, *yazawin* and *phonesavadan,* respectively, both literally mean "the history of rulers" or "chronicle of kings." It becomes difficult, in this context, to reconstruct the life-world of nonelites, even if they are located at the court center. They typically appear in the record as statistical abstractions: so many laborers, so many conscripts, taxpayers, padi planters, so many bearers of tribute. Rarely do they appear as historical actors, and when they do, as in the case of a suppressed revolt, you can be sure that something has gone terribly wrong. The job of peasants, you might say, is to stay out of the archives.

Hegemonic histories centered on courts and capital cities introduce other distortions as well. They are, forcibly, histories of "state spaces"; they neglect or ignore altogether both "nonstate spaces" beyond their reach and the long periods of dynastic decline or collapse when there is hardly a state at all. In a truly evenhanded, year-by-year, chronology of precolonial, mainland Southeast Asian states, most of the pages would be blank. Are we to pretend, along with the official chronicles, that because there was no dynasty in control, there was no history? Beyond the problem of blank pages, however, the nature of the official histories of the court center systematically exaggerates the power, the coherence, and the majesty of the dynasty.[74] The court documents that survive are largely tax and land records on the one hand and hymns of praise, assertions of power, and claims to legitimacy on the other; the latter are meant to persuade and to amplify power, not to report facts.[75] If we take the cosmological bluster emanating from the court centers as indicative of facts on the ground, we risk, as Richard O'Connor has noted, "impos[ing] the imperial imaginings of a few great courts on the rest of the region."[76]

The independent nations of mainland Southeast Asia add a new layer of historical mystification. As the successor states, ethnically and geographically, to the classical kingdoms, they have their own interest in embellishing the glory, continuity, and beneficence of their ancestors. Furthermore, the histories of the classical states have been mined and distorted in the interest of identifying a protonation and a protonationalism that could be of use against contemporary enemies, both foreign and domestic. Thus early artifacts such as Dong Son drums (large bronze ceremonial objects dating from roughly 500 BCE to the beginning of the common era and found throughout highland Southeast Asia and southern China) or local uprisings have been appropriated as national and/or ethnic achievements when, at the time, such identities made no sense at all. The result is an historical fable that projects the nation and its dominant people backward, obscuring discontinuity, contingency, and fluid identities.[77] Such accounts serve, as Walter Benjamin reminded us, to naturalize the progression and necessity of the state in general and the nation-state in particular.[78]

The inadequacies of mandala, dynastic, capital-city, text-based histories are so manifest, even when read skeptically, that they are chiefly useful as self-interested descriptions and cosmological claims. During the greater part of the historical record, and especially in the uplands, there was no state or "hardly-a-state." What states there were tended to be personal creations that were tenuous and fragmented, and that seldom outlasted their founder by long. Their cosmological claims and ideological reach were far greater than their practical control over human labor and grain.[79]

Here it is crucial to distinguish the "hard" power of the state from its economic and symbolic influence, which was far wider. The precolonial state, when it came to extracting grain and labor from subject populations, could project its power only within a fairly small radius of the court, say, three hundred kilometers, and that undependably and only during the dry season. The economic reach of the precolonial state, on the other hand, was far wider but based on voluntary exchange. The higher the value and smaller the weight and volume of the commodity (think silk and precious gems as opposed to charcoal or grain), the greater the reach. The symbolic reach of the state—its regalia, titles, costumes, its cosmology—traveled far and wide as ideas that have left a deep impression in the hills, even as they were often deployed in revolts against valley kingdoms. While the valley kingdom's hard power was a minute fraction of its expansive imperial imaginings, its reach as a market of physical or, especially, symbolic commodities was far greater.

What if we replaced these "imperial imaginings" with a view of Southeast Asian history as dominated by long periods of normative and normalized statelessness, punctuated by occasional, and usually brief, dynastic states that, when they dissolved, left in their wake a new deposit of imperial imaginings? In a critique of overly state-centric histories, Anthony Day points us in just this direction: "What would the history of Southeast Asia look like, however, if we were to take the turbulent relations between families as normative rather than a departure from the norm of the absolutist state which must 'deal with disorder'?"[80]

THE ELEMENTARY UNITS OF POLITICAL ORDER

Abandoning the tunnel vision of the court-state view, as urged by Day and O'Connor and actually pursued some considerable distance by Keith Taylor, we attempt an account of the elementary units of political order in mainland Southeast Asia.[81] I emphasize the term *political order* to avoid conveying the mistaken impression that outside the realm of the state lay mere disorder. Depending on the location and date, such units might range from nuclear families to segmentary lineages, bilateral kindreds, hamlets, larger villages, towns and their immediate hinterlands, and confederations of such towns. Confederations appear to constitute the most complex level of integration that had any stability at all. They consisted of small towns located on terrain favorable to wet-rice cultivation, with its concentration of population, together with an allied population in the adjacent hills. Alliances of such "wet-rice archipelagoes" were common, although they too were short-lived and their constituent members rarely surrendered their freedom of action. Traces of these patterns survive in place names throughout the entire region: Xishuang Banna ("twelve village rice fields") in Yunnan, Sipsong Chutai ("twelve Tai lords") along the Vietnamese-Laotian border and Negri Sembilan ("nine realms") in western Malaysia, and Ko Myo ("nine towns") in Burma's Shan states. In this respect, the largest quasi-permanent building blocks in the region were the Malay *negeri/Negara,* the Tai *muang,* and the Burmese *main* (မိုင်း),

each of which represented a potential fund of manpower and grain, located, in the most favorable cases, athwart a valuable trade route.

Assembling such potential nodes of power into a political and military alliance was itself a small, and usually evanescent, miracle of statecraft. Bringing many such units together under central rule was exceptionally rare and normally short-lived. When the political confection it represented disintegrated, it tended to fragment into its constituent units: the petty state-lets, small villages, hamlets, and lineages. New agglomerations might arise, orchestrated by a new and ambitious political entrepreneur, but they were always a contingent alliance of the same elementary units. The symbolic and ideological format for state-making was known and observed by ambitious local leaders with even the slightest pretense to wider power. State mimicry—what I have called cosmological bluster—was copied from the Chinese or Indic high forms, with rudimentary materials and in miniature, right down to the most petty village chiefs.

If larger political units were radically unstable, the elementary units themselves were hardly timeless blocks of building material. We must see these units themselves as in almost constant motion: dissolving, splitting, relocating, merging, and reconstituting. The households and individuals within a hamlet or lineage were themselves in motion over time. A settlement might remain in place over, say, half a century, but because of residents coming and leaving, their linguistic and ethnic identification might shift dramatically.[82] Here demography played a central role, the population density in Southeast Asia being, in 1600, one-sixth that of India and one-seventh that of China. The existence of an open frontier operated like an automatic brake on what the state could extract. Motivated by factors as disparate as epidemics, famines, taxes, corvée labor, conscription, factional conflict, religious schism, shame, scandal, and the desire to change one's luck, it was relatively simple for households and entire villages to move. Thus, over time, the membership of any elementary unit was in flux, as was the very existence of the unit itself. If there was an element of stability here, it resided in the ecology and geography of places favorable to human settlements. A well-watered plain situated on a navigable river or a trade route might occasionally be abandoned, but it was just as likely to be reinhabited when conditions permitted. Such locations were, of course, the typical cores of the negeri, the muang, the maín.

Fluid as they were, these elementary units were the only building blocks available to the would-be state-maker. In the absence of an ambitious strongman, or when the wider polity inevitably shattered, the "remains" were once again the elementary units. Is an intelligible history possible under such circumstances? I believe that it is, although it is surely not a dynastic history. The units in question do have a history, do observe a rough logic in formation, combination, and dissolution, and do exhibit a certain autonomy vis-à-vis dynastic or modern states. They have a history, but that history is on a different plane from state or dynastic history. For all their fluidity, they are the relatively constant features of the landscape, while the successful dynastic state is rare and ephemeral. The contingency of the "state" invites us to treat it less as a unity than as a "complex web of contractual mutualities."[83] For when it does splinter, as Akin Rabibhadana observed about the early nineteenth-century Siamese state, "the component parts of the system tended to split off in order to save their own lives."[84]

Making sense of innumerable small units, seemingly in constant movement, might seem impossible. It is surely more daunting than dynastic history, but we are not without guidance from those who have sought to understand comparable systems. In the case of Southeast Asia, there are many studies of social structure that seek to grasp the logic behind the fluidity. First, most famous, and most controversial among them is Edmund Leach's *Political Systems of Highland Burma.* Subsequent work along these lines in the highlands, not to mention studies of the Malay world, where shifting petty states, a mobile population, and a distinction between upstream and downstream, unruled and ruled populations also is at work, is richly suggestive. Beyond Southeast Asia, however, we may look again to the encounter between states and nomadic, stateless populations in the Middle East. The case for beginning with the elementary unit of the household and treating villages, tribes, and confederations as provisional and shaky alliances has also been used to brilliant effect for eighteenth-century North American society in the Great Lakes region by Richard White.[85] And, finally, we may profitably look back to Thucydides' *Peloponnesian War,* which describes a world of peoples, some with kings, some without, whose fickle loyalties and unreliable cohesion is a source of constant anxiety to the statesmen of each of the major antagonists: Athens, Sparta, Corinth, and Syracuse—each of them, in turn, a confederation.[86]

One challenge for a non-state-centric history of mainland Southeast Asia consists in specifying the conditions for the aggregation and disaggregation of its elementary units. The problem has been succinctly put by one observer of a somewhat comparable flux between states and their autonomous hinterlands: "There comes a time when one realizes that one is dealing, really, with molecules which sometimes unify in the form of a vague confederation, sometimes, just as easily, disaggregate. Even their names offer no consistency or certainty."[87] If the fluidity of the molecules themselves is an inconvenience for anthropologists and historians, imagine the problem it poses for the dynastic official or would-be state-builder, the colonial official, and the modern state functionary. State rulers find it well nigh impossible to install an effective sovereignty over people who are constantly in motion, who have no permanent pattern of organization, no permanent address, whose leadership is ephemeral, whose subsistence patterns are pliable and fugitive, who have few permanent allegiances, and who are liable, over time, to shift their linguistic practices and their ethnic identity.

And this is just the point! The economic, political, and cultural organization of such people is, in large part, a strategic adaptation to avoid incorporation in state structures. These adaptations are all the more feasible in the mountainous hinterlands of state systems: that is to say, in places like Zomia.

> Here [Sumatra] I am the advocate of despotism. The strong arm of power is necessary to bring men together, and to concentrate them into societies.... Sumatra is, in great measure, peopled by innumerable petty tribes, subject to no general government.... At present people are as wandering in their habits as the birds of the air, and until they are congregated and organized under something like authority, nothing can be done with them.[88]

In the early nineteenth century, as in the classical mainland states, Sir Stamford Raffles, quoted above, understood that the precondition of colonial rule was the concentration of population and sedentary agriculture. He required a nonfugitive people whose labor and production were legible and hence appropriable by the state. We turn our attention next, then, to an understanding of the logic and dynamics behind the creation of state spaces in mainland Southeast Asia.

ENDNOTES

1. *Guiyang Prefectural Gazetteer,* quoted in Mark Elvin, *The Retreat of the Elephants: An Environmental History of China* (New Haven: Yale University Press, 2004), 236–37.

2. *Gazetteer of Upper Burma and the Shan States,* compiled from official papers by J. George Scott, assisted by J. P. Hardiman, vol. 1, part 1 (Rangoon: Government Printing Office, 1893), 1: 154.

3. Elizabeth R. Hooker, *Religion in the Highlands: Native Churches and Missionary Enterprises in the Southern Appalachian Area* (New York: Home Missions Council, 1933), 64–65.

4. Valley peoples and states may make further vernacular distinctions between those who are sedentary and live in villages and those who live in the forest and are presumptively nomadic.

5. The relationship between Bedouin pastoralists and urban Arabs, as it concerns state-making and civilization, pervades the writings of the great fourteenth-century Arab historian and philosopher Ibn Khaldun.

6. Recent archeological evidence appears to indicate that widespread copper mining and metallurgy on an industrial scale, associated elsewhere with state formation, was practiced in northeast Thailand without any evidence of state centers. It appears to have been an off-season craft of agriculturists on a surprising scale. See Vincent Pigott, "Prehistoric Copper Mining in Northeast Thailand in the Context of Emerging Community Craft Specialization," in *Social Approaches to an Industrial Past: The Archaeology and Anthropology of Mining,* ed. A. B. Knapp, V. Pigott, and E. Herbert (London: Routledge, 1998), 205–25. I am grateful to Magnus Fiskesjö for bringing this to my attention.

7. Anthony Reid, *Southeast Asia in the Age of Commerce, 1450–1680,* vol. 1, *The Lands Below the Winds* (New Haven: Yale University Press, 1988), 15. China, less Tibet, at 37 persons per square kilometer was more densely populated than the South Asian subcontinent at 32 per square kilometer. Europe at that time had roughly 11 persons per square kilometer.

8. Richard A. O'Connor, "Founders' Cults in Regional and Historical Perspective," in *Founders' Cults in Southeast Asia: Polity, and Identity,* ed. Nicola Tannenbaum and Cornelia Ann Kammerer, Yale Southeast Asia Monograph Series no. 52 (New Haven: Yale University Press, 2003), 269–311, quotation from 281–82. For a quite different and largely unilinear account of the rise of states generally, see Allen W. Johnson and Timothy Earle, *The Evolution of Human Societies: From Foraging Group to Agrarian State,* 2nd ed. (Stanford: Stanford University Press, 2000).

9. Richard A. O'Connor, "Agricultural Change and Ethnic Succession in Southeast Asian States: A Case for Regional Anthropology," *Journal of Asian Studies* 54 (1995): 968–96.

10. See, in this connection, Michael Mann, *The Sources of Social Power* (Cambridge: Cambridge University Press, 1986), 63–70.

11. Charles Tilly, *Coercion, Capital, and European States, AD 990–1992* (Cambridge, Mass.: Blackwell, 1990), 162.

12. Encouragement of sedentarism is perhaps the oldest "state project," a project related to the second-oldest state project of taxation. It was at the center of Chinese statecraft for millennia through the Maoist period, when People's Liberation Army soldiers by the thousands were digging terraces to get the "wild" Wa to plant irrigated wet rice.

13. Hugh Brody, *The Other Side of Eden: Hunters, Farmers, and the Shaping of the World* (Vancouver: Douglas and McIntyre, 2000).

14. Sanjay Subramanyum, "Connected Histories: Notes toward a Reconfiguration of Early Modern Eurasia," *Modern Asian Studies* 31 (1997): 735–62.

15. For an excellent account of this process in Vietnam and Indonesia, see Rodolphe de Koninck, "On the Geopolitics of Land Colonization: Order and Disorder on the Frontier of Vietnam and Indonesia," *Moussons* 9 (2006): 33–59.

16. The colonial and early postcolonial regimes, like the classical states, had considered these areas *terra nullius* or *inutile*—as in the traditional distinction between *La France utile* and *La France inutile*—in the sense that they did not repay the costs of administration in terms of grain or revenue. Though forest and hill products might be valuable and though their populations might be captured as slaves, they were considered to lie well outside the directly administered, profitable grain core on which state power and revenue depended. These areas were, under colonialism, typically governed by so-called indirect rule, whereby traditional authorities were supervised and made tributary rather than replaced. Under Han administration from the Yuan Dynasty through much of the Ming, such zones were governed, as we shall see, under the tusi system, a Chinese form of indirect rule.

17. Hill populations have in quite a few cases, and for their own reasons, adopted lowland religions as their own. The symbolic appropriation of lowland religions has, however, not necessarily implied incorporation in the lowland state. See, for example, Nigel Brailey, "A Reinvestigation of the Gwe of Eighteenth Century Burma," *Journal of Southeast Asian Studies* 1, no. 2 (1970): 33–47. See also the discussion in Chapter 8.

18. Patricia M. Pelley, *Post-Colonial Vietnam: New Histories of the National Past* (Durham: Duke University Press, 2002), 96–97.

19. This official account has been effectively contradicted in Keith Taylor's "Surface Orientations in Vietnam: Beyond Histories of Nation and Region," *Journal of Asian Studies* 57 (1998): 949–78.

20. These four groups, each now represented by a nation-state, have absorbed all of the many earlier states of the region with the exception of Cambodia and Laos, which have, for their part, incorporated nonstate spaces of their own.

21. Geoff Wade, "The Bai-Yi Zhuan: A Chinese Account of Tai Society in the 14th century," paper presented at the 14th IAHA Conference, Bangkok, May, 1996, appendix 2, 8. Cited in Barbara Andaya, *The Flaming Womb: Repositioning Women in Early Modern Southeast Asia* (Honolulu: University of Hawai'i Press, 2006), 12.

22. Willem van Schendel, "Geographies of Knowing, Geographies of Ignorance: Southeast Asia from the Fringes," a paper for the workshop Locating Southeast Asia: Genealogies, Concepts, Comparisons and Prospects, Amsterdam, March 29–31, 2001.

23. Jean Michaud, *Historical Dictionary of the Peoples of the Southeast Asian Massif* (Lanham, Md.: Scarecrow, 2006), 5. See also Jean Michaud, ed., *Turbulent Times and Enduring Peoples: Mountain Minorities in the Southeast Asian Massif* (Richmond, England: Curzon, 2000).

24. Michaud, *Historical Dictionary,* 2. Adding the lowland populations now in the hills would raise the figure by perhaps another fifty million, a figure that is increasing daily.

25. Ernest Gellner, "Tribalism and the State in the Middle East," in *Tribes and State Formation in the Middle East,* ed. Philip Khoury and Joseph Kostiner (Berkeley: University of California Press, 1990), 109–26, quotation from 124. Analogies to the Pashtuns, Kurds, and Berbers are less apposite because, in these three cases, the people in question have—or better, are assumed to have—a common culture. No such cultural cohesion is presumed for the great mountain kingdom discussed here, although some of its peoples (for example, Dai, Hmong, Akha/Hani) are far flung across the region. But for a perceptive account of Islamic sectarianism in the hills, see Robert LeRoy Canfield, *Faction and Conversion in a Plural Society: Religious Alignments in the Hindu-Kush,* Anthropological Papers, Museum of Anthropology, University of Michigan, 50 (Ann Arbor: University of Michigan, 1973).

26. Laos is a partial exception inasmuch as, like Switzerland, it is largely a "mountain state" with a small valley plain along the Mekong that it shares with Thailand.

27. See, in this connection, Sidney Pollard's suggestive *Marginal Europe: The Contribution of Marginal Lands since the Middle Ages* (Oxford: Clarendon, 1997).

28. Other explicit proponents of a systematic view from the periphery include Michaud, *Turbulent Times and Enduring Peoples,* especially the Introduction by Michaud and John McKinnon, 1–25, and Hjorleifur Jonsson, *Mien Relations: Mountain Peoples, Ethnography, and State Control* (Ithaca: Cornell University Press, 2005).

29. F. K. L. Chit Hlaing [F. K. Lehman], "Some Remarks upon Ethnicity Theory and Southeast Asia, with Special Reference to the Kayah and Kachin," in *Exploring Ethnic Diversity in Burma,* ed. Mikael Gravers (Copenhagen: NIAS Press, 2007), 107–22, esp. 109–10.

30. Fernand Braudel, *The Mediterranean and the Mediterranean World in the Age of Philip II,* vol. 1, trans. Sian Reynolds (New York: Harper and Row, 1966).

31. Reid, *Southeast Asia in the Age of Commerce,* vol. 1.

32. Van Schendel, "Geographies of Knowing," 10, puts it nicely: "If seas can inspire scholars to construct Braudelian regional worlds, why not the world's largest mountain ranges?" But this did not happen. Instead, excellent studies of various parts of Zomia continued to be done, but these did not address an audience of fellow "Zomianists," nor did they have the ambition to build up a Zomia perspective that could offer a new set of questions and methodologies to the social sciences.

33. The "anarchy," of course, was entirely in the eye of the beholder. Hill peoples were in no doubt about who they were, even if, for the colonial official, they were illegible.

34. E. R. Leach, "The Frontiers of Burma," *Comparative Studies in Society and History* 3 (1960): 49–68.

35. For a fine analysis of gender relations among the Lahu, see Shanshan Du, *Chopsticks Only Work in Pairs: Gender Unity and Gender Equality among the Lahu of Southwest China* (New York: Columbia University Press, 2002).

36. Nan Chao/Nan-zhuao and its successor, the Dali Kingdom in southern Yunnan, from roughly the ninth century to the thirteenth; Kengtung/Chaing-tung/Kyaingtung, a trans-Salween/Nu kingdom in the Eastern Shan States of Burma, independent from roughly the fourteenth century until its conquest by the Burmese in the seventeenth; Nan, a small independent kingdom in the Nan River Valley in northern Thailand; Lanna, near the present site of Chiang Mai in Thailand, and independent from roughly the thirteenth to the eighteenth century, allowing for a Burmese conquest in the mid-sixteenth century. It is diagnostic that each

of these kingdoms was dominated by the padi-planting, Tai-speaking peoples most frequently associated with state-making in the hills.

37. Janet Sturgeon, "Border Practices, Boundaries, and the Control of Resource Access: A Case from China, Thailand, and Burma," *Development and Change* 35 (2004): 463–84.

38. Van Schendel, "Geographies of Knowing," 12.

39. Braudel, *The Mediterranean,* 1: 32, 33. Braudel fails here, I think, to note those peoples who carry, as it were, their civilizations on their backs wherever they go: Roma (Gypsies) and Jews, for example.

40. Ibn Khaldun, *The Muqaddimah: An Introduction to History,* 3 vols., trans. Franz Rosenthal, Bollinger Series 43 (New York: Pantheon, 1958), 1: 302.

41. O. W. Wolters, *History, Culture, and Region in Southeast Asian Perspectives* (Singapore: Institute for Southeast Asian Studies, 1982), 32. Wolters's citation is from Paul Wheatley, "Satyanrta in Suvarnadvipa: From Reciprocity to Redistribution in Ancient Southeast Asia," in *Ancient Trade and Civilization,* ed. J. A. Sabloff et al. (Albuquerque: University of New Mexico Press, 1975), 251.

42. Quoted in Andrew Hardy, *Red Hills: Migrants and the State in the Highlands of Vietnam* (Honolulu: University of Hawai'i Press, 2003), 4.

43. Owen Lattimore, "The Frontier in History," in *Studies in Frontier History: Collected Papers, 1928–1958* (Oxford: Oxford University Press, 1962), 469–91, quotation from 475.

44. Edmund Leach, *The Political Systems of Highland Burma: A Study of Kachin Social Structure* (Cambridge: Harvard University Press, 1954).

45. Thomas Barfield, "The Shadow Empires: Imperial State Formation along the Chinese-Nomad Frontier," in *Empires: Perspectives from Archaeology and History,* ed. Susan E. Alcock, Terrance N. D'Altroy, et al. (Cambridge: Cambridge University Press, 2001), 11–41. Karl Marx identified such parasitic, militarized peripheries engaged in slave-raiding and plunder on the fringe of the Roman Empire as "the Germanic mode of production." For the best account of such secondary state formation by the Wa people, see Magnus Fiskesjö, "The Fate of Sacrifice and the Making of Wa History," Ph.D. thesis, University of Chicago, 2000.

46. I borrow the term from Gonzalo Aguirre Beltrán, who argues that much of the post-conquest indigenous population of Spanish America could be found "in areas that are particularly hostile or inaccessible to human movement" and marginal to the colonial economy. For the most part, he has in mind rugged mountainous areas, although he includes tropical jungles and deserts. Aguirre Beltrán tends to see such areas more as "survivals" of precolonial populations rather than environments to which populations fled or were pushed. *Regions of Refuge,* Society of Applied Anthropology Monograph Series, 12 (Washington, D.C., 1979), 23 and passim.

47. Michaud, *Historical Dictionary,* 180, quotation from 199. Elsewhere, writing about the hill populations of Vietnam (the "montagnards"), he echoes the theme. "To some extent montagnards can be seen as refugees displaced by war and choosing to remain beyond the direct control of state authorities, who sought to control labor, tax productive resources, and secure access to populations from which they could recruit soldiers, servants, concubines, and slaves. This implies that montagnards have always been on the run." Michaud, *Turbulent Times and Enduring Peoples,* 11.

48. See Christine Ward Gailey and Thomas C. Patterson, "State Formation and Uneven Development," in *State and Society: The Emergence and Development of Social Hierarchy and Political Centralization,* ed. J. Gledhill, B. Bender, and M. T. Larsen (London: Routledge, 1988), 77–90.

49. Fiskesjö, "Fate of Sacrifice," 56.

50. The classic texts elaborating this argument include Pierre Clastres, *Society against the State: Essays in Political Anthropology,* trans. Robert Hurley (New York: Zone, 1987); Aguirre Beltrán, *Regions of Refuge;* Stuart Schwartz and Frank Salomon, "New Peoples and New Kinds of People: Adaptation, Adjustment, and Ethnogenesis in South American Indigenous Societies (Colonial Era)," in *The Cambridge History of Native Peoples of the Americas,* ed. Stuart Schwartz and Frank Salomon (Cambridge: Cambridge University Press, 1999), 443–502. For a review of recent evidence, see Charles C. Mann, *1491: New Revelations of the Americas before Columbus* (New York: Knopf, 2005).

51. Felix M. Keesing, *The Ethno-history of Northern Luzon* (Stanford: Stanford University Press, 1976); William Henry Scott, *The Discovery of the Igorots: Spanish Contacts with the Pagans of Northern Luzon,* rev. ed. (Quezon City: New Day, 1974).

52. See, for example, Bruce W. Menning, "The Emergence of a Military-Administrative Elite in the Don Cossack Land, 1708–1836," in *Russian Officialdom: The Bureaucratization of Russian Society from the Seventeenth to the Twentieth Century,* ed. Walter MacKenzie Pinter and Don Karl Rowney (Chapel Hill: University of North Carolina Press, 1980), 130–61.

53. Leo Lucassen, Wim Willems, and Annemarie Cottaar, *Gypsies and Other Itinerant Groups: A Socio-historical Approach* (London: Macmillan, 1998).

54. Martin A. Klein, in "The Slave Trade and Decentralized Societies, *Journal of African History* 42 (2001): 49–65, observes that rather more centralized African societies often became predatory slave-raiders themselves (further reinforcing centralizing tendencies) and that decentralized societies often retreated to hills and forest zones of refuge when they were available, as well as fortifying their settlements to evade slave raids. See also J. F. Searing, "'No Kings, No Lords, No Slaves': Ethnicity and Religion among the Sereer-Safèn of Western Bawol (Senegal), 1700–1914," *Journal of African History* 43 (2002): 407–29; Dennis D. Cordell, "The Myth of Inevitability and Invincibility: Resistance to Slavers and the Slave Trade in Central Africa, 1850–1910," in *Fighting the Slave Trade: West African Strategies,* ed. Sylviane A. Diouf (Athens: Ohio University Press, 2003), 50–61; and for an attempt at a statistical analysis, Nathan Nunn and Diego Puga, "Ruggedness: The Blessing of Bad Geography," special section of the *American Historical Review* devoted to "Geography, History, and Institutional Change: The Causes and Consequences of Africa's Slave Trade," March 2007.

55. The term *mandala,* borrowed from south India, describes a political landscape of court centers radiating power outward through alliances and charisma, but having no fixed frontiers. It is an inherently plural term in the sense that it conjures up a number of contending mandalas jockeying for tribute and allies, with each mandala's sway waxing and waning—or disappearing altogether—depending on the circumstances. See I. W. Mabbett, "Kingship at Angkor, *Journal of the Siam Society* 66 (1978): 1058, and, especially, Wolters, *History, Culture, and Region.*

56. Scholarship on Southeast Asia as a whole is far less guilty of this charge than, say, scholarship on India or China. As a crossroads and contact zone, the borrowing and adaptations of religious beliefs, symbols of authority, and forms of political organization that originated elsewhere could hardly be overlooked. Mandala elites themselves flaunted such trappings. The "hill effects" on valley culture and social organization, however, are typically ignored.

57. The cases of the Minagkabau and the Batak on Sumatra, who long cultivated irrigated rice and developed an elaborate culture but did not create states, reminds us that while irrigated rice is nearly always a precondition of state formation, it is not sufficient.

58. The same process is roughly applicable, it seems, to our understanding of the formation of the Han system at a much earlier period.

59. Gilles Deleuze and Felix Guattari, *A Thousand Plateaus: Capitalism and Schizophrenia,* trans. Brian Massum (Minneapolis: University of Minnesota Press, 1987), 360.

60. Clastres, *Society against the State.* There are many such shatter zones in Africa that developed as populations threatened with capture for the slave trade fled into areas of relative safety. One such area is the Lamé-speaking zone along the current Guinea-Liberian border. Michael McGovern, personal communication, November 2007.

61. M. P. Griaznov, *The Ancient Civilization of Southern Siberia,* trans. James Hogarth (New York: Cowles, 1969), 97–98, 131–33, cited in Deleuze and Guattari, *A Thousand Plateaus,* 430.

62. Lattimore, "Frontier in History," 472.

63. Ernest Gellner, *Saints of the Atlas* (London: Weidenfeld and Nicolson, 1969), 1–2.

64. Ibid., 1–2, 14, 31.

65. Quoted in Richard Tapper, "Anthropologists, Historians, and Tribespeople on Tribe and State Formation in the Middle East," in *Tribes and State Formation in the Middle East,* ed. Philip Khoury and Joseph Kostiner (Berkeley: University of California Press, 1990), 48–73, quotation from 66.

66. The stripping down of social structure to simpler, minimal forms, just as the resort to variable and mobile subsistence practices and fluid identities, has been shown to enhance adaptability to a capricious natural and political environment. See in this connection Robert E. Ehrenreich, Carole L. Crumley, and Janet E. Levy, eds., *Heterarchy and the Analysis of Complex Societies,* Archeological Papers of the American Anthropological Society, no. 6 (1995).

67. This point is missed, I think, in the perennial debates about whether Southeast Asian classical states were more dependent on trade or on manpower. A positional advantage at a river junction, a mountain pass, a jade or ruby mine had to be held militarily against rival claimants.

68. Georges Coedès, *The Indianized States of Southeast Asia* (Honolulu: East-West Center Press, 1968), originally published in France in 1948.

69. J. C. van Leur, *Indonesian Trade and Society* (The Hague: V. van Hoeve, 1955), 261.

70. John Smail, "On the Possibility of an Autonomous History of Modern Southeast Asia," *Journal of Southeast Asian History* 2 (1961): 72–102.

71. Peter Bellwood, "Southeast Asia before History," chapter 2 of *The Cambridge History of Southeast Asia,* ed. Nicholas Tarling, vol. 1, *From Early Times to 1800* (Cambridge: Cam-bridge University Press, 1992), 90.

72. Compared with other cultural zones, the maritime states of Southeast Asia, located at or near the estuary of rivers, left little in the way of physical evidence behind. The long search for the remains of Srivijaya is perhaps the most striking case in point. See in this context Jean Michaud, *Historical Dictionary,* 9, who notes that both building materials and burial practices in the hills leave little in the way of archeological traces. In this connection it should be added that, even in the lowlands, commoners were often forbidden to build structures with brick, stone, or even teak, lest it become a potential fortification in a rebellion. Hjorleifur Jonsson, personal communication, June 6, 2007.

73. The obverse of this fact is that a kingdom that does not leave a paper trail is unlikely to appear in the record at all. Georges Condominas notes that the Lua' kingdom(s) of highland and Khmer Southeast Asia, despite leaving ruins and oral legends of its founding by the marriage of a Lawa king and a Mon queen who brought Buddhism to the hills, has left hardly a trace because it apparently had no writing system. *From Lawa to Mon, from Saa' to Thai: Historical and Anthropological Aspects of Southeast Asian Social Spaces,* trans. Stephanie Anderson et al., an Occasional Paper of Anthropology in Association with the Thai-Yunnan Project, Research School of Pacific Studies (Canberra: Australian National University, 1990).

74. Such chronicles do, then, the symbolic work of the state. I am indebted to Indrani Chatterjee for pointing this out to me.

75. One major exception is found in the Burmese *Sit-tans,* administrative records that are devoted largely to providing an inventory of taxable property and economic activity and population according to their tax status. See Frank N. Trager and William J. Koenig, with the assistance of Yi Yi, *Burmese Sit-tàns, 1784–1826: Records of Rural Life and Administration,* Association of Asian Studies monograph no. 36 (Tucson: University of Arizona Press, 1979).

76. Richard A. O'Connor, "Review of Thongchai Winichakul, *Siam Mapped: A History of the Geo-body of a Nation*" (Honolulu: University of Hawai'i Press, 1994), *Journal of Asian Studies* 56 (1997): 280. A telling example is the official Burmese court version of a diplomatic letter from the Chinese emperor in which it appears that the Chinese emperor as the emperor of the East is addressing the Burmese king as the emperor of the West and that the two are coequals bestriding the civilized world. As Than Tun remarks, "In all probability, this Burmese version of the address from China is quite different from its original though it is the one acceptable to the Burmese king who admits no other monarch as his superior." *Royal Orders of Burma, A.D. 1598–1885,* part 1, *A.D. 1598–1648,* ed. Than Tun (Kyoto: Center for Southeast Asian Studies, 1983), 3: 1. Official court histories remind me of my high school newspaper, *The Sun Dial,* whose motto was "We Mark Only the Hours That Shine."

77. One of the first efforts to correct this myopia may be found in Taylor, "Surface Orientations." It should be noted that the important work of demystifying nationalist histories is, finally, well under way in Southeast Asia.

78. Walter Benjamin, "Theses on the Philosophy of History," in *Illuminations,* ed. Hannah Arendt (New York: Schocken, 1968), 255–56. I am grateful to Charles Lesch for bringing this to my attention in his un-published paper "Anarchist Dialectics and Primitive Utopias: Walter Benjamin, Pierre Clastres, and the Violence of Historical Progress," 2008.

79. See Herman Kulke, "The Early and Imperial Kingdom in Southeast Asian History," in *Southeast Asia in the 9th to 14th Centuries,* ed. David G. Marr and A. C. Milner (Singapore: Institute for Southeast Asian Studies, 1986), 1–22. Bronson makes a related point that the northern two-thirds of South Asia has, over the past three millennia, produced "exactly two moderately durable, region-spanning states: the Gupta and the Mughal. Neither of these nor any of the smaller states lasted longer than two centuries and anarchical interregna were everywhere prolonged and severe." Bennett Bronson, "The Role of Barbarians in the Fall of States," in *The Collapse of Ancient States and Civilizations,* ed. Norman Yoffee and George L. Cowgill (Tucson: University of Arizona Press, 1988), 196–218.

80. Anthony Day, "Ties That (Un)Bind: Families and States in Pre-modern Southeast Asia," *Journal of Asian Studies* 55 (1996): 398. Day is here criticizing the state-centric aspect of the important historiographic work by Anthony Reid and Victor Lieberman.

81. See Taylor, "Surface Orientations." Taylor imaginatively examines several periods in the early history of the area now called Vietnam, while scrupulously avoiding reading back modern national or regional narratives for which there is no contemporary evidence.

82. See in this connection Sara (Meg) Davis's critique of Condominas, "Premodern Flows and Postmodern China: Globalization and the Sipsongpanna Tai," *Modern China* 29 (2003): 187: "Villagers shifted between villages and towns, federations of villages and states split and reformed, and the nobility was sometimes compelled to travel far and wide to hold a constituency together. . . . Such continual and steady movement and change make the region difficult to characterize, though we can note three constants: Village affiliation, strong traditions of independence, and freedom of movement."

83. Anthony Reid, "'Tradition' in Indonesia: The One and the Many," *Asian Studies Review* 22 (1998): 32.

84. Akin Rabibhadana, "The Organization of Thai Society in the Early Bangkok Period, 1782–1873," Cornell University, Thailand Project, Interim Report Series, no. 12 (July 1969), 27.

85. Richard White, *The Middle Ground: Indians, Empires, and Republics in the Great Lakes Region, 1650–1815* (Cambridge: Cambridge University Press, 1991).

86. Thucydides, *The Peloponnesian War,* trans. Rex Warner (New York: Penguin, 1972).

87. Basile Nikitina, quoted, in French, by Tapper in "Anthropologists, Historians, and Tribespeople," 55; my translation.

88. Sir Stamford Raffles, cited by Reid in "'Tradition' in Indonesia," 31.

Cities, People, and Language

BY JAMES C. SCOTT

And the Colleges of the Cartographers set up a Map of the Empire which had the size of the Empire itself and coincided with it point by point.... Succeeding generations understood that this Widespread Map was Useless, and not without Impiety they abandoned it to the Inclemencies of the Sun and the Winters.
— Suarez Miranda, *Viajes de varones prudentes (1658)*

An aerial view of a town built during the Middle Ages or the oldest quarters (*medina*) of a Middle Eastern city that has not been greatly tampered with has a particular look. It is the look of disorder. Or, to put it more precisely, the town conforms to no overall abstract form. Streets, lanes, and passages intersect at varying angles with a density that resembles the intricate complexity of some organic processes. In the case of a medieval town, where defense needs required walls and perhaps moats, there may be traces of inner walls superseded by outer walls, much like the growth rings of a tree. A representation of Bruges in about 1500 illustrates the pattern. What definition there is to the city is provided by the castle green, the marketplace, and the river and canals that were (until they silted up) the lifeblood of this textile-trading city.

The fact that the layout of the city, having developed without any overall design, lacks a consistent geometric logic does not mean that it was at all confusing to its inhabitants. One imagines that many of its cobbled streets were nothing more than surfaced footpaths traced by repeated use. For those who grew up in its various quarters, Bruges would have been perfectly familiar, perfectly legible. Its very alleys and lanes would have closely approximated the most common daily movements. For a stranger or trader arriving for the first time, however, the town was almost certainly confusing, simply because it lacked a repetitive, abstract logic that would allow a newcomer to orient herself. The cityscape of Bruges in 1500 could be said to privilege local knowledge over outside knowledge, including that of external political authorities.[1] It functioned spatially in much the same way a difficult or unintelligible dialect would function linguistically. As a semipermeable membrane, it facilitated communication within the city while remaining stubbornly unfamiliar to those who had not grown up speaking this special geographic dialect.

Historically, the relative illegibility to outsiders of some urban neighborhoods (or of their rural analogues, such as hills, marshes, and forests) has provided a vital margin of political safety from control by outside elites. A simple way of determining whether this margin exists is to ask if an outsider would have needed a local guide (a native tracker) in order to find her way successfully. If the answer is yes, then the community or terrain in question enjoys at least a small measure of insulation from outside intrusion. Coupled with patterns of local solidarity, this insulation has proven politically valuable in such disparate contexts as eighteenth- and early nineteenth-century urban riots over bread prices in Europe, the Front de Libération Nationale's tenacious resistance to the French in the Casbah of Algiers,[2] and the politics of the bazaar that helped to bring down the Shah of Iran. Illegibility, then, has been and remains a reliable resource for political autonomy.[3]

Stopping short of redesigning cities in order to make them more legible (a subject that we shall soon explore), state authorities endeavored to map complex, old cities in a way that would facilitate policing and control. Most of the major cities of France were thus the subject of careful military mapping (reconnaissances militaires), particularly after the Revolution. When urban revolts occurred, the authorities wanted to be able to move quickly to the precise locations that would enable them to contain or suppress the rebellions effectively.[4]

States and city planners have striven, as one might expect, to overcome this spatial unintelligibility and to make urban geography transparently legible from without. Their attitude toward what they regarded as the higgledy-piggledy profusion of unplanned cities was not unlike the attitude of foresters to the natural profusion of the unplanned forest. The origin of grids or geometrically regular settlements may lie in a straightforward military logic. A square, ordered, formulaic military camp on the order of the Roman castra has many advantages. Soldiers can easily learn the techniques of building it; the commander of the troops knows exactly in which disposition his subalterns and various troops lie; and any Roman messenger or officer who arrives at the camp will know where to find the officer he seeks.... Other things being equal, the city laid out according to a simple, repetitive logic will be easiest to administer and to police.

Whatever the political and administrative conveniences of a geometric cityscape, the Enlightenment fostered a strong aesthetic that looked with enthusiasm on straight lines and visible order. No one expressed the prejudice more clearly than Descartes: "These ancient cities that were once mere straggling villages and have become in the course of time great cities are commonly quite poorly laid out compared to those well-ordered towns that an engineer lays out on a vacant plane as it suits his fancy. And although, upon considering one-by-one the buildings in the former class of towns, one finds as much art or more than one finds in the latter class of towns, still, upon seeing how the buildings are arranged—*here a large one, there a small one*—and how *they make the streets crooked and uneven*, one will say that *it is chance more than the will of some men using their reason that has arranged them thus*."[5]

Descartes's vision conjures up the urban equivalent of the scientific forest: streets laid out in straight lines intersecting at right angles, buildings of uniform design and size, the whole built according to a single, overarching plan.

The elective affinity between a strong state and a uniformly laid out city is obvious. Lewis Mumford, the historian of urban form, locates the modern European origin of this symbiosis in the open, legible baroque style of the Italian city-state....[6] [T]he baroque redesigning of medieval cities—with its grand edifices, vistas, squares, and attention to uniformity, proportion, and perspective—was intended to reflect the grandeur and awesome power of the prince. Aesthetic considerations frequently won out over the existing social structure and the mundane functioning of the city. "Long before the invention of bulldozers," Mumford adds, "the Italian military engineer developed, through his professional specialization in destruction, a bulldozing habit of mind: one that sought to clear the ground of encumbrances, so as to make a clear beginning on its own inflexible mathematical lines."[7]

The visual power of the baroque city was underwritten by scrupulous attention to the military security of the prince from internal as well as external enemies. Thus both Alberti and Palladio thought of main thoroughfares as military roads (*viae militaires*). Such roads had to be straight, and, in Palladio's view, "the ways will be more convenient if they are made everywhere equal: that is to say that there will be *no part in them where armies may not easily march*."[8]

There are, of course, many cities approximating Descartes's model. For obvious reasons, most have been planned from the ground up as new, often utopian cities.[9] Where they have not been built by imperial decrees, they have been designed by their founding fathers to accommodate more repetitive and uniform squares for future settlement.[10] A bird's-eye view of central Chicago in the late nineteenth century (William Penn's Philadelphia or New Haven would do equally well) serves as an example of the grid city.

From an administrator's vantage point, the ground plan of Chicago is nearly utopian. It offers a quick appreciation of the ensemble, since the entirety is made up of straight lines, right angles, and repetitions.[11] Even the rivers seem scarcely to interrupt the city's relentless symmetry. For an outsider—or a policeman—finding an address is a comparatively simple matter; no local guides are required. The knowledge of local citizens is not especially privileged vis-à-vis that of outsiders. If, as is the case in upper Manhattan, the cross streets are consecutively numbered and are intersected by longer avenues, also consecutively numbered, the plan acquires even greater transparency.[12] The aboveground order of a grid city facilitates its underground order in the layout of water pipes, storm drains, sewers, electric cables, natural gas lines, and subways—an order no less important to the administrators of a city. Delivering mail, collecting taxes, conducting a census, moving supplies and people in and out of the city, putting down a riot or insurrection, digging for pipes and sewer lines, finding a felon or conscript (providing he is at the address given), and planning public transportation, water supply, and trash removal are all made vastly simpler by the logic of the grid.

Three aspects of this geometric order in human settlement bear emphasis. The first is that the order in question is most evident, not at street level, but rather from above and from outside.... The symmetry is either grasped from a representation ... or from the vantage point of a helicopter hovering far above the ground: in short, a God's-eye view, or the view of an absolute ruler. This spatial fact is perhaps inherent in the process of urban or architectural planning itself, a process that involves miniaturization and scale models upon which patron and planner gaze down, exactly as if they were in a helicopter.[13] There is, after all, no other way of visually imagining what a large-scale construction project will look like when it is completed except by a miniaturization of this kind. It follows, I believe, that such plans, which have the scale of toys, are judged for their sculptural properties and visual order, often from a perspective that no or very few human observers will ever replicate.

The miniaturization imaginatively achieved by scale models of cities or landscapes was practically achieved with the air-plane. The mapping tradition of the bird's-eye view, evident in the map of Chicago, was no longer a mere convention. By virtue of its great distance, an aerial view resolved what might have seemed ground-level confusion into an apparently vaster order and symmetry. It would be hard to exaggerate the importance of the airplane for modernist thought and planning....

A second point about an urban order easily legible from outside is that the grand plan of the ensemble has no necessary relationship to the order of life as it is experienced by its residents. Although certain state services may be more easily provided and distant addresses more easily located, these apparent advantages may be negated by such perceived disadvantages as the absence of a dense street life, the intrusion of hostile authorities, the loss of the spatial irregularities that foster coziness, gathering places for informal recreation, and neighborhood feeling. The formal order of a geometrically regular urban space is just that: formal order. Its visual regimentation has a ceremonial or ideological quality, much like the order of a parade or a barracks. The fact that such order works for municipal and state authorities in administering the city is no guarantee that it works for citizens. Provisionally, then, we must remain agnostic about the relation between formal spatial order and social experience.

The third notable aspect of homogeneous, geometrical, uniform property is its convenience as a standardized commodity for the market. Like Jefferson's scheme for surveying or the Torrens system for titling open land, the grid creates regular lots and blocks that are ideal for buying and selling. Precisely because they are abstract units detached from any ecological or topographical reality, they resemble a kind of currency which is endlessly amenable to aggregation and fragmentation. This feature of the grid plan suits equally the surveyor, the planner, and the real-estate speculator. Bureaucratic and commercial logic, in this instance, go hand in hand....

The vast majority of Old World cities are, in fact, some historical amalgam of a Bruges and a Chicago. Although more than one politician, dictator, and city planner have devised plans for the total recasting of an existing city, these dreams came at such cost, both financial and political, that they have rarely left the drawing boards. Piecemeal planning, by contrast, is far more common. The central, older core of many cities remains somewhat like Bruges, whereas the newer outskirts are more likely to exhibit the marks of one or more plans. Sometimes, as in the sharp contrast between old Delhi and the imperial capital of New Delhi, the divergence is formalized.

Occasionally, authorities have taken draconian steps to retrofit an existing city. The redevelopment of Paris by the prefect of the Seine, Baron Haussmann, under Louis Napoleon was a grandiose public works program stretching from 1853 to 1869. Haussmann's vast scheme absorbed unprecedented amounts of public debt, uprooted tens of thousands of people, and could have been accomplished only by a single executive authority not directly accountable to the electorate.

The logic behind the reconstruction of Paris bears a resemblance to the logic behind the transformation of old-growth forests into scientific forests designed for unitary fiscal management. There was the same emphasis on simplification, legibility, straight lines, central management, and a synoptic grasp of the ensemble. As in the case of the forest, much of the plan was achieved. One chief difference, however, was that Haussmann's plan was devised less for fiscal reasons than for its impact on the conduct and sensibilities of Parisians. While the plan did create a far more legible fiscal space in the capital, this was a by-product of the desire to make the city more governable, prosperous, healthy, and architecturally imposing.[14] The second difference was, of course, that those uprooted by the urban planning of the Second Empire could, and did, strike back. As we shall see, the retrofitting of Paris foreshadows many of the paradoxes of authoritarian high-modernist planning that we will soon examine in greater detail.

The plan shows the new boulevards constructed to Haussmann's measure as well as the prerevolutionary inner boulevards, which were widened and straightened.[15] But the retrofit, seen merely as a new street map, greatly underestimates the transformation. For all the demolition and construction required, for all the new legibility added to the street plan, the new pattern bore strong traces of an accommodation with "old-growth" Paris. The outer boulevards, for example, follow the line of the older customs (octroi) wall of 1787. But Haussmann's scheme was far more than a traffic reform. The new legibility of the boulevards was accompanied by changes that revolutionized daily life: new aqueducts, a much more effective sewage system, new rail lines and terminals, centralized markets (Les Halles), gas lines and lighting, and new parks and public squares.[16] The new Paris created by Louis Napoleon became, by the turn of the century, a widely admired public works miracle and shrine for would-be planners from abroad.

At the center of Louis Napoleon's and Haussmann's plans for Paris lay the military security of the state. The redesigned city was, above all, to be made safe against popular insurrections.... Barricades had gone up nine times in the twenty-five years before 1851. Louis Napoleon and Haussmann had seen the revolutions of 1830 and 1848; more recently, the June Days and resistance to Louis Napoleon's coup represented the largest insurrection of the century. Louis Napoleon, as a returned exile, was well aware of how tenuous his hold on power might prove.

The geography of insurrection, however, was not evenly distributed across Paris. Resistance was concentrated in densely packed, working-class quartiers, which, like Bruges, had complex, illegible street plans.[17] The 1860 annexation of the "inner suburbs" (located between the customs wall and the outer fortifications and containing 240,000 residents) was explicitly designed to gain mastery over a *ceinture sauvage* that had thus far escaped police control. Haussmann described this area as a "dense belt of suburbs, given over to twenty different administrations, built at random, covered by an inextricable network of narrow and tortuous public ways, alleys, and dead-ends, where a nomadic population without any real ties to the land [property] and without any effective surveillance, grows at a prodigious speed."[18] Within Paris itself, there were such revolutionary *foyers* as the Marais and especially the Faubourg Saint-Antoine, both of which had been determined centers of resistance to Louis Napoleon's coup d'état.

The military control of these insurrectionary spaces—spaces that had not yet been well mapped—was integral to Haussmann's plan.[19] A series of new avenues between the inner boulevards and the customs wall was designed to facilitate movement between the barracks on the outskirts of the city and the subversive districts. As Haussmann saw it, his new roads would ensure multiple, direct rail and road links between each district of the city and the military units responsible for order there.[20] Thus, for example, new boulevards in northeastern Paris allowed troops to rush from the Courbevoie barracks to the Bastille and then to subdue the turbulent Faubourg Saint-Antoine.[21] Many of the new rail lines and stations were located with similar strategic goals in mind. Where possible, insurrectionary quartiers were demolished or broken up by new roads, public spaces, and commercial development....

The reconstruction of Paris was also a necessary public-health measure. And here the steps that the hygienists said would make Paris more healthful would at the same time make it more efficient economically and more secure militarily. Antiquated sewers and cesspools, the droppings of an estimated thirty-seven thousand horses (in 1850), and the unreliable water supply made Paris literally pestilential. The city had the highest death rate in France and was most susceptible to virulent epidemics of cholera; in 1831, the disease killed 18,400 people, including the prime minister. And it was in those districts of revolutionary resistance where, because of crowding and lack of sanitation, the rates of mortality were highest.[22] Haussmann's Paris was, for those who were not expelled, a far healthier city; the greater circulation of air and water and the exposure to sunlight reduced the risk of epidemics just as the improved circulation of goods and labor (healthier labor, at that) contributed to the city's economic well-being. A utilitarian logic of labor productivity and commercial success went hand in hand with strategic and public-health concerns.

[. . .]

As happens in many authoritarian modernizing schemes, the political tastes of the ruler occasionally trumped purely military and functional concerns. Rectilinear streets may have admirably assisted the mobilization of troops against insurgents, but they were also to be flanked by elegant facades and to terminate in imposing buildings that would impress visitors.[23] Uniform modern buildings along the new boulevards may have represented healthier dwellings, but they were often no more than facades. The zoning regulations were almost exclusively concerned with the visible surfaces of buildings, but behind the facades, builders could build crowded, airless tenements, and many of them did.[24]

The new Paris, as T. J. Clark has observed, was intensely visualized: "Part of Haussmann's purpose was to give modernity a shape, and he seemed at the time to have a measure of success in doing so;

he built a set of forms in which the city appeared to be visible, even intelligible: Paris, to repeat the formula, was becoming a spectacle."[25]

Legibility, in this case, was achieved by a much more pronounced segregation of the population by class and function. Each fragment of Paris increasingly took on a distinctive character of dress, activity, and wealth—bourgeois shopping district, prosperous residential quarter, industrial suburb, artisan quarter, bohemian quarter. It was a more easily managed and administered city and a more "readable" city because of Haussmann's heroic simplifications.

As in most ambitious schemes of modern order, there was a kind of evil twin to Haussmann's spacious and imposing new capital. The hierarchy of urban space in which the rebuilt center of Paris occupied pride of place presupposed the displacement of the urban poor toward the periphery.[26] Nowhere was this more true than in Belleville, a popular working-class quarter to the northeast which grew into a town of sixty thousand people by 1856. Many of its residents had been disinherited by Haussmann's demolitions; some called it a community of outcasts. By the 1860s, it had become a suburban equivalent of what the Faubourg Saint-Antoine had been earlier—an illegible, insurrectionary *foyer*. "The problem was not that Belleville was not a community, but that it became the sort of community which the bourgeoisie feared, which the police could not penetrate, which the government could not regulate, where the popular classes, with all their unruly passions and political resentments, held the upper hand."[27] If, as many claim, the Commune of Paris in 1871 was partly an attempt to reconquer the city ("la reconquete de la Ville par la Ville")[28] by those exiled to the periphery by Haussmann, then Belleville was the geographical locus of that sentiment. The Communards, militarily on the defensive in late May 1871, retreated toward the northeast and Belleville, where, at the Belleville town hall, they made their last stand. Treated as a den of revolutionaries, Belleville was subjected to a brutal military occupation.

[. . .]

THE CREATION OF SURNAMES

Some of the categories that we most take for granted and with which we now routinely apprehend the social world had their origin in state projects of standardization and legibility. Consider, for example, something as fundamental as permanent surnames.

A vignette from the popular film *Witness* illustrates how, when among strangers, we do rely on surnames as key navigational aids.[29] The detective in the film is attempting to locate a young Amish boy who may have witnessed a murder. Although the detective has a surname to go on, he is thwarted by several aspects of Amish traditionalism, including the antique German dialect spoken by the Amish. His first instinct is, of course, to reach for the telephone book—a list of proper names and addresses—but the Amish don't have telephones. Furthermore, he learns, the Amish have a very small number of last names. His quandary reminds us that the great variety of surnames and given names in the United States allows us to identify unambiguously a large number of individuals whom we may never have met. A world without such names is bewildering; indeed, the detective finds Amish society so opaque that he needs a native tracker to find his way.

Customary naming practices throughout much of the world are enormously rich. Among some peoples, it is not uncommon for individuals to have different names during different stages of life (infancy, childhood, adulthood) and in some cases after death; added to these are names used for joking, rituals, and mourning and names used for interactions with same-sex friends or with in-laws. Each name is specific to a certain phase of life, social setting, or interlocutor. A single individual will frequently be called by several different names, depending on the stage of life and the person addressing him or her. To the question "What is your name?" which has a more unambiguous answer in the contemporary West, the only plausible answer is "It depends."[30]

For the insider who grows up using these naming practices, they are both legible and clarifying. Each name and the contexts of its use convey important social knowledge. Like the network of alleys in Bruges, the assortment of local weights and measures, and the intricacies of customary land tenure, the complexity of naming has some direct and often quite practical relations to local purposes. For an outsider, however, this byzantine complexity of names is a formidable obstacle to understanding local society. Finding some one, let alone situating him or her in a kinship network or tracing the inheritance of property, becomes a major undertaking. If, in addition, the population in question has reason to conceal its identity and its activities from external authority, the camouflage value of such naming practices is considerable.

The invention of permanent, inherited patronyms was, after the administrative simplification of nature (for example, the forest) and space (for example, land tenure), the last step in establishing the necessary preconditions of modern statecraft. In almost every case it was a state project, designed to allow officials to identify, unambiguously, the majority of its citizens. When successful, it went far to create a legible people.[31] Tax and tithe rolls, property rolls, conscription lists, censuses, and property deeds recognized in law were inconceivable without some means of fixing an individual's identity and linking him or her to a kin group. Campaigns to assign permanent patronyms have typically taken place, as one might expect, in the context of a state's exertions to put its fiscal system on a sounder and more lucrative footing. Fearing, with good reason, that an effort to enumerate and register them could be a prelude to some new tax burden or conscription, local officials and the population at large often resisted such campaigns.

[. . .]

Until at least the fourteenth century, the great majority of Europeans did not have permanent patronymics.[32] An individual's name was typically his given name, which might well suffice for local identification. If something more were required, a second designation could be added, indicating his occupation (in the English case, smith, baker), his geographical location (hill, edgewood), his father's given name, or a personal characteristic (short, strong). These secondary designations were not permanent surnames; they did not survive their bearers, unless by chance, say, a baker's son went into the same trade and was called by the same second designation.

[. . .]

A connection between state building and the invention of permanent patronyms exists for four-teenth- and fifteenth-century Eng-land. In England only wealthy aristocratic families tended to have fixed surnames. In the English case such names referred typically to families' places of origin in Normandy (for example, Baumont, Percy, Disney) or to the places in England that they held in fief from William the Conqueror (for example, Gerard de Sussex). For the rest of the male population, the standard practice of linking only father and son by way of identification prevailed.[33] Thus, William Robertson's male son might be called Thomas Williamson (son of William), while Thomas's son, in turn, might be called Henry Thompson (Thomas's son). Note that the grandson's name, by itself, bore no evidence of his grandfather's identity, complicating the tracing of descent through names alone. A great many northern European surnames, though now permanent, still bear ... particles that echo their antique purpose of designating who a man's father was (Fitz-, O'-, -sen, -son, -s, Mac-, -vich).[34] At the time of their establishment, last names often had a kind of local logic to them: John who owned a mill became John Miller; John who made cart wheels became John Wheelwright; John who was physically small became John Short. As their male descendants, whatever their occupations or stature, retained the patronyms, the names later assumed an arbitrary cast.

The development of the personal surname (literally, a name added to another name, and not to be confused with a permanent patronym) went hand in hand with the development of written, official documents such as tithe records, manorial dues rolls, marriage registers, censuses, tax records, and land records.[35] They were necessary to the successful conduct of any administrative exercise involving large numbers of people who had to be individually identified and who were not known personally by the authorities. Imagine the dilemma of a tithe or capitation-tax collector faced with a male popula-tion, 90 percent of whom bore just six Christian names (John, William, Thomas, Robert, Richard, and Henry). Some second designation was absolutely essential for the records, and, if the subject suggested none, it was invented for him by the recording clerk. These second designations and the rolls of names that they generated were to the legibility of the population what uniform measurement and the cadastral map were to the legibility of real property. While the subject might normally prefer the safety of anonymity, once he was forced to pay the tax, it was then in his interest to be accurately identified in order to avoid paying the same tax twice. Many of these fourteenth-century surnames were clearly nothing more than administrative fictions designed to make a population fiscally legible. Many of the subjects whose "surnames" appear in the documents were probably unaware of what had been written down, and, for the great majority, the surnames had no social existence whatever outside the document.[36] Only on very rare occasions does one encounter an entry, such as "William Carter, tailor," that implies that we may be dealing with a permanent patronym.

The increasing intensity of interaction with the state and statelike structures (large manors, the church) exactly parallels the development of permanent, heritable patronyms. Thus, when Edward I clarified the system of landholding, establishing primogeniture and hereditary copyhold tenure for manorial land, he provided a powerful incentive for the adoption of permanent patronyms. Taking one's father's surname became, for the eldest son at least, part of a claim to the property on the father's death.[37] Now that property claims were subject to state validation, surnames that had once been mere bureaucratic fantasies took on a social reality of their own. One imagines that for a long time English subjects had in effect two names—their local name and an "official," fixed patronym. As the frequency of interaction with impersonal administrative structures increased, the official name came to prevail in all but a man's intimate circle. Those subjects living at a greater distance, both socially and geographically, from the organs of state power, as did the Tuscans, acquired permanent patronyms much later. The upper classes and those living in the south of England thus acquired permanent surnames before the lower classes and those living in the north did. The Scottish and Welsh acquired them even later.[38]

State naming practices, like state mapping practices, were inevitably associated with taxes (labor, military service, grain, revenue) and hence aroused popular resistance. The great English peasant rising of 1381 (often called the Wat Tyler Rebellion) is attributed to an unprecedented decade of registrations and assessments of poll taxes.[39] For English ... peasants, a census of all adult males could not but appear ominous, if not ruinous.

The imposition of permanent surnames on colonial populations offers us a chance to observe a process, telescoped into a decade or less, that in the West might have taken several generations. Many of the same state objectives animate both the European and the colonial exercises, but in the colonial case, the state is at once more bureaucratized and less tolerant of popular resistance. The very brusqueness of colonial naming casts the purposes and paradoxes of the process in sharp relief.

Nowhere is this better illustrated than in the Philippines under the Spanish.[40] Filipinos were instructed by the decree of November 21, 1849, to take on permanent Hispanic surnames. The author of the decree was Governor (and Lieutenant General) Narciso Claveria y Zaldua, a meticulous administrator as determined to rationalize names as he had been determined to rationalize existing law, provincial boundaries, and the calendar.[41] He had observed, as his decree states, that Filipinos generally lacked individual surnames, which might "distinguish them by families," and that their practice of adopting baptismal names drawn from a small group of saints' names resulted in great "confusion." The remedy was the *catalogo*, a compendium not only of personal names but also of nouns and adjectives drawn from flora, fauna, minerals, geography, and the arts and intended to be used by the authorities in assigning permanent, inherited surnames. Each local official was to be given a supply of surnames sufficient for his jurisdiction, "taking care that the distribution be made by letters [of the alphabet]."[42] In practice, each town was given a number of pages from the alphabetized catalogo, producing whole towns with surnames beginning with the same letter. In situations where there has been little in-migration in the past 150 years, the traces of this administrative exercise are still perfectly visible across the landscape: "For example, in the Bikol region, the entire alphabet is laid out like a garland over the provinces of Albay, Sorsogon, and Catanduanes which in 1849 belonged to the single jurisdiction of Albay. Beginning with *A* at the provincial capital, the letters *B* and *C* mark the towns along the coast beyond Tabaco to Tiwi. We return and trace along the coast of Sorsogon the letters *E* to *L*; then starting down the Iraya Valley at Daraga with *M*, we stop with *S* to Polangui and Libon, and finish the alphabet with a quick tour around the island of Catanduanes."[43]

The confusion for which the decree is the antidote is largely that of the administrator and the tax collector. Universal last names, they believe, will facilitate the administration of justice, finance, and public order as well as make it simpler for prospective marriage partners to calculate their degree of consanguinity.[44] For a utilitarian state builder of Claveria's temper, however, the ultimate goal was a complete and legible list of subjects and taxpayers. This is abundantly clear from the short preamble to the decree: "In view of the extreme usefulness and practicality of this measure, the time has come to issue a directive for the formation of a civil register [formerly a clerical function], which may not only fulfill and ensure the said objectives, but may also serve as a basis for the statistics of the country, guarantee the collection of taxes, the regular performance of personal services, and the receipt of payment for exemptions. It likewise provides exact information of the movement of the population, thus avoiding unauthorized migrations, hiding taxpayers, and other abuses."[45]

Drawing on the accurate lists of citizens throughout the colony, Claveria envisioned each local official constructing a table of eight columns specifying tribute obligations, communal labor obligations, first name, surname, age, marital status, occupation, and exemptions. A ninth column, for updating the register, would record alterations in status and would be submitted for inspection every month. Because of their accuracy and uniformity, these registers would allow the state to compile the precise statistics in Manila that would make for fiscal efficiency. The daunting cost of assigning surnames to the entire population and building a complete and discriminating list of taxpayers was justified by forecasting that the list, while it might cost as much as twenty thousand pesos to create, would yield one hundred thousand or two hundred thousand pesos in continuing annual revenue.

What if the Filipinos chose to ignore their new last names? This possibility had already crossed Claveria's mind, and he took steps to make sure that the names would stick. Schoolteachers were ordered to forbid their students to address or even know one another by any name except the officially inscribed family name. Those teachers who did not apply the rule with enthusiasm were to be punished. More efficacious perhaps, given the minuscule school enrollment, was the proviso that forbade priests and military and civil officials from accepting any document, application, petition, or deed that did not use the official surnames. All documents using other names would be null and void.

Actual practice, as one might expect, fell considerably short of Claveria's administrative utopia of legible and regimented taxpayers. The continued existence of such non-Spanish surnames as Magsaysay or Macapagal suggests that part of the population was never mustered for this exercise. Local officials submitted incomplete returns or none at all. And there was another serious problem, one that Claveria had foreseen but inadequately provided for. The new registers rarely recorded, as they were supposed to, the previous names used by the registrants. This meant that it became exceptionally difficult for officials to trace back property and taxpaying to the period before the transformation of names. The state had in effect blinded its own hindsight by the very success of its new scheme.

With surnames, as with forests, land tenure, and legible cities, actual practice never achieved anything like the simplified and uniform perfection to which its designers had aspired. As late as 1872, an attempt at taking a census proved a complete fiasco, and it was not tried again until just before the revolution of 1896. Nevertheless, by the twentieth century, the vast majority of Filipinos bore the surnames that Claveria had dreamed up for them. The increasing weight of the state in people's lives and the state's capacity to insist on its rules and its terms ensured that.

Universal last names are a fairly recent historical phenomenon. Tracking property ownership and inheritance, collecting taxes, maintaining court records, performing police work, conscripting soldiers, and controlling epidemics were all made immeasurably easier by the clarity of full names and, increasingly, fixed addresses. While the utilitarian state was committed to a complete inventory of its population, liberal ideas of citizenship, which implied voting rights and conscription, also contributed greatly to the standardization of naming practices. The legislative imposition of permanent surnames is particularly clear in the case of Western European Jews who had no tradition of last names. A Napoleonic decree ... in 1808 mandated last names.[46] Austrian legislation of 1787, as part of the emancipation process, required Jews to choose last names or, if they refused, to have fixed last names chosen for them. In Prussia the emancipation of the Jews was contingent upon the adoption of surnames.[47] Many of the immigrants to the United States, Jews and non-Jews alike, had no permanent surnames when they set sail. Very few, however, made it through the initial paperwork without an official last name that their descendants carry still.

The process of creating fixed last names continues in much of the Third World and on the "tribal frontiers" of more developed countries.[48] Today, of course, there are now many other state-impelled standard designations that have vastly improved the capacity of the state to identify an individual. The creation of birth and death certificates, more specific addresses (that is, more specific than something like "John-on-the-hill"), identity cards, passports, social security numbers, photographs, fingerprints, and, most recently, *dna* profiles have superseded the rather crude instrument of the permanent surname. But the surname was a first and crucial step toward making individual citizens officially legible, and along with the photograph, it is still the first fact on documents of identity.

THE DIRECTIVE FOR A STANDARD, OFFICIAL LANGUAGE

The great cultural barrier imposed by a separate language is perhaps the most effective guarantee that a social world, easily accessible to insiders, will remain opaque to outsiders.[49] Just as the stranger or state official might need a local guide to find his way around sixteenth-century Bruges, he would need a local interpreter in order to understand and be understood in an unfamiliar linguistic environment. A distinct language, however, is a far more powerful basis for autonomy than a complex residential pattern. It is also the bearer of a distinctive history, a cultural sensibility, a literature, a mythology, a musical past.[50] In this respect, a unique language represents a formidable obstacle to state knowledge, let alone colonization, control, manipulation, instruction, or propaganda.

Of all state simplifications, then, the imposition of a single, official language may be the most powerful, and it is the precondition of many other simplifications. This process should probably be viewed, as Eugen Weber suggests in the case of France, as one of domestic colonization in which various foreign provinces (such as Brittany and Occitanie) are linguistically subdued and culturally incorporated.[51] In the first efforts made to insist on the use of French, it is clear that the state's objective was the legibility of local practice. Officials insisted that every legal document—whether a will, document of sale, loan instrument, contract, annuity, or property deed—be drawn up in French. As long as these documents remained in local vernaculars, they were daunting to an official sent from Paris and virtually impossible to bring into conformity with central schemes of legal and administrative standardization. The campaign of linguistic centralization was assured of some success since it went hand in hand with an expansion of state power. By the late nineteenth century, dealing with the state was unavoidable for all but a small minority of the population. Petitions, court cases, school documents, applications, and correspondence with officials were all of necessity written in French. One can hardly imagine a more effective formula for immediately devaluing local knowledge and privileging all those who had mastered the official linguistic code. It was a gigantic shift in power. Those at the periphery who lacked competence in French were rendered mute and marginal. They were now in need of a local guide to the new state culture, which appeared in the form of lawyers, *notaires*, schoolteachers, clerks, and soldiers.[52]

A cultural project, as one might suspect, lurked behind the linguistic centralization. French was seen as the bearer of a national civilization; the purpose of imposing it was not merely to have provincials digest the Code Napoleon but also to bring them Voltaire, Racine, Parisian newspapers, and a national education.... Where the command of Latin had once defined participation in a wider culture for a small elite, the command of standard French now defined full participation in French culture. The implicit logic of the move was to define a hierarchy of cultures, relegating local languages and their regional cultures to, at best, a quaint provincialism. At the apex of this implicit pyramid was Paris and its institutions: ministries, schools, academies (including the guardian of the language, l'Académie Française). The relative success of this cultural project hinged on both coercion and inducements.... Standard (Parisian) French and Paris were not only focal points of power; they were also magnets. The growth of markets, physical mobility, new careers, political patronage, public service, and a national educational system all meant that facility in French and connections to Paris were the paths of social advancement and material success. It was a state simplification that promised to reward those who complied with its logic and to penalize those who ignored it.

THE CENTRALIZATION OF TRAFFIC PATTERNS

The linguistic centralization impelled by the imposition of Parisian French as the official standard was replicated in a centralization of traffic. Just as the new dispensation in language made Paris the hub of communication, so the new road and rail systems increasingly favored movement to and from Paris over interregional or local traffic. State policy resembled, in computer parlance, a "hardwiring" pattern that made the provinces far more accessible, far more legible, to central authorities than even the absolutist kings had imagined.

Let us contrast, in an overly schematic way, a relatively uncentralized network of communication, on one hand, with a relatively centralized network, on the other. If mapped, the uncentralized pattern would be the physical image of the actual movements of goods and people along routes *not* created by administrative fiat. Such movements would not be random; they would reflect both the ease of travel along valleys, by watercourses, and around defiles and also the location of important resources and ritual sites. Weber captures the wealth of human activities that animate these movements across the landscape: "They served professional pursuits, like the special trails followed by glass makers, carriers or sellers of salt, potters, or those that led to forges, mines, quarries, and hemp fields, or those along which flax, hemp, linen, and yarn were taken to market. There were pilgrimage routes and procession trails."[53]

If we can imagine, for the sake of argument, a place where physical resources are evenly distributed and there are no great physical barriers to movement (such as mountains or swamps), then a map of paths in use might form a network resembling a dense concentration of capillaries. The tracings would, of course, never be entirely random. Market towns based on location and resources would constitute small hubs, as would religious shrines, quarries, mines, and other important sites.[54] In the French case as well, the network of roads would have long reflected the centralizing ambitions of local lords and the nation's monarchs. The point of this illustrative idealization, however, is to depict a landscape of communication routes that is only lightly marked by state centralization....

Beginning with Colbert, the state-building modernizers of France were bent on superimposing on this pattern a carefully planned grid of administrative centralization.[55] Their scheme, never entirely realized, was to align highways, canals, and ultimately rail lines to radiate out from Paris like the spokes of a wheel.... The layout was designed "to serve the government and the cities and lacking a network of supporting thoroughfares had little to do with popular habit or need. Administrative highways, a historian of the center called them, [were] made for troops to march on and for tax revenues to reach the treasury."[56]

[. . .]

As a centralizing aesthetic, the plan defied the canons of commercial logic or cost-effectiveness. The first phase of the grid, the line from Paris east to Strasbourg and the frontier, ran straight through the plateau of Brie rather than following the centers of population along the Marne. By refusing to conform to the topography in its quest of geometric perfection, the railway line was ruinously expensive compared to English or German railroads. The army had also adopted the Ponts et Chaussées logic, believing that direct rail lines to the borders would be militarily advantageous. They were proven tragically wrong in the Franco-Prussian War of 1870–71.[57]

This retrofitting of traffic patterns had enormous consequences, most of which were intended: linking provincial France and provincial French citizens to Paris and to the state and facilitating the deployment of troops from the capital to put down civil unrest in any department in the nation. It was aimed at achieving, for the military control of the nation, what Haussmann had achieved in the capital itself. It thus empowered Paris and the state at the expense of the provinces, greatly affected the economics of location, expedited central fiscal and military control, and severed or weakened lateral cultural and economic ties by favoring hierarchical links. At a stroke, it marginalized outlying areas in the way that official French had marginalized local dialects.

CONCLUSION

Officials of the modern state are, of necessity, at least one step—and often several steps—removed from the society they are charged with governing. They assess the life of their society by a series of typifications that are always some distance from the full reality these abstractions are meant to capture. Thus the foresters' charts and tables, despite their synoptic power to distill many individual facts into a larger pattern, do not quite capture (nor are they meant to) the real forest in its full diversity. Thus the cadastral survey and the title deed are a rough, often misleading representation of actual, existing rights to land use and disposal. The functionary of any large organization "sees" the human activity that is of interest to him largely through the simplified approximations of documents and statistics: tax proceeds, lists of taxpayers, land records, average incomes, unemployment numbers, mortality rates, trade and productivity figures, the total number of cases of cholera in a certain district.

These typifications are indispensable to statecraft. State simplifications such as maps, censuses, cadastral lists, and standard units of measurement represent techniques for grasping a large and complex reality; in order for officials to be able to comprehend aspects of the ensemble, that complex reality must be reduced to schematic categories. The only way to accomplish this is to reduce an infinite array of detail to a set of categories that will facilitate summary descriptions, comparisons, and aggregation. The invention, elaboration, and deployment of these abstractions represent, as Charles Tilly has shown, an enormous leap in state capacity—a move from tribute and indirect rule to taxation and direct rule. Indirect rule required only a minimal state apparatus but rested on local elites and communities who had an interest in withholding resources and knowledge from the center. Direct rule sparked widespread resistance and necessitated negotiations that often limited the center's power, but for the first time, it allowed state officials direct knowledge of and access to a previously opaque society.

Such is the power of the most advanced techniques of direct rule, that it discovers new social truths as well as merely summarizing known facts. The Center for Disease Control in Atlanta is a striking case in point. Its network of sample hospitals allowed it to first "discover"—in the epidemiological sense—such hitherto unknown diseases as toxic shock syndrome, Legionnaires' disease, and AIDS. Stylized facts of this kind are a powerful form of state knowledge, making it possible for officials to intervene early in epidemics, to understand economic trends that greatly affect public welfare, to gauge whether their policies are having the desired effect, and to make policy with many of the crucial facts at hand.[58] These facts permit discriminating interventions, some of which are literally lifesaving.

The techniques devised to enhance the legibility of a society to its rulers have become vastly more sophisticated, but the political motives driving them have changed little. Appropriation, control, and manipulation (in the nonpejorative sense) remain the most prominent. If we imagine a state that has no reliable means of enumerating and locating its population, gauging its wealth, and mapping its land, resources, and settlements, we are imagining a state whose interventions in that society are necessarily crude. A society that is relatively opaque to the state is thereby insulated from some forms of finely tuned state interventions, both welcomed (universal vaccinations) and resented (personal income taxes). The interventions it does experience will typically be mediated by local trackers who know the society from inside and who are likely to interpose their own particular interests. Without this mediation—and often with it—state action is likely to be inept, greatly overshooting or undershooting its objective.

An illegible society, then, is a hindrance to any effective intervention by the state, whether the purpose of that intervention is plunder or public welfare. As long as the state's interest is largely confined to grabbing a few tons of grain and rounding up a few conscripts, the state's ignorance may not be fatal. When, however, the state's objective requires changing the daily habits (hygiene or health practices) or work performance (quality labor or machine maintenance) of its citizens, such ignorance can well be disabling. A thoroughly legible society eliminates local monopolies of information and creates a kind of national transparency through the uniformity of codes, identities, statistics, regulations, and measures. At the same time it is likely to create new positional advantages for those at the apex who have the knowledge and access to easily decipher the new state-created format.

The discriminating interventions that a legible society makes possible can, of course, be deadly as well. A sobering instance is wordlessly recalled by a map produced by the City Office of Statistics of Amsterdam, then under Nazi occupation, in May 1941.[59] Along with lists of residents, the map was the synoptic representation that guided the rounding up of the city's Jewish population, sixty-five thousand of whom were eventually deported.

The map is titled "The Distribution of Jews in the Municipality." Each dot represents ten Jews, a scheme that makes the heavily Jewish districts readily apparent. The map was compiled from information obtained not only through the order for people of Jewish extraction to register themselves but also through the population registry ("exceptionally comprehensive in the Netherlands")[60] and the business registry. If one reflects briefly on the kind of detailed information on names, addresses, and ethnic backgrounds (determined perhaps by names in the population registry or by declaration) and the cartographic exactitude required to produce this statistical representation, the contribution of legibility to state capacity is evident. The Nazi authorities, of course, supplied the murderous purpose behind the exercise, but the legibility provided by the Dutch authorities supplied the means to its efficient implementation.[61] That legibility, I should emphasize, merely amplifies the capacity of the state for discriminating interventions—a capacity that in principle could as easily have been deployed to feed the Jews as to deport them.

Legibility implies a viewer whose place is central and whose vision is synoptic. State simplifications of the kind we have examined are designed to provide authorities with a schematic view of their society, a view not afforded to those without authority. Rather like US highway patrolmen wearing mirrored sunglasses, the authorities enjoy a quasi-monopolistic picture of selected aspects of the whole society. This privileged vantage point is typical of all institutional settings where command and control of complex human activities is paramount. The monastery, the barracks, the factory floor, and the administrative bureaucracy (private or public) exercise many state-like functions and often mimic its information structure as well.

State simplifications can be considered part of an ongoing "project of legibility," a project that is never fully realized. The data from which such simplifications arise are, to varying degrees, riddled with inaccuracies, omissions, faulty aggregations, fraud, negligence, political distortion, and so on. A project of legibility is immanent in any statecraft that aims at manipulating society, but it is undermined by intrastate rivalries, technical obstacles, and, above all, the resistance of its subjects.

State simplifications have at least five characteristics that deserve emphasis. Most obviously, state simplifications are observations of only those aspects of social life that are of official interest. They are *interested*, utilitarian facts. Second, they are also nearly always written (verbal or numerical) *documentary* facts. Third, they are typically *static* facts.[62] Fourth, most stylized state facts are also *aggregate* facts. Aggregate facts may be impersonal (the density of transportation networks) or simply a collection of facts about individuals (employment rates, literacy rates, residence patterns). Finally, for most purposes, state officials need to group citizens in ways that permit them to make a collective assessment. Facts that can be aggregated and presented as averages or distributions must therefore be *standardized* facts. However unique the actual circumstances of the various individuals who make up the aggregate, it is their sameness or, more precisely, their differences along a standardized scale or continuum that are of interest.

The process by which standardized facts susceptible to aggregation are manufactured seems to require at least three steps. The first, indispensable step is the creation of common units of measurement or coding. Size classes of trees, freehold tenure, the metric system for measuring landed property or the volume of grain, uniform naming practices, sections of prairie land, and urban lots of standard sizes are among the units created for this purpose. In the next step, each item or instance falling within a category is counted and classified according to the new unit of assessment. A particular tree reappears as an instance of a certain size class of tree; a particular plot of agricultural land reappears as coordinates in a cadastral map; a particular job reappears as an instance of a category of employment; a particular person reappears bearing a name according to the new formula. Each fact must be recuperated and brought back on stage, as it were, dressed in a new uniform of official weave—as part of "a series in a total classificatory grid."[63] Only in such garb can these facts play a role in the culmination of the process: the creation of wholly new facts by aggregation, following the logic of the new units. One arrives, finally, at synoptic facts that are useful to officials: so many thousands of trees in a given size class, so many thousands of men between the ages of eighteen and thirty-five, so many farms in a given size class, so many students whose surnames begin with the letter *A*, so many people with tuberculosis. Combining several metrics of aggregation, one arrives at quite subtle, complex, heretofore unknown truths, including, for example, the distribution of tubercular patients by income and urban location.

To call such elaborate artifacts of knowledge "state simplifications" risks being misleading. They are anything but simpleminded, and they are often wielded with great sophistication by officials. Rather, the term "simplification" is meant in two quite specific senses. First, the knowledge that an official needs must give him or her a synoptic view of the ensemble; it must be cast in terms that are replicable across many cases. In this respect, such facts must lose their particularity and reappear in schematic or simplified form as a member of a class of facts.[64] Second, in a meaning closely related to the first, the grouping of synoptic facts necessarily entails collapsing or ignoring distinctions that might otherwise be relevant.

Take, for example, simplifications about employment. The working lives of many people are exceptionally complex and may change from day to day. For the purposes of official statistics, however, being "gainfully employed" is a stylized fact; one is or is not gainfully employed. Also, available characterizations of many rather exotic working lives are sharply restricted by the categories used in the aggregate statistics.[65] Those who gather and interpret such aggregate data understand that there is a certain fictional and arbitrary quality to their categories and that they hide a wealth of problematic variation. Once set, however, these thin categories operate unavoidably as if all similarly classified cases were in fact homogeneous and uniform.... There is, as Theodore Porter notes in his study of mechanical objectivity, a "strong incentive to prefer precise and standardizable measures to highly accurate ones," since accuracy is meaningless if the identical procedure cannot reliably be performed elsewhere.[66]

To this point, I have been making a rather straightforward, even banal point about the simplification, abstraction, and standardization that are necessary for state officials' observations of the circumstances of some or all of the population. But I want to make a further claim, one analogous to that made for scientific forestry: the modern state, through its officials, attempts with varying success to create a terrain and a population with precisely those standardized characteristics that will be easiest to monitor, count, assess, and manage. The utopian, immanent, and continually frustrated goal of the modern state is to reduce the chaotic, disorderly, constantly changing social reality beneath it to something more closely resembling the administrative grid of its observations. Much of the statecraft of the late eighteenth and nineteenth centuries was devoted to this project. "In the period of movement from tribute to tax, from indirect rule to direct rule, from subordination to assimilation," Tilly remarks, "states generally worked to homogenize their populations and break down their segmentation by imposing common languages, religions, currencies, and legal systems, as well as promoting the construction of connected systems of trade, transportation, and communication."[67]

As the scientific forester may dream of a perfectly legible forest planted with same-aged, single-species, uniform trees growing in straight lines in a rectangular flat space cleared of all underbrush and poachers,[68] so the exacting state official may aspire to a perfectly legible population with registered, unique names and addresses keyed to grid settlements; who pursue single, identifiable occupations; and all of whose transactions are documented according to the designated formula and in the official language. This caricature of society as a military parade ground is overdrawn, but the grain of truth that it embodies may help us understand the [State's] grandiose plans.... [69] The aspiration to such uniformity and order alerts us to the fact that modern statecraft is largely a project of internal colonization, often glossed, as it is in imperial rhetoric, as a "civilizing mission." The builders of the modern nation-state do not merely describe, observe, and map; they strive to shape a people and landscape that will fit their techniques of observation.[70]

[. . .]

State officials can often make their categories stick and impose their simplifications, because the state, of all institutions, is best equipped to insist on treating people according to its schemata. Thus categories that may have begun as the artificial inventions of cadastral surveyors, census takers, judges, or police officers can end by becoming categories that organize people's daily experience precisely because they are embedded in state-created institutions that structure that experience.[71] The economic plan, survey map, record of ownership, forest management plan, classification of ethnicity, passbook, arrest record, and map of political boundaries acquire their force from the fact that these synoptic data are the points of departure for reality as state officials apprehend and shape it. In dictatorial settings where there is no effective way to assert another reality, fictitious facts-on-paper can often be made eventually to prevail on the ground, because it is on behalf of such pieces of paper that police and army are deployed.

These paper records are the operative facts in a court of law, in an administrative dossier, and before most functionaries. In this sense, there are virtually no other facts for the state than those that are contained in documents standardized for that purpose. An error in such a document can have far more power—and for far longer—than can an unreported truth. If, for example, you want to defend your claim to real property, you are normally obliged to defend it with a document called a property deed, and to do so in the courts and tribunals created for that purpose. If you wish to have any standing in law, you must have a document that officials accept as evidence of citizenship, be that document a birth certificate, passport, or identity card. The categories used by state agents are not merely means to make their environment legible; they are an authoritative tune to which most of the population must dance.

ENDNOTES AND REFERENCES

1. As one might expect, independent towns were likely to privilege local knowledge far more than royal towns, which were designed with administrative and military order in mind.

2. The Casbah's illegibility, however, was not insurmountable. The FLN's resistance there was eventually broken, although at great long-run political cost, by determined police work, torture, and networks of local informers.

3. The inability of many US municipal authorities to effectively govern inner cities has prompted attempts to bring back the "cop on the beat" in the form of "community policing." The purpose of community policing is to create a cadre of local police who are intimately familiar with the physical layout of the community

and especially the local population, whose assistance is now judged vital to effective police work. Its aim is to turn officials who had come to be seen as outsiders into insiders.

4. I am grateful to Ron Aminzade for sending me the explanatory notes (*mémoires*) meant to accompany two of the maps the military officials had prepared as part of this *haute reconnaissance* in the city of Toulouse in 1843. They come from the *Archives de l'Armée, Paris*, dossier MR 1225. They note the streets or terrain that would be difficult to traverse, watercourses that might impede military movement, the attitude of the local population, the difficulty of their accents, the locations of markets, and so on.

5. René Descartes, *Discourse on Method*, trans. Donald A. Cress (Indianapolis: Hackett, 1980), p. 6, quoted in R. P. Harrison, *Forests: The Shadow of Civilization*, (Chicago: University of Chicago Press, 1992) pp. 111–12.

6. Lewis Mumford, *The City in History: Its Origins, Its Transformations, and Its Prospects* (New York: Harcourt Brace Jovanovich, 1961), p. 364.

7. Ibid., p. 387.

8. Quoted in ibid., p. 369.

9. Thomas More's utopian cities, for example, were to be perfectly uniform, so that "he who knows one of the cities will know them all, so exactly alike are they, except where the nature of the ground prevents" (More's *Utopia*, quoted in ibid., p. 327).

10. St Petersburg is the most striking example of the planned utopian capital, a metropolis that Dostoyevsky called the "most abstract and premeditated city in the world." See Marshall Berman, *All That Is Solid Melts into Air: The Experience of Modernity* (New York: Penguin, 1988), chap. 4. The Babylonians, Egyptians, and, of course, the Romans built "grid-settlements." Long before the Enlightenment, right angles were seen as evidence of cultural superiority. As Richard Sennett writes, "Hippodamus of Miletus is conventionally thought the first city builder to conceive of these grids as expressions of culture; the grid expressed, he believed, the rationality of civilized life. In their military conquests the Romans elaborated the contrast between the rude and formless camps of the barbarians and their own military forts, or castra" (*The Conscience of the Eye: The Design and Social Life of Cities* [New York: Norton, 1990], p. 47).

11. Well, almost. There are a few streets—among them Lincoln, Archer, and Blue Island—that follow old Indian trails and thus deviate from the geometric logic.

12. It may have occurred to the reader that certain grid sections of upper Manhattan and Chicago are, despite their formal order, essentially ungoverned and dangerous. No amount of formal order can overcome massive countervailing factors such as poverty, crime, social disorganization, or hostility toward officials. As a sign of the illegibility of such areas, the Census Bureau acknowledges that the number of uncounted African-Americans was six times the number of uncounted whites. The undercount is politically volatile since census figures determine the number of congressional seats to which a state is entitled.

13. See the mind-opening book by the geographer Yi-Fu Tuan, *Dominance and Affection: The Making of Pets* (New Haven: Yale University Press, 1984).

14. The plan created not only a more legible fiscal space but also the fortunes of the small coterie who used their inside knowledge of the plan to profit from real-estate speculation.

15. There was an older, quasi-planned, baroque city bequeathed to Paris by her absolutist rulers, especially those prior to Louis XIV, who for his part chose to lavish his planning on a "new space," Versailles.

16. As Mark Girouard notes, the plan included public facilities and institutions such as parks (notably the huge Bois de Boulogne), hospitals, schools, colleges, barracks, prisons, and a new opera house (*Cities and People: A Social and Architectural History* [New Haven: Yale University Press, 1985], p. 289). Roughly a century later, against greater odds, Robert Moses would undertake a similar retrofit of New York City.

17. Mumford writes, "Were not the ancient medieval streets of Paris one of the last refuges of urban liberties? No wonder that Napoleon III sanctioned the breaking through of narrow streets and culs-de-sac and the razing of whole quarters to provide wide boulevards. It was the best possible protection against assault from within" (*The City in History*, pp. 369–70).

18. Quoted in Louis Girard, *Nouvelle histoire de Paris: La deuxième république et le second empire, 1848–1870* (Paris, 1981), p. 126. Cited in J. M. Merriman, *Aux marges de la ville: Faubourgs et banlieues* (Paris: Seuil, 1994), p. 15. The parallels with the later *ceinture rouge*, the leftist working-class suburbs ringing Paris, are striking. Soweto and other black townships in South Africa under apartheid, although established explicitly for the purposes of segregation, also became illegible, subversive spaces from the perspective of the authorities.

19. Since the planners lacked a reliable map of the city, the first step was to build temporary wooden towers in order to achieve the triangulation necessary for an accurate map. See David H. Pinkney, *Napoleon III and the Rebuilding of Paris* (Princeton: Princeton University Press, 1958), p. 5.

20. Quoted in Jeanne Gaillard, *Paris, la ville, 1852–1870* (Paris, 1979), p. 38, cited in Merriman, *Aux marges de la ville*, p. 10.

21. Ibid., pp. 8–9.

22. Pinkney, *Napoleon III*, p. 23. A commonplace of demographic history has been that urban populations in Western Europe, beset with epidemics and generally high mortality, did not successfully reproduce themselves until well into the nineteenth century; the growth of cities came largely from in-migration from the healthier countryside. Although this position has been challenged, the evidence for it is still convincing. See the judicious synthesis and assessment by Jan de Vries, *European Urbanization, 1500–1800* (Cambridge: Harvard University Press, 1984), pp. 175–200.

23. Merriman, *Aux marges de la ville*, pp. 7–8. See also T. J. Clark, *The Painting of Modern Life: Paris in the Art of Manet and His Followers* (Princeton: Princeton University Press, 1984), p. 35. Louis Napoleon's and Haussmann's mania for straight lines was the butt of many jokes. A character in a play by Edmond About, for instance, dreams of the day when the Seine itself will be straightened, because, as he says, "its irregular curve is really rather shocking" (quoted in Clark, *The Painting of Modern Life*, p. 35).

24. Pinkney, *Napoleon III*, p. 93.

25. Clark, *The Painting of Modern Life*, p. 66. For a superb analysis of how tidy Orientalist expositions depicting Old Cairo, the peasant village, and so on gave Arab visitors to Paris a completely new way of seeing their society, see Timothy Mitchell, *Colonizing Egypt* (Berkeley: University of California Press, 1991), especially chaps. 1–3.

26. Gaillard, *Paris, la ville*, p. 568, quoted in Merriman, *Aux marges de la ville*, p. 20.

27. David Harvey, *Consciousness and the Urban Experience* (Baltimore: Johns Hopkins University Press, 1985), p. 165, quoted in Merriman, *Aux marges de la ville*, p. 12. See also David Harvey, *The Urban Experience* (Baltimore: Johns Hopkins University Press, 1989), which covers much of the same ground.

28. Jacques Rougerie, *Paris libre, 1871* (Paris, 1971), p. 19, quoted in Merriman, *Aux marges de la ville*, p. 27.

29. I owe this astute observation about *The Witness* to Benedict Anderson. More generally, his analysis of the census and the map as totalizing classificatory grids, particularly in colonial settings, has greatly influenced my thinking here. See Anderson, *Imagined Communities: Reflections on the Origin and Spread of Nationalism* (London: Verso, 1983), and also the remarkable book by Thongchai Winichakul, *Siam Mapped: A History of the Geo-Body of a Nation* (Honolulu: University of Hawaii Press, 1994).

30. See, for example, William E. Wormsley, "Traditional Change in Imbonggu Names and Naming Practices," *Names* 28 (1980): 183–94.

31. The adoption of permanent, inherited patronyms went far, but not the whole way. How is a state to associate a name, however unique and unambiguous, with an individual? Like identity cards, social security numbers, and pass systems, names require that the citizenry cooperate by carrying them and producing them on the demand of an official. Cooperation is secured in most modern state systems by making a clear identity a prerequisite for receiving entitlements; in more coercive systems, harsh penalties are exacted for failure to carry identification documents. If, however, there is widespread defiance, individuals will either fail to identify themselves or use false identities. The ultimate identity card, then, is an ineradicable mark on the body: a tattoo, a fingerprint, a DNA "signature."

32. To my knowledge, Iceland is the only European nation that had not adopted permanent surnames by the late twentieth century.

33. In the West, women, domestic servants, and tied laborers were typically the last to adopt surnames (and to be given the vote), because they were legally subsumed as minors in the charge of the male head of family.

34. Other surnames referring to fathers are not quite so obvious. Thus the name "Victor Hugo" would originally have meant simply "Victor, son of Hugo."

35. I am indebted to Kate Stanton, an astute research assistant, for her background research on this issue.

36. See C. M. Matthews, *English Surnames* (London: Weidenfeld and Nicolson, 1966), pp. 35–48.

37. As Matthews notes, "The humble peasant with only one virgate of land was as anxious to claim it by right of being his father's eldest son as the rich man inheriting a large estate. The land could be claimed and awarded only at the Manorial Court, being held 'by copy of the Court Roll' [that is, being a copyhold], which meant that the life tenant's name was inscribed there on permanent record. This system provided a direct incentive to men to keep the same surname that had been put down on the roll for their father and grandfather" (ibid., p. 44). And given the vagaries of the mortality rate in fourteenth-century England, younger sons might want to keep the name as well, just in case.

38. In historical documents one can occasionally glimpse a moment when a permanent surname seems to gel. Under Henry VIII in the early sixteenth century, for example, a Welshman who appeared in court was asked for his name, and he answered, in the Welsh fashion, "Thomas Ap [son of] William, Ap Thomas, Ap Richard, Ap Hoel, Ap Evan Vaughan." He was scolded by the judge, who instructed him to "leave the

old manner, ... whereupon he after called himself Moston, according to the name of his principal house, and left that name to his posteritie" (William Camden, *Remains Concerning Britain*, ed. R. D. Dunn [1605; Toronto: University of Toronto Press, 1984], p. 122). This "administrative" last name almost certainly remained unknown to Thomas's neighbors.

39. See the classic study by Rodney Hilton, *Bond Men Made Free: Medieval Peasant Movements and the English Rising of 1381* (New York: Viking Press, 1977), pp. 160–64.

40. I am particularly grateful to Rosanne Ruttan, Otto van den Muijzenberg, Harold Conklin, and Charles Bryant for putting me on the track of the Philippine case. The key document is Domingo Abella, ed., *Catalogo alfabetico de Apellidos* (Manila: National Archives, 1973). See also the short account in O. D. Corpuz, *The Roots of the Filipino Nation,* vol. 1 (Quezon City: Aklahi Foundation, 1989), pp. 479–80. For a perceptive analysis of naming and identity formation among the Karo-Batak of colonial East Sumatra, see Mary Margaret Steedly, "The Importance of Proper Names: Language and 'National' Identity in Colonial Karoland," *American Ethnologist* 23, no. 3 (1996): 447–75.

41. For nearly three hundred years, the Spanish calendar for the Philippines had been one day ahead of the Spanish calendar, because Magellan's expedition had not, of course, adjusted for their westward travel halfway around the globe.

42. Abella, *Catalogo alfabetico de Apellidos*, p. viii.

43. Ibid., p. vii.

44. As if the Filipinos did not have perfectly adequate oral and written genealogical schemes to achieve the same end.

45. Abella, *Catalogo alfabetico de Apellidos*, p. viii.

46. For the best treatment of permanent patronyms in France and their relation to state-building, see the insightful book by Anne Lefebvre-Teillard, *Le nom: Droit et histoire* (Paris: Presses Universitaires de France, 1990). She examines the process whereby state officials, both administrative and judicial, gradually authorized certain naming practices and limited the conditions under which names might be changed. The civil registers, along with the *livret de famille* (family pass book), established toward the end of the nineteenth century, became important tools for police administration, conscription, civil and criminal justice, and elections monitoring. The standard opening line of an encounter between a policeman and a civilian—"Vos papiers, Monsieur"—dates from this period. Having experienced the "blinding" of the administration caused by the destruction of civil registers in the burning of the Hôtel de Ville (city hall) and the Palais de Justice at the end of the Commune in 1871, officials took care to keep duplicate registers.

47. Robert Chazon, "Names: Medieval Period and Establishment of Surnames," *Encyclopedia Judaica* (Jerusalem and Philadelphia: Keter Publishers and Coronet Books, 1982), 12:809–13. In the 1930s the Nazis passed a series of "name decrees" whose sole purpose was to distinguish what they had determined as the Jewish population from the Gentile population. Jews who had Aryan-sounding names were required to change them (or to add "Israel" or "Sarah"), as were Aryans who had Jewish-sounding names. Lists of approved names were compiled, and contested cases were submitted to the Reich Office for Genealogical Research. Once the administrative exercise was complete, a person's name alone could

single out him or her for deportation or execution. See Robert M. Rennick, "The Nazi Name Decrees of the Nineteen Thirties," *Journal of the American Name Society* 16 (1968): 65–88.

48. Turkey, for example, adopted surnames only in the 1920s as a part of Ataturk's modernization campaign. Suits, hats (rather than fezzes), permanent last names, and modern nationhood all fit together in Ataturk's scheme. Reze Shah, the father of the deposed Shah, ordered all Iranians to take the last name of their town of residence in order to rationalize the country's family names. Ali Akbar Rafsanjani thus means Ali Akbar from Rafsanjan. Although this system has the advantage of designating the homes of the generation that adopted it, it certainly doesn't clarify much locally in Rafsanjan. It may well be that the state is particularly concerned with monitoring those who are mobile or "out of place."

49. Dietary laws that all but preclude commensality are also powerful devices for social exclusion. If one were designating a set of cultural rules in order to wall off a group from surrounding groups, making sure its members cannot easily speak to or eat with others is a splendid beginning.

50. This is true despite the fact, as Benedict Anderson insightfully points out, that the "national past" is so often fitted with a bogus pedigree.

51. Eugen Weber, *Peasants into Frenchmen: The Modernization of Rural France, 1870–1914* (Stanford: Stanford University Press, 1976), chap. 6. Weber points out that in the last twenty-five years of the nineteenth century, fully half of the Frenchmen reaching adulthood had a native tongue other than French. See Peter Sahlins's remarkable book *Boundaries: The Making of France and Spain in the Pyrenees* (Berkeley: University of California Press, 1989) for a discussion of French language policy at its periphery. Although administrative official languages have a lineage that goes back to at least the sixteenth century, the imposition of a national language in other spheres comes in the mid-nineteenth century at the earliest.

52. For an illuminating analytical account of this process, see Abram de Swaan, *In Care of the State* (Oxford: Polity Press, 1988), especially chap. 3, "The Elementary Curriculum as a National Communication Code," pp. 52–117.

53. Ibid., p. 197.

54. For a careful depiction of the geography of standard market areas, see G. William Skinner, *Marketing and Social Structure in Rural China* (Tucson: Association of Asian Studies, 1975).

55. Much of the following material on the centralization of transport in France comes from the fine survey by Cecil O. Smith, Jr., "The Longest Run: Public Engineers and Planning in France," *American Historical Review* 95, no. 3 (June 1990): 657–92. See also the excellent discussion and comparison of the Corps des Ponts et des Chaussées with the US Army Corps of Engineers in Theodore Porter, *Trust in Numbers: The Pursuit of Objectivity in Science and Public Life* (Princeton: Princeton University Press, 1995), chap. 6.

56. Weber, *Peasants into Frenchmen,* p. 195.

57. Smith, "The Longest Run," pp. 685–71. Smith claims that the Legrand Star meant that many reservists being mustered for World War I had to funnel through Paris, whereas, under a more decentralized rail plan, there would have been far more direct routes to the front: "Some reservists in Strasbourg [were] journeying via the capital to don their uniforms in Bordeaux before returning to fight in Alsace." General Von Möltke observed that he had six different rail lines for moving troops from the North German Confederation to the war zone between the Moselle and the Rhine, while French troops coming to the front had to detrain

at Strasbourg or Metz, with the Vosges mountains in between. Finally, and perhaps most important, once Paris was surrounded, the Legrand Star was left headless. After the war, the high command insisted on building more transverse lines to correct the deficiency.

58. See Ian Hacking, *The Emergence of Probability: A Philosophical Study of Early Ideas About Probability, Induction, and Statistical Inference* (Cambridge: Cambridge University Press, 1975).

59. I am extraordinarily grateful to the City Museum of Amsterdam for staging the fine and unsparing exhibition "Hunger-winter and Liberation in Amsterdam" and the accompanying catalogue, *Here, back when …* (Amsterdam: City Museum, 1995).

60. *Here, back when …*, p. 10.

61. Since, as we know best from the case of Anne Frank, a good many citizens were willing to hide Jews in the city and the countryside, deportation as a systematic administrative exercise eventually failed. As the Jewish population became increasingly opaque to the authorities, they were increasingly forced to rely on Dutch collaborators who became their local trackers.

62. Even when these facts appear dynamic, they are usually the result of multiple static observations through time that, through a "connect the dots" process, give the appearance of continuous movement. In fact, what actually happened between, say, observation A and observation B remains a mystery, which is glossed over by the convention of merely drawing a straight line between the two data points.

63. This is the way that Benedict Anderson puts it in *Imagined Communities,* p. 169.

64. I am grateful to Larry Lohmann for insisting to me that officials are not necessarily any more abstract or narrow of vision in their representation of reality than laypeople are. Rather, the facts that they need are facts that serve the interests and practices of their institutional roles. He would have preferred, I think, that I drop the term "simplification" altogether, but I have resisted.

65. There are at least three problems here. The first is the hegemony of the categories. How does one classify someone who usually works for relatives, who may sometimes feed him, let him use some of their land as his own, or pay him in crops or cash? The sometimes quite arbitrary decisions about how to classify such cases are obscured by the final result, in which only the prevailing categories appear. Theodore Porter notes that officials in France's Office of National Statistics report that even trained coders will code up to 20 percent of occupational categories differently (*Trust in Numbers,* p. 41). The goal of the statistical office is to ensure the maximum reliability among coders, even if the conventions applied to achieve it sacrifice something of the true state of affairs. The second problem, to which we shall return later, is how the categories and, more particularly, the state power behind the categories shape the data. For example, during the recession in the United States in the 1970s, there was some concern that the official unemployment rate, which had reached 13 percent, was exaggerated. A major reason, it was claimed, was that many nominally unemployed were working "off the books" in the informal economy and were not reporting their income or employment for fear of being taxed. One could say then and today that the fiscal system had provoked an off-stage reality that was designed to stay out of the data bank. The third problem is that those who collect and assemble the information may have special interests in what the data show. During the Vietnam War the importance of body counts and pacified villages as a measure of counterinsurgency

success led commanders to produce inflated figures that pleased their superiors—in the short run—but increasingly bore little relation to the facts on the ground.

66. The goal is to get rid of intersubjective variability on the part of the census takers or coders. And that requires standard, mechanical procedures that leave no room for personal judgment. See Porter, *Trust in Numbers,* p. 29.

67. Charles Tilly, *Coercion, Capital, and European States,* A.D. *990–1992* (Oxford: Blackwell, 1990), p. 100.

68. Indicative of this tendency in scientific forestry is the substantial literature on "optimum control theory," which is imported from management science. For an application and bibliography, see D. M. Donnelly and D. R. Betters, "Optimum Control for Scheduling Final Harvest in Even-Aged Forest Stands," *Forest Ecology and Management* 46 (1991): 135–49.

69. The caricature is not so far-fetched that it does not capture the lyrical utopianism of early advocates of state sciences. I quote the father of Prussian statistics, Ernst Engel: "In order to obtain an accurate representation, statistical research accompanies the individual through his entire earthly existence. It takes account of his birth, his baptism, his vaccination, his schooling and the success thereof, his diligence, his leave of school, his subsequent education and development, and, once he becomes a man, his physique and his ability to bear arms. It also accompanies the subsequent steps of his walk through life; it takes note of his chosen occupation, where he sets up his household and his management of the same, if he saved from the abundances of his youth for his old age, if and when and at what age he marries and whom he chooses as his wife—statistics look after him when things go well for him and when they go awry. Should he suffer shipwreck in his life, undergo material, moral, or spiritual ruin, statistics take note of the same. Statistics leave a man only after his death—after it has ascertained the precise age of his death and noted the causes that brought about his end" (quoted in Ian Hacking, *The Taming of Chance* [Cambridge: Cambridge University Press, 1990], p. 34). One could hardly ask for a more complete list of early nineteenth-century state interests and the paper trail that it generated.

70. Tilly, echoing the colonial theme, describes much of this process within the European nation-state as the replacement of indirect rule with direct rule (*Coercion, Capital, and European States,* pp. 103–26).

71. This process is best described by Benedict Anderson: "Guided by its [the colonial state's] imagined map, it organized the new educational, juridical, public-health, police and immigration bureaucracies it was building on the principle of ethnoracial hierarchies which were, however, always understood in terms of parallel series. The flow of subject populations through the mesh of differential schools, courts, clinics, police stations and immigration offices created 'traffic-habits' which in time gave real social life to the state's earlier fantasies" (*Imagined Communities,* p. 169). A related argument about the cultural dimension of state-building in England can be found in Philip Corrigan and Derek Sayer, *The Great Arch: English State Formation as Cultural Revolution* (Oxford: Blackwell, 1991).

Understanding Inner-City Poverty

Resistance and Self-Destruction under U.S. Apartheid

BY PHILIPPE BOURGOIS

I did not run fast enough out the door of the video arcade crackhouse to avoid hearing the lookout's baseball bat thud twice against a customer's skull. I had misjudged the harsh words Caesar, the lookout, had been exchanging with a drug-intoxicated customer to be the aggressive but ultimately playful posturing that is characteristic of much male interaction on the street. Pausing on the curb in front of the crackhouse, I tried to decide from the continued sound of scuffling inside whether or not I should call for medical emergency. Reassured when I saw the beaten young man crawl out the door amidst a parting barrage of kicks and howling laughter, I walked two doors down the block to my tenement where I was living at the time in the primarily Puerto Rican neighborhood of East Harlem, New York. Confused by my impotence in the face of the violence of my crack dealer friends, I ended my fieldwork early that night and tried to recover from my own anger and rushing adrenaline by rocking my newborn son to sleep. My baby's appreciative gurgles, however, did not erase from the back of my mind the sound of Caesar's baseball bat thudding on the drug addict's skull.

The following evening, I forced myself to return to the crackhouse where I was spending much of my time conducting research on inner-city poverty and social marginalization (figure 13–1). I rebuked Caesar for his "overreaction" to the obnoxious customer the night before. Caesar was only too pleased to engage me in a playful argument. Half way through our verbal jousting, he grabbed my tape recorder out of my shirt pocket, turned it on, and spoke directly into the microphone. He

Figure 13–1. The Game Room video arcade and crackhouse. (Photo by author)

wanted to make sure I had a clear record of his riposte so that it could be included as a direct quote in the book on street culture and the underground economy that I was writing at the time:

Nah, Felipe, you just don't understand. It's not good to be too sweet sometimes to people, man, because they're just gonna take advantage of you.

That dude was talking shit for a long time, about how we weak; how he control the block; and how he can do whatever he wants.

I mean, we were trying to take it calm like, until he starts talkin' this'n'that, about how he gonna drop a dime on us [report us to the police].

That's when I grabbed the bat—I looked at the axe that we keep behind the Pac-Man but then I said, "No; I want something that's going to be short and compact. I only gotta swing a short distance to clock him.

[Now shouting out the video arcade doorway for everyone outside to hear] You don't control nothin', because we rocked your bootie. Ha! Ha! Ha!

[Turning back to me] That was right when you ran out the door, Felipe. You missed it. I had gotten wild.

You see, Felipe, you can't be allowing people to push you around in this neighborhood, or else you get that reputation, like: "That homeboy's soft."

Primo, the manager of the crackhouse, further confirmed Caesar's story and raised the credibility of his violent persona by noting with a chuckle that he had only barely managed to subdue Caesar after the second blow of the baseball bat to keep Caesar from killing the offending customer while he lay semiconscious on the floor.

THE LOGIC OF VIOLENCE IN STREET CULTURE

Most readers might interpret Caesar's behavior and public rantings and ravings to be those of a dysfunctionally antisocial psychopath. In the context of the underground economy, however, Caesar's braggadocio and celebration of violence are good public relations. Periodic public displays of aggression are crucial to his professional credibility. They ensure his long-term job security. When Caesar shouted his violent story out the door of the crackhouse for everyone in the vicinity to hear, he was not bragging idly or dangerously; on the contrary, he was advertising his effectiveness as a lookout, and confirming his capacity for maintaining order at his work site. Another side benefit that Caesar derives from his inability to control his underlying rages is a lifelong monthly Social Security Insurance check for being—as he puts it—"a certified nut case." He periodically reconfirms his emotional disability by occasional suicide attempts.

In short, at age nineteen, Caesar's brutality has allowed him to mature into an effective career as crackhouse lookout. Aside from providing him with what he considers to be a decent income, it also allows him on a personal and emotional level to overcome the terrified vulnerability he endured growing up in East Harlem. Born to a sixteen-year-old heroin addict, he was raised by a grandmother who beat him regularly, but whom he loved dearly. Sent to reform school for striking a teacher with a chair, Caesar admitted,

> I used to cry every day; be a big sucker. I was thinking suicide. I missed my moms. I mean 'buela [Granma]—you've met her.
>
> Plus I was a little kid back then—like about twelve or thirteen—and I'd get *beat* down by other kids and shit. I was getting my ass kicked. I used to get hurt.
>
> It was a nasty reform school. I used to see the counselors holding down the kids naked outside in the snow.

Being smart and precocious, Caesar soon adapted to the institutionalized violence of his school and developed the skills that eventually allowed him to excel in the underground economy:

> So then, I just learned. I used to fight so wild that they wouldn't bother me for awhile. I would go real crazy! Real crazy, every time I would fight. Like I would pick up a chair or a pencil or something and really mess them up. So they'd thought I was wild and real crazy.
>
> I mean, I always got into fights. Even if I lost, I always started fights. That let me relax more, because after that nobody messed with me.

ANTHROPOLOGICAL APPROACHES TO POVERTY AND THE INNER CITY

Caesar and his immediate supervisor, Primo, were merely two members out of a network of some twenty-five Puerto Rican retail crack sellers whom I befriended in the more than four years that I lived and worked in East Harlem at the height of what politicians and the media called "the crack epidemic," extending roughly from 1985 to 1991. As a cultural anthropologist engaged in the research methodology of "participant-observation fieldwork," or "ethnography," I can only collect "accurate data" by violating the canons of traditional, positivist research. We anthropologists have to become intimately involved with the people we study, striving to establish long-term, respectful, and usually mutually empathetic relationships. We attempt to suspend our value judgments in order to immerse ourselves in the common sense of the people we live with.

Researchers who are not cultural anthropologists have a hard time believing that useful, reliable data can be generated from the small samples of people that we study using participant-observation, qualitative methods. This is because quantitative-oriented researchers who collect data via surveys or by consulting published censuses do not understand the intensity of the relationship one must develop with each individual in one's sample in order to obtain information that addresses the cultural contexts and processual dynamics of social networks in holistic contexts. Anthropologists do not correlate discrete statistical variables; rather, they explain (or evoke) the reasons (or accidents) for why and how social relations unfold within their indigenous (and global) contexts. Ideally, anthropologists develop an organic relationship to a social setting where their presence only minimally distorts indigenous social interaction. We must seek out a legitimate social role within the social scene we are studying in order to develop friendships (and sometimes enmities) that allow us (with informed consent) to observe behavior directly in as unobtrusive a manner as possible. A major task of participant-observers is to put themselves "in the shoes" of the people they study in order to "see local realities" through "local eyes." Obviously, on an absolute level, such an achievement is impossible and possibly even dangerous, as it implies a power imbalance. Indeed, the premise that the "essence" of a group of people or a culture can be understood and described by an outsider and translated into academic analytic categories can lead to stereotyping. Postmodernists have criticized ethnography as being predicated on a totalizing modernist fantasy that is ultimately oppressive. Anthropologists risk imposing ethnocentric, power-laden, analytic categories and exotifying images onto the unsuspecting people they study in the name of an arrogantly assumed ethnographic academic authority. To avoid imposing in the name of science images that "other" the people they study, ethnographers need to be self-reflexively critical and to recognize that no single, simple reality or essence of a culture necessarily exists. Cultures and social processes are inevitably both more—but also less—than what can be captured in one outsider's attempt to reduce them into a coherent ethnographic monograph or article. Nevertheless, for the sake of defining participant-observation in a meaningful way, suffice it to say that cultural anthropologists, for all the problems that cross-cultural reportage implies, try to get as close as possible to local, everyday worlds without disrupting and judging them. The overall goal is to obtain a holistic perspective on the internal logics of and external constraints on the way processes unfold while at the same time recognizing humbly that cultures and social meanings are fragmented and multiplicitous.

In the case of my work with crack dealers in East Harlem, before even being able to initiate my research formally, I had to confront the overwhelming reality of racial- and class-based segregation in urban America. Initially, it felt as if my white skin signaled the terminal stage of a contagious disease sowing havoc in its path. Busy street comers emptied amidst a hail of whistles whenever I walked by as nervous drug dealers scattered in front of me, certain that I was an undercover narcotics agent. Conversely, the police made it clear to me that I was violating unconscious apartheid laws by throwing me spread-eagled against building walls to search me for weapons and drugs when they encountered me on their patrols. From their perspective, the only reason for a "white boy" to be in the neighborhood after dark is to buy drugs. As a matter of fact, the first time the police stopped me, I naively tried to explain to them in a polite voice that I was an anthropologist studying social marginalization. Convinced I was making fun of them, they showered me with a litany of curses and threats. They then escorted me to the nearest bus stop and ordered me to leave East Harlem, "and go buy your drugs in a white neighborhood ya' dirty mother . . ."

It was only through my long-term physical presence, residing in the neighborhood, and my polite perseverance on the street that I was able to overcome these racial and class boundaries and eventually earn the respect and full cooperation of the dealers operating on my block. It helped when they saw me getting married and having a baby. By the time my son was old enough to be baptized in the local church, I was close enough to several of the dealers to invite them to the party at my mother's apartment downtown.

In contrast, I was never able to communicate effectively with the police. I learned, however, always to carry a "picture I.D." showing my correct local address, and I always forced myself to stare at the ground politely and mumble effusive "yes sirs" in a white, working-class, New York accent whenever they stopped me. Unlike most of the crack dealers I spent time with, I was never beaten or arrested— only occasionally threatened and sometimes politely queried and advised to "find a cheap apartment in Queens instead."

I am convinced that it is only by painstakingly violating urban apartheid that I was able to collect meaningful data on inner-city poverty. Methodologically, it is only by establishing lasting relationships based on mutual respect that one can begin to ask provocative personal questions and expect to engage in substantive conversations about the complex experience of extreme social marginalization in the United States. Perhaps, this is why the experience of poverty and social marginalization is so poorly understood. The traditional, quantitative-oriented survey methodologies of upper-middle-class sociologists or criminologists tend to collect fabrications. Few people on the margins of society trust outsiders when they ask invasive personal questions, especially concerning money, drags, and alcohol. In fact, nobody—whether rich or poor—likes to answer such indiscrete, incriminating queries.

Historically, inner-city poverty research has been more successful at reflecting the biases of an investigator's society than at analyzing the experience of poverty or documenting race and class apartheid. The state of poverty and social marginalization research in any given country emerges almost as a litmus for gauging contemporary social attitudes towards inequality and social welfare. This is particularly true in the United States, where discussions of poverty almost immediately become polarized around moralistic value judgments about individual self-worth, and frequently degenerate into stereotyped conceptions of race. In the final analysis, most people in the United States—rich and poor alike—believe in the Horatio Alger myth of going from rags to riches. They are also intensely moralistic about issues of wealth; perhaps this stems from their Puritanical/Calvinist heritage. Even progressive leftist academics in the United States secretly worry that the poor may actually deserve their fate. As a result they often feel compelled to portray the inner city in an artificially positive manner that is not only unrealistic but is also theoretically and analytically flawed.

This ideological context for inner-city poverty research in the United States is probably best epitomized by the best-selling books of the anthropologist Oscar Lewis in the 1960s. He collected thousands of pages of life-history interviews with an extended family of Puerto Ricans who migrated to East Harlem and the South Bronx in search of employment. Some thirty years later, his culture of poverty theory remains at the center of contemporary polemics around the inner city in the United States. Despite his being a social democrat in favor of expanding government poverty programs, his theoretical analysis offers a psychological reductionist—almost blame-the-victim—explanation for the transgenerational persistence of poverty. On some level it sounded the death knell for the Great Society dreams of the Johnson administration and helped disabuse the dream of the early 1960s that poverty in America could be eradicated. If anything, thirty years later, his theory resonated more than ever with the campaigns for individual responsibility and family values that were so celebrated by politicians in U.S. national elections during the 1990s. In a 1966 *Scientific American* article, Lewis wrote,

> By the time slum children are six or seven, they have usually absorbed the basic attitudes and values of their subculture. Thereafter they are psychologically unready to take full advantage of changing conditions or improving opportunities that may develop in their lifetime....
> It is much more difficult to undo the culture of poverty than to cure poverty itself.

In their anger and frustration over the way Lewis's family-based and Freudian-influenced focus on impoverished Puerto Rican immigrants confirms conservative American biases, liberal social scientists have often fallen into the trap of glorifying the poor and denying any empirical evidence of personal self-destruction. When I moved into the same inner-city neighborhood where the Puerto Rican families that Lewis studied had lived more than thirty years ago, I was determined to avoid his failure to examine structural inequality, while at the same time documenting the way oppression is painfully internalized in the day-to-day life of the persistently poor. Striving to develop a political economy perspective that takes culture and gender seriously, and which also recognizes the link between individual actions and social/structural determination, I focused on how an oppositional street culture of resistance to exploitation and social marginalization is contradictorily self-destructive to its participants. In fact, street dealers, addicts, and criminals become the local agents administering the destruction of their surrounding community.

THE DOLLARS AND SENSE OF DRUGS

Given the extraordinary economic importance of illicit drugs and the destructive impact they have on people's lives, inner-city researchers have to address the issue of substance abuse and the role of drugs in the underground economy. The easiest dimension of drug dealing for outsiders to understand is its economic logic. On a worldwide scale, illegal drugs have become an immense, multibillion-dollar business. Tragically, in the United States during the 1980s and through the 1990s, the crack/cocaine and heroin industries have been the only dynamically growing, equal-opportunity employers for inner-city men. For example, the street in front of my tenement was not atypical and within a two-block radius I could obtain heroin, crack, powder cocaine, hypodermic needles, methadone, valium, angel dust (an animal tranquilizer), marijuana, mescaline, bootleg alcohol, and tobacco. Within one hundred yards of my stoop there were three competing crackhouses selling vials at two, three, and five dollars. Two additional retail outfits sold powder cocaine in ten- and twenty-dollar plastic-sealed packages, patented with a neatly carved, rubber stamp logo. Immediately above the particular crackhouse camouflaged as a video arcade where I spent most of my time, two legally registered doctors administered a "pill mill," writing several dozen prescriptions for opiates, stimulants, and sedatives every day. This added up to several millions of dollars worth of drugs per year. In the projects opposite my tenement, the New York City Housing Authority Police arrested a fifty-five-year-old mother and her twenty-two-year-old daughter while they were "bagging" twenty-one pounds of cocaine into ten-dollar, quarter-gram "jumbo" vials of adulterated product worth approximately one million dollars on the street. The police found twenty-five thousand dollars in small-denomination bills in this same apartment.

In other words, many millions of dollars worth of business takes place within a stone's throw of the youths growing up in East Harlem tenements and housing projects. Drug dealing in the underground economy offers youths—primarily males—a career with real possibilities of upward mobility. Like most other people in the United States, drug dealers are merely scrambling to obtain their "piece of the pie" as fast as possible. In feet, in their pursuit of success they are following the minute details of the classical Yankee model for upward mobility: up-by-the-bootstraps via private entrepreneurship. Perversely, they are the ultimate rugged individualists braving an unpredictable frontier where fortune, fame, and destruction are all just around the comer—and where competitors are ruthlessly hunted down and shot.

Despite the obvious economic incentives, most of East Harlem's residents shun drugs and work nine-to-five plus overtime at legal jobs. The problem, however, is that this law-abiding majority has lost control of public space. They have been pushed onto the defensive, living in fear, or even in contempt, of their neighborhood. Worried mothers and fathers are forced to maintain children double-locked behind apartment doors in determined attempts to keep street culture out. Their primary goal is to save up enough money to move to a safe, working-class neighborhood.

The drug dealers in this book, consequently, represent only a small minority of East Harlem's population, but they have managed to set the tone for public life. They force local residents, especially women and the elderly, to live in fear of being assaulted or mugged. Most important, on a daily basis, the street-level drug dealers offer a persuasive, even if violent and self-destructive, alternative lifestyle—what I call street culture—to the youths growing up around them. The drug economy is the material base for street culture, and its expansion during the 1980s and 1990s unconsciously rendered street culture even more appealing and fashionable.

On a subtler level, street culture is more than economic desperation or greediness; it is also a search for dignity and a refusal to accept the marginalization that mainstream society imposes on children who grow up in the inner city. As noted earlier, it can be understood as a culture of resistance—or at least of opposition—to economic exploitation and cultural denigration. Concretely, this takes the form of refusing low wages and poor working conditions, and of celebrating marginalization as a badge of pride—even if it is ultimately self-destructive.

Once again, an argument with Caesar clearly illustrates this dynamic. In this particular confrontation, Caesar was responding to the chiding of a legally employed, undocumented, new-immigrant Mexican who was sitting on a stoop near the crackhouse accusing Puerto Ricans of being lazy. Caesar replied,

Figure 13–2. Vacant lot next to the tenement where the author lived. (Photo by author)

That's right my man! We is real vermin lunatics that sell drugs. We don't wanna be a part of society. What do we wanna be working for? Puerto Ricans don't like to work. Okay, maybe not all of us, 'cause there's still a lot of strict folks from the old school that still be working. But the new generation, no way!

We have no regard for nothing. The new generation has no regard for the public. We wanna make easy money, and that's it. *Easy* now mind you. We don't wanna work hard. That's the new generation for you.

Now the old school was for when we was younger, and we used to break our asses. I had all kinds of stupid jobs … scrap metal sorting, dry cleaning, advertising agencies.

But not no more [putting his arm around Primo]. Now we're in a rebellious stage. We rather evade taxes; make quick money; and just survive. But we're not satisfied with that either, ha!

Figure 13–3. Abandoned tenement repopulated by its former superintendent with stuffed animals. (Photo by author)

HISTORY AND POLITICAL ECONOMY

Caesar's words need to be placed in their historical and structural context lest they serve to confirm racist stereotypes and psychological-reductionist explanations for violence, substance abuse, and ultimately for poverty itself. Indeed, that is one of the weaknesses of ethnographic accounts; they risk becoming voyeuristic constructions of a dehumanized, sensationalized "exotic" other in a political and economic vacuum. Upon closer examination, one can discern that Caesar's celebration of unemployment, crime, and substance abuse is integrally related to labor market forces, historical developments, and even international political confrontations that are well beyond his control.

Most fundamentally, the unfortunate strategic geopolitical location of the island of Puerto Rico in the Caribbean has always made it a military prize for world superpowers, resulting in a particularly distorted legacy of economic and political development. This was as true under Spanish colonialism as it is under the contemporary United States-sponsored political control of the territory. An artifice of the Cold War to check the influence of neighboring Cuba, Puerto Rico continues to bear the ambiguous status of "Free Associated Commonwealth." Puerto Ricans who remain on their native island are forbidden from voting in Federal elections, despite being subject to U.S. military selective service. Soon after the U.S. marines invaded the island in 1898, the economy was taken over by U.S. agro-export corporations and Puerto Rico was subjected to one of the most rapid and dislocating economic transformations that any Third World nation has ever undergone in modern history. To add insult to injury in the post-World War II decades, in an attempt to upstage the Cuban state-run socialist experiment, the United States dubbed Puerto Rico's development strategy "Operation Bootstrap" and declared it to be a magnificent success of free market investment incentives. Perhaps the best index of the human failure of Puerto Rico's economic model, however, is provided by the fact that between a third and half of the island's population have been forced to leave their native island to seek work and sustenance abroad since the late 1940s. More Puerto Ricans live outside Puerto Rico today than inside. Like all new immigrants arriving in the United States throughout history, Puerto Ricans have been confronted by racism and cultural humiliation. This is exacerbated by the phenotypical fact that, unlike the Irish, the Jews, and the Italians who arrived in New York City before them, most Puerto Ricans do not have white skin.

In other words, New York-born Puerto Ricans are the descendants of an uprooted people in the midst of a marathon sprint through economic history propelled by realpolitik forces rather than by humanitarian or even by any straightforward economic logic. In diverse permutations, over the past two or three generations their parents and grandparents went (1) from semisubsistence peasants on private hillside plots or local haciendas (2) to agricultural laborers on foreign -owned, capital-intensive agro-export tropical plantations, (3) to factory workers in export-platform shanty towns, (4) to sweat-shop workers in New York City ghetto tenements, (5) to service-sector employees in high-rise, inner-city housing projects. Over half of those who remained on the island are so impoverished today that they qualify for food stamps. Those who made it to New York City endure the highest family poverty rates of all ethnic groups in the nation, except for Native Americans.

FROM MANUFACTURING TO SERVICE AND THE CRACK ALTERNATIVE

The Puerto Rican experience in New York City has been further exacerbated by the fact that most Puerto Ricans arrived on the U.S. mainland in the post-World War II period in search of factory work precisely at the historical moment when those kinds of jobs were leaving U.S. metropolitan areas. Over the past three decades, multinational corporations have restructured the global economy by moving their factory production facilities overseas to countries with lower labor costs. The personal disruption of living through the structural transformation of New York's economy as an entry-level laborer was clearly articulated by the crack dealers in their life-history tape recordings. Almost all the crack dealers and addicts whom I interviewed over the years—especially the older ones—worked at one or more legal jobs in their early youth. In fact, most entered the labor market at a younger age than the typical middle-class American. This was the case for Primo, the manager of the video arcade crackhouse.

> I was like fourteen or fifteen playing hooky and pressing dresses and whatever they were making on the steamer. They was cheap, cheap clothes.
>
> My mother's sister was working there first, and then her son, my cousin Hector—the one who's in jail now—was the one they hired first, because his mother agreed: "If you don't want to go school, you gotta work."
>
> So I started hanging out with him. I wasn't planning on working in the factory. I was supposed to be in school; but it just sort of happened.

Teenage Primo's marginal factory moved out of East Harlem within a year of his employment there. He became merely one more of the half-million manufacturing workers in New York City to lose their livelihood almost overnight as factory employment dropped 50 percent from 1963 to 1983. Of course, instead of understanding himself as the victim of a structural transformation, Primo remembers with pleasure and even pride the extra income he earned for clearing the machines out of the factory space: "Them people had money, man. Because we helped them move out of the neighborhood. It took us two days—only me and my cousin, Hector. Wow! It was work. They gave us seventy bucks each."

Caesar, the crackhouse lookout, had a similar experience working as a high school dropout in a metal-plating, costume jewelry factory. At this stage in their lives, had Caesar and Primo not been confined to the weakest sector of manufacturing in a period of rapid job loss, their teenage working-class dream might have stabilized. Formerly, when most entry-level jobs were found in factories, the contradiction between an oppositional street culture and traditional, working-class, shop-floor culture—especially when it was protected by a union—was less pronounced. In the factory, being tough and violently macho is accepted behavior; a certain degree of opposition to management is expected and is considered masculine.

DISRESPECT AT WORK

Manufacturing jobs have been largely replaced by service-sector employment in New York's expanded, finance-driven economy. At the entry-level, the fastest growing niche for high school dropouts, or even college graduates, is office support work in the administrative headquarters of the multinational corporations that have moved their production plants overseas. The problem, of course, is that the oppositional street identity that is so effective and appealing in the burgeoning underground economy does not allow for the humble, obedient social interaction that professional office workers demand from their subordinates. A qualitative change has occurred in the tenor of social interaction in service-sector employment. Workers in a mail room or behind a photocopy machine cannot publicly maintain their cultural autonomy. Most concretely, they have no union; more subtly, there are few fellow workers surrounding them to insulate them and to provide them with a culturally based sense of class solidarity. Instead they are besieged by supervisors and bosses from an alien, hostile, and obviously dominant culture. When these office managers are not intimidated by street culture, they ridicule it.

Obedience to the norms of high-rise, office-corridor culture is interpreted as overwhelmingly humiliating by street culture standards—especially for males. On the street, the trauma of experiencing a threat to one's personal dignity has been frozen linguistically in the commonly used phrase "to diss," which is short for, "to disrespect." One does not have to dig deeply to obtain stories of deep humiliation due to the loss of personal and cultural autonomy experienced by the dealers in their previous bouts of service-sector employment. This was the case for Primo when he worked as a messenger for a trade publication magazine.

> When my boss be talking to people in the office, she would say, "He's illiterate," as if I was really that stupid that I couldn't understand what she was talking about, 'cause I'd be standing right there.
>
> So what I did one day was, I just looked up the word, "illiterate" in the dictionary, and I saw that she's saying to her associates that I'm stupid or something.
>
> I'm stupid! You know like [pointing to himself], "He doesn't know nothin.'"
>
> Well, I am illiterate anyway.

Although Primo resented being called illiterate, the most profound dimension of his humiliation was being obliged to look up in the dictionary the word used to insult him. In contrast, in the underground economy, he does not have to risk this kind of threat to his self-worth: "My boss, Papo [the crackhouse owner], he would never disrespect me that way. He wouldn't tell me that, because he's illiterate too."

When Primo attempted to show initiative and answer the telephone when his supervisors were busy, he was rebuked for scaring away customers with his Puerto Rican accent. Another crack dealer, Leroy, who operated his own independent sales point on a neighboring block (plate 2), had also been profoundly humiliated when he worked as a messenger because a white woman fled from him shrieking down the hallway of a high-rise office building. He had ridden in the elevator with the terrified woman and, coincidentally, had stepped off on the same floor with her to make a delivery. Worse yet, he had been trying to act as a debonair man at the time, allowing her to step off the elevator first.

> She went in the elevator first, but then she just waits there to see what floor I press. She's playing like she don't know what floor she wants to go to, because she wants to wait for me to press my floor. And I'm standing there and I forgot to press the button. I'm thinking about something else—don't know what was the matter with me. And she's thinking like, "He's not pressing the button; I guess he's following me!"

Leroy struggles to understand the terror that his dark skin inspires in white office workers. He confided this to me early in our relationship, and I noticed that, like most Americans, he becomes uncomfortable when talking across class and ethnic boundaries about race relations:

> It's happened before. I mean after awhile you become immune to it. Well, when it first happens, it like bugs you, "That's messed up; how they just judge you."
>
> But I understand a lot of them. How should I say it? A lot of white people ... [looking nervously at me] I mean Caucasian people [flustered, putting his hand gently on my shoulder]. If I say white, don't get offended, Felipe.
>
> But those other white people, they never even experienced Puerto Rican or black people. So automatically they think something wrong with you. Or you know, they think you out to rob them or something.
>
> It irks me; like, you know, it clicks my mind; makes me want to write a [rap] rhyme. I always write it down.

Of course, as a crack dealer, Leroy no longer has to confront these dimensions of class and racial humiliation.

POLARIZATION AROUND GENDER

In addition to their obvious racial conflict, service-sector confrontations also include a tense gender dynamic. Most of the supervisors at the lowest levels of the service sector are women, and street culture forbids males from accepting public subordination across gender lines. Typically, in their angrier memories of disrespect at work, many of the male crack dealers would refer to their female bosses in explicitly sexist language, often insulting their body parts, and dismissing them with street-slang, sexualized curses. They also specifically describe themselves and the other males around them at work as effeminate. Caesar was particularly incensed:

I lasted in the mail room for like eight months at this advertising agency that works with pharmaceutical stuff. They used to trust me.

But I had a prejudiced boss. She was a ho' [prostitute]. She was white. I had to take a lot of crap from that fat, ugly ho', and be a wimp.

I didn't like it, but I kept on working, because … [shrugging] you don't want to mess up the relationship. So you just be a punk.

Oh my God! I hated that head supervisor. That ho' was *really* nasty. She got her rocks off on firing people, man. You can see that on her face, boy. She made this one guy that worked with me cry—and beg for his job back.

This structural workplace confrontation that polarizes relations between young, inner-city men and white-collar, upwardly mobile women parallels another profound transformation in traditional gender power relations occurring within working-poor immigrant families. The loss of decently paid factory jobs that provide union family benefits for health and retirement makes it increasingly impossible for men to fulfill old-fashioned patriarchal dreams of being an omnipotent provider for a wife and several children. At the same time, dramatic increases in labor force participation among Puerto Rican women, as well as the broader cultural redefinitions of increased individual rights and autonomy for women occurring throughout all levels of U.S. society since the late 1960s, have thrown into crisis the traditional family model of the conjugal household dominated by an authoritarian man.

Males, however, are not accepting the new rights and roles that women have been earning over the past few decades; instead, they attempt to reassert violently their grandfather's lost autocratic control over their households and over public space. This is exacerbated in the inner-city Puerto Rican case by the persistence of a rural-based memory of large, male-dominated, farming households "blessed" with numerous children. Males who are no longer effective heads of households often experience the rapid structural transformations of their generation as a dramatic assault on their sense of masculine dignity. In the worst-case scenario, as males become impotent economic failures in the service economy, they lash out against the women and children they can no longer support economically or control ideologically. Concretely, this takes the form of fists in the face at home and gang rape in the crackhouse.

IN SEARCH OF SOLUTIONS

The crisis that has accompanied the complicated historical rearrangement of gender-power relations over the past few decades is glossed by political leaders into superficial slogans such as "the crisis in family values" or "Just say no to drugs." This kind of psychological-reductionist and blame-the-victim moralism obfuscates the structural inequalities around race, class, and gender that must be addressed if real improvements in the lives of the poor are to occur. Politicians and the media expect to find simple, quick-fix solutions to the persistent poverty that is increasingly concentrated in urban cores—whether it be in the teeming shantytowns of nonindustrial nations, the working-class public housing suburbs of European cities, or the postindustrial wastelands of U.S. inner-city neighborhoods.

Of all the industrialized nations, the United States is the most extreme with respect to income inequality and ethnic segregation. By the end of the twentieth century, only Russia and Rwanda imprisoned larger proportions of their populations than the United States. No other wealthy, industrialized country came close to having such a large proportion of its citizens living below the poverty line.

The inner city represents the United States' greatest domestic failing, hanging like a sword of Damocles over the larger society. The only force sustaining this precariously suspended sword is the fact that drug dealers, addicts, and street criminals internalize their rage and desperation. They direct their brutality against themselves and their immediate community rather than against their structural oppression.

If the United States were to serve as an international model for political and economic development at the dawn of the twentieth century it should be as a model for what not to imitate. The balance of structural economic power that penalizes and humiliates the working poor and pushes them into the underground economy serves few people's interests. The public policy response of building bigger and more expensive prisons is irrational from both an economic cost/benefit analysis and also a humanitarian perspective. Finally, the painful and prolonged self-destruction of people like Primo and Caesar and their families and loved ones is cruel and unnecessary.

There are no simple, technocratic formulas for implementing the public policies that might provide equitable access to shelter, employment, sustenance, and health. The first step out of the impasse requires a fundamental ethical and political reevaluation of basic socioeconomic models. Anthropologists, because of their participant-observation methods and their culturally relative sensibilities can play an important role in fostering a public debate over the human cost of poverty. The challenge is clearly in front of us. Do we have the intellectual and political energy to confront it both at home and abroad?

ACKNOWLEDGMENTS

I thank my neighbors, the crack dealers, and their families who invited me into their homes and lives in East Harlem. I changed everyone's name and camouflaged the street addresses to protect individual privacy. The article was written with support from the National Institute on Drug Abuse (grant R01-DA10164). I also want to thank the following institutions for their generous financial support while I conducted fieldwork in East Harlem: the Harry Frank Guggenheim Foundation, the Russell Sage Foundation, the Social Science Research Council, the Ford Foundation, the Wenner-Gren Foundation for Anthropological Research, the United States Bureau of the Census, and the National Institute on Drug Abuse (grant R03 DA06413-01). I thank Harold Otto for transcribing the tape recordings, Joelle Morrow for typing the article with me, and Ann Magruder for inputting the final edits. A preliminary version appeared in French in Actes de la recherche en sciences sociales 94 (1992): 59–78.

SUGGESTIONS FOR FURTHER READING

Anderson, Elijah. 1978. *Place on the Corner.* Chicago: University of Chicago Press.

Bourgois, Philippe. 1998. "The Moral Economies of Homeless Heroin Addicts: Confronting Ethnography, HIV Risk, and Everyday Violence in San Francisco Shooting Encampments." *Substance Use and Misuse* 33, no. 11:2323–51.

_____. 1995. *In Search of Respect: Selling Crack in El Barrio.* New York: Cambridge University Press.

Connolly, Deborah. 2000. *Homeless Mothers: Face to Face with Women and Poverty.* Minneapolis: University of Minnesota Press.

Davis, Mike. 1990. *City of Quartz: Excavating the Future in Los Angeles.* London, New York: Verso.

Dehavenon, Anna Lou. 1994. "Monitoring Emergency Shelter for Homeless Families in New York City." *Practicing Anthropology.* 16, no. 4: 12–16.

Devine, John. 1996. *Maximum Security: The Culture of Violence in Inner-City Schools.* Chicago: University of Chicago Press.

Hamid, Ansley. 1990. "The Political Economy of Crack-Related Violence." *Contemporary Drug Problems* 17, no. 1: 31–79.

Katz, Michael. 1995. *Improving Poor People: The Welfare State, the "Underclass," and Urban Schools as History.* Princeton, NJ: Princeton University Press.

Leacock, Eleanor Burke, ed. 1971. *The Culture of Poverty: A Critique.* New York: Simon and Schuster.

Lewis, Oscar. 1966. *La Vida: A Puerto Rican Family in the Culture of Poverty—San Juan and New York.* New York: Random House.

Liebow, Elliot. 1993. *Tell Them Who I Am: The Lives of Homeless Women.* New York: Penguin Books.

Macleod, Jay. 1995 [1987]. *Ain't No Makin' It: Aspirations and Attainment in a Low-Income Neighborhood.* Boulder, CO: Westview Press.

Rigdon, Susan M. 1988. *The Culture Facade: Art., Science, and Politics in the Work of Oscar Lewis.* Urbana: University of Illinois Press.

Rodriguez, Clara. 1989. *Puerto Ricans: Born in the USA.* Boston: Unwin Hyman.

Sassen, Saskia. 1991. *The Global City: New York, London, Tokyo.* Princeton, NJ: Princeton University Press.

Scheper-Hughes, Nancy. 1992. *Death without Weeping: the Violence of Everyday Life in Brazil.* Berkeley: University of California Press.

Steinberg, Stephen. 1981. "The Culture of Poverty Reconsidered." In *The Ethnic Myth: Race, Ethnicity, and Class in America,* 106–28. New York: Atheneum.

Tonry, Michael. 1995. *Malign Neglect: Race, Crime, and Punishment in America.* New York: Oxford University Press.

Wacquant, Loïc. 1997. "Three Pernicious Premises in the Study of the American Ghetto." *International Journal of Urban and Regional Research.* 21, no. 2: 341.

Waterston, Alisse. 1993. *Street Addicts in the Political Economy.* Philadelphia: Temple University Press.

Williams, Terry. 1992. *The Crackhouse: Notes from the End of the Line.* Reading, MA: Addison-Wesley.

Willis, Paul. 1981. *Learning to Labor: How Working Class Kids Get Working Class Jobs.* New York: Columbia University Press.

Wilson, William Julius. 1996. *When the Work Disappears: the World of the New Urban Poor.* New York: Knopf.

Wojcicka Scharff, Jagna. 1998. *King Kong on Fourth Street: Families and the Violence of Poverty on the Lower East Side.* Boulder, CO: Westview Press.

Post-Soviet Body Politics
Crime and Punishment in the Pussy Riot Affair

BY ANYA BERNSTEIN

O n the crisp morning of February 21, 2012, five young women walked into the Moscow's Cathedral of Christ the Savior. Situated in the heart of the Russian capital, the cathedral is one of the tallest Orthodox churches in the world. Wearing a blaze of color in sleeveless dresses, neon tights, and their signature balaclava ski masks, they jumped on the altar, turned their backs to the lavish icon screen, took out their electric guitars, and began a song that was a mix of punk-rock riffs and traditional Orthodox chant. The lyrics criticized the close relations between the Russian Patriarch Kirill and President Putin, the Orthodox Church's conservative anti-woman and anti-LGBT rhetoric, while the refrain—styled as a traditional Orthodox prayer chant—addressed the Mother of God directly, pleading her to "oust Putin" and "become a feminist." The women were apprehended by security before they could finish—a key moment in the trial that would follow, when a judge determined that it mattered very much just which of their lyrics were leashed upon confused onlookers. Following their initial release from the church, they mixed a video of their performance with a more elaborately scored soundtrack and scenes recorded elsewhere days earlier, and released their work on YouTube. Less than two weeks later three members of the group were arrested, and a long trial commenced that would make this "punk prayer" world famous.[1] The members of the all-female collective known as Pussy Riot were eventually found guilty on charges of "hooliganism motivated by religious hatred" and received two-year prison sentences in distant, all-female Russian labor camps.

While global press coverage was quick to describe the conflict in classic terms: believers against atheists, nationalists against internationalists, or the liberal intelligentsia against the conservative *narod* (people), local debates presented a far more complicated picture. Although most Pussy Riot supporters indeed generally belonged to the intelligentsia, even the most staunch defenders made sure to clarify that they separated the act itself from the state's response to it. Although the frequent consensus among the band's supporters was that the performance venue was a decidedly poor choice, most very much disagreed that such offences should be punishable with a prison sentence. As the trial progressed, there eventually appeared within Russia a vocal opposition to Pussy Riot's imprisonment; however, a large part of the population was still clearly hostile to the women, with many demanding even harsher punishment, calling for the maximum seven-year prison sentence. Still others, while hostile to the group, did not think Pussy Riot should serve a prison sentence at all, invoking, instead, a radically *different* kind of punishment.

Strikingly, the Pussy Riot affair provoked unprecedented debates over the usefulness and varied meanings of *corporal* punishment in Russia, from flogging and birching, to even tarring and feathering. As time passed, the narratives around the trial increasingly came to focus specifically on the three convicted female bodies. These bodies first appeared to the public as anonymous and hidden behind their colorful balaklavas. They later came unmasked, only to be hidden again, this time behind iron bars and inside the glass cage where Russian courts keep defendants during hearings.

What these bodies thematized and made increasingly visible to contemporary Russians and their observers around the world was the spectacular violence of sovereign power. Indeed, many Russians interpreted these young women as a threat to the very core of the Russian state and especially its recently elaborated doctrine of "sovereign democracy." Drawing on the scholarship on sovereignty and the body—with an added attention to notions of gender at work in "the political"—I argue that under conditions of postsocialist transformation in Russia, the bodies of the Pussy Riot participants became vital sites for the enactment of sovereignty for a wide range of citizens.[2] These three female bodies, which became increasingly vulnerable during the trial and subsequent imprisonment but at the same time stunned the audiences by their stubborn vitality, were remarkably multivalent. For some, their punishment ratified and strengthened the legitimacy of the Russian polity, while for others it revealed both the brutality and ultimate impotence of the Russian state. What united these diverse perspectives, and what invites us to reflect here on their consequences for contemporary sovereignty in Russia, was an implicit narrative of sacrifice—the legitimacy and desirability of which is still hotly debated—through which sovereign violence inscribed itself upon Pussy Riot's bodies.

THE BODIES OF THE CONDEMNED

In the days immediately following the performance in the cathedral and before the arrest of the two women,[3] the punk-prayer was a subject of discussion among diverse if sometimes otherwise arcane Moscow circles, including members of the arts world, select Orthodox clergy, grassroots Orthodox and nationalist groups, and the radical feminist community. These particular publics were created and brought in virtual dialogue by the series of conflicts between contemporary artists and the Orthodox Church that have been going on since the late 1990s, when the first post-Soviet art trial found a well-known Moscow conceptual artist guilty of "inciting religious hatred." The case became notorious as the first post-Soviet "blasphemy trial," a stunning reversal of course in a country where militant blasphemy against religion was something that was close to official ideology for most of the twentieth century.[4]

In the case of Pussy Riot, a surprisingly unanimous negative reaction ensued from all of the above communities, albeit for largely diverse reasons. The celebrated gallery owner and art critic Marat Guelman, who previously supported artists condemned by the Orthodox Church, wrote that the punk-prayer was offensive and inappropriate, as it was done in a "sacred" space, as opposed to the "profane" space of a gallery.[5] Indeed, all of the artists previously condemned by the church had performed in galleries and museums. The feminist community took issue with one member of Pussy Riot, Nadezhda (Nadya) Tolokonnikova, who as part of another well-known radical art-collective, Voina, had participated in a notorious stunt titled, "Kiss the Cop," whereby members of the collective forcefully kissed policewomen on the street. Some feminists viewed this controversial performance as constituting violence against women.[6] One of the most unexpected responses, however, came from a religious intellectual, a senior deacon Andrei Kuraev, who wrote the following on his blog on the day of the Pussy Riot performance:

I would offer them some *bliny* (traditional Russian thin pancakes), pour them a cup of honey wine, and invite them to come back for the forgiveness ceremony. And if I were a layman elder, I would also give them a fatherly pinch… To bring them back to their senses…. And it's *Maslenitsa* time (the week before Lent in the Orthodox calendar, similar to Mardi Gras): the time for the social cosmos to turn upside down.[7]

While this turned out to be by far the most benevolent response by a senior Orthodox leader, his seemingly playful message strategically depoliticized Pussy Riot's performance in his choice of mythical and carnivalesque imagery. It further delegitimized the women by infantilizing them, portraying them as children who committed a prank that should be at best ignored. But it is the idea of "pinching" the "girls" as an appropriate reaction of an adult Russian male that resonated, spiraling the symbolic violence and drawing their bodies further into the orbits of the state.

On the same day, a well-known journalist and TV presenter, Maksim Shevchenko wrote: "I think Orthodox women should catch and flog these little bitches with birch rods. Let them also have a 'performance'."[8] An influential conservative intellectual, Egor Kholmogorov, opined that, "If I was work-ing for this church, I would first call the TV crews and then undress them, cover them with feathers and honey, shave their heads, and kick them out to the freezing cold in front of the cameras."[9] In the coming days and months, the blogosphere exploded with cruel fantasies, often of a sexual character, such as the calls "to strip them naked," "to have them tarred and feathered," "to strip them naked and tie them to the whipping post," to "spank" (*otshlepat'*), "flog" (*vyporot'*), "whip" (*vysech'*), and "birch" them (*otkhlestat' rozgami*), or to "give them "a fatherly spanking" (*otecheski otshlepat'*). Speaking outside the courthouse on the first day of the trial, Boris Nemtsov, an opposition politician and leader of a liberal-democratic coalition that is regularly critical of Putin, said, "If I could get my way, I would spank these girls and let them go. What is going on here is sadism and cruelty."[10] On the opposite end of the political spectrum, Gennadii Ziuganov, the leader of the Russian Communist Party and the main opposition to Putin's "United Russia," stated: "I would take a good leather belt, give them a good spanking, and then send them back to their children and parents. This would be a good administrative punishment for them. And I would tell them not to engage in such blasphemy anymore."[11] Putin himself referred to the performance in the Cathedral as "witches' gathering" (*shabash*) and did not fail to mention that he was informed of the women's involvement in group sex during one of their previous performances. In an awkward attempt at humor, he quipped that group sex can be better than "individual" sex, because one can always "slack off" (*sachkanut'*).[12] Indeed, the Russian left, the right, and the centrists became unwittingly united by drawing Pussy Riot's bodies into these discourses of desire.

THE RETURN OF THE REPRESSED?

Indeed, Many Russians were dissatisfied with imprisonment as an appropriate form of "reeducation" for Pussy Riot. As if to illustrate the erotic and phantasmatic dimension of political domination, the initial violent reactions by public figures triggered heated debate on the return of corporal punishment. The results of a survey conducted by sociologists from the Russian Center for the Study of Public Opinion in the wake of the trial scandalized liberal circles revealing that 27% of the population would support the reintroduction of corporal punishment for defendants such as Pussy Riot.[13] Russia's oft-remarked split identity, once again, became the focus of debate, as bewildered liberal commentators sorrowfully concluded that finally, "we are more definitely the West of the East rather than the East of the West."[14]

Medieval precedents aside, over the course of the nineteenth century Russian spectacles of sovereign violence, such as theatrical corporal punishments, were gradually being replaced by the disciplinary practices of the penitentiary system—not unlike the trajectory that Foucault famously traced for western Europe.[15] A quintessential instrument of imperial sovereignty, the *knout*, a stiff thong of rawhide fastened by a bronze ring to a braided leather whip attached to a wooden stick, also served as a boundary establishing mechanism between various social groups, ethnicities, and genders. Thus, already in 1795, the wealthier estates were exempted from being whipped with a *knout*. While lower-class women were flogged as much as men, the redefinitions of gender eventually led to their exemption. It was argued that not only women were biologically weaker than men, but the shame of being naked and lashed in public compromised their femininity and maternal roles and therefore threatened the broader social order.[16] While women were viewed as crucially important to the empire given their reproductive capacity, they were also increasingly viewed as dangerous as a result of their potentially uncontrolled sexuality. Thus, it was believed that public punishments might exacerbate the case, as the sense of shame would make women "turn to depravity," destroying "family happiness" and corrupting "the morals of her female intimates and friends."[17] As reproductive function became increasingly important in discourses on women and the nation, at first pregnant women, then breast-feeding women, and then, during the Great Reforms,[18] in 1863 most women became exempt.[19]

Yet, despite the arguments against reforms advanced by conservative Russians such as writer Fyodor Dostoyevsky (he insisted that, counter the spirit of the Great Reforms, there was a certain authenticity in pain suffered from the birch-rod, which led him to oppose the cold rationality of the European legal system and "bourgeois hypocrisy"[20]), women's exemption from corporal punishment did not lead to liberation. On the contrary, women's punishment essentially became privatized, as they became subjects to punishment only by their husbands, thus reinforcing the status of a peasant male and "constituting the family as his inviolable domain and reinforcing the wife's 'private' status."[21] Given this historical background of women's corporal punishment in Russia, what do we make of the current calls to violently punish Pussy Riot? Are we witnessing, to use Freud's auspicious phrase, a "return of the repressed," a coming back of the socially and judicially unacceptable desires, a kind of affective counter-modernity?

A closer look at the punitive discourses around Pussy Riot reveals an interesting range of perceptions across varied modes of punishment and suffering. Contemporary champions of flogging argued that while administrative punishment, such as a fine, would be too little, prison would be too much. Prisons do not re-educate people, they break them or make them into real criminals.[22] Corporal punishment in these discourses inevitably emerges as something more authentic, more sincere, a sign of Russian national distinctiveness, superior to the "western" bourgeois rationality of the judiciary system, similar to the way wife-beating was praised by Dostoyevsky as "part of Russian folkways."[23] Yet, unlike other contexts where whipping has been advocated as a way to ritually purify the violator with the purpose of his or her subsequent reintegration into the community,[24] re-inclusion did not appear to be the issue at hand. Prison, it was argued, needs to be avoided, because it would might make the women into heroines and martyrs while corporal punishment—where as some proponents stressed, shame is more important than pain—would humiliate them and make everyone forget the "dumb prank."

As some of Pussy Riot's opponents argued, it was preferable that the women suffer a certain kind of social death through the shame of corporal punishment and subsequent societal forgetting, as long as perceptions of sacrifice and martyrdom were avoided. Thus Pussy Riot may (or rather should) have been killed (or whipped, or tarred and feathered), but they were not to be sacrificed. Yet, killing without sacrifice (despite what Agamben famously argued) proved an impossibility in this context, as such acts of sovereign violence necessarily create sacrificial victims.[25] Indeed, as the case continued to stir Russia, multiple sacrificial processes revealed themselves as essential to the reconstitution of political sovereignty through the Pussy Riot's bodies, first degraded and then reconstituted, much as the moral nation itself, in a sanctified domain. But first, as all sacrificial victims, they required purification.

In my article in Critical Inquiry 40 (Autumn 2013): 220–241, I demonstrate that this purification was achieved through a deliberate evacuation of what is often understood as "the political" in Russia. As the trial progressed, the prosecution consistently denied what they referred to as a "political motif," resulting in the final charge of "hooliganism motivated by religious hatred." I also make the case that despite the calls of those who warned that the women should not be turned into martyrs, their punishment—although arguably following the letter of the law—ended up acquiring a distinctly sacrificial character. Some stressed ascetic denial and martyrdom, emphasizing Christian-like self-sacrifice, while others emphasized the ways in which Pussy Riot became an inadvertent medium for ritual action and communication between multiple actors. What these discourses seem to share is a rather well worn theme throughout human history: the use of women's bodies as the means of communicative practices—sacrifice, hierarchical discipline, and legal warnings. Pussy Riot's bodies, almost inevitably, became appropriated and saturated with signification as they became objects of violence and, at the same time, sites of its vital resistance. In the end, it was not the extensive international support or the condemnation of the government by its vocal opponents at home, but a public recognition of the sacrificial undertones to Pussy Riot's trial that turned out to be so challenging for the Russian government's triumphant pageant of sovereign rule.

Read more in: Anya Bernstein, "An Inadvertent Sacrifice: Body Politics and Sovereign Power in the Pussy Riot Affair," *Critical Inquiry* 40 (Autumn 2013): 220–241.

Anya Bernstein *is Assistant Professor of Anthropology and Social Studies at Harvard University. Her book "Religious Bodies Politic: Rituals of Sovereignty in Buryat Buddhism" will be published by the University of Chicago Press this fall. Bernstein's current project focuses on religion and politics in contemporary Russia, exploring the issues of secularism, body politics, and imaginaries of death and immortality.*

ENDNOTES

1. There were five members of the group in the Cathedral, but only three were arrested. Pussy Riot does not have a fixed membership, and many participants remain anonymous.

2. For approaches to sovereignty that focus on the body as the site and object of sovereign power, see, for example, Giorgio Agamben, *Homo Sacer: Sovereign Power and Bare Life*, trans. Daniel Heller-Roazen (Stanford, 1998); Michel Foucault, *Discipline and Punish: The Birth of the Prison*, trans. Alan Sheridan (Vintage, 1979); Achille Mbembe, "Necropolitics," trans. Libby Meintjes, *Public Culture* 15, no. 1 (2003):11–40; Thomas Blom Hansen and Finn Stepputat, *Sovereign Bodies: Citizens, Migrants, and States in the Postcolonial World* (Princeton, 2005).

3. They were arrested March 3, 2012. The third convicted participant, Ekaterina Samutsevich was arrested on March 16, 2012.

4. As of today, Russia does not use the word "blasphemy" as a legal term. Instead, until 2013, the court deployed a law roughly parallel to the European hate speech laws, as per Article 282 of the Russian Criminal Code. After the Pussy Riot trial, a new law on "offending religious feelings" was proposed and approved relatively quickly, making public offenses of religion punishable with fines and imprisonment up to three years. For the discussion of the art-trials from 1998–2010, see Anya Bernstein, "Caution, Religion! Iconoclasm, Secularism, and Ways of Seeing in Post-Soviet Art Wars." Upcoming in *Public Culture* Fall 2014.

5. Marat Guelman, blog entry, February 21, 2012, http://maratguelman.livejournal.com/2558067.html

6. "Oni nazvali sebia feministkami," March 2, 2012, http://feministki.livejournal.com/1560428.html?thread=59057772

7. Andrei Kuraev, "Maslenitsa v khrame Khrista Spasitelia," February 2, 2012, http://diak-kuraev.livejournal.com/285875.html

8. "Smeshenie neba i preispodnei," *Vzgliad: delovaia gazeta,* February 21, 2012, http://www.vz.ru/opinions/2012/2/21/563022.html

9. Quoted in Vladimir Abarionov, "Sviato mesto Pussy Riot," *Grani.ru,* February 27, 2012, http://grani.ru/opinion/abarinov/m.195956.html

10. Elena Kostiuchenko, "V Khamovnicheskom sude zavershen pervyi den' slushanii po delu Pussy Riot," *Novaya Gazeta,* July 30, 2012, http://www.novayagazeta.ru/news/58666.html

11. "Ziuganov: Vyporol by Pussy Riot khoroshim remnem," *Vzgliad: delovaia gazeta,* August 21, 2012, http://vz.ru/news/2012/8/21/594406.html

12. "Vladimir Putin: Interview telekanalu *Russia Today*," September 6, 2012, http://kremlin.ru/news/16393

13. "Bit' ili ne bit', vot v chem vopros, ili o vozrozhdenii telesnykh nakazanii v Rossii," September 19, 2012, http://wciom.ru/index.php?id=459&uid=113045

14. Ekaterina Dobrynina, "Chetvert' rossiian toskuet po rozgam," *Rossiiskaia gazeta,* September 19, 2012, http://www.rg.ru/2012/09/19/nakasanie-site.html

15. Foucault, *Discipline and Punish*.

16. Abby M. Schrader, *Languages of the Lash. Corporal Punishment and Identity in Imperial Russia* (Northern Illinois, 2002).

17. Laura Engelstein, *The Keys to Happiness: Sex and the Search for Modernity in Fin-De-Siecle Russia* (Cornell, 1992), p. 73.

18. The 1860s and 1870s are known in Russia as the period of the "Great Reforms," which resulted in the emancipation of serfs and the progressive changes in the judicial, military, and administrative systems introduced during the rule of Alexander II.

19. Schrader, p. 144. The only women who were still subject to corporal punishment at that time were exiled convicts. The practice of punishing the banished women persisted until 1893, and all corporal punishment was abolished in 1903.

20. Svetlana Boym, *Another Freedom: The Alternative History of an Idea* (Chicago, 2012), pp.103–159.

21. Engelstein, *The Keys to Happiness*, pp. 74–75. Similar privatization of punishment was applied to minors.

22. "Surov ili spravedliv prigovor Pussy Riot?" *Komsomol'skaia Pravda,* August 17, 2012, http://www.kp.ru/radio/stenography/41898/

23. Boym, *Another Freedom*, p. 115

24. Mark Goodale and Sally Engle Merry, *The Practice of Human Rights: Tracking Law Between the Local and the Global* (Cambridge, 2007), p. 221.

25. Agamben 1998. I thank Jean Comaroff for bringing this point to my attention. She makes this argument in Jean Comaroff, "Beyond the Politics of Bare Life: AIDS and the Global Order." *Public Culture* 19, no. 1 (2007): 197–219.

World Markets
Anthropological Perspectives

BY JANE SCHNEIDER

From an anthropological perspective, the world is a vastly uneven playing field in which a hegemonic "free market culture" and disruptive "market forces" move outward from centers of concentrated power and wealth to exert pressure on peripheries that are more or less vulnerable to their impact. By "free market culture" is meant a set of dispositions, values, and practices that gravitate around the following principles, associated with market-friendly laws and institutional arrangements. The first is an expectation that the drive for gain is the mainspring of human behavior, so that all humans, if given a chance, will instinctively welcome the opportunities for choice offered by markets and choose "rationally" to maximize individual advantage. The second is a conviction that markets are efficient engines of technological innovation and progress, and should therefore be allowed to operate without cumbersome regulations and controls. Third is a firm belief in the capacity of unfettered markets to deliver human happiness—a decent, even pleasing standard of living not only for society's elites, but also for its middle and working classes. This principle shades into, without being the same as, "consumer culture" and "political democracy." That markets might also create unhappiness, disrupting lives and widening the gap between the haves and the have-nots, is, according to the fourth principle of free market culture, a temporary condition, often explainable by the unworthiness of the have-nots (they are lazy, rent-seeking, risk avoiding, prone to cronyism, profligate, live for the moment, have too many children, and so on).

Rooted in the scientific, technological, and commercial breakthroughs of early modern Europe, then reinforced and disseminated through the intellectual movement of the Enlightenment, the French Revolution, the heady power of industry, and the inventions of advertising and shopping, free market culture was a Western creation, even if markets, and other market cultures, were not. By the late twentieth century, however, we find its dispositions, values, and practices, summarized by the word *capitalism*, to have spread throughout the world. This dispersal corresponds to the independence movements and projects for agricultural and industrial development that have unfolded in Europe's former colonies since the Second World War. And yet, despite these transformations, the world remains a vastly unequal place.

This said, it is important to know that anthropology is the site of continuous, productive disagreement regarding, precisely, the vastness of the gulf between, to use a shorthand expression, "the West and the rest." Are European societies, whose institutions and values already favored free markets before the twentieth century, radically different from societies that have experienced these markets as an intrusion from the outside? Are the differences narrowing? Is there a risk in overstating them in the first place? Will Europeans inevitably continue to spread their culture and institutions throughout the world, or is this a Eurocentric conclusion that blinds us to the precocious development of the Asian Pacific before the nineteenth century, and to its recent spectacular "comeback" after an interlude of European expansion? There is, and has been, little consensus among anthropologists on these questions.

For example, since its inception, the discipline has produced passionate arguments on both sides of the rationality debate: for some, all humans are capable of enlightened self-interest, strategize to maximize benefits and minimize costs, and intrinsically value the expression of rational choice— conforming, thereby, to one of the core principles of free market culture. For others, the very idea of a universal humanity, or a set of motives that are universally human, is dangerous to the recognition and maintenance of valuable cultural differences—alternative rationalities—around the world. Most anthropologists fall between these extremes, yet the fact that both positions have long been represented in the discipline is the source of its considerable ability to self-correct. Anthropologists in general retreat from abstract modeling, document complexity, and are intrigued by the contradictions and unanticipated surprises of human life. This quality, which is enhanced by the tradition of fieldwork, is evident in the following brief review of a succession of anthropological arguments regarding world markets in the different epochs of capitalism.

ANTHROPOLOGISTS AND OTHERS: EARLY ENCOUNTERS

Argonauts of the Western Pacific, written by Bronislaw Malinowski in 1922, is a classic starting place for anthropologists' first reflections on the universality of free market culture. In it Malinowski analyzes the vast network of exchange that he observed in the Trobriand Islands of the South Pacific, in which men dared to travel by canoe over open seas to trade with distant partners for ornamental arm bands and necklaces made of shell. The resulting chain of relations, the "Kula ring," bore no resemblance to a market, he argued, and the shell objects no relation to money. Like Europeans contemplating the crown jewels, Trobrianders related to these objects with reverence, manifesting a keen interest in whom, and how prestigious, the previous owners had been. Although Malinowski laid out the Kula system in a chapter on "tribal economics," he depicted it as simultaneously economic, political, magical, and ceremonial-religious. By contrast, market systems, based on economizing behaviors, were "economic."

Malinowski's Trobriand Islands ethnography led some of his successors to classify objects of exchange as gifts or commodities. Common English usage associates gifts with selfless, disinterested generosity; it associates commodities with wealth accumulation and the satisfaction of individual desires. But although this simple dichotomy, which is isomorphic with the notion of a radical gap between "the West and the rest," surfaces from time to time in anthropological writing, it is consistently challenged. Already in the 1940s, British anthropologist Raymond Firth, observing that Malay fishermen competed with each other for glory or honor by strategically choosing among alternatives, declared that striving to maximize individual advantage is a human universal. One has only to adjust for the desired ends to be able to apply formal economic modeling everywhere. Firth's approach, and critique of Malinowski, inspired many subsequent anthropologists, some of whom attributed the hypothesis of a great divide between capitalist and noncapitalist, Western and non-Western societies, to other anthropologists' overly romantic view of "them" and/or "antimarket mentality."

An especially productive rethinking of these issues derives from the work of French anthropologist Marcel Mauss, whose pathbreaking 1924 essay, *The Gift,* made ample use of Malinowski's data. Mauss minimized the altruistic side of gift giving, stressing instead the side having to do with power. Defining gift exchange as a "total social phenomenon"—at once moral, religious, and economic—and considering gifts to include services, rituals, brides, land, and rank, as well as "things," he argued that the human compunction to give, receive, and repay is also fundamentally political. In a far from voluntary manner, givers lavishly disperse what they have in order to stave off receivers' sentiments of envy or resentment—sentiments that might otherwise lead to magical retribution in the form of evil eye, and even to open war. Once given, gifts compel reciprocity, the spirit of the giver being embodied in them, adding moral weight. Although different from a commodity economy, a gift economy should not be considered its opposite: gift-exchange is neither solidary, harmonious, nor egalitarian. At the same time as it levels wealth, giving fosters indebtedness, allowing creditors to accumulate power, which can then be translated back into wealth.

Mauss developed a similarly qualified picture of market society, based on observations of his native France. Citing his fellow citizens' rivalry to spend on wedding ceremonies and entertaining their friends, he argued that gift exchange was far from banished among the French. Moreover, charity was as much a part of French custom as shopping in department stores. The French would hardly dispute that holders of excessive wealth should seek to neutralize the envy of others by adopting a self-sacrificing, ascetic life-style or indulging in generosity. Obviously influenced by socialist ideology, Mauss saw workers giving life and labor to their communities as well as to their bosses; of course they would make revolutionary demands if denied a share in the profit. Although the laws of the free market might dictate otherwise, solutions to this problem lay in notions of group morality expressed through aristocratic philanthropy, social insurance, and public welfare. Since all of these redistributive measures were evident in France, its market society did not appear to be radically at odds with the moral and economic arrangements of the Trobriands.

Mauss's double-edged solution to reducing the distance between "them and us"—his bridging of the conceptual gap between gifts and commodities—resonates well with recent ethnographic accounts of entrepreneurship in various parts of the world. For example, a study by Italo Pardo of the relatively poor residents of central Naples finds them engaged in "strong, continuous interaction" between moral values of generosity or "good-heartedness" and clever practices for making money, between bestowing favors out of genuine benevolence and using the "favor system" to get ahead, between lovingly tending the shrines of local saints and souls of the dead and presumptuously expecting their blessings and even miracles. More or less moral actors—irreverent and humorously self-deprecating—these small-scale Neapolitan entrepreneurs are above all motivated to construct a "good life" as manifested in the symbolic display of material possessions, a reputation for giving and hosting, and signs that the saints have supported—not undermined—the health of their families.

EUROPEAN COLONIALISM, NEO-COLONIALISM, AND WORLD MARKETS

During the period of European colonial expansion, and in many respects during a neocolonial period following independence, Europe's colonies and dependent regions produced primary products (agricultural and mineral resources) for world markets, importing industrial goods manufactured in metropolitan "core" regions in exchange. The result was a substantially unequal pattern, referred to as "uneven development," which favored the further industrial growth of Western Europe, North America, and eventually Japan. Through market relations as well as outright plunder, some peripheral regions were actually "de-developed," drawn to specialize in the production of a single crop or mineral, which left them wide open to the disappointment of extremely low value-added returns and the chaotic effects of swings in commodity prices.

How anthropologists approached this situation is reflected in their conflicting reception of the work of Hungarian economist Karl Polanyi in the 1950s and 1960s. In his 1944 book, *The Great Transformation*, Polanyi questioned European capitalism as a unique and strange phenomenon. This was not because of its deep entanglement with markets and money and profits, all of which predated capitalism by centuries and had a well-established historic presence on every continent on earth. The "great" transformation was specific to the eighteenth-century English countryside, where, with the backing of the state and in the name of agricultural improvement, a fiction was created that land, and labor, and capital are nothing but commodities, reducible to quantified measures of cost and benefit. Stripped of their rights to land through Parliamentary Acts of Enclosure and the formation of a land market, former peasants became agricultural or industrial workers, required to sell their labor for a wage in a brand new institution: a market for labor. A forceful moral critic of this historic shift, although less radical in his prescribed remedies than Marx and Engels, Polanyi argued that humans, robbed of the "protective covering" of culturally sensitive definitions of land and labor, would "perish from the effects of social exposure." No wonder that, by the middle of the nineteenth century, new forms of protection (specifically, labor and welfare legislation), were on the horizon.

In a second book, coauthored with anthropologist Conrad Arensberg, Polanyi outlined three stages in the emergence of full-fledged "market societies," defined as having markets for land, labor, and capital as well as goods and services. At the simplest, and presumably the earliest, level of this evolutionist scheme were societies whose economies were structured by reciprocity—the exchange of gifts. A principle of redistribution dominated societies that were more complex and later in time. Here chiefly regimes and state bureaucracies siphoned up the social product, allocating it then to various claimants, based on some combination of need, calculated interest, and the maintenance of patron-client relations. (Socialist command economies might be said to fall under the rubric of "redistribution." Anthropologists have noted a strong continuity between Western discourses about "Oriental" societies, said to have subordinated markets and individual liberties to "despotic" states made tyrannous by the absence of private property, and discourses about both Chinese and Russian variants of Communism. Dramatizing Western history as dynamic, youthful, and energetic, these discourses caricature the Oriental/Communist "other" as stagnant: bogged down by "dynastic cycles," then stifled by collectivization.) In Polanyi's rendering, systems of reciprocity and redistribution did not lack contact with markets. Within them, however, world markets were restricted to quarantined "ports of trade," such that market forces would not penetrate and dissolve customary relations of land and labor.

Polanyi provoked a lively critique among anthropologists in the Firth tradition, who accused him of fundamentally disliking markets, romantically overplaying the altruism and solidarity of noncapitalist societies, and exaggerating the difference between these societies and the West. Yet others of the profession found his work attractive. At the time of the Vietnam War, American anthropologists attempting to understand the outbreak of peasant revolutions and independence movements in Europe's former colonies were an especially receptive audience. For example, Eric Wolf's comparative study, *Peasant Wars of the Twentieth Century* (1969), traced six instances of peasant unrest (Vietnam among them) to peasants' loss of access to land and engagement with world markets—interrelated consequences of colonial expansion and the worldwide quest for cotton, jute, sugar, rubber, coffee, and other tropical commodities that Europeans desired.

For both the colonial and postcolonial periods, clashing concepts of property—divergent meanings attached to resources—have continued to capture the attention of anthropologists. Thanks to recent archival as well as ethnographic studies, researchers are reconstructing the awkward and contested formation of land and labor markets in the heavily colonized regions of Africa and Asia. There now exists, for example, a fascinating literature on the transformation of the "cattle complex" in eastern and southern Africa. Here, prior to colonialism, cattle-keeping societies rarely ate these animals or put them to tasks that Westerners considered useful, viewing them rather as an important storehouse of wealth (figure 15–1). As John and Jean Comaroff (1990) propose in discussing the case of Tshidi Barolong, a Tswana people resident along today's South Africa-Botswana border, cattle also served as metaphors for society—the kind of "total social phenomenon" that interested Mauss. Only men had, and herded, cattle. Through cattle, paid out as bridewealth, they garnered access to women's childbearing and food-producing capacities. Chiefly men, who possessed the largest herds, harnessed spiritual powers by sacrificing cattle to ancestors and making cattle payments to ritual specialists. Finally, men who were rich in cattle gained power, for cattle could be deployed in building up loyal, militarily ready clienteles.

Contradicting this pattern, Christian missionaries of the early contact period promoted concepts of private property in land and cattle; of the retention and investment of wealth; of men farming instead of women; of the complete restructuring of farming practice through the use of cattle for traction; and of the reorientation of agricultural production toward world markets. In the context of these changes, Tshidi men with the largest herds acquired the lion's share of the land, while others were dispossessed. Subsequently, the colonial state imposed a head tax, coercing landless men into migration streams that fed the labor markets of agricultural and mining enterprises in South Africa. Former chiefs, no longer recipients of tribute and fines, became tax collectors instead. Although in a much-diminished position, they at least had a respectable money income and could live at home with their families. Poor men, by contrast, had to leave, remitting their meager wages to their womenfolk, who stayed behind to raise subsistence crops and care for children and old people.

Significantly, the Tshidi continue to reckon transactions that concern enduring social relationships—payments for bridewealth, healing, court-imposed fines, and loans between patrons and clients—in terms of nominal cattle known as "cows without legs," cattle whose value does not fluctuate with the price of an ox in the marketplace but instead reflects the quality of the ties between the exchanging parties. Anthropologist James Ferguson has recorded the frustration of Western development experts in Lesotho upon encountering similar practices in the early 1980s. Not even a worsening drought in those years, and the likelihood that many cattle would die, could compel their sale in the market.

The Lesotho communities studied by Ferguson have retained a concept of property that interdicts marketing livestock except in times of emergency or because of a dire need for food and shelter. To do so under other conditions—to cross what is essentially a "livestock-cash barrier"—is to succumb to utter humiliation. This "bovine mystique," as Ferguson calls it, should not be seen as a stubborn remnant of traditionalism, surviving into the present as if by inertia. Rather, it is part of a wider complex in which 70 percent of household income derives from the remitted wages of emigrant men, working in South Africa's mines and industries. The men, for their part, invest some of their earnings in cattle. Unlike cash, this investment is not subject to the constant demands of wives and children for money—demands that are sometimes intensified by wives' suspicion that husbands dissipate their earnings on beer and other women near the place of work.

Protected from women's demands, cattle constitute a retirement fund for the migrant men. By loaning cows to others of the home community to milk, breed, or otherwise use, they earn prestige and a place for themselves, notwithstanding their long-term absence. And the cattle can be sold in old age if necessary. So important are these considerations that Lesotho men in general, and older men in particular, ideologically reinforce the "bovine mystique," even as women ridicule them for being "old-fashioned."

THE GLOBAL FACTORY

Since the 1970s, industrial production for world markets has spread to every continent, incorporating volumes of new workers, some into factories, others into workshops, still others through work that is done by the piece in their homes. Accelerating the flow of rural-to-urban migration, this change undoes the characterization of former colonies and neocolonial dependencies as predominantly agrarian. The old pattern of uneven development, in which dominated peoples produced primary products for an industrialized metropolitan "core," is substantially broken; industrial commodities are manufactured the world over and can flow from the former colonies, often glossed as the Third World, to the first free market societies as frequently as they flow in the other direction.

Anthropologists have been interested in the provenience and condition of laborers in the various worksites of the global factory: their social and geographical distance from a place of origin, their ethnic mix, their composition with regard to gender and age—how many of them are young and female—and the discipline to which they are subjected at work and home. Under some conditions, wage work is liberating—a breath of fresh air when compared to the servile labor that often accompanies monocrop agriculture. For many young women, earning wages has constituted an opportunity to escape patriarchal surveillance. Best of all, perhaps, wages and piece-rates enable the acquisition of markers of modernity. The spread of the global factory has gone hand-in-hand with the transformation of villages and towns, as cash incomes get poured into new or restructured houses for ordinary folk. Boasting a larger size, previously unheard of building materials, and the wonders of electricity, such dwellings justify to their proud owners the sacrifices of hard work. Motivated to obtain them, workers may respond with enthusiasm to a development-oriented government that promotes the concept of a hard work ethic through the schools and mass media.

At the same time, field research into the local effects of the global factory suggests that many new industrial workers experience the labor market as a terrain of constraint and insecurity, from which they have little relief. A problem that has received particular attention is the situation of young women workers in unregulated export-processing zones such as Ciudad Juárez, just over the Mexican border from the United States. Here wage earners, employed by transnational corporations, far from being liberated or allowed to spend on themselves, remit what they earn to their parents. Anthropological studies have also shown that factory managers mobilize parental authority as reinforcement in disciplining the young women at work.

Transnational corporations pose other problems. Assisted by innovations in communications technology, they operate with an ever-wider reach, at the same time maintaining an anchor in the (frequently Western) home country. Yet they do not necessarily own all of the firms that manufacture the goods they market. An anthropological study of a shoe-producing town in rural Taiwan illustrates how the meanings of work, of marketing, and of consumption—interconnected activities that span the continents—can veer off in directions that have virtually nothing to do with one another. In Taiwan, shoes are cut and stitched for the Nike Corporation by a multiplicity of small, independently owned factories and workshops. Religion is everywhere. A traditional network of interconnected temples crisscrosses the island, offering a ready-made communications grid for contracting and subcontracting arrangements between local and parent firms. New religions are also present: Yiguan Dao, for example, emphasizes cultivating the Dao as a way to ward off the imminent destruction of the world.

Yiguan Dao's daily rituals of bowing and kowtowing mimic the motions of machines, while the urgency of its Armageddon-like message reflects the intensity of work. In the peak seasons of heavy deadlines, the workday runs from 8 A.M. to 9 P.M. on weekdays, with an hour's break for lunch and a half hour's break for dinner, and from 8 to 6 on Saturdays and alternate Sundays. Symbols of modernity broadcast the payoff: bowling alleys and stock brokerages commingle with spirit mediums and rice paddies. Women doing piecework, such as silk-screening logos, sit before modest but modernized houses; entrepreneurs enjoy palatial homes and BMWs. Meanwhile, on the other side of the world, the transnational, Nike, conducts marketing research, designs and redesigns shoes to stay ahead of fashion trends (the average life of a shoe style fell from seven years to ten months between 1971 and 1989), and purchases advertising and promotion. Owning the "swoosh" trademark and distribution system, if not the retail stores, it encourages U.S. consumers to believe that athletic prowess, indeed the cult of athleticism, can be accessed through Nike sneakers.

Whether giant transnationals subcontract with foreign manufacturers or establish foreign plants of their own, a driving motivation is often that of escaping high labor costs and environmental regulations at home. This puts the new industrial locales under pressure to keep wages low and turn a blind eye as aquifers disappear and emissions and effluents foul the air and water. Ian Skoggard, the anthropologist who researched shoe production in Taiwan, notes that the images highlighted in Nike's New York shrine to athletes, with its Fifth Avenue address, Greek columns, and videos of sponsored players and teams, would be tarnished if a consumer campaign were to dwell on the oppressive gender relations that contribute to disciplining the labor of women among its Asian suppliers.

In the past, when peripheral regions were reduced to simplified, agrarian forms of production, being a Third World consumer was not much fun. Colonial merchants foisted shoddy and often inappropriate goods off on people through a "truck system" of company stores. Miners and agricultural workers purchased supplies for home and work in these stores, which were located at or near the work site, and were often forced to take part or all of their wage in kind. The storekeepers, who at first were Europeans, advanced them credit, further tying them in to world markets. More than this, they aggressively pushed items for which there was apparently no demand at the behest of wholesalers higher up in the commodity chain.

By contrast, the world of the global factory is a world of global desire. Truck marketing has disappeared, indigenous merchants and shopkeepers have replaced foreigners in local markets, and distributors are highly attentive to consumer demand. Out of this new situation comes an interesting anthropological debate as to how vulnerable and manipulated these new consumers are. Some anthropologists, evoking the pessimism about consumer culture fostered by the Frankfurt school of social theory at the end of World War II, are convinced that market forces retain the upper hand: clever marketers and advertisers coerce people's labor or docility through unnecessarily multiplying their wants and needs.

There is, however, a strong research tradition within anthropology to the contrary. Goods that embellish the house, adorn the body, and serve as gifts to kin and friends, not to mention goods that ease the tasks of everyday living, both resonate with preexisting cultural values and assist people in the creation of new social identities—new projects for life—appropriate to their participation in the modem world. No matter that these goods are produced by distant powers (some, of course, may be produced locally, given the terms of the global factory); no matter even that advertisers promote them to audiences that have been targeted through marketing research. The point is to discover how buyers use, and construct the meanings of, soaps and perfumes, Nikes and jeans, washing machines and televisions sets, and television advertising itself.

There is much to be learned about these issues from Daniel Miller's (1997) ethnography of Trinidad, where, he claims, capitalism is more taken for granted than in Europe. Miller prefers the term *capitalism,* to *markets* because it suggests a phenomenon with political and historical dimensions rather than an abstract force of nature, propelled by its own logic, as in "market forces." Trinidadians, it seems, identify with and feel they have a right to what capitalism is famous for giving the world: reliable, high-quality commodities sold under recognized brands at affordable prices.

The qualities that make one brand more attractive than another are not necessarily self-evident— for example, the preference in Trinidad for Chinese shiny peanuts over American salted peanuts remains a mystery. Yet the distributors of commodities, for the most part Trinidadians of African and Indian as well as European descent, can hardly be said to be manipulating demand. On the contrary, Miller (1997) shows that their advertising and promotional campaigns are to a large extent driven by processes of competition and emulation among themselves. Often it is a matter of waiting to see which among a number of competing firms takes the lead in investing in some innovation or other, perhaps an innovation deriving from a U.S. or European trade show. Miller's most developed examples come from the manufacturers and distributors of soft drinks (called sweet drinks), whose flavors, packaging, and labels have proliferated to such a degree under this kind of competitive pressure as to create confusion for those who must load the trucks and stock the shelves. In the fray, foreign brands like Canada Dry and Coca-Cola, made locally under franchise, do extremely well, especially as mixers for mm. (One is reminded of William Roseberry's description of coffee entrepreneurs of the

1980s competing to develop the gourmet coffee market in the United States: every so often one of a multitude of uncharted experiments worked.)

It should finally be noted that commodities manufactured in the First World do not necessarily rob Third World consumers of the autonomy and the joy of producing cultural artifacts of their own. Industrially manufactured yams have been shown to be a tremendous boon to handloom weavers, enabling them to concentrate their energies on the more artistic and interesting aspects of the textile craft. Chemical dyestuffs are tremendously attractive to dyers who must otherwise labor intensely for decades to get good reds from natural dyes, always, from their point of view, coming up short. By the same token, and in tune with Dick Hebdige's (1979) analysis of punk style in late-twentieth-century London, anthropologists appreciate that people can deploy consumer goods in shocking, theatrical ways to resist consumerism. They reject, in other words, the facile assumption that runaway shopping and purchasing mean a homogenization (or Americanization) of diverse cultural practices or the erosion of cultural creativity altogether. And yet, a few anthropologists have warned of going too far in the direction of celebrating consumers for their capacity to fashion something of their own definition from the goods they buy. For millions of people worldwide, the need and desire for consumer goods seals their participation in labor markets, even at the cost of long-distance migration, the separation of families, and the sense of earning less—for women, far less—than one's worth.

FINANCIAL MARKETS AND STRUCTURAL ADJUSTMENT

The emergence of the global factory both gained from and further encouraged the worldwide liberalization of finance, which dates to the economic downturn of the United States in the late 1960s and early 1970s as Japan, Germany, and the oil-producing countries challenged its dominant position. Out of the resulting crisis came a negotiated end to the post-World War II Bretton Woods monetary system. The Bretton Woods Accords defined economies as national; the movement of money in and out of them was necessarily subject to national controls. In modifying the Accords, a contrary argument w as made that if nation-states deregulated money flows and freed up markets from what are called "distortions"—namely, state subsidies and monopolies, price controls, and restrictions on imports—then investment capital would gravitate toward less-developed regions where returns on labor are greater, stimulating these regions toward fuller development with benefits for the whole. In the imagined world that would thus be created, commodities would be produced wherever the conditions for producing them were optimal, with tremendous leaps in manufacturing efficiency and the multiplication of wealth through worldwide trade.

Miller characterizes this vision of the future as "pure capitalism"—a concept that he contrasts with the "organic capitalism" practiced in a place like Trinidad where firms, including transnational firms, are part of a regional institutional trajectory whose norms and precedents have accumulated over time. The choice of the word "pure" evokes the principles of free market culture outlined at the beginning of this essay, but directs our attention to specific institutions that distill the logic of markets, abstracted from any regional or historical context, and promote the resulting model with missionary zeal. Key examples of promotional institutions are major U.S. schools of business and finance, the central banks and treasury departments of the first industrialized countries, Wall Street firms, and the heavily American-influenced International Monetary Fund, World Bank, and International Financial Corporation, a World Bank subsidiary. In Miller's view, these source-points of "pure capitalism" have played an ideological role in history no less potent than that played by various Communist Parties, whose leaders believed they could shape diverse social realities into conformity with a utopian ideal. If anything, the late 1980s collapse of Communism and its associated command economies has vastly enlarged the terrain in which the free market gospel can be preached.

As liberalization advanced over the 1980s and 1990s, governments around the world created fledgling stock markets in the hope of supplementing bank-based systems of investment and avidly set out to attract private foreign capital, promising its unfettered entry and exit. In glossy brochures, they advertised minimal regulation, tax benefits, low wages, labor peace, free-floating national currencies, extravagandy modem "world trade centers," and gorgeous hotels and beaches—each a bargaining chip in the competitive courtship dance for major money. Meanwhile, in the capital-rich locations, institutional investors like mutual funds with decidedly short-term investment horizons multiplied, as did a series of innovations in financial instruments modeled on commodities futures. Enhanced through information-age technology, these instruments allow transnational investors to speculate on currency spreads, interest rate movements, bond prices, and various swaps and options, in the hopes of hedging their other operations in a world of unhinged values. Significantly, public discourse ceased referring to Europe's former colonies and dependencies as "underdeveloped" or "developing" countries. The new language, invented by officials at the International Finance Corporation in the mid-1980s, is "emerging markets." As the shift implies, world financial markets are not merely about allocating resources for the old, quasipolitical goal of development. Speculative profit-seeking activity, encouraged by governments' abdication of the power to regulate, has multiplied astronomically, and with it the danger of downturns becoming crashes.

Although it is too soon for there to be much anthropological writing on this startling new moment in the history of world markets, we can anticipate contributions that follow in the footsteps of research done in Latin America during the 1980s; for that continent, if for somewhat different reasons, offered a preview of the instability of today. As is well known, the first phase of financial liberalization after the oil crisis of 1973–74 saw U.S. banks embark on a lending boom to Asian, African, and above all, Latin American countries—a boom that was already unraveling by 1981. Unable to sustain confidence that the loans and investments would be repaid, the affected governments undertook programs of "structural adjustment," which the IMF mandated as a quid pro quo for negotiating more realistic terms. The main features of the adjustment were to raise interest rates so as to staunch capital flight, reorient production around exports, and drastically cut government services and programs as a step toward lowering the public deficit. State-owned industries were either closed down or privatized;

agricultural and industrial enterprises found it difficult to borrow. And, in an unhappy coincidence, millions of people lost both their jobs and the possibility of government-funded "safety net" assistance.

Thrown back on their communities and families, or thrown out into the swelling streams of migrants, these dispossessed people—industrial laborers as well as peasants—caught the attention of ethnographers who charted their course. June Nash's (1994) comparison of Mayan farmers in the highlands of Chiapas, Mexico, with tin miners in Bolivia (figure 15–2) is exemplary, both because of her long-term familiarity with these two situations dating to the 1960s, and because she also studied the surprisingly parallel instance of laid-off General Electric workers in Pittsfield, Massachusetts. Her writings tell of the intensification of subsistence economies among people who had long depended on the market for most of their daily provisioning. In Bolivia, wives had traditionally kept vegetable gardens and raised guinea pigs for protein, but now they also undertook lengthy trips to visit kinfolk in the rich farming hinterland of Cochabamba. In Pittsfield, men turned to hunting for wild turkey and pheasant, and to fishing, only to discover that encroaching urban sprawl and industrial pollution had jeopardized these resources. Another quite predictable response was intensified out-migration: more highland Mayan men left for the lowland coffee plantations than had been the case before; many Pittsfield families pulled up stakes and scattered. When the Bolivian government closed the tin mines in 1986, thousands of miners departed for the coca-producing areas near the border with Brazil or for Brazil and Argentina.

At first, the tin miners did not take off. Together with their families and sympathetic schoolteachers, they mobilized a "March for Life," and, when that was repressed by government troops, they staged a hunger strike. In Pittsfield, by contrast, neither union nor community generated a collective response. Nash proposes that these differences reflect contrasts in what Miller would call "organic capitalisms"—the specific regional histories of past engagements with the market. For the highland Maya, Nash's third case, these past engagements involved, on the one hand, male out-migration to coffee plantations and, on the other hand, an inward-turning pattern of conflict in the home communities. Between her first visit in 1957 and 1980, villagers acquired electricity, paved streets, and cement block houses with television aerials on them. In the same period, they lost their sense of control over local ancestral spirits whom they believed had abandoned them to take up residence in a non-Indian town. They also started to level accusations of witchcraft against innovative leaders and entrepreneurs, especially those who did not make generous contributions to the local fiesta cycle. This inward-turning mode of coping with anxiety about change carried over into the 1980s when, as a consequence of debt restructuring, the costs for transport, fertilizer, and credit doubled. Different from the Bolivian tin miners, who directed their anger outward, at state officials, and from Pittsfield's passive unemployed, the Mayan highlanders became embroiled in a rising rate of intracommunity violence. Traditional local authorities, heavily identified with folk-Catholicism, expelled younger men and women, many of whom professed attraction to reform Catholic and Protestant religious movements.

The IMF missionaries of "pure capitalism" present the steps of structural adjustment as a necessary "strong medicine" which, if followed as prescribed, can restore a country's ability to attract investment capital. But in cases where excessive debt is traceable to instability in the economic environment—for example the post-boom collapse of world prices for a strategic export like oil or tin—governments must immediately scramble to find alternative sources of livelihood for their people, or watch them embark on the dangerous path of seeking illegal entry into First World countries. A well-worn alternative in desperate times is the artisan production of indigenous arts and crafts (weavings, embroideries, batiks, carpets, woodcarvings, ironwork, and ceramics), which not only garner income, but also confer pride and prestige. How reliable such production can be in a worldwide context of structural adjustment is another matter, however. Anthropological research points to the challenges of gaining and maintaining a competitive edge.

One issue is how the distribution system is organized. A study of weavings from Oaxaca, Mexico, traces government programs encouraging their manufacture back to the 1940s, when the opening of the Pan-American Highway first brought tourists to the region. In certain designated towns, local merchants began putting out materials to weaving households with whom they had a godparent relation, and in which family labor could be exploited. The strongest merchants were those who had accumulated startup capital during earlier bouts of migration to the United States and who benefited, as well, from U.S. commercial contacts. Then came the 1980s debt crisis and the drastic devaluation of the peso. In this context, U.S. importers flooded into Mexico, advantaged by cheap airfares, hotels, rented cars, and interpreters. The Oaxacan merchants lost ground to these interlopers just as the differential between wholesale and retail prices approached 1,000 times. The Oaxacan weavers lost, too. Whereas the local merchants had recycled their profits into the fiesta system and community public works, the interlopers felt no compulsion to distribute their earnings in Oaxacan weaving towns.

American intermediaries of Oaxacan textiles, wedded to the pure capitalist principle that commodities should be made wherever it is cheapest to make them, tried to get the Oaxacan weavers to incorporate "Oriental" carpet motifs into their designs, just as they had given weavers in India Zapotec motifs to copy. Interestingly, these projects met resistance, for although the resulting textiles might have retained their exotic, handcrafted appearance, the artisans worried that an "inauthentic" product would lose market share.

Anthropologists writing on arts and crafts point out that the word *authenticity* means different things to different people. Governments promoting "commercial" or "tourist" arts, and exporters seeking to market them, often go to great lengths to depict these commodities as faithful to an unchanging, ancestral tradition, laden with cultural meaning. This is because the ultimate consumers, perhaps out of nostalgia for pasts that never were, want to be reassured that what they are buying is "real," not spurious or fake. Indeed, highly educated tourists and collectors covet objects that were not only originally made for "the natives," but used by them as well. Yet this does not mean that arts and crafts defined as "authentic" by those who market and consume them are in fact all that old or unchanged. Art and craft producers have long modified their wares to fit with First World lifestyles, transforming, let us say, indigenous blouses and shawls into alien place mats and pillow covers. More to the point, many apparently "authentic" crafts originated during the first colonial contact, or as "trinkets" to appeal to the earliest tourists and collectors. One can argue, in fact, that all art and craft traditions are hybrids of multicultural interactions and that all of them change through time. Yet if "native" craftsmen and artists are unable to define and maintain a discrete ethnic identity, they risk losing out to more efficient, if "inauthentic," competitors. Hence the recent plea of Inuit carvers to the Canadian government that soapstone sculptures, a relatively new tourist art, are "theirs"; whites and other outsiders should not be carving them (figure 15–3). In their case, as in countless others, the viability of art and craft production will ultimately rest on the ("distorting") intervention of governmental and nongovernmental (NGO) support.

Tourism is closely intertwined with art and craft manufacture as a moneymaking activity to fall back on or cultivate when the economic order is in disarray. Tourist markets, including "ecotourism" or the marketing of nature, are in some ways the reciprocal of migration, bringing First World people to Third World places, hopefully to boost, not destroy, the local economy. Migrant flows and tourist flows interact in complex ways. A by now well-documented trajectory is that of immigrants not merely remitting wages to family members in the home country, but saving and investing in home-country businesses related to tourist development—hotels, restaurants, guest houses, even street peddling stands. Here, too, competition is daunting, whether from better capitalized international players, from other tourist destinations, or from the inherent contradiction of the tourist industry itself, which is that the more a place attracts visitors, the fewer visitors will eventually want to go there.

And still, the arts and crafts and tourist options seem so much healthier than other alternatives that have been seized upon in recent years by people dispossessed of their livelihood—in particular, narcotics production and trafficking, and the tragic commerce in sex work. In the case of the latter, rural families make ends meet in part through the remitted earnings of one or more daughters, deployed through networks of kin in a city of the same nation or abroad and at risk of contracting the HIV infection.

Meanwhile, recovery through agriculture or industry has been rendered more challenging by some very recent First World developments: bioengineering applied to crops and animals, with the result of vastly increasing agricultural productivity; and the growing presence of truly cheap labor in the form of new immigrants. The latter constitute a wellspring of servants and errand boys in support of the gentrification of professional and managerial elites, and a highly exploitable labor pool for go-getting, immigrant-owned businesses. Among the latter are the infamous sweatshops that signal the return of clothing manufacturing from cheaper locales "off-shore."

Not surprisingly, the anthropological literature offers two quite different perspectives on the renewed assertion of "pure capitalism" in these First World settings. In one, illustrated by Igor Kopytoff's well-known essay, "The Cultural Biography of Things" (1986), market forces are characterized as acultural—as an inexorable march toward ever greater calculation and abstraction in human affairs, facilitated by ever-expanding technological upgrades in the instruments of exchange. At the same time, even in the United States, the most highly commercialized, monetized society on earth, this march, or drive, is held to be counteracted by localized cultural values. Culturally sensitized individuals and groups at times erect barriers to the circulation of commodities, for example, by boycotting goods deemed to have been produced under morally reprehensible conditions. As the word "biography" implies, there is another, more everyday respect in which culture confronts economism. Things, the argument goes, move in and out of commodity status as people redefine their meaning, conferring on them "biographies" that change through time.

Charting a different course, Roger Rouse (1995) suggests that in the United States, the market has *become* the culture. Over the last two decades, the champions of free markets in corporations, advertising firms, and the media have fostered a broad consensus around an ethos of buying and selling, investing and borrowing, shopping and consuming, and around the idea of consumption as a measure of self-worth. Thanks to their hegemony—to their propagation of this ethos through entertainment, persuasion, and the evocation of desire—it is now totally normal for young people to acquire credit cards as a rite of passage. That billboards have invaded more public spaces; that stores are open around the clock; that stock market quotations fill the airwaves; and that prisons are entrusted to franchises are but a few indications of the extent to which commercial values are taken for granted and embedded in everyday life.

TOWARD THE FUTURE

A possible conclusion from this review is that, while the myriad organic capitalisms of the world might be credited with raising standards of living, and enabling the assumption of a modern identity, in many countries the destabilizing consequences of the push to "purify" these capitalisms and compel their conformity with free market culture has wreaked a kind of counterproductive havoc. In light of this, many anthropologists are tempted to "relativize" this culture, to make it strange. Perhaps its strangest feature is a moral one. For beyond celebrating rational-choice behavior as a human universal, and beyond defining markets as the source of all progress, the dispositions, values, and practices of pure capitalism imply a moral economy of good and bad. The good are those who by investing in a resource make it more efficient and productive to the benefit of all; the bad, or potentially bad, are those who interfere with this process. Because investment is inherently destabilizing as well as enhancing, however, not least because it may be followed by disinvestment, this moral economy must go to some lengths to represent the victims of destabilization as merely transitory casualties of change. Disparaged as free-riders or "cronyistic" if they band together to impede progress, such persons are otherwise expected to accept the argument that their society will eventually recover and they will be reabsorbed. Implied is a shallow, exonerative understanding of what dislocation means to families and communities, especially in places that will not easily regain their economic health.

From an anthropological perspective, discourses on the assumed temporariness of market dislocations and the incipient moral or political indictment of those who would protest are interesting for having developed earlier in England than in other places in the West, and for being most forcefully articulated in English and Anglo-American variants of capitalism. Perhaps—an anthropologist might imagine—this radical instance of market culture grew out of the history of English agriculture, in which moves toward the privatization of property were already evident in the Middle Ages, well before the eighteenth-century Enclosure Acts that so troubled Polanyi, and in contrast with medieval agriculture in, for example, France. However it was first established, the "pure" variant of capitalism surely gained support from the English state and from English successes with industrial technology, colonialism, and imperialism—successes that Anglo-Americans built upon in the twentieth century. In the 1980s, the governments of Ronald Reagan in the United States and Margaret Thatcher in England renewed the premises of a moral economy that would purge itself of sentimentalism—the disparaging word for an undue concern with those whose lives are disrupted by market forces. This purging set the stage for the promotion of financial liberalization worldwide.

And this brings us to a final arena of anthropological reflection on the future direction of world markets. If free market culture in its most radical and demanding form indeed had particular historical roots, so that it is experienced by many as alien and in need of modulation, will it forever be the case that the terms of this culture shape the world's most powerful and well-capitalized international institutions? Or, in a context of capital flight and chain-linked global recession, might other values and practices, alternative understandings and discourses, come to the fore, not only within individual states, but also in wider, transnational networks?

Anthropologists typically seek to recognize and question Eurocentric imaginings of the world. The argument recently put forth by Andre Guilder Frank in his provocative book, *ReOrient* (1998), that until the late eighteenth century the Chinese people were more productive and "developed" than Europeans, is one they are prepared to seriously consider. Were China to become a world power again, would its cultural values and practices influence the worldwide values and practices of capitalism? Anthropologists now working in China have proposed that personalized Chinese relations of kinship, friendship, and patronage, known as *guanxi*, have actually facilitated, not sapped, the efficiency of light industrial manufacturing firms, nominally still owned by villages and towns. Perhaps firms of this type will outlive the current pressures for structural adjustment to serve as a future challenge to "pure capitalism" which, despite the chaos that it is known to be capable of creating, is hegemonic today.

SUGGESTIONS FOR FURTHER READING

Blim, Michael. 1997. "Can Not-Capitalism Lie at the End of History, or Is Capitalism's History Drawing to an End?" *Critique of Anthropology* 17, no. 4: 351–63.

Burke, Timothy. 1996. *Lifebuoy Men, Lux Women: Commodification, Consumption, and Cleanliness in Modem Zimbabwe.* Durham, NC: Duke University Press.

Comaroff, Jean, and John L. Comaroff. 1990. "Goodly Beasts, Beastly Goods: Cattle and Commodities in a South African Context." *American Ethnologist* 17, no. 2: 195–217.

Ferguson, James. 1994. *The Anti-Politics Machine: "Development," Depoliticization, and Bureaucratic Power in Lesotho.* Minneapolis: University of Minnesota Press.

Frank, Andre Gunder. 1998. *ReOrient: Global Economy in the Asian Age.* Berkeley and Los Angeles: University of California Press.

Graburn, Nelson H. H. 1999. "Ethnic and Tourist Arts Revisited" In *Unpacking Culture: Art and Commodity in Colonial and Postcolonial Worlds,* ed. Ruth B. Phillips and Christopher B. Steiner, 335–53. Berkeley and Los Angeles: University of California Press.

Hebdige, Dick. 1979. *Subculture: The Meaning of Style.* London: Methuen.

Kopytoff, Igor. 1986. "The Cultural Biography of Things." In *The Social Life of Things: Commodities in Cultural Perspective,* ed. Arjun Appadurai, 64–95. Cambridge: Cambridge University Press.

Miller, Daniel. 1997. *Capitalism: An Ethnographic Approach.* Oxford: Berg.

Nash, June. 1994. "Global Integration and Subsistence Insecurity," *American Anthropologist* 96, no. 1: 7–31.

Ong, Aiwah. 1987. *Spirits of Resistance and Capitalist Discipline: Factory Women in Malaysia.* Albany: State University of New York Press.

Pardo, Italo. 1996. *Managing Existence in Naples.* Cambridge and New York: Cambridge University Press.

Roseberry, William. 1996. "The Rise of Yuppie Coffees and the Reimagination of Class in the United States." *American Anthropologist* 98, no. 4: 762–76.

Rothstein, Frances Abrahamer, and Michael L. Blim, eds. 1992. *Anthropology and the Global Factory: Studies of the New Industrialization in the Late Twentieth Century.* New York: Bergin and Garvey.

Rouse, Roger. 1995. "Thinking through Transnationalism: Notes on the Cultural Politics of Class Relations in the Contemporary United States," *Public Culture* 7: 535–602.

Schiller, Nina Glick; Linda Basch; and Cristina Blanc-Szanton, eds. 1992. *Toward a Transnational Perspective on Migration: Race, Class, Ethnicity, and Nationalism Reconsidered.* Annals of the New York Academy of Sciences, vol. 645. New York: New York Academy of Sciences.

Schneider, Jane. 1978. "Peacocks and Penguins: the Political Economy of European Cloth and Colors." *American Ethnologist* 5, no. 4: 413–37.

Skoggard, Ian. 1998. "Transnational Commodity Flows and the Global Phenomenon of the Brand." In *Consuming Fashion: Adorning the Transnational Body*, ed. Anne Brydon and Sandra Niessen, 57–71. Oxford: Berg.

Smart, Allen. 1997. "Oriental Despotism and Sugar-Coated Bullets: Representations of the Market in China." In *Meanings of the Market: the Free Market in Western Culture*, ed. James G. Carrier, 159–95. Oxford: Berg.

Stephen, Lynn. 1993. "Weaving in the Fast Lane: Class, Ethnicity, and Gender in Zapotec Graft Commercialization." In *Crafts in the World Market: the Impart of Global Exchange on Middle American Artisans,* ed. June Nash, 25–59. Albany: State University of New York Press.

Wolf, Eric R. 1969. *Peasant Wars of the Twentieth Century.* New York: Harper and Row.

The Organ Detective
A Career Spent Uncovering a Hidden Global Market in Human Flesh

BY ETHAN WATTERS

Tracking the organ trade, anthropologist Nancy Scheper-Hughes visited African and South American dialysis units, organ banks, police morgues, and hospitals. She interviewed surgeons, patient's rights activists, pathologists, nephrologists, and nurses. So why aren't more people listening to her?

When she first heard about the organ thieves, the anthropologist Nancy Scheper-Hughes was doing fieldwork in northeastern Brazil. It was 1987, and a rumor circulating around the shantytown of Alto do Cruzeiro, overlooking the town of Timbaúba, in a sugarcane farming region of Pernambuco, told of foreigners who traveled the dirt roads in yellow vans, looking for unattended children to snatch up and kill for their transplantable organs. Later, it was said, the children's bodies would turn up in roadside ditches or in hospital dumpsters.

Scheper-Hughes, then an up-and-coming professor at the University of California-Berkeley, had good reason to be skeptical. As part of her study of poverty and motherhood in the shantytown, she had interviewed the area's coffin makers and the government clerks who kept the death records. The rate of child mortality there was appalling, but surgically eviscerated bodies were nowhere to be found. "Bah, these are stories invented by the poor and illiterate," the manager of the municipal cemetery told her.

And yet, while Scheper-Hughes doubted the literal truth of the tales, she was unwilling to dismiss the rumors. She subscribed to an academic school of thought that swore off imposing Western notions of absolute or objective truth. As much as she wanted to show solidarity with the beliefs of her sources, she struggled with how to present the rumors in her 1992 book, *Death Without Weeping: The Violence of Everyday Life in Brazil.*

In the end, she argued that the organ stealing stories could only be understood in light of all the bodily threats faced by this impoverished population. In addition to pervasive hunger and thirst, the locals also faced mistreatment at the hands of employers, the military, and law enforcement. The medical care available, she suggested, often did more harm than good. Local health care workers and pharmacists gave the malnourished and chronically ill locals the catchall diagnosis of nervos and prescribed tranquilizers, sleeping pills, vitamins, and elixirs. The locals were well aware that wealthier people in their country and abroad had access to better medical care—including exotic procedures like tissue and organ transplants.

"The people of the Alto can all too easily imagine that their bodies may be eyed longingly as a reservoir of spare parts by those with money," Scheper-Hughes wrote in Death Without Weeping. The stories of transplant teams murdering local children and harvesting their organs persisted, she wrote, "because the 'misinformed' shantytown residents are onto something. They are on the right track and are refusing to give up on their intuitive sense that something is seriously amiss." The book, which was widely praised and nominated for the National Book Critics Circle Award, solidified her reputation as one of the leading anthropologists of her generation.

In 1995, Scheper-Hughes was the sole anthropologist invited to speak at a medical conference on the practice of organ trafficking held in Bellagio, Italy. Although there remained no solid evidence that people were being murdered for viable organs, rumors similar to the ones Scheper-Hughes had documented in Brazil had now spread from South America to Sweden, Italy, Romania, and Albania. In France, one popular story told of children being abducted from Euro Disney for their kidneys. The conference organizers asked Scheper-Hughes to explain the persistence of this gruesome meme.

The trade in kidneys particularly fascinated her. Unlike the trade in heart valves or corneas, kidneys were being shipped from country to country inside the living bodies of sentient individuals.

If the other participants at the conference, who were mainly transplant surgeons, were hoping to learn from Scheper-Hughes what was factual and what was false among these rumors, they were likely disappointed. She told them the stories were "true at that indeterminate level between fact and metaphor," as she'd later write. Looking back, she feels certain that the surgeons—whom she thinks of as bright and skilled, like fighter pilots, but not very intellectual—didn't really understand her more theoretical analyses. "We were speaking different languages," she told me.

Still, Scheper-Hughes made the best of her time among the doctors. In Bellagio, she decided to do some on-the-fly ethnographic research into the current practices of transplant surgeons. As she spoke with them during boat rides on Lake Como or while touring the olive groves of Villa Serbelloni, the doctors answered her questions candidly. One surgeon told her that he knew of patients who had traveled to India to purchase kidneys. She remembers an Israeli surgeon telling her that Palestinian laborers were "very generous" with their kidneys, and often donated to strangers in exchange for "a small honorarium." A heart surgeon from Eastern Europe admitted his concern that medical tourism would encourage doctors from his country to harvest organs from brain-dead donors who were "not quite as dead as we might like them to be." In these new practices, Scheper-Hughes began to understand, human organs and tissue generally moved from south to north, from the poor to the rich, and from brown-skinned to lighter-skinned people.

While none of the surgeons' accounts confirmed the kidnapping-for-organs rumors, Scheper-Hughes came to believe that the "really real" traffic in human body parts, as she has called it, was ripe for further study. "There were so many unanswered questions," she recalls. "How were patients finding out about available organs in other countries? Who were the poor people who were selling their body parts? Nobody had gone into the trenches to find out."

Scheper-Hughes' investigation of the organ trade would be a test case for a new kind of anthropology. This would be the study not of an isolated, exotic culture, but of a globalized, interconnected black market—one that crossed classes, cultures, and borders, linking impoverished paid donors to the highest-status individuals and institutions in the modern world. For Scheper-Hughes, the project presented an opportunity to show how an anthropologist could have a meaningful, real-time, and forceful impact on an ongoing injustice. "There is a joke in our discipline that goes, 'If you want to keep something a secret, publish it in an anthropology journal,'" she once told me. "We are perceived as benign, amusing characters." Scheper-Hughes had grander ambitions. She decided it was time, as she puts it, to stop following the rumors and start following bodies.

In her writing, Scheper-Hughes has described her years of research into the international black market for organs as a disorienting "descent into Hades." When she discusses the topic in person, she is animated and energetic. At 69, Scheper-Hughes presents a brassy mix of grandmother and urban hipster. On the winter day when I visited her home near the U.C. Berkeley campus, her hair was short, spiked, and highlighted with streaks of magenta, and she wore a short-sleeved shirt that revealed a stylized tattoo of a turtle—a gift, she said, from her son for her 60th birthday. As she talked about her dozens of international journeys to interview surgeons, donors, recipients, and various intermediaries, she showed me her office, which had formerly been the home's garage. Inside were thousands of files, stored in dozens of large plastic bins and black file cabinets, along with drawers full of cassette tapes and field notebooks.

Since the mid-1990s, Scheper-Hughes has published some 50 articles and book chapters about the organ trade, and she is currently in the process of synthesizing that material into a book, tentatively titled A World Cut in Two. Over the years, she has had an outsize impact on the intellectual trends in her field, and her study of the organ trade is likely to be her last major statement on the meaning and value of the discipline to which she has devoted her life. Whether this body of work represents a triumph of anthropological research or a cautionary tale about scholarly vigilantism is already a hotly disputed question among her colleagues.

When Scheper-Hughes began to focus on the organ trade in the 1990s, she was a leading voice in a contentious debate about the future of anthropology, which was then in the midst of a long-brewing identity crisis. In the 1940s and 1950s, anthropologists had carried the banner of science into the field. Back in those days, a graduate student heading out to complete an ethnography of some far-flung people could be expected to carry with him a copy of George Murdock's **Outline of Cultural Materials**, which lists more than 500 categories, cultural institutions, and behaviors under headings like "family," "religious practices," "agriculture," and so on. Anthropologists were expected to document kinship relations and answer straightforward questions like: How is food stored and preserved? Are farm crops grown for animal fodder? Does the groom move in with the bride's family after marriage, or vice versa? Because everyone was collecting the same types of information, the data could be replicated and updated, and cultures large and small could be classified and compared. Anthropologists of the era sought to create a taxonomy of human social behavior, and the doggedness and objectivity of the researcher were prized.

Scholars who came of age in the political tumult of the 1960s rejected this model. Scheper-Hughes was among a cohort of anthropologists who suggested that the scientific, taxonomic approach was just imperialism in another form, and that any claims of objectivity or literal truth were ultimately illusory or, worse, an excuse for exploitation and violence.

Of course, there remained a question: If not just collecting and cataloging facts about other cultures, what should anthropologists be doing? In a 1995 debate with the anthropologist Roy D'Andrade in the pages of Current Anthropology, Scheper-Hughes argued for what she called a "militant anthropology," in which practitioners would become traitors to their class and nation by joining political battles arm in arm with their subjects. The job of the anthropologist wasn't simply to document the quotidian but to strip away appearances and reveal the hidden forces and ideologies that leave people dominated and oppressed. To do this, she suggested throwing off the traditional guise of the academic—in "the spirit of the Brazilian 'carnavalesque'"—and joining the powerless in their fight against bourgeois institutions like hospitals and universities.

"The new cadre of 'barefoot anthropologists' that I envision," she wrote, "must become alarmists and shock troopers—the producers of politically complicated and morally demanding texts and images capable of sinking through the layers of acceptance, complicity, and bad faith that allow the suffering and the deaths to continue."

D'Andrade and others saw grave danger for the discipline in Scheper-Hughes' call to the barricades (or to the carnival). D'Andrade believed that Scheper-Hughes and her intellectual allies were leading the field away from an objective science and toward what he called a "moral model" based on the simplistic duality of the oppressed and the oppressor. Her militant style of anthropology, he feared, would turn a once promising discipline into an exercise in "moralistic pamphleteering."

"With the moral model, the truth ain't exactly the thing that everyone strives for," D'Andrade, who is now retired and living in Northern California, told me. "What you strive for is a denunciation of a real evil." I asked him who prevailed in his public debate with Scheper-Hughes. "I believed that after the kerfuffle that people would get back to asking, 'How do you know something is true or not?' But in the end, the moral model swept the country and cultural anthropology stopped being anything that a self-respecting social scientist would call a science. The hegemony of the Scheper-Hughes position became total."

Another loose consensus that emerged out of the debates of the 1990s was a widely shared belief that cultural anthropology's focus on far-away, exotic societies had run its course: Why shouldn't anthropologists turn their gaze on institutions that have real power in the modern world—banks, multinational corporations, courts, and governmental agencies? Or, for that matter, transplant units in major hospitals?

At the time, there were only a handful of papers in the medical literature addressing the rise of the global organ market. Since the 1970s, live organ transplants had changed from experimental proce- dures to a common practice in the United States, most European and Asian countries, half a dozen South American nations, and four countries in Africa. In 1983, the introduction of the immunosup- pressant drug cyclosporine dramatically increased the potential donor pool for any given patient. By the mid-1990s, there were hints in the medical literature of the rise of a new phenomenon: transplant tourism. In 1989, a small article had appeared in The Lancet reporting an inquiry into allegations that four Turks had been brought to Humana Hospital Wellington, in London, to sell their kidneys. Other research suggested that the selling of kidneys from living donors was rapidly growing in India, and that in China human organs were being harvested from the bodies of executed prisoners.

The Organ Recruits: Scheper-Hughes found that Brazilians—often men trying to support families—were being trafficked to South Africa to sell their kidneys to patients from third countries. Alberty da Silva (pictured) contributed an organ to a woman from Brooklyn. (Photo: Organs Watch)

While most governments and international medical associations condemned the sale of human organs, laws and professional guidelines were inconsistent and often poorly enforced. What was clear was that the demand for organs outstripped the supply in nearly every country. In the United States, despite significant public outreach campaigns to encourage donations, there were already more than 37,000 people on organ waiting lists. Each year 10 percent of patients waiting for a heart transplant died before a donated organ could become available.

Scheper-Hughes' research into the organ trade began in earnest not long after the Bellagio confer- ence, when she teamed up with the event's organizer, a medical historian at Columbia University named David Rothman; his wife, Sheila, a professor of sociomedical sciences at Columbia; and Lawrence Cohen, a fellow anthropologist from U.C. Berkeley. The four decided to spread out across the globe, dividing up the burgeoning global hot spots for transplant tourism. The Rothmans would focus their research on China; Cohen would investigate India; and Scheper-Hughes would travel mainly to Brazil and South Africa.

The research got off to a swift start. During breaks from teaching in the late 1990s, Scheper- Hughes visited African and South American dialysis units, organ banks, police morgues, and hospitals to interview surgeons, pathologists, nephrologists, nurses, patient's rights activists, and public of- ficials. "It became like detective work," she told me. "I used a simple snowballing technique. I'd go to a morgue or a transplant ward and I'd get one person to tell me something—and then ask, 'Where do I go from here?' I found it enormously satisfying to begin to put the pieces together."

Her collaborators, too, quickly made headway. While reliable estimates of how many transplants were happening on the black market were difficult to come by, evidence that this market existed appeared nearly everywhere the collaborators looked. In India, Cohen found people selling their kidneys to private transplant clinics that catered to patients all over the world, despite a 1994 law that made such transactions illegal. Selling kidneys, he discovered, had become so common in India that some poor parents even talked of selling an organ to raise a dowry for a daughter. David Rothman, for his part, had become convinced that a Chinese anti-crime campaign was associated with a growing enterprise that sold organs from executed prisoners.

In both Brazil and South Africa, Scheper-Hughes discovered that the dead bodies of many poor people were harvested, without permission, for useful tissues—corneas, skin, heart valves—to be exported to wealthier countries. In São Paulo, she worked with a city council member who had been tracking illegal commerce in human tissue taken from the cadavers of indigents and nursing-home patients. He showed her documents suggesting that more than 30,000 pituitary glands had been shipped to the United States over a three-year period. In South Africa, the director of a research unit in a public medical school showed her documents approving the sale of heart valves to medical centers in Austria and Germany. She also discovered, at private medical centers in both Brazil and South Africa, that kidneys from live donors were being bought and sold.

In 1998, while Scheper-Hughes was still writing up her first major papers on her field research, she and her collaborators met at a Starbucks in Tokyo during a medical ethics conference to compare notes. The material they were turning up seemed so remarkable that they brainstormed starting an organization called Organs Watch, which would serve as a repository for information on global transplant activity and a center for future research. By 1999, they had secured a $230,000 grant from the Open Society Institute, along with a commitment from the University of California, to help create the new organization.

As she gathered more information on Rosenbaum and his ties to multiple American hospitals, Scheper-Hughes made another unusual decision for an anthropologist: She began to share her findings with U.S. law enforcement.

But the collaboration between the Rothmans and Scheper-Hughes was short-lived. Scheper-Hughes' first major article on the organ trade, which she published in April 2000 in Current Anthropology, chronicled her findings in the morgues and hospitals in Brazil and South Africa; it was also so impassioned that it sounded, at times, like the setup for a horror movie. "Global capitalism and advanced biotechnology have together released new medically incited 'tastes' for human bodies, living and dead, for the skin and bones, flesh and blood, tissue, marrow, and genetic material of 'the other,'" she wrote. She called organ and tissue transplant a "post-modern form of human sacrifice" and accused transplant surgeons of conspiring to invent an "artificially created need ... for an ever-expanding sick, aging, and dying population."

Some anthropologists saw the paper as groundbreaking. Elliott Leyton, of Memorial University of Newfoundland, wrote that the paper was nothing less than the "beginning of a long-awaited moral vindication of much of modern anthropology, lost for so long in the contemplation of its own navel." Other anthropologists, however, felt that Scheper-Hughes played fast and loose with source identification, and that her writing came off more like muckraking journalism than anthropology.

To her collaborator David Rothman, Scheper-Hughes' rhetoric didn't seem like scholarship at all. He was particularly taken aback by her contention that doctors were intentionally creating the demand for transplants. Rothman remembers traveling with his wife (and co-collaborator) to Berkeley in November of 1999 to attend the public launch of Organs Watch. "When Sheila and I saw the website that had been created, we were—let me see if I can get the right word—disturbed," Rothman said. "It was sensationalistic, emotive, and provocative, with pictures of bodies but no charts. We realized that we operated in very different ways from Nancy." After a heated argument, the Rothmans cut ties with Scheper-Hughes and ended their work with Organs Watch. But Scheper-Hughes was just getting started.

As soon as organs watch went public in 1999, Scheper-Hughes began to receive hundreds of leads through emails and phone calls from people who claimed behind-the-scenes knowledge of the tissue and organ trade. She began to personally track down many of the stories. "I was traveling in a blur, like a whirling dervish," she said.

She also began to push what she acknowledged were the accepted ethical boundaries of anthropological research. On her trips, as she wrote in a 2006 paper published in the Annals of Transplantation, she sometimes posed as a patient seeking a transplant or as someone looking to purchase a kidney for a sick family member. On a visit to Turkey, she pretended to be shopping for a kidney for a sick husband at a flea market near a minibus station in Askaray, a poor immigrant neighborhood of Istanbul. She found an unemployed baker who said he was willing to sell one of his kidneys, and she went so far as to sit with him at a local cafe to negotiate a price. At other times, she wrote, she'd simply walk into hospitals or clinics to confront a surgeon or an administrator or to learn what she could from patients. When stopped or questioned by staff or security, she would identify herself as "Dr. Scheper-Hughes," knowing that the questioner wouldn't likely suspect that she was referring to her doctorate in anthropology. Faced with what she called an international "organs Mafia," Scheper-Hughes argued in a 2009 article for Anthropology News that she had no choice but to abandon many accepted rules of her profession. "When one researches organized, structured and largely invisible violence," she wrote, "there are times one must ask if it is more important to strictly follow a professional code or to intervene."

Her research during this period yielded a wealth of information and insight into the illicit networks of organ brokers. The trade in kidneys particularly fascinated her. Unlike the trade in cadaveric heart valves or corneas, kidneys were being shipped from country to country inside the living bodies of sentient individuals. In the Philippines, kidney sellers she interviewed often pulled up their shirts, displaying their nephrectomy scars with evident pride. They spoke of the surgery as a sacrifice made for their families, and members of their community sometimes compared their abdominal incisions to the lance wounds Christ received on the cross. In Moldova, as she reported in a 2003 paper published in the Journal of Human Rights, people who had sold their kidneys were considered so morally and physically compromised that they were treated as social pariahs. "That son of a bitch left me an invalid," one Moldovan paid donor said of his surgeon. Young Brazilian men who had been flown to South Africa to sell their kidneys described to Scheper-Hughes how the experience had gained them a pass into the world of tourism and medical marvels. One told her that his main regret was not having spent more time in the hospital. "There were clean sheets, hot showers, lots of food," he recalled. As he recovered, he went down to the hospital courtyard and bought himself his first cappuccino. "It was like ambrosia," he said. "I really felt like a big tourist." In the end, some attested that they would make the deal again, and some regretted the decision. "They treated me OK until they got what they wanted," another seller told her. "Then I was thrown away like garbage."

In her travels, Scheper-Hughes was also able to develop some relationships with kidney brokers, the middlemen who sought out donors in poor countries and neighborhoods. One convicted broker, Gadalya "Gaddy" Tauber, gave her lengthy interviews while serving out his sentence in Henrique Dias military prison in Recife, Brazil. Tauber, she learned, had facilitated a trafficking scheme that sent poor Brazilians to a private medical center in South Africa to supply kidneys for Israeli transplant tourists. He employed a number of "kidney hunters," some of whom were young men who had already donated their kidneys, to find new recruits. In the end, it wasn't difficult. Once the first young men came back from surgery centers in South Africa showing off their thick rolls of cash, Tauber and his associates had more willing donors than they needed. They began to drop the price they offered to donors from $10,000 to $6,000 and then to $3,000, Scheper-Hughes reported in a 2007 profile of Tauber.

Scheper-Hughes' portrayals of organ donors, recipients, and even brokers like Tauber show a great deal of nuance and empathy. At other times, however—particularly when she writes about transplant doctors, bioethicists, or members of the "transplant establishment"—her writing turns markedly more strident.

Where Are the Bodies
The Haunting of Indonesia

BY ADRIAN VICKERS

Controversies about the 1965–66 killings of communists in Indonesia have revolved around questions of "how many?" and "who was responsible?" The killings are the subject of strong dispute at present as Islamic groups utilize anticommunist sentiments within complex power plays. While there is general agreement that at least 500,000 people accused of being communists were killed in the period following an attempted coup in 1965, public discourse in Indonesia plays down the significance of the killings through a series of rhetorical strategies aimed at placing the burden of responsibility on the communists themselves. Thus attempts to create a national reconciliation process have been stalled, as have attempts to more accurately document the burial sites of those killed. By examining the social and cultural problems surrounding the bodies of the victims, this paper demonstrates the complexity of issues of corporeality and haunting. Examples from Bali and Java show how hard it is to memorialize the killings, and thus the difficulties of incorporating the killings into national discourse.

In Indonesia in the months and years immediately following September 30, 1965, 500,000 people accused of being communists—according to conservative estimates—were systematically murdered. Hundreds of thousands of others were imprisoned, and millions suffered curtailment of their human rights. These killings brought Major-General Suharto to power. For the period that he remained president, from 1967 to 1998, public discussion of the killings was forbidden, and state agencies actively intervened to censor any mention of the killings in public documents.[1] The killings were the basis of not just a new regime, but a new version of

Adrian Vickers, "Where Are the Bodies: The Haunting of Indonesia," *The Public Historian,* vol. 32, no. 1, pp. 45-58. Copyright © 2010 by University of California Press. Reprinted with permission.

the Indonesian state, and the authorized account of the origins of Suharto's regime was an important legitimizing mythology.

During the Suharto or New Order era, the killings were marked by absence. People had to act as if the killings had never occurred, despite the fact that millions of people were affected as political prisoners, family of victims, witnesses, and perpetrators; the legitimizing mythology was at odds with local ontology. The post-Suharto period is one in which this huge gulf in comprehension of the killings is being bridged, but it is a measure of the efficacy of New Order ideology that it is proving very difficult to reconcile the two understandings.

Visiting Balinese villages in the late 1970s and 1980s, I was struck by the number of empty house-yards in otherwise densely populated villages. I was told that these had been the houses of victims of the killings. After the families were taken to graveyards and slaughtered, the houses were burned down. In Bali these empty living places, *karang suung*, were dangerous, the kinds of spaces populated by ghosts and malicious spirits who could bring misfortune to those around them. These are some of the negative elements of what anthropologist Graeme MacRae calls the *"niskala* landscape,"[2] the space inhabited by forces that are outside sensory perception. These forces are nevertheless considered part of Balinese reality. Similar kinds of what we would call "spirit beliefs" exist in Java, although modern rationalists, including Muslim modernists, disdain these kinds of beliefs.[3] This kind of rationality does not extend too far beyond a small group, since even members of the family of a former president and religious leader have documented how the Presidential Palace in Jakarta is haunted.[4] Another anthropologist, James T. Siegel, argues that in Java people have beliefs about the dead that accord them a different status than ascribed in Western practices and beliefs. The dead can be imagined, says Siegel, as a source of blessings if treated properly and their graves visited. This is not to say that people on Java do not feel grief, but they imagine their relationship to the dead in ways different from those that Siegel or I might feel.[5]

Java and Bali were the islands where the anticommunist killings were most intense. Given the currency of spirit beliefs in daily life on these two islands, the fate and handling of the dead is an important consideration in understanding the impacts of the killings on Indonesian society, and the lack of resolution of this suffering in public life. An inkling of this comes from discussions of the Bali bombings of October 11, 2002 in Kuta, where in the gossip and conspiracy theory surrounding the event, some local sources explained the choice of site as stemming from the fact that there were so many 1965 killings around where the Sari Club had been.[6]

WESTERN AND INDONESIAN HISTORIOGRAPHY OF THE KILLINGS

The historiography of the 1965 killings is still very sparse. In the Suharto years—and still now—by far the largest number of both Western and Indonesian accounts is taken up with the question of what happened during the so-called coup of September 30, 1965, in which a small group of army officers attempted to seize power, only to be defeated in the following days by a rightist group from the military led by Suharto. In the Suharto period, the standard account of the coup attributed it to the Communist Party of Indonesia, the *PKI*, and created a mythology around the killings of six generals by the coup group. The coup group was known as the 30th September Movement (*Gerakan Tigapuluh September* or G30S, but this was punned into "Gestapu" by the Indonesian military propaganda arm drawing on World War II references that were current at the time. In response, deposed president Sukarno referred to the events as *"Gestok"* (the 1st October Action), thus asserting that this was really a seizure of power by Suharto. In the New Order mythology, the generals who did not die in their houses were tortured and their bodies were sexually mutilated by members of the PKI-affiliated Indonesian Women's Movement, *Gerwani*. The torture and mutilations were a fabrication, but are enshrined in a monument that commemorates the generals as "Heroes of the Revolution." The monument is contemporary with a state-sponsored film made by leading director Arifin C. Noer (*The Treachery of the G30S-PKI*).[7] School texts and other statements by the then government made this standard version overwhelming. The monument to the dead generals also includes a life-size diorama showing communists torturing one of the captured generals.[8]

This account is important because it erases the subsequent killings of communists from history. It provides a powerful image of monstrous communists that precludes any possible sympathy; it makes the victims of the killings so inhuman that the death of 500,000 people is seen as just retribution for the deaths of six. At the time of the coup this emotional equation was established first of all with publicity about the death of a little girl, five-year old Ade, the daughter of General Nasution. She was killed in the crossfire when the coup group unsuccessfully attempted to shoot her escaping father. The second element that established the equation was the concept that in 1965 it was a matter of "kill or be killed." Rumor had it that the PKI was organizing an armed take-over of power and would wipe out all its enemies, so the actions of the killers was simply self-protection. A rumor was in circulation in Jakarta in 1965 that a boat-load of arms from China was coming to the PKI (this was another fabrication, possibly introduced by the CIA), and members of political parties opposed to the PKI were also later shown death lists allegedly drawn up by the PKI, with their opponents' names on them. These lists now seem to have been inventions of the military.[9] Such accounts of causality make it clear that the regime that took power bore no responsibility for the events. The only acknowledged perpetrators were communists, and the only acknowledged "victims" were anticommunist generals and a little girl. This official account naturalized the massacres that followed, and made the perpetrators into agents of justice and self-defense. In the popularly accepted version of the killings, they were spontaneous reactions by the general population against the PKI, but planned actions for which the military bore primary responsibility for planning and leading the carrying out of mass murder. Both perpetrators and victims became anonymous.

Few versions of the story countered this official version, and those that existed were in English and were not accessible in Indonesia. One of the only detailed accounts of the killings appeared soon after the events, and was based both on the author's experience as a journalist, and apparently on access to U.S. reports.[10] This account, like many of those that followed, detailed the processes of violence, where killings of people accused of being communists were carried out not just with the swift execution of the firing squad, but through torture, beheadings, and the hacking of bodies into pieces. These stories fit with the oral accounts that I have collected over the years that talk of dead bodies jamming up waterways and systematic slitting of throats of intended victims to save bullets. People from East Java spoke of finding human body parts in fish long after the bodies had disappeared.

Very few Western journalists ventured outside Jakarta during the killings, so there was very little information getting out to the world, and western newspaper editors frequently did not publish the stories of those few journalists based in Jakarta because they were unverified.[11] One of the rare publications on the subject was Harry Aveling's edited collection of translations of Indonesian short stories about the killings and their aftermath.[12] A few journalistic accounts produced in the 1970s added to the picture, and the journal *Indonesia* published a number of primary sources,[13] but no original research on the subject was carried out until the late 1980s, when Robert Cribb edited a collection of primary sources and analyses of different aspects of the killings.[14] The long-term perceptions of the killings and their implications for the lived experience of those who remain are not explicitly dealt with in the English-language literature.

The period after the fall of Suharto, with its relaxation of censorship, has seen the appearance of thousands of new books in Indonesia on Indonesian history and politics, books that would never have been allowed to appear before 1998. The best sellers in Indonesian bookshops over the last ten years consistently have included large numbers of books on the 1960s. As with the general historiography, much of this literature is concerned with the coup rather than the killings, but even so there have been a number of significant accounts of the killings themselves, including autobiographical accounts of survivors. The first major account was Hermawan Sulistyo's publication of his earlier Ph.D. thesis.[15] This book dealt with the killings in East Java, carried out by members of the group Ansor, a "youth wing" of the traditionalist Muslim body Nahdlatul Ulama or NU. As someone closely aligned with NU and its future president, Abdurrahman Wahid or Gus Dur, Sulistyo has been accused of being more sympathetic with the killers than their victims, but nevertheless his account details the processes of killings in a clearer fashion than previous accounts.

Gus Dur's presidency was also marked by the first steps in creating a process of national reconciliation, and Sulistyo was involved in that process as a presidential advisor. Gus Dur, as someone whose family members were involved in the killings, issued a public apology to the victims (*korban*) of 1965, a category that includes the hundreds of thousands of political prisoners and family members of those killed and imprisoned. This and other aspects of Gus Dur's antihierarchical approach to his office led to a strong backlash against him, especially from the military, who worked closely with the political party of Megawati Sukarnoputri to remove Gus Dur in a constitutional coup. The attempts to set up a national reconciliation process persist, but at the time of writing these remain stalled at the level of the national Constitutional Court. One of the key bodies pursuing this aim is a nongovernment organization affiliated with NU, Syarikat, which has dedicated itself to documenting the experiences of victims. Their main documentation to date has been a series of videotapes of interviews with women who were political prisoners and otherwise victims of the New Order regime. These interviews have largely been carried out by young school and university students who have a deep commitment to finding out what their parents' and grandparents' generations would never talk about. Interestingly, many of these researchers are now too young to have experienced the New Order.[16]

Syarikat arose after other groups had already begun the process of attempting to document the killings and incarcerations from the point of view of those who were imprisoned. For most of these groups "reconciliation" has meant acknowledgement of their suffering and of what occurred. Although members of the different "victims' groups"[17] might want some kind of calling to account of the perpetrators, collectively they know that this is too ambitious an aim in an Indonesia where the heirs and collaborators of the perpetrators still hold political power. This was a movement led by older political activists, most of them now dead, and began in the late New Order period, largely thanks to the tireless efforts of ex-Gerwani member Sulami. The organization that she set up, the Foundation for Victims of the Killings (LPKP), received strong motivation from the publication of her own memoirs, which followed on the prison writings of Indonesia's most famous author and a member of the organization, Pramoedya Ananta Toer.[18] After their own memoirs came the writings of other former political prisoners, notably Putu Oka Sukanta and Hersri Setiawan.[19]

Budiawan, in a publication again based on a Ph.D. thesis, has documented the killings from the angle of the New Order's psychology of state terror.[20] A number of other oral historical accounts have been published, but some of these have not been well documented, and have involved heavy editing and re-writing.[21] A clearer picture of the lead-up to the killings and their course has been provided by an oral history team working under the activists Ayu Ratih and Hilmar Farid, in collaboration with the historian John Roosa.[22] The opening up of the Indonesian publishing industry since 1998 has also produced an Indonesian translation of one of the most important publications on political conflict in Bali, Geoffrey Robinson's *Dark Side of Paradise*.[23] This publication, along with the translation of Cribb's edited volume, for the first time gave Balinese readers access to detailed knowledge of the extent and nature of the killings. Balinese author Degung Santikarma, the son of a leftist political leader killed in 1965, has been the most senior Balinese author contributing to the analysis of the killings and the lack of public acknowledgement of the events.[24]

A reaction to sympathetic accounts of the post-1965 period has been a recent set of books that go back to blaming the PKI, both for the killings of the generals and for other actions, such as the land reform movement of the early 1960s that led to local conflicts over land control. These accounts make explicit the New Order implication that the killings were "natural" reactions to the "brutality" and "terrorism" of the PKI, and attribute all blame to the victims.[25] They demonstrate the impossibility of opening up the period for public debate, since both sides more often engage in polemics. Attempts at public discussion are often just restatements of the New Order version of events. For example a television program on "the need for reconciliation of victims and perpetrators" shown on local television in Yogyakarta in 2003 saw a promilitary representative angrily declaring that the "real facts" of 1965 were that the PKI killed six generals, and refusing to acknowledge that there was any possibility of going beyond those "facts."[26]

A BALINESE ACCOUNT

For generations of Indonesians born after the killings, sorting out "the facts" has been difficult. One of the most moving independent accounts of the killings comes from a young Balinese writer, I Ngurah Suryawan (b. 1979).[27] This is one of the few books to detail the impacts of the killings on both victims and killers, and to deal with the physical sites of killings and the problems of the bodies of the dead. It stands out because it does not begin with the advocacy that comes from the positions of the other writers and public figures with more direct personal connections. His book is an important attempt to bridge the gap between the continued lived experience of the killings and public representation of them.

Suryawan's account is based on his own attempts to understand the stories in his family and village. The first of these stories is of his grandmother's telling that *Pekak* (Grandfather) Wayan, their former next door neighbor, was going to be part of a mass ritual for the elevation of the souls of the dead. In his case because he was *"mati Gestok"* his corpse was never found. Suryawan did not understand what *"mati Gestok,"* literally "killed in the 1st October Action" meant, and his book reflects the journey to find out.[28]

Bali was, probably after the Kediri area of East Java, the site of the most intense killings, with at least 80,000 killed (out of a then population of one-and-a-half million), mainly at the end of 1965 and the first quarter of 1966. In other areas killings went on until at least 1968. This book is written with a splendidly poetic style (although it suffers from lack of editing), as Suryawan narrates his encounters with those who were killers, witnesses, and families of victims. The wife of a member of the Nationalist Party (PNI) killings squads (called *Tameng*) tells of how the killers would gather at her house after they had transported their victims to the local graveyards and beaches for slaughter. They came still with blood on their hands to eat *lawar*, the festive pork dish, and drink *arak*, home-brewed rice whisky. Like many working in Indonesian universities, Suryawan lacked access to most of the Western sources that would have added to his account, but the details he provides of one particular part of West Bali, the site which had one of the largest concentrations of communists on the island, are significant in terms of what they add to our general understanding.

What is clear from Suryawan's account is that many of the conventional narratives of the killings in Bali are open to question, and when he attempted to document specific mass killings, his sources tended to disagree wildly. An example of the conventional narrative is the story that the mass killings in the Jembrana area were sparked by an initial aggression of the PKI, in which an army intelligence officer and two members of the Muslim "youth" group Ansor were killed.[29] While one of Suryawan's informants confirms the standard account, another casts doubt on it, arguing that those killed may actually have been killed by the military as a way of stirring up anti-PKI sentiment. This, and other aspects of Suryawan's accounts, tend to confirm what is now becoming clear in Indonesia as more people speak about the period: that much of the killing was provoked and led by the military, who provided specific death lists to the various militias with which they worked. One of the sinister phrases that is repeated by different people Surywan interviewed is *"kene garis,"* literally "ruled out," of someone on these lists.

While this role had already been long documented in the Western academic literature, it is only just beginning to penetrate the Indonesian accounts.

Another aspect of complexity that arises is the diversity of approaches to killings, with the army playing a key regulatory role. For example, one of the Jembrana leaders of the Nationalist Party (PNI) groups was notorious for raping women alleged to be PKI, usually just before killing them. But as Suryawan shows, this man was actually taken to court and convicted of rape (although his sentence, three years, was absurdly low), partly because other members of anticommunist groups were repelled by his actions. Likewise, the military curbed looting of the property of victims.

The photographs in Suryawan's book illustrate open landscapes, surprisingly empty for overpopulated Bali: the beach at Candikusuma; a "tourist object"; a bridge; and an imposing old Chinese shop. All of these are major killing sites, and those who know and use these sites regularly treat them with care, fencing them off and putting up shrines. When killings occurred, usually people were taken from one village to be executed in the graveyard of another, to avoid too many local ramifications. Bodies from elsewhere were dumped at Candikusuma, and mass executions by firing-squad were performed there. The bodies were left to be washed out to sea, although digging in the sand years afterwards has turned up many skulls. Where people were killed in their houses, the houses had to be burned down and the sites ritually purified with big offering ceremonies. The reasons why become clear in the discussion of the big old Chinese shop, *Toko Wong*. Prisoners were collected here, but were subject to mass slaughter in the many over-crowded rooms in the shop, where the blood was said to have reached the level of the skirtings. Informants were loathe to identify the shop because they felt talking about it would affect its business. People often report hearing noises coming from the shop, such as screams, or the sounds of a mass of voices. One of the local people known as a notorious "sadist" who led the slaughter in the shop rooms is said to have gone mad, and to have fits whenever he walks anywhere near the shop.[30]

HAUNTINGS AND PURIFICATIONS

The madness of the killers is a common motif in stories of the killings on Bali.[31] Strangely, many killers were people who allegedly were themselves communists. In other areas I have heard it said that they killed in order to prove themselves politically pure, although one of Suryawan's more chilling stories is of a man who took part in slaughters because he wanted to take a kind of generalized revenge for the murder of his own communist brother. Other killers are described in Suryawan's book, as with other general accounts I have heard, as having been co-opted by the military from other groups and compelled to join in. Such people are the ones described as having gone mad. The *Toko Wong* slaughters in particular weigh on the minds of witnesses and participants.

The madness of the Toko Wong "sadist" and other killers is the first of many types of haunting. In Bali there are many types of beings who live beyond the realm of the senses. In general belief a "bad death" (*salah pati*), such as by suicide or bad accident, consigns the spirit of the deceased to inhabiting lonely sites such as ravines or forests. Such ghosts, *tonya* or *memedi*, can be grouped with the *wong gamang*, "spirit people" who live in communities similar to human social units, and who have to be "fed" with offerings to be kept happy.[32] When placated they can look after their local human communities, as was told to me of the village of Serangan, off the coast of Badung. Serangan is a "hot earth" (*gumi panas*) village, an area where power we might call spiritual is concentrated, and had, before a large tourist development disturbed it, a quiet coastline where the *wong gamang* lived. According to accounts of Serangan people told to me in 1994, the *wong gamang* played a major role in 1965, protecting the village from the slaughters of other areas.

Similarly, the late Klungkung (East Bali) artist, Mangku Mura, described for me in 1996 the effects of banning cockfighting in his area of Bali in the period prior to 1965. Cockfights are felt by many Balinese to be important because they involve the spilling of blood, and thus appease adverse forces. According to Mangku Mura, his portion of the village of Kamasan in Klung kung, Banjar Siku, defied the government order and persisted with cockfights in this period. Because of these cockfights, Banjar Siku remained free from the killings, even though the poor sharecroppers of that part of the village were involved in leftist groups, whereas the rest of Kamasan was subject to large-scale slaughters.

There are many Balinese forms of offerings and ceremonies involving the invisible world. Most ceremonies include sets of offerings to high and lower spirits, or forces of the upper and lower worlds, often referred to as gods and demons. These ceremonies can also include ways of dealing with human death, as found in elaborate sets of death, cremation, and postcremation ceremony that move humans from the world of living to the world of the dead, including preparing souls for reincarnation, or ultimate apotheosis that frees the soul from the cycles and birth and death.

Immediately at the time of killings some villages or sections of villages took action to purify them-selves. Suryawan describes how one village leader, Dewa Rai, was murdered in his own house, the killing having been jointly committed by all community members so no one person was to blame. This kind of communal acceptance of responsibility is common in Southeast Asia, but in this case it meant the whole community had to make expensive and elaborate offerings on the site of the killing, since blood had been spilt there instead of at the graveyards where others were executed.[33]

The returning presence of the bodies under the landscape of Java and Bali is described in detail by Suryawan, as he meets with people who regularly find skulls and other skeletal remains when floods occur or parts of the landscape dug up for new developments, as with the river mouth at Perancak, and Ijogading Bridge in Negara, a major killing site since upgraded. Suryawan seeks out the wells into which bodies are reputed to have been dumped, one of which is called the Crocodile Hole (*Lubang Buaya*) after the site in Jakarta where the bodies of the generals were dumped on the night of September 30, 1965. When attempting to visit this spot and a nearby house, his guide, a local, calls off the visit after seeing a headless man and a Chinese woman, although Suryawan did not see these figures.[34]

On July 23, 2007 Anak Agung Bagus Sutedja, Governor of Bali up to 1966, was cremated, with the body absent.[35] In Sutedja's case there was great uncertainty as to whether he had survived the events of 1965. Sutedja, as governor, was close to President Sukarno, and strongly favored the left.

He, like the leading political figure from a powerful house of Badung Regency, I Gede Puger, are often described as PKI in conversation with Balinese, but this is not true, as neither were members of the Party, who often referred to them as "running dogs of Capitalism."[36] After the coup in Jakarta, Sutedja was summoned to the capital. The last record of his presence in Jakarta is a note dated December 10, 1965, summoning him from his hotel to meet with Sukarno. According to his family, Sutedja disappeared from Jakarta in the middle of 1966, and there are many legends that he had survived and gone into exile to Europe, or perhaps was living in other parts of Indonesia. Such legends took on an almost messianic dimension, and his son consulted many spirit mediums (*balian*) to try to locate him. By 2005, when it was permissible to talk about the disappeared, the family finally decided that he was dead and that his lost spirit needed to be placated, so a large cremation was organized.[37]

Such ceremonies had been held over many decades since the killings. At first they were held quietly, as with large mass postcremation rituals (*mukur*). The period leading up to a large world-wide purification ceremony, the *Eka Dasa Rudra*, held in 1979, saw many—including those from the village of Kamasan where I was living at the time—take the opportunity to purify the souls of the dead. Prior to the 1990s these matters could not be publicly discussed, particularly as the Suharto regime had run periodic purges of those in society who were held to have "an unclean environment," code for PKI family members or links. Only in the post-Suharto period have there been open attempts to make such spiritual rehabilitations public.

One such highly publicized attempt took place on Java in 2000, where an organization devoted to documenting the killings attempted an exhumation and reburial of the dead. Filmed by Lexy Rambadeta, the villagers of Dempes, Wonosobo in Central Java used a death list to exhume one grave.[38] This grave was estimated by the leader of the exhumation group, a legal representative, as containing twenty-one bodies, all of whom were taken from the local prison to be killed. Those murdered included a village head and university lecturers. The details of the list are matched against the memories of family members, and a ring is used by a woman, Sudjiyem, to identify her husband. At the end of the process one family attempts to bury its dead, but is stopped by an angry mob from a local Muslim youth group, carrying signs reading "PKI not welcome here."[39] Although the potential physical conflict was averted, the scenes are ugly, and demonstrate the emotional nature of the exercise. Such violent agitations continue to mean that processes of reconciliation are stymied at each level of politics, as when lobby groups led by Muslim leaders from the NU body stymied reform of the school curriculum in 2007, leading to book-burnings that extended beyond text books from the new curriculum into anything with "communist associations." The involvement of former Ansor members from NU in the killings means that most do not want the issues reopened. This is also the case of those who were part of the PNI political party, now the major component of the Indonesian Democratic Party of Struggle (*Partai Demokrat Indonesia-Perjuangan* or PDI-P) led by Megawati Sukarnoputri. The recognition of vested interests by these two groups in politics will stymie any further developments in the process of reconciliation. I have also heard that on Bali police and military intelligence harassment of members of "Victims' Groups" continues, and that some of Suryawan's informants were subject to such harassment. There is further ambiguity over the attitude of the current president, Susilo

Bambang Yudhoyono, an ex-military officer whose father-in-law was General Sarwo Edhy, the military leader of the killings in Java and Bali. Although the military can exert power and influence in the state, their collective role in the killings will not be dealt with, either nationally or internationally.

UNRESOLVED LANDSCAPES

The ease with which Suryawan was able to redefine his own local landscape seems throughout his book to shock him. For those who remembered the killings and were involved, as participants, family, or witnesses, these are landscapes littered with bones, peopled by spirit beings who can visit misfortune on the living. Surywan's accounts of the haunting of the landscape, and the highly charged atmosphere around discussion of the killings, illustrates why reconciliation is so difficult to achieve, especially in the absence of agreed-upon facts. The ghosts themselves thus constitute unacknowledged facts in the public culture of the Indonesian state.

Balinese and Javanese spiritualism adds another dimension to the political problems of dealing with the killings of the 1960s. The burden of the killings is a psychic one, one that has on-going ramifications for the living. Over the last decade, the freedom to lighten this burden by ritual means has eased the lives of many, but national and local politics are still dominated either by the personnel who held power during the Suharto period, or by those who have a vested interested in the Suharto-era mythology of the origins of the New Order state. Identifying the victims of the killings as victims, let alone discussing the responsibility of the perpetrators, remains extremely difficult. Because the political situation distorts and even stifles public debates, the meanings of such rituals and their acknowledgement in the wider political sphere are not yet part of Indonesian public discourse.

The physical landscape of Java and Bali is contested, because it is a landscape polluted on many levels. One of the most recent attempts to reconcile the physical and felt landscapes is the building of a garden, the *Taman 1965*, or garden monument to the victims of 1965, built by a prominent local non-government organization leader, Agung Alit, whose brother Degung Santikarma has done much to open up public discussions of the killings in Indonesian newspapers, public debates, and conference papers. As children of one of the political leaders murdered in the killings, Agung Alit and Degung have used their public identity to challenge the uneasy landscape and to create new sites where meanings of the killings can be explored. The *Taman 1965* is then a new kind of ritual of reconciliation, attempting through the use of charged physical space to acknowledge and clarify the existence of the killings and their long-term effects. Thus it is a reconciliation of individual felt knowledge with public lack of acknowledgment. As yet the Indonesian state has no way of dealing with this difference, and is unable to identify or confront the perpetrators. Until this changes, such rituals and memorial spaces will have to suffice.

ENDNOTES

1. Confidential sources have told me how mention of the killings was removed from publications even during the 1990s. See Adrian Vickers, "Reopening Old Wounds: Bali and the Indonesian Killings," *Journal of Asian Studies* 57, no. 3 (August 1998): 774–85.

2. Graeme MacRae, "Economy, Ritual and History in a Balinese Tourist Town." Ph.D. dissertation, University of Auckland, 1997, 183.

3. Clifford Geertz, *The Religion of Java* (Glencoe, IL: Free Press, 1961).

4. Yenny Zannuba Wahid, "The Ghosts of the Palace," *Latitudes*, April 2002, 75–77.

5. James T. Siegel, "Images and Odors in Javanese Practices Surrounding Death," *Indonesia* 36 (October 1983): 1–14.

6. Although another local story attributed the club's destruction to the fact that it was on the site of a children's graveyard.

7. Arswendo Atmowiloto, *Pengkhianatan G30s/PKI* (Jakarta: Pustaka Sinar Harapan, 1988).

8. Katharine E. McGregor, *History in Uniform: Military Ideology and the Construction of Indonesia's Past* (Singapore: NSUS Press, 2006).

9. Yusuf Hasyim, "Killing Communists," in *Indonesia in the Soeharto Years: Issues, Incidents and Images*, ed. John H. McGlynn et al. (Singapore and Leiden: Lantar, 2007).

10. John Hughes, *The End of Sukarno: A Coup That Misfired, a Purge That Ran Wild* (London: Angus & Robertson, 1968).

11. Ross Tapsell, "Australian Reporting of the Indonesian Killings of 1965–66: The Media as The 'First Rough Draft of History'," *Australian Journal of Politics and History* 54, no. 2 (2008): 211–24.

12. H. Aveling, ed., *Gestapu: Indonesian Short Stories on the Abortive Communist Coup of 30th September 1965* (Honolulu: University of Hawaii, 1975).

13. "Report from East Java," *Indonesia* 41 (April 1986): 134–49; Ibu Marni, "I Am a Leaf in the Storm," Trans. Anton Lucas, *Indonesia* 49 (1989): 49–60; Brian May, *The Indonesian Tragedy* (London: Routledge, 1978); Peter Polomka, *Indonesia since Sukarno* (Harmondsworth: Penguin, 1971); Pipit Rochijat, "Am I PKI or Non-PKI?," Trans. Ben Anderson, *Indonesia* 40 (1985): 37–56.

14. Robert Cribb, ed., *The Indonesian Killings 1965–1966: Studies from Java and Bali* (Clayton, Vic.: Monash University Center of Southeast Asian Studies, 1990).

15. Hermawan Sulistyo, *Palu Arit Di Ladang Tebu: Sejarah Pembantaian Massal Yang Terlupakan (Jombang-Kediri 1965-1966)* (Jakarta, Indonesia: Kepustakaan Populer Gramedia, 2000).

16. Discussions (2005–2008) with Rumekso Setiawan, a leading figure of Syarikat with whom I have worked very closely, and also with Syarikat members (2006–2007) and one of the school teachers of a student film maker (2007).

17. Although the general term used is *korban* or victim (the word can also mean "corpse"), various of the survivors of the period, such as leftist journalist, publisher, and former political prison Jusuf Issak reject the label of "victims"—"I wasn't a victim, I was an opponent of Suharto" (personal communication, 2005).

18. Sulami, *Kisah Nyata Wanita Di Penjara 20 Tahun, Karena Tuduhan Makar Dan Subversi, Perempuan-Perempuan Dan Penjara* (Jakarta: Cipta Lestari, 1999); Pramoedya Ananta Toer, *Nyanyi Sunyi Seorang Bisu,* 2 vols. (Jakarta: Lentera, 1995 & 1997).

19. Hersri Setiawan, *Diburu Di Pulau Buru* (Yogyakarta: Galang Press, 2006); Hersri Setiawan, *Aku Eks Tapol* (Yogyakarta: Galang Press, 2003); Putu Oka Sukanta, *Mearjut Harkat* (Yogy karta: Insist Press, 1999).

20. Budiawan, *Mematahkan Pewarisan Ingatan: Wacana Anti-Komunis Dan Politik Rekonsiliasi Pasca-Soeharto,* Tim Penerjemah Elsam, Hersri Setiawan, and Eddi Riyadi Terre trans., 1st ed. (Jakarta: Lembaga Studi dan Advokasi Masyarakat, 2004).

21. Sulastomo, *Hari-Hari Yang Panjang: 1963–1966* (Jakarta: Kompas, 2000).

22. John Roosa, Hilmar Farid, and Ayu Ratih, *Tahun Yang Tak Pernah Berakhir: Memahami Pengalaman Korban 65: Esai-Esai Sejarah Lisan* (Jakarta: Kompas, Lembaga Studi dan Advokasi Masyarakat, 2004).

23. Robert Cribb, ed., *The Indonesian Killings: Pembantaian PKI di Jawa dan Bali, 1965–1966* (Yogyakarta, 2003); Geoffrey Robinson, *Sisi Gelap Pulau Dewata: Sejarah Kekerasan Politik* (Yogyakarta: MataBangsa, 2006); Geoffrey Robinson, *The Dark Side of Paradise: Political Violence in Bali* (Ithaca, NY: Cornell University Press, 1995).

24. E.g. Degung Santikarma, "Menulis Sejarah Dan Membaca Kuasa: Politik Pasca-1965 Di Bali," in *Perspektif Baru: Penulisan Sejarah Indonesia,* ed. Henk Schulte Nordholt, Bambang Purwanto, and Ratna Saptari (Jakarta: Yayasan Obor Indonesia/KITLV-Jakarta/Pustaka Larasan, 2008, 2008): Degung Santikarma, "Monument, Document and Mass Grave: The Politics of Representing Violence in Bali," in *Beginning to Remember: The Past in the Indonesian Present,* ed. Mary S. Zurbuchen (Singapore: Singapore University Press, 2005), 312–23.

25. A. Kasdi, *Kaum Merah Menjarah: Aksi Sepihak PKI/BTI Di Jawa Timur 1960–1965* (Yogyakarta: Jendela, 2001); Aminuddin Kasdi and G. Ambar Wulan, *G.30s. PKI/1965: Bedah Ceasar* (sic) *Dewan Revolusi Indonesia* (Surabaya: Java Pustaka Media Utama, 2005): Ridwan Saidi, *Lakon Politik 'Che Guevara Melayu': Dokumentasi Teror PKI 1955–1960* (Jakarta: IPS, 2006).

26. TVRI Yogyakarta, Perlukah Rekonsiliasi Korban-Pelaku (Yogykarta, 2003).

27. I Ngurah Suryawan, *Ladang Hitam Di Pulau Dewa: Pembantaian Massal 1965 Di Bali* (Yogyakarta: Galang Press, 2007), 49–50.

28. Ibid.

29. This story was the basis of my own earlier account of how the killings started as a civil conflict in Bali, in Ibid., 149; Adrian Vickers, *Bali: A Paradise Created* (Ringwood, Vic.: Penguin, 1989), 171.

30. Suryawan, *Ladang Hitam Di Pulau Dewa: Pembantaian Massal 1965 Di Bali,* 159.

31. Further confirmed by Degung Santikarma in his discussions with me about people in his village, a point he also follows up in his own publications on the killings in the Badung district in South Bali.

32. Margaret J. Wiener, *Visible and Invisible Realms: Power, Magic, and Colonial Conquest in Bali* (Chicago: University of Chicago Press, 1995), 53–54.

33. Suryawan, *Ladang Hitam Di Pulau Dewa: Pembantaian Massal 1965 Di Bali,* 133.

34. Ibid., 216.

35. Gembong, "Tunggangi Lembu Maketu, Dikawal Singa Jantan: A.A. Bagus Sutedja Dipelebon," *Warta Bali*, January 17, 2007. Suryawan includes photographs of the cremation, but no details.

36. The last comment came from the late Prof. I Gusti Ngurah Bagus. Suryawan also repeats the error in his descriptions of Puger.

37. Suryawan, *Ladang Hitam Di Pulau Dewa: Pembantaian Massal 1965 Di Bali*, 166–172.

38. Lexy Junior Rambadeta, *Mass Grave* (Indonesia, 2003).

39. The full footage from Rambadeta's film is only included in a longer documentary by Chris Hilton, *Shadow Play* (2001).

Killing the Documentary
An Oscar-Nominated Filmmaker Takes Issue with 'The Act of Killing'

BY JILL GODMILOW

I n March 2013, I bought a ticket to a screening at the Museum of Modern Art. There was a big buzz about a new film called "The Act of Killing" and I wanted to see it.

In the theater, first I was fascinated, then puzzled, then increasingly disturbed by the film's shock therapy approach to the horrors of political life in Indonesia. After an hour, I walked out, stepping on the toes and handbags of mesmerized audience members. I walked not because talk of murders by murderers made me queasy. These stories, told by low-level assassins, employed during General Suharto's 1965 coup to depose left-leaning President Sukarno and to destroy all his opponents, aren't new. (Estimates range from 500,000 to two million accused "communists" and ethnic Chinese were slaughtered.) I walked out because I was miserable in my viewer's seat—shackled in the intolerable position the film suggested I should be comfortable in. I wasn't.

Two months later, perplexed by the rave reviews trailing the film from festival to festival, I went to see it again when it opened in theaters. "The Act of Killing" now began with a new introduction by the filmmaker. Addressing the camera, Joshua Oppenheimer gives the audience permission to laugh when there is something funny. Why do we need his permission to laugh? Is he demanding that we feel comfortable watching boastful reconstructions of mass butchery by the death squads of Medan? What is he nervous about? Oppenheimer also reminds us that we are all capable of good and evil ... that any among us could be tempted. Hmmm?

Since then, the raves, awards and prizes have continued. No critic seems to be examining—at least in print or on the net—what there is to learn from this "unruly documentary artivism": the new moniker for non-fiction films which assert their status as both art and activism and thus the license they claim to refuse compliance with certain classic codes of ethical documentary filmmaking.

In my opinion, unruly artivist films are obliged to produce useful experience. Good filmmaking comes down to education—education of the senses, including the sixth sense, as the Buddhists would have it, the mind. Unruly or not, the questions to ask of all films remain the same: How is the audience constructed by the film—that is, to whom is the film addressed—and how? What generalizations are made about the represented...and about us/them differences? What information is privileged or repressed? What arguments are made? Is the experience of the film useful? How are we changed by it?

I suspect that the critics—like the rest of us—don't know what to do with their engagement with this "bold" film. Without noting any personal discomfort, they stab wildly, flattering the film with platitudes: *audacious, timeless, explosive, shattering, horribly brilliant, shocking, transporting, unprecedented, bizarre, hypnotic, surreal, disturbing, timeless, unforgettable, unmissable, essential, stunning, a minor miracle, a new form of cinematic surrealism, an absolute and unique masterpiece, a radical development in the documentary form, unprecedented in the history of cinema, every frame is astonishing, and so on.*

I read these vague and awkward phrases as fumbling attempts to avoid the writers' own confusion. Or perhaps the critics lack the energy, or the means, or both, to confront what has happened to them in their cinema seats. Yes, they have endured extreme sensation—sensation way off their critical charts. They can say they've never seen anything like this before, and they haven't. Yet, without analysis of their own experience in the theater—and perhaps not wishing to be left off the cheerleading bandwagon—they jump on and more amazed raves flow forth.

As far as I have been able to discover, no critic has admitted discomfort in the face of this "candy-colored moral migraine" (J. Hoberman). Here and there are tiny hints: Nicolas Rapold wrote from the film's premiere, "Toronto shock and outrage at the grotesque spectacle of impunity settles into*helpless numbness* [emphasis mine] over the course of the 116-minute running time." Anthony Lane, in the The New Yorker, queries: "Unforgettable though such scenes may be, however, is it wise to weave such fantasies—however distressing or therapeutic—around the practice of evil when the facts of the case are, to most viewers, so obscure?" Jonathan Rosenbaum, on his blog: "Maybe there's some other use value for his showcase of the feelings of mass murderers that I haven't yet been able to tease out of this material." So far, only Nick Fraser, a BBC Commissioning Editor, and the independent critic, Jennifer Merin, both at About.com, have written negatively about the film—elegantly and succinctly. The rest of the critics have handled this hot and "revered" documentary without respect for the Indonesian people, or, it's my understanding, for the film's international audiences.

Throughout the film, Oppenheimer encourages his collaborators to produce ostentatiously surreal and violent dramatic film reconstructions of their death squad activities. Ever since Robert Flaherty asked his Inuit collaborator, Nanook the Bear, (his real name was "Allakariallak") to fake the capture of a seal in 1922—at the very beginning of ethnographic film tourism—we have seen hundreds of social actors perform "real" re-enactments of their lives for the cameras of documentary filmmakers. There is nothing new in "The Act of Killing" but carnage, and the special, cozy relationship we are urged to enjoy with the killers. Perhaps this is exactly what the critics are avoiding with their raves—that they have been duped into admiring, for an hour or two, the cool Rat Pack killers of Medan.

Collaboration is a way to share, with the social actors represented, responsibility for a film's acts of description, strategies and arguments...a way to "keep it clean." Some of the most useful films I've seen in the last twenty years—non-fiction and otherwise—have been the products of collaboration with the social actors represented, in unique and disparate ways. Carolyn Strachan and Allessandro Cavadini's "Two Laws," Kent MacKenzie's "The Exiles," and Rolf de Heer and Peter Djigirr's "Ten Canoes" come quickly to mind.

First on this list should be Rithy Pahn's "S-21: The Khmer Rouge Killing Machine"—the perfect counter model to "The Act of Killing." In S-21, the two survivors of the infamous Cambodian prison and their Khmer Rouge prison guards are brought together in a patient reenactment of their crimes, which the traumatized guards cannot otherwise recollect. "The Act of Killing" is also a collaboration of sorts, but for me a non-productive, uncomfortable, even unclean one.

Here are six warnings based on what I saw in "The Act of Killing," a dangerous model for the future. I write here to start a dialog with other filmmakers where there is none—not yet. It is up to us to learn from this film and work hard to avoid its miscalculations and mistakes.

DON'T MAKE HISTORY WITHOUT FACTS

In spite of the scale of their deeds, the Medan gangsters featured in "The Act of Killing" are, in fact, no more than foot soldiers and footnotes to a much larger drama—a 50-year sequence of upheavals, which permitted a paranoid and aggressive U.S., with other allies, to depose left-leaning leaders and popular movements in any way they saw fit—all over the world. It began in Iran in 1953, then in Indonesia, 1965, Vietnam, Laos and Cambodia starting in 1965, in Chile, 1973, then in El Salvador and Nicaragua, 1979, in Guatemala in 1982, in Iraq, 2001, and then some. There is no mention in Oppenheimer's film of the role of the U.S. in the Indonesian massacres, or of the bigger Cold War drama.

It is irresponsible, even obscene, to take up the current abysmal Indonesian political condition without laying out the history of who was complicit in the military overthrow of President Sukarno and the massacre that followed, activities that threaten citizens even today. The U.S. Embassy in Jakarta supplied the right-wing Indonesian military with lists of up to 5,000 suspected Communists for elimination. (Steeped in the "domino theory", which argues that if one state in a region came under the influence of communism, then the surrounding states would follow in a chain reaction, President Lyndon Johnson was dedicated to the "containment" of China's and the Soviet Union's capacity to spread communism throughout Asia. Johnson continued to support Suharto's "New Order" coup until the general had terrorized and then completely secured the country.)

Without context, there is only sensation and spectacle. Yet there is the illusion of learning and caring. After two hours of "The Act of Killing," we leave the theater with a fantasy degree in Indonesian history … credentialed, but ignorant, and absolved. Instead of offering useful history and analysis, the film's exploitation of the Medan thugs actually rebunkers the traces of the 1965 genocide and its aftermath, further perpetuating the crimes.

THINK TWICE BEFORE REPRESENTING DISPLAYS OF VIOLENCE PERPETRATED ON LITTLE BROWN PEOPLE BY OTHER LITTLE BROWN PEOPLE

Consider whether your film helps anybody understand anything useful, especially when representing people of another color, or any other category of human, in unique and complex historical situations.

Horror shows, like the terrorizing of the Indonesian people, make us gasp in horror and disbelief. Yet, as with all liberal-consensus documentaries, we feel we are doing some civic duty by just witnessing the troubles. We feel we have "cared." Then, when the film ends, as the lights are coming up, we recuperate ourselves in our cinema seats, semi-consciously, with the unspoken sentiment, "Thank God that's not me… nor mine." (Thank God I don't live in a gangster paradise, as Indonesia is represented in this film.) The horror show is over and we can go home, enlightened, ennobled, refreshed … absolved.

After 60 odd years of "underdeveloped" and "third world" geopolitical constructions by "first world" cultures, to step into "third world" waters requires respect and extreme caution to avoid unconsciously generating chauvinistic representations. There is no evidence in this film—and there should be—that the Indonesian people are capable of resistance to domination and terror. The history books and filmed records tell us they are capable. (For example, witness Joris Iven's "Indonesia Calling," a 1946 documentary film about trade union seamen, waterside workers and passionate Indonesian freedom fighters, refusing to service Dutch ships containing arms and ammunition destined for Indonesia to suppress the country's independence movement. There is "A Poet: Unconcealed Poetry" ("Puisi tak terkuburkan"), by the Indonesian filmmaker, Garin Nugroho, made in 2000…the first Indonesian film to revisit the 1965 massacres. And more recently, the 2011 documentary Dongeng Rangkas. There are others.)

The Swedish filmmaker and University of Minnesota scholar Dag Yngvesson, currently writing a PhD dissertation on Indonesian Cinema, has watched "The Act of Killing" at many different Indonesian screenings and describes the relation of us (western filmmaker/western audience) vs. them (Indonesian subjects) in this way: "As 'The Act of Killing' uses the information it has gathered to shock its Indonesian audience into accepting the truth of its representations, it simultaneously reduces its local viewers, who are implicitly "in" the film, to the level of not yet democratic, not yet enlightened, and, at some level, still in need of a caring outsider to help guide them on the path to positive change."

In a recent panel presentation, Yngvesson expanded his analysis of how "The Act of Killing" secures the post-colonial country of Indonesia to our understanding of a doomed state:

Yet each moment of creativity, and each ostensibly 'free' admission of violence, lechery, or lack of remorse from its participants ultimately serves to tighten the reigns of Oppenheimer's discursive control. Using their candid descriptions, he feeds both local and international audiences an Indonesia that is too easily digested, shocking atrocities and all, and settles comfortably within the pre-processed realm of the known. Well-stocked with ideas born of the Geneva Convention and the International Criminal Court at The Hague, Oppenheimer places his interlocutors, and their film, in a hermetically sealed story-world where a typically crumbling, underdeveloped nation is neatly divided along axes of good and evil by the contemporary standards of international law.

DON'T PRODUCE FREAK SHOWS OF THE CRIMINAL, OPPRESSED, "THE PRIMITIVE"

Don't herd "others-than-us" into cinema cages and then examine their "peculiarities" of action, speech, their fears, their limitations, their despotisms, as if they are foreign to the natural, the human... the family of man. Don't wantonly project unexamined political criteria, especially on a people with a long history of colonial subjugation. And, as importantly, refuse to make any representations that suggest that the others-than-us are needy of our caring, filmic intervention.

BE FAIR TO YOUR SOCIAL ACTORS

With gentle encouragement from the director, the movie gangsters of Medan serve themselves up as willing subjects to be consumed. There is a pining for the spotlight, for the opportunity to exhibit their power. However, to "empower" social actors in documentary, when the "actors" don't realize how they will be seen on the world stage (in this film as immoral, grotesque, juvenile and pathetic) is a questionable practice. Many times over we have witnessed, on film and elsewhere, debased, paramilitary mad men in the pay of power. There is nothing new here about these particular criminals—nothing except their ignorance of their own exploitation in the cinema.

The writer, Jeremy Mohler, has suggested that Anwar Congo, the central figure in the film, might have been pleased to tell his tales to an American filmmaker, as he and his mates were hugely enamored of the American action films that were banned by Sukarno's left leaning government in the 60's. Mohler writes, "Congo and his buddies resemble the lower-level gangsters in The Sopranos (1999–2007), eager to please the bosses but unaware of the larger games being played above them." Because

Congo's corrupt bosses received funding, weaponry, manpower and kill lists from the CIA, Congo might have understood, naively, that the American documentary director would thus be delighted with his lurid accounts of murder, since that's just what the U.S. aid was paying for. I base this speculation on Yngvesson's account of Congo's sense of betrayal on seeing the finished film.

Yet a few months after the highly successful launch of Oppenheimer's film at several major Western film festivals, in an Al Jazeera follow-up report inspired by "The Act of Killing" (Vaessen 2012), Congo weeps during a Skype conversation with his former admirer, who is now safely back in Europe: "I very much feel that what you've produced has made things very difficult for me." Oppenheimer indicates that he understands Anwar's predicament, but assures Congo that he will never forget his bravery in opening his story to the world, revealing "how people can commit evil acts."

Oppenheimer has indeed succeeded in documenting, and drawing mass attention to, a predicament both uniquely horrifying, and, at the same time, rather typical in the discourse of the Third World: that of gross human rights violations, and, in this case, genocide, at the hands of a corrupt regime and its supporters. The film is thus both problematic and also potentially powerful as a local political tool, depending on the context in which it is shown and what other sources of information viewers have to process its sweeping claims.

Congo, having heard Oppenheimer out via Skype, says nothing, but instead raises himself, still streaming tears, and walks away, leaving laptop and camera alone in the room. For him, and Indonesia, there will be no ending scene, plane ticket home, or "180 degree turn" that leads to an unambiguous truth.

Oppenheimer has said, on the record, that he would be in danger if he returned to Indonesia...in danger, perhaps, from the government, but maybe from the gangsters themselves.

AVOID BUILDING A FILM ON THE BEDROCK OF PORNOGRAPHY

Pornography is the use of other people's "reality" for our pleasure. In "The Act of Killing," our pornographic interest is generated primarily by the gangsters' ignorance of us watching and disapproving. It's titillating to stand on the safe side of a one-way mirror...unseen, amazed, judging...as the gangster's cinema fantasies grow more and more grandiose. The film keep stimulating wonder, and titillating narrative questions: "How far will the gangsters go... especially on camera?" "Don't they know we are watching them... aghast?" "Why have they been tolerated for so long?" There are adequate answers and explanations of the gangsters' performances but explanations would dampen audience fascination with the sideshow.

Don't titillate us with others' sad condition, with the Medan gangsters' demonstrations of their power and their Hollywood fantasies. Rather, try to de-titillate or de-pornographize such experiences, so that the underlying structural forces producing and protecting these criminal behaviors are laid bare.

There are many techniques to do this: Harun Farocki de-pornographized napalm in "Inextinguishable Fire." Trinh T. Minh-ha de-pornographized African villagers in "Reassemblage." Alain Resnais de-pornographized the atomic bomb in "Hiroshima Mon Amour."

DON'T COMPROMISE YOUR AUDIENCE

As the cameras roll, Congo proudly demonstrates his preferred killing technique (strangling with piano wire…"less blood") then carefully directs the re-enactment of it on film. Because the American director stands in for viewers, we enjoy, vicariously, his intimate, non-judging, comfortable collaboration with Congo. As the filmmaker's accomplices, we are unable to separate from identifying with his methods of seduction—cameras, crew, make up, props, costumes, and extravagant lighting instruments—so that the gangsters can squeeze, in their inept way, sinister, and sometimes absurdly romanticized, movie experience from their histories.

Normally, in non-fiction film—for better or for worse—we are left alone with our Judeo-Christian "thou-shalt-not-kill" and certainly our "thou-shalt-not-kill-and-boast-about-it" judgments. But here, both our invisibility behind the camera, and our comfortable and confident superior moral position has been eroded by our partnership with the unseen but very present director, who keeps encouraging the gangsters' boasting demonstrations.

We want to trust the director but we are not used to this treatment and so we squirm… we squirm, rationalize and hope… hoping, for almost two hours, that the end of the film will loose the narrative straightjacket we have suffered by Congo's finally realizing remorse. We feel deeply compromised by the intimacy and collusion. We struggle to exercise our own judgment. Our occasional snickerings at the glamorized fantasies are but feeble attempts to twist ourselves out of this excruciating dilemma. The filmmaker has forced a trade of our moral reasoning for grotesque cinema thrills.

AVOID USING DOCUMENTARY FOR CONFESSIONS AND/OR PRIMAL THERAPY

When, at long last, we see Congo in pain, unable to retch… seemingly weakened by the memories he has been attempting to reproduce for the screen, the narrative has completed its task and the audience is relieved of tension…I guess. Theoretically we have been "paid back" for our time and interest, but the payback is unsatisfying and we feel it. Congo's remorse is not useful for anything except resolving the film's narrative and rationalizing the compromising footage that preceded it. Congo's retching can't stack up against the murders. It can't unravel the director's web of intentions. It offers nothing in the way of restorative justice. And it can't explain how it was possible for Indonesia to be turned on its political/social ass almost overnight and why it remains in its ghastly condition today. It can't explain anything that we want to understand. That would require a different kind of film.

Poor Congo. On the "Act of Killing" website, the director explains, "He needs the filmmaking to address his own nightmares so he can live with himself. He's trying to deal with his pain. He's trying to experience his pain." The unseen but ever present filmmaker captures his audience with daring tales of murder, and then rationalizes audience discomfort with the suggestion that we have witnessed the saving of one person's soul. Congo's pain is not our business. We are not priests. We cannot pardon anybody. This witnessing makes us feel helpless and distraught. Confessions are private matters unless part of a reconciliation process.

As with scenes of people praying and meditating on camera, it's hard to believe that these are not performances of self for the camera… perhaps, even unconsciously … performed to pay back the filmmaker's expensive investment in the social actor's participation in the film. I trust that I am not the only one in the audience who has speculated that Congo felt he owed the American filmmaker an ending, and delivered it.

The possibility that Congo dutifully performed retching for the American filmmaker had apparently never occurred to Oppenheimer. Errol Morris, one of the executive producers of the film, queried the director about this issue, and, as reported in Morris' Slate article in July, 2013, Oppenheimer was very disturbed by the suggestion that Congo's participation in his film had not brought him to remorse, that the retching—like the gangsters' other productions, was a required performance, that Anwar was not seriously interested in confessing guilt. Oppenheimer responded:

You're raising a very, very scary thought. It's so disturbing in some way that it would've been hard for me to maintain my relationship with Anwar, if this were an operating assumption. It could be right. If Anwar doesn't have a past and also has these at the very most echoes, reverberations or stains from what he's done that he doesn't recognize, and if the final moment is maybe yet another moment of performance, if he then disappears into the night and we're left in this shop of empty handbags, and there's no connection to the past on that roof, then it's almost too chilling for me to contemplate what the whole movie is really saying. It's a disturbing thought.

It is a disturbing thought.

AFTERTHOUGHTS

One afternoon, in a dentist's office, I leafed through People magazine's December 30, 2013 issue. There were many top ten lists, among them the Top 10 Movies of the Year. Sandwiched between #3, "American Hustle" and #5, "Gravity," was #4, "The Act of Killing," summarized as: "The year's most stunning documentary unmasks men responsible for mass killings in Indonesia as both boastful and pathetic—and disturbingly, still in power." Hot stuff—but that's entertainment. And entertainment, combined with Judeo-Christian high moral education, is what liberal-consensus audiences seem to desire. It's what gets nominated for Academy Awards.

Perhaps distribution of this film should be limited to the numbed and fearful Indonesia people, among whom—and I take the director's word on this—the portrayal of Congo's movie fantasies, and now Congo's discomfort and guilt are sparking renewed interest in examining the last 48 years of Indonesian history. The director suggests that Congo's cheesy re-enactments will help reduce fear of the right wing state, which has ruled with violence and intimidation all those years. I hope it does. But I would suggest that the possibility of empowerment has been eclipsed. This would have required input, real collaboration between the perpetrators and victims.

The education of the rest of us has failed. Without education, we are likely to stay silent the next time our politicians see it in their interest to destabilize another peoples' government, by any means necessary.

The Question of Collaborators

Moral Order and Community in the Aftermath of the Khmer Rouge

BY EVE MONIQUE ZUCKER

AN EPILOGUE AS PRELUDE

I t was near to the end of my fieldwork in Cambodia when Pu [Uncle] Thon offered to take me to see the sites that had comprised the old village of O'Thmaa before Pol Pot came and everything was destroyed.[1] The original village had consisted of four parts, each with its own place name and located at a distance from each other. Each part contained a group of households whose members were related by birth or marriage. Unlike today when the houses line the main road, the four parts formed a loose arc that together formed O'Thmaa village.

On the morning of the tour, we set off on the oxcart road behind my house passing the Thmaa Khmouch or ghost/spirit rock on our right. The base of this boulder is littered with old bottles and ancient ceramic jugs and bowls, which had been used as receptacles for the ash remains of ancestors that the villagers say lived perhaps a century ago. Turning westward, we continued until we reached a stretch of rice paddy where the first of these homesteads once stood. Pu Thon explained:

> This place was called Bung Srei. There were four houses here.... In the house of Yiey [Grandmother] Hom there were four people originally; now no one is left. Her two children, both Khmer Rouge soldiers from 1970 to 1972, were accused by someone from the village, not a Khmer Rouge, of being White Khmer and killed. One of these sons was married to Yiey Na, the daughter of Ta [Grandfather] Som.

The next is the house of Yiey Na and no one is left. She was the daughter of Ta Sok. Her husband who was the son of Yiey Hom was a Khmer Rouge soldier but was killed after being accused by a villager of being White Khmer.

We continued westward toward the O'Thmaa creek and came to Ta En's garden near the giant mango trees and small stream:

This place is O'Ta Rom and is named after the ancestor guardian spirit named Rom. We believed in these spirits before the war. There were three houses here. The first was the house of Von. His wife is Yiey Oak.

Pu Thon told me that Von was a member of the Khmer Rouge who had his head cut off by the American-backed government under Lon Nol (1970–1975). The Lon Nol Government was at war with the Khmer Rouge, who were fighting a revolutionary war to seize power in the country and install an extremist Marxist-Leninist-inspired government that later decimated over one-fifth of the population (approximately 1.7 million people) in an effort to "cleanse" the nation. The Khmer Rouge Regime lasted from 1975 to 1979 under the leadership of Pol Pot.

Pu Thon's narrative continues:

Lon Nol's soldiers cut off Von's head and sent it to their commander. It was the custom at that time. Von was a Khmer Rouge soldier who had gone to the "Struggle in the Forest" [he had joined the revolutionary movement that was based in the forests] with the Khmer Rouge in the late 1960s. He was the first cousin of Cheun. All of his family is dead except Yiey Oak and her son Som.

Next is the house of Ta Chan. He was the village chief under Sihanouk [the monarch who held power before being ousted by Lon Nol] and first cousin of Ta Von. Chan's daughter married Ta En. Chan worked with Ta Kam who was the deputy village chief. Both were village chiefs for a long time. Chan was killed by Lon Nol. Everyone in his family is now dead except two daughters; one here in the village who is married to Ta En, and the other in Sre Ambel. His wife died of illness.

And so the tour continued, with each household having lost some, or all, of its members to the Khmer Rouge, Lon Nol, or each other. I tell this story here to start at the place where the old society ended. And now the story I tell begins.

INTRODUCTION

The villagers were only beginning to recover from the terror and devastation of the 1970s when the Khmer Rouge entered the highland village of O'Thmaa and its surrounding communities, having recently returned to their villages in late 1998. This homecoming has not been easy. In addition to having to physically rebuild their village, villagers also had to reestablish the village as a moral entity, a community based on sets of mostly kin ties, forming a reciprocal web of obligations among people.[2]

Much of the work on the aftermath of violence and the healing process that has followed has focused on the individual or collective "memory" of violence (Antze and Lambek 1996; Rittner and Roth 1993; Robben and Suárez-Orozco 2000). I focused on how aspects of the moral order that were broken or damaged were being repaired in efforts to heal from the past. How were the actions and roles of collaborators linked to their social and moral position within the community, and how did this positioning vary across communities?

BACKGROUND TO RESEARCH

My research spanned two neighboring communities in a mountainous region of Kompong Speu province in southwestern Cambodia. The first of these two communes I call Prei Phnom and the second I call Doung Srei. Each of them consists of a collection of villages. I based myself in Prei Phnom's westernmost village, which I call O'Thmaa, bordering on the wilderness of the Cardamom mountain range. I made regular excursions to the other villages in Prei Phnom commune as well as to several in Doung Srei.

At the time of my research in 2003, O'Thmaa had a population of 175 people dispersed over 40 households. There were few elders in the community, especially men, because of the war and the large number of executions that had occurred within the village in the early 1970s. From 1970 until the mid-1990s, all men and many women old enough to become soldiers were conscripted by the Khmer Rouge, the government, or both. This lack of elders had significant repercussions for this community, where elders were considered the symbolic vessels of moral and traditional knowledge and therefore played important roles in the transmission and practice of religious and social events. Moral knowledge is acquired over a lifetime; such knowledge is considered to be wisdom in old age. Being morally wise means not only knowing right from wrong but also knowing the ways of the ancestors who are considered imbued with the best moral qualities, including honesty, wisdom, and virtue. An elder in Cambodia symbolically becomes like a living, and therefore accessible, ancestor.

The vast majority of villagers in the communities where I worked considered themselves Theravada Buddhists; however, 10 percent of O'Thmaa's population were Methodist Christians. Indigenous animist and Hindu "Brahman" practices interlaced the practices of villagers of both of these faiths. These villagers occupied the lowest ranks of Cambodia's socioeconomic ladder due to high illiteracy rates, continuous forced displacement since 1970, a shortage of arable land, and an overall lack of resources. Before the war they cultivated small rice paddies and gardens, and subsidized their living through trade in forest products such as resin, aloewood, and betel. Today people again tend rice paddies and gardens, but at the point of my study had been unable to grow sufficient rice and food to sustain them throughout the year. Instead, they relied on the illicit sale of forest products and aid from development agencies.

A HISTORY OF CONFLICT

The geographic locale of the community has also had significant historical consequences for its residents. The area is mountainous, forested, and only thirty km from the main highway, making it an ideal base for guerrilla warfare campaigns. The villagers explained to me that the area was put to this use in three separate historical instances. The first of these episodes took place in the late 1940s and early 1950s when the Khmer Independence movement (Khmei Issarak), with the support of the Vietnamese, used the area as a base from which to launch guerrilla attacks on the French colonial government. Later in the late 1960s and early 1970s, the area was taken again, this time by the Khmer Rouge and by the North Vietnamese. During this period, the Khmer Rouge established a base of operations in the area under one of their top leaders, famous for his brutality. The Khmer Rouge conscripted villagers at this time as soldiers and local leaders.

According to the villagers, the Vietnamese presence in the area lasted only a little more than a year, but the Khmer Rouge entrenched themselves and began implementing their insidious policies while continuing their fight through the American bombings of 1973, and onward. Between late 1970 and early 1972, the majority of villagers initially joined the Khmer Rouge up on a nearby mountain to flee the war and the Lon Nol government army. After a brief return to the village, most were forcibly evacuated by the Khmer Rouge to a cooperative where they were forced to eat, work, and sleep collectively. In April 1975, the civil war ended with a Khmer Rouge victory. They called their new state Democratic Kampuchea, which lasted four years until 1979 when Vietnam seized power. In its four years of existence, Pol Pot and his cohort exercised torture, mass executions, starvation, and devastation on the people of Cambodia, leaving close to two million people dead. When Vietnam took the country, the Khmer Rouge (including soldiers from the village) were forced to flee to the Thai border. However, by the late 1980s the Khmer Rouge had regained a foothold in this village region, making it a base and a battle zone up through the mid- to late 1990s.

The historical significance of the region is implied in the name the Khmer Rouge bestowed on it: Prei Brayut, or "The Forest of the Struggle," the place from which they launched and fought their revolution. Later the region became known as a "base" (moulitan) area, a place that came under Khmer Rouge control relatively early in the revolution, and from which they conscripted their soldiers and low-level leaders. These "base people" or "old people" were considered less corrupt than the "new people" of the urban centers, who were believed to have been contaminated by foreign ideologies (Him 2000; Kiernan 1996; Pin and Man 2000; Ung 2000).

Through all of this, most of the surviving people from the commune where I stayed were forcibly relocated numerous times. It was not until the 1990s that the residents resettled their villages; most villagers did not return to O'Thmaa until after 1998 when they began to rebuild their lives after nearly thirty years of absence.

TA KAM: THE STORY OF A VILLAGE ELDER

What follows is the story of one recent returnee to the village who I call Ta Kam. His story is told from three vantage points: mine, the villagers', and his own.

My Story of Ta Kam

It was on my first journey to O'Thmaa that I met Ta [grandfather] Kam. I found him constructing a bamboo platform for his thatched hut on the side of the village's northern slope. His face and body, both lean and angular from a lifetime of work and poverty, were topped by closely cropped silver hair that contrasted with the dark caramel of his skin. Ta Kam explained that he had only just returned to O'Thmaa. He had been born in this village and owned a parcel of land through his first wife, but lived in Doung Srei with his sister's family. He had returned to O'Thmaa to help his daughter farm.

At the time, I found his homecoming extraordinary for it brought into stark relief the rupture and continuity that seemed to characterize this village. I thought that it must have been a profound experience for him to return to see those he had known since his childhood and perhaps with whom he had had little contact for two or three decades. Ta Kam had said he was seventy-eight, and so I asked him about an old woman I had met earlier in the village, who appeared roughly the same age. He said only that he knew her and that she was a bit older than him. I found this strange in a village with such a small population.... Surely he must have more of a sense of connection with her. But he said little about her and seemed to dismiss the topic.

I did not meet Ta Kam again for four months. I made several attempts to visit him but was repeatedly told that he was away in the forest or the other commune. One rainy September evening I decided to try again. Remembering his hospitality, I was looking forward to seeing him and so I was quite pleased to find him at home that evening. Unfortunately Ta Kam was ill and my companion and I found him lying on the raised platform of his hut when we arrived. Even so, he welcomed us with warmth and grace. Ta Kam's manner was reminiscent of the archetypal traditional Khmer elder—grandfatherly, self-effacing, wise, and kind. On a later visit, he agreed to tell me his life story.

After that I did not meet with Ta Kam for several months, but would catch occasional glimpses of him along the road with his worn red-and-white checked *kramar* (scarf) tied into a small bundle and slung over his shoulder. He was always dressed the same, in a threadbare white shirt, mid-length trousers, and wide-brimmed hat; he would be clutching a walking staff. Thin, gaunt, poorly attired, and making incredibly long treks under Cambodia's sweltering sun, he gave the appearance of an ascetic or pilgrim.

Over time, I learned a bit more about him. I was told that he often attended ceremonies at the temple in Doung Srei commune where he served as an *achaa* (Buddhist layman) and that he was related by blood *(sach-chiem)* as well as marriage *(sach-tlay)* to most of the people of the village. Nonetheless, I also observed that he had little or no interaction with the other villagers. No one seemed to show much interest or regard for him, unlike his daughter who seemed to enjoy good relations with most villagers. It was only much later that I was able to understand Ta Kam's peculiar relationship with the villagers.

Their Story of Ta Kam

In the final months of my fieldwork, the village development chief,[3] Sau, whom I knew quite well, and I were discussing the executions that had occurred in the village in the early 1970s after the Khmer Rouge had come to the area. I remarked how I had noticed there were a disproportionate number of widows (26 percent of village households at the time were headed by widows)[4] in O'Thmaa as compared to other villages in the area. Agreeing, Sau explained:

> During that time they had a chief like I am today. He wanted to have a good face and so he would issue complaints against people here to the commune leadership and they believed him. They would come then and catch these people and take them away to kill them.... Some of the people committed no wrong—but he accused them anyway to gain face (reputation). That village chief was Ta Kam.

Ta Kam, whom I had perceived as a warm, grandfatherly elder was in fact a killer—a collaborator.

After this it must not have taken long for word to spread that I now knew about this village secret, for I began to hear stories from other villagers as well. I learned that Ta Kam had been the vice village chief under Lon Nol and then was elected by the villagers to be the acting village chief under the Khmer Rouge. Ta Kam thus doubly betrayed the villagers. As leader he would have been expected to behave morally and offer the villagers some protection in exchange for their support. He not only failed to do this but also transgressed his role by sacrificing them to promote his own welfare and longevity. Ta Kam had now become in the words of one villager: "that Ta, who caught the people to take to kill."

Viewed as a killer of his own people, Ta Kam was shunned by the villagers. He did not speak or talk with anyone beyond his daughter and was notably absent at the annual village harvest festival. One former Khmer Rouge soldier who had lost his father to Ta Kam explained the present-day relationship between the villagers and Ta Kam as follows:

> That Ta, he doesn't dare to look at anyone young or old in the face. No one really likes him either. They don't want to be friendly with him; they hate him. If people wanted to they could

take revenge *(songsuck)* against him at any time. But people think it is over now and so they don't want to fight and claim or demand *(tiem tia)* retribution for their parents' blood.

I now understood why no one would talk to Ta Kam when he came to the village and why he was rarely mentioned. People saw him as lacking morality and concerned only for his own promotion and welfare. In other words, they said he was ambitious in the negative sense, meaning that he willfully sought to better his position at the expense of others, was ignorant, and did not know right from wrong. Ta Kam sacrificed his neighbors and kinsmen to the Khmer Rouge and yet, remarkably, the children and wives of those he killed did not seek revenge. They said the past was behind them and they had no desire to continue fighting, suggesting that they have found a means by which to heal from their wounds, even if Ta Kam's living presence still continued to haunt them as a reminder of their lost loved ones.

Over time people were willing to share their stories with me, but they were still reticent about talking about Ta Kam. When they spoke about that terrible episode in the past they more often commented that the people of that generation committed evil deeds against one another for reasons that are not understood. One might anticipate that the villagers would also shun Ta Kam's daughter, but instead she enjoyed warm social relations with most villagers. This appeared antithetical to the idea that families are morally affiliated, an idea that informed the practice of arrests and executions under the Khmer Rouge in O'Thmaa when cadres and their entire families, including babies, were arrested and killed as traitors. This view of families seems to stem from broader Khmer beliefs about kinship ties in hierarchical relations of politics and violence. Not blaming the family as a whole provided villagers with another means of healing; the tear in the community was contained through their welcoming of the daughter. Because most villagers were related to Ta Kam by blood or by marriage, there was a vested interest in keeping his family within the community while surgically removing him.

Ta Kam's Story of Himself

It is important to humanize Ta Kam, for he is actually a real person and it is as such that villagers related to him, and because his story contextualizes the village's circumstances.

Ta Kam was born in O'Thmaa in 1923 to a family that had lived in the area for generations. Like other villagers at the time, most of his children died in infancy; later, a son taken by the Khmer Rouge died under Pol Pot. Ta Kam said he had relations in every village across the two communes, but when asked about his relations in O'Thmaa he said there was only his daughter and a couple of nephews. His account of his childhood was sparse. There was no school. He helped his parents tend their rice paddy and garden and helped collect forest products for consumption and trade. One of the significant events that Ta Kam remembers from his childhood was seeing a French hunter astride an elephant, accompanied by some Khmer soldiers. He explained that he hid himself in the forest at the time because he feared the Frenchman just as he would fear soldiers or policemen. In another act of evasion, he later avoided an encounter with a delegation sent from the district governor's office to conscript boys for military service. These encounters with outsiders of higher social rank and representing larger systems of power are important in understanding Ta Kam's later acts and the history of the village.

When Issarak and Vietnamese forces entered the area during the war of independence, Ta Kam was forced to flee with other villagers to the mountains in the north for four years. At age thirty-five, he went to work at a nearby mountain where the former king Norodom Sihanouk was building a residence. He recalls that there were twenty households in O'Thmaa when he left and twenty-five by the time the Khmer Rouge had entered the area in early 1970, when he was forty-seven. "Then," Ta Kam explained, "Pol Pot came to the area and they were killing everyone except me and a few others who managed to survive." He said he had not seen these other survivors since that time.

He continued with this period from 1970 to 1975, a particularly bloody chapter in O'Thmaa's history:

> Before 1975 I didn't do any work [meaning he held no special position]. I was just like other people, someone eking out a living. The war happened and some people fled to the forest, but I didn't. After that the Khmer Rouge pushed me to drive a cart and carry cloth, rice seed, and other stuff [again, he was not in a position of power].

Ta Kam later admitted that he had fled to the forest, but qualified this by saying: "Here we had a lot of trouble and had to flee to the mountains to live."

When I asked him whether he was ever made to be the village chief, he stated he had not, and that he had "always gone to the temple." He said he had never been a monk, but at the request of Doung Srei's temple monks and laymen he had served the monastery there as part of an effort to look after his next life.

THE PROBLEM OF THE COLLABORATOR AND A LACK OF ELDERS

In Ta Kam's life narrative he presented himself as a passive entity subject to the will of more powerful circumstances. The villagers do not agree. They said that he was elected by them to be village chief and he accepted the position. He was not forcibly conscripted by the Khmer Rouge. For them, he was not a victim but an opportunist who, motivated by ambition, perpetrated acts against his own people. Moreover, his actions were directed locally on his extended kin and community, violating the tacit collective identity of villagers as victims of outsiders and circumstance. Up to now, villagers had not talked openly about Ta Kam's place within village history. As a member of the former village he was one of them, and therefore his actions were in some sense viewed as a reflection on the villagers' character as a whole. Yet he was also no longer one of them, as he himself had chosen to live elsewhere. The villagers were apparently willing to see him socially erased. Ta Kam could not be forgiven as a victim of circumstance, for he violated the terms of this discourse by transgressing a boundary of insiders and outsiders.

Ta Kam's presence, however, is not the only obstacle to the village's recovery from the trauma of the past. There is also a problem of absence of elders—that is, moral elders. People say that Prei Phnom "lacks elders" after the war, and that traditional knowledge and practice in this commune is therefore relatively weak. This, they say, explains why the people of Prei Phnom have lost interest in traditional practices and knowledge and instead have turned toward "modern" ideologies and ways. The commune chief of Prei Phnom explained to me:

> The young people don't know much about the ancient traditions and the old people who did are dead now. These days the younger folks are into popular modern ideas.

Historical texts suggest that in Cambodia the restoration of order following chaotic historical episodes is sought not by innovation, but through a return to the ancestral traditions of the past (Chandler 1998). Prei Phnom has an inadequate number of elders to transmit the cultural heritage that might fill in and enrich the present. Ironically, Ta Kam is one of the few remaining elders of O'Thmaa. As one of the oldest members of the original village, he is well versed in its traditional knowledge, practices, myths, and stories. However, because of his own past, his knowledge is inaccessible to the next generation for it is tainted.

To sum up, Ta Kam represents a blockage to the remaking of moral order in several ways. First, his presence prevents people from forgetting the treacherous past of the village. Second, he blocks the transmission of an older moral order since he cannot legitimately pass on traditional knowledge. Third, he opposes the moral order itself by having inverted the structural order that places elders and ancestors in a morally elevated position. And finally, his presence reminds people of his role in the painful loss of their loved ones.

It may seem uncanny, then, that Ta Kam acts as a Buddhist layman in the neighboring commune, where he serves the needs of the monastery. Ta Kam himself describes no rupture in his telling explanation of his religious activities: "I am only looking after my next life." For him, it seems, the process of mending the moral order is less problematic than it is for the children of his victims, and one wonders whether he ever really perceived a breach in it in the first place.

CONCLUSION

Local collaborators such as Ta Kam pose difficulties to the process of rebuilding the social and moral order of villages such as O'Thmaa. However, villagers have found some means of reconstructing their communities and rebuilding trust in the wake of decades of violence, forced evacuations, destruction of families, and betrayal by members of their own community. Through such acts as forgiving soldiers on both sides by invoking a narrative of "victims of circumstance," or by practicing forgiveness through the acceptance of Ta Kam's daughter into the community, we see an effort to heal the wounds of the past. Finally and significantly, we also see that despite the opportunity to avenge the deaths of their loved ones by retaliating against Ta Kam, villagers have turned away from violence in an effort to allow healing and move on with their lives.

EPILOGUE

This chapter was based on fieldwork in 2001–2003. Having recently been back to the village (2010), I find that Ta Kam has now returned to the village and his presence is accepted by the villagers. He is now nearly ninety years old and is seen by the younger generation as an elder and a Buddhist layman. This younger generation does not carry the sentiments that the older generation does; to them the Khmer Rouge past is remote. There are very few living elders left in the village who are anywhere close to Ta Kam's age. In addition, the younger generation who were children and teenagers during the Khmer Rouge time are also significantly less in number than those who are now in their twenties.

NOTES

1. The names of all personages and places in the village area have been given aliases to protect their privacy.
2. For further reading, see also Ebihara 1968; Overing 2003; Yan 1996; and Zucker 2006.
3. The village development chief is elected as leader to represent the village in matters having to do with development projects initiated by development agencies and organizations. The development chief has de facto if not de jure responsibility for handling intervillage issues and politics.
4. This figure comes from data from the Lutheran World Federation and corresponds with data collected from the village chiefs and commune offices. O'Thmaa, as the most western village, has the highest percentage of widows, followed by its two neighbors immediately to the east. This is not coincidental, for all three of these villages fell under the same leadership and were moved to the same cooperative.

20 Another World
Theme Parks and Nature

BY SUSAN G. DAVIS

Sea World's experiences are manufactured by a relatively small number of people working for a very large organization; they are disseminated from a narrow point of origin for wide reception and consumption. In this sense, the theme park is industrially produced popular culture. Viewed this way, from its landscaping to its performing whales to its television commercials, Sea World is more than just another example of a universal human tendency to enjoy nature. Rather, the theme park's oceanscapes are an example of the private production of visions of nature and ideas about animals, images and ideas that spread out into the larger culture. To unpack the meanings of places like Sea World, it is useful to speak of theme-parked nature as an industrial product and to look closely at the industry that produces it.

At the same time, of course, the Sea World parks are popular culture in the sense that a large number of people, more than 11 million a year in fact, enthusiastically enjoy them. But what has created this enthusiasm? Fascination with nature and animals has deep roots in Western culture, and so, while the industrial history of the theme park needs analysis, Sea World's manufactured marine visions must be located in this cultural history. The present-day surge of commercial nature imagery is not a transparent matter of commerce bringing the previously unseen into focus, but a case of selecting natural things to see and inventing ways to see them.[1] Sea World adds to this history, producing and mobilizing a stream of intertwined ideas. Its innovation is to make remote ocean worlds visible to a mass public and bring previously little-known sea animals to fame, even as it folds these novelties into older nature stories.

SEA WORLD'S FOREBEARS

The beginnings of this industry are usually dated from the 1955 opening of Disneyland in Anaheim, California, but its roots run deep in the history of popular and commercial culture. Theme park ancestors include the older amusement park and its peripatetic forebears, the circus and carnival, and the industrial expositions and world's fairs of the nineteenth and twentieth centuries.[2] Historians consider turn-of-the-century Coney Island prototypical, a mass commercial recreation synthesizing carnivalesque fun with the celebration of technological progress.[3] Urban resorts like Coney Island, along with smaller pleasure gardens, were inexpensive, widely popular gathering places for European immigrants, working people, and youth, providing a shared experience of the freedoms of the industrial city and offering connections to the new meanings of the culture of consumption. Their proprietors profited from the freeing up of leisure time attendant on the ten-hour day, and they catered to a large working and middle class seeking cheap amusements.[4] Social historians' evaluation of the amusement park is complex. These pleasure worlds provided a realm of liberty that undermined older gender barriers and allowed unmarried women, in particular, freedom from the constraints of factory and family. They gave a wide spectrum of Americans a place to shed harsh work discipline and self-restraint, a public place to learn to play. But at the same time, like much of the rest of commercial recreation, amusement parks and World's Fairs were racially segregated. Their displays carefully connected leisure to the basic lessons of white superiority and American imperialism. In this sense, there was nothing innocent about their pleasures.[5]

Between about 1900 and 1920, organized amusement zones modeled on Coney Island's resorts sprang up in most metropolitan areas in the United States. During the Great Depression, the amusement park business suffered, and it did not rebound until its wide working- and middle-class audience found itself amid the unparalleled post-World War II economic boom. Higher per capita income, the reemergence of leisure time in the 1950s, and the advent of the paid vacation in the 1960s gave the amusement park business new energy and direction. In the first two decades following the war, a building boom nearly doubled the number of amusement parks, from 400 counted in 1954 to 786 tallied in 1967.[6]

As American prosperity and the amusement park industry expanded, the parks themselves were profoundly reorganized. By all accounts, Disneyland, completed in 1955, was the model. At Disneyland, the amusement park shed its petty commercial connections, and the principles of the theme park were decisively laid out. In the late 1960s and early 1970s, many large national corporations followed Disney into the theme park industry, seeking the profits to be made from entertainment, mass leisure, and the expanding tourism industry.[7] Enthusiastically aided by local and state governments, this "minor stampede" resulted in a U.S. landscape dotted with elaborate, themed leisure zones as development corporations absorbed older parks, built new ones, and cloned successful single ventures into chains of similar parks.[8] By 1993, *Amusement Business,* the industry's leading trade journal, estimated that the more than seven hundred theme and amusement parks in North America had an attendance exceeding 255 million. Attendance at the fifty largest parks was about 143.3 million in that year, or more than half the combined Canadian and U.S. populations.[9] In the 1980s and 1990s, waves of corporate mergers, takeovers, and leveraged buyouts gathered under the wings of still larger corporations the chains constructed in the 1970s, so that in 1993 about 40 percent of all theme park visits were made to parks owned by conglomerates. In 1995, corporately owned chains accounted for 90 percent of attendance at the fifty largest North American parks.[10] Meanwhile, many small and locally owned amusement parks, some of them survivors of the thirties, continue to go out of business.

Disneyland's designers had sparked the two-decades-long theme park boom by inaugurating not just a new park style but a new kind of cultural product. The structure of the theme park and its cultural ingredients differ in some important ways from those of its forerunners. The early parks were certainly completely commercial ventures, making their profits from a high volume of admissions, rides, games, and concessions, all offered at low prices. But the first theme park was commercial with a new intensity: it built advertising and modern marketing into its amusements, and in fact it placed them at the core of its activities. As is well known, Disneyland's success derived from its founder's foresighted connection with the fledgling ABC television network. Together, Disney and ABC developed *The Disneyland Show* to showcase the Anaheim park: the show promoted the park while the park promoted the show and the network. Disneyland imagistically and physically converted Disney media products into tourist attractions. This new genre was a medium of mass communication, one that literally made film physical and spatial.[11]

As it has developed, the theme park is exhaustively commercial, a virtual maze of advertising, public relations, and entertainment. Whether Sea World, Disneyland, or Six Flags Over Texas, the theme park is the site of carefully controlled sales of goods (food and souvenirs) and experiences (architecture, rides, and performances) "themed" to the corporate owner's proprietary images. But theme parks are advertising culture in another way too, and here again Disneyland led the reworking of the amusement park's economy and organization. While the early amusement park was often built by metropolitan capital (for example, railway companies had trolley parks and brewers had beer gardens), Disney followed the example of the twentieth-century world's fair or industrial exposition and involved national corporations as investing partners. Consumer goods manufacturers like Carnation received exclusive sales, marketing, and advertising rights at Disneyland in return for cash investments to help start up particular displays or rides.[12] As at the world's fairs, these displays in many cases promoted a product, a technology, or a corporate vision of the future.[13] This pattern has been expanded over several decades, and the theme park has been used to concretize and demonstrate visions of the social future. Today corporate sponsors collaborate in promotions, sharing advertising costs while they fold their general social stance into the recreational landscape.[14]

The contemporary theme park is, in theory, open to all who can pay. In contrast to the amusement park, where raucous mixing was framed by racial hierarchy, it appears broadly democratic. But spatial and locational changes altered the meanings of the amusement park and defined the theme park as a new kind of experience, in some ways more restricted than before. Where early twentieth-century amusement parks had been built within short distances of urban neighborhoods or connected to them by cheap public transport, the new theme parks went up far beyond the outskirts of town. In the 1950s, land in the exurb was cheap, federal policies dictated the connection of vast interurban areas with the new interstate highway system, and housing policies set the stage for massive suburban growth.[15] By the 1980s, Anaheim, San Diego, and Orlando were no longer the sleepy outskirts but the centers of vast tourism districts.[16] From the beginning, this geographical pattern in tourism development tended to cut the urban and inner-city working class out of the theme park market. As one park marketing director put it, not mincing any words, "Once you got out of those old neighborhoods, you left a lot of trouble, a lot of tough people and rowdy teenagers behind. That was the real breakthrough." The new audience would be mainly white, suburban, and middle-class, although in this manager's opinion the important social dimension "wasn't color so much as class."[17] Navigating the interstate to the theme park required, of course, a car and a parent free to drive it, which limited the access of the amusement park's younger and poorer audience.

Similarly, pricing strategies helped shift the cultural meanings of the theme park as they revealed the developers' conception of their customers. Whereas the older amusement park charged no admission but collected a separate fee for each ride or attraction, in the 1960s the Six Flags parks initiated "pay-one-price," a high admission fee allowing unlimited access to rides and shows.[18] Although a convenience for the visitor, the single price eliminated nonpaying access, and the meaning of a visit to the park shifted from a casual, often spur-of-the-moment recreation to a planned excursion. Pay-one-price tended to define the customers as those who could save enough to pay a high fee, and it tended to define them as families—or groups under parental control.[19] The theme park offered families on vacation a carefully packaged tourist experience whose meanings were based on recombinations of familiar content, novel location, and the expanded technologies of perceptual control.

It was this corporately shaped product that became so widely popular, promoted through the 1970s and 1980s as the focus of middle-class travel plans and, increasingly, business conventions and professional-society meetings. As the parks steadily flourished, they influenced the landscape around them. While in the 1970s theme parks were stand-alone tourist attractions, by the 1990s they became the core of vast leisure and resort complexes such as those in Orlando, Florida; Orange County, California; and Las Vegas, Nevada.[20] Theme park companies are now involved in developing entire urban entertainment districts. The famous Universal Studios Tours parks in Hollywood and Florida (owned by MCA) have expanded outward into malls surrounding them. Called CityWalks, these are in fact attempts at small, themed residential and working cities.[21] Similar zones are being built in Germany and France, and in Tokyo and Osaka, Japan.[22] At the same time, urban planners and shopping mall designers draw heavily from theme park technique.

In the 1990s, the theme park industry's most striking development has been the integration of the chains built in the sixties and seventies into enormous conglomerate corporations. The "big five" owners are Disney, Anheuser-Busch, Time-Warner, Paramount Viacom, and Universal-MCA, a subsidiary of Seagrams Co. Together these five chains comprise twenty-nine parks in North America, with combined attendance totaling more than 119 million visits in 1995. Four of these chains are nestled within mass media conglomerates, with Disney dominant; its American parks alone account for 47.2 million visits in 1995.[23] Time-Warner's attendance, an estimated 24,3 million, probably ranked second in 1995; the company estimates that 85 percent of the U.S. population lives within a day's drive (three hundred miles) of a Six Flags park.[24] The Busch Entertainment Corporation's nine parks garnered about 20 million visitors in 1995; about 13 million people visited a Paramount park and 12.7 million visited an MCA park in the same year.[25]

THE CASH MACHINE

The theme park is a good investment for a corporate conglomerate, since it is a machine for the rapid generation of cash. Immediate profits are made in much the same way as in other mass entertainment industries, such as movies, rock concerts, and big-league sports. Admissions make up perhaps as much as 50 percent of revenues; roughly another 50 percent comes from sales of food, drinks, souvenirs, and other merchandise inside the park. But unlike the rock concert and more like the shopping mall, the theme park depends heavily on the construction of a landscape and the careful planning of human movement through space. The spatial rationale of the theme park is to cluster commercial opportunities represented by concessions, including everything from hot dog stands to designer boutiques, around attractions, which can range from rides and simulator theaters to animal, human, or robotic performances. Event scheduling, architecture, and landscaping help move customers through concessions at speeds and intervals that have been carefully studied and determined to enhance sales.

Because of the overriding importance of concession sales measured in sales per capita, or "per caps," managerial and perceptual control are central to any theme park. The old amusement park was a complex mix of often sleazy entertainments run by subcontracting performer-entrepreneurs or concessionaires. By all accounts it was this cheap and explicitly carnivalesque heritage that Walt Disney rejected as he planned Disneyland. By contrast, the theme park specializes in experiential homogeneity.[26] Replacing the petty carnival and midway entrepreneurs with the corporation's own centrally produced and managed attractions, Disney and his followers gained control over profits, the quality of concessions, and—just as important to advertisers and sponsors—image and style. This totalizing effort is captured in the industry phrase "to theme." Surface stylistic characteristics are highly coordinated in "theming," but more important, the meanings the park contains are centrally produced to be as nonconflictual as possible. Paradoxically, this overall uniformity is expressed as a rich variety of artifacts, cultures, histories, styles, texts, architectures, and performances.

The production of an environment that pays so much attention to experience is costly, requiring centralized monitoring of a range of factors. Temporary and long-term problems demand solution; theme park companies are divided into departments filled with specialists in traffic flow; design and signing; maintenance and sanitation; interaction between the park and its patrons ("guest relations"); the quality, tone, style, and content of performances; food and drinks; and souvenirs and concessions, One theme park designer writes that "in the final analysis everyone views the design of the theme as a complete unit in which all elements, major and minor, work together in a harmonious relationship. This means keeping contradictions to an absolute minimum."[27] Indeed, the concept of the "themed environment," the fully designed, highly coordinated "land" with all services, performances, and concessions designed and provided in-house, was arguably Disney's major contribution to the industry and perhaps to American culture.[28]

As is well known, park themes vary. The industry leader Disney's overarching theme is the corporation's imaginative work and media products, "The Magic Kingdom." During the 1970s the other park chains could not draw on an animated film heritage, but they did find pieces of cultural history to mine as themes. National history, once over lightly, was the original narrative of the Six Flags company; now it specializes in mind-blowing roller coaster rides themed to action movies.[29] As I will show, the Sea World chain discovered the charisma of marine mammals and the benefits of specializing in marine nature and wildlife. Media conglomerates' acquisition of most parks located in large markets has resulted in a wave of retheming as parks display and cross-promote the entertainment products of the parent companies. These products include a wide variety of animated films and live-action film and television, television cartoon and comic strip characters, books and magazines, sports teams and sports heroes, music and music television celebrities. The promise of limitless opportunities to cross-promote (in entertainment industry terms, to "support") goods and imagery and the vast potential for interlocking products and overlapping promotional activities is what has attracted MCA, Viacom, and Time-Warner to theme parks.[30]

Cross-promotional possibilities have been evident for at least three decades, but only the recent merging of huge media companies and the collation of a wide range of media products have allowed its full promise to become clear. Today, the overlap of marketing, advertising, and content has become the essence of media profitability, especially since licensed merchandise sales can now far outstrip the revenues from the original media product.[31] In the marketing language of the 1990s, each product—the television show, the animated film, the rental video, the theme park, and the Pocahontas pajamas—adds value to all the others.

In an industry dominated by mass media conglomerates, Sea World is both typical and an anomaly. Its parent company, Anheuser-Busch, stands out for its lack of major media holdings and Hollywood connections.[32] Although Sea World was a relative latecomer when it opened in 1964, its history parallels that of the parks industry as a whole. Begun as a single park developed by a group of Southern California investors, Sea World was quickly expanded into a chain which then changed corporate hands several times: The publishing, real estate, and insurance firm Harcourt Brace Jovanovich (HBJ) bought the first three Sea Worlds in 1977 in hopes of combining the marine exhibits with its own extensive educational publishing and filmstrip enterprises. This promise was never realized. When HBJ was threatened by a takeover attempt from a consortium put together by the predatory British publisher and financier Robert Maxwell, HBJ pulled all the available cash out of the theme parks division, sucking the Sea Worlds dry of funds for anything beyond day-to-day operations. The parks raised admissions prices and laid off nearly half their on-site workers, but when fiscal restructuring failed to right HBJ's ship, the Sea Worlds were put up for sale and purchased by Anheuser-Busch in 1989.[33]

Anheuser-Busch had been in the amusement parks industry in the old days, setting up brewery tours and picnic grounds around its plants in Tampa and Pasadena. The Tampa amusement park was expanded into a botanical and zoological garden in the 1970s (felicitously called Busch Gardens: Africa: The Dark Continent).[34] Later, Anheuser-Busch diversified by building Busch Gardens: The Old Country, a history park near Williamsburg, Virginia, and acquiring Sesame Place, a TV-themed children's play park in Langhorne, Pennsylvania.[35] With the purchase of the HBJ holdings, Anheuser-Busch owned the largest group of theme parks in the United States.

Anheuser-Busch's parks are very successful. While none of the biggest theme park chains report attendance figures, it is likely that Anheuser-Busch's nine parks together have the third largest total attendance of the five United States theme park conglomerates.[36] At a conservative guess, the four Sea Worlds together entertain about 11.6 million paying visitors annually, and most of these are North Americans.[37] These visits alone evidence wide exposure to and interest in Anheuser-Busch's colorful worlds of the sea. And Busch Entertainment is expanding abroad with the Gran Tibidabo theme park in Salou, Spain.

The theme park business is ancillary but important to the brewer. As a giant beverage and food producer, Anheuser-Busch controls 43 percent of the U.S. beer market. In 1993 the company saw about $11.6 billion in sales worldwide, and in 1995 it bought a half interest in China's national Tsing-Tsao brewery and announced an aggressive plan to expand into beer making in all of Asia.[39] Although the parks appear only tangentially related to the beer product, with their *Sesame Street* character tie-ins and their nature education theme, they do help provide a useful "family image" for the Budweiser brand in particular. The Sea Worlds also help further beer's association with the great outdoors, picking up a longtime Busch family association with wildlife management,[40] By associating the brewing conglomerate with conservation, the parks help deflect concern over industrial pollution and large-scale waste production.[41]

Unlike other theme park owners, Anheuser-Busch has no significant media holdings or outlets to help integrate its parks into a cross-promotional marketing and merchandising strategy. Sea World has never had a film product or long-running television series to make up the core of its marketing, although it airs annual television entertainment specials and buys prime-time advertising.[42] Lacking a Mickey Mouse or Bugs Bunny, Anheuser-Busch and Sea World rely heavily on Shamu, the trademarked killer whale, which is also a licensed image, park logo, and corporate icon. But Anheuser-Busch's ability to exploit the whale mascot is limited, at least compared to what Disney can do with one of its characters. Although the company bought the rights to an animated, feature length film that would promote Shamu and the parks to movie and television audiences, licensing rights have been tied up in a legal Gordian knot.[43] Meanwhile, Time-Warner, owner of the Six Flags parks, has done well with two action adventure films starring a killer whale named Keiko. *Free Willy* was spun off into *Free Willy 2: The Journey Home* and an animated Saturday morning television show. Following an imbroglio over the treatment of Keiko at a theme park in Mexico, Time-Warner helped invent a "Free Keiko/Free Willy" rehabilitation campaign that not surprisingly also promotes the film products. Ironically, despite the Warner films' anti-theme park, anticaptivity story lines, Sea World claims that all their parks have profited from an increased general interest in killer whales stirred up by the movies and the Keiko controversy.[44]

INDUSTRIAL NATURE MAGIC

The lack of a direct film or television tie-in has encouraged Sea World to carefully cultivate nature as the theme park's central story. Although the park always includes human and land animal entertainments, recreated ocean environments and marine animals—from invertebrates to birds to mammals—are the central theme of the Sea Worlds; the performing whales are the central attractions, and management calls them its "core product." Superficially, the ways that the different Sea World parks present nature seem varied; the oceans' rich variety is one theme at all the parks. Occasionally there are regional variations. Sea World in Orlando, for example, features manatees that cannot be seen at Sea World in San Diego; conversely, the killer whales are on display at all four parks. But despite the detail in the dioramas and the range of species within individual parks, Sea World's nature is standardized. As we will see, nature displays for mass audiences rely on stock techniques and the corporate search for a consistent product. Indeed, in addition to being visually dazzling, Sea World's nature spectacles must be consistent and predictable precisely because they express a corporate worldview.

In the theme park-world's fair tradition, other corporations are involved with Sea World. The park subsidizes some of its displays though corporate partnerships, and park brochures refer to the Sea World "family of sponsors." In San Diego, ARCO helps present the Penguin Encounter, the Skytower Ride is brought to you by Southwest Airlines, and am/pm mini markets helps fund the Shark Encounter. But many other businesses and manufacturers, from Kodak to Pepsi-Cola, take part in joint promotional and advertising ventures inside and outside the park. Southwest Airlines also provides Sea World with a "flying billboard" in the form of *Shamu One.*, a black-and-white-painted Boeing 737 lined inside with wall-to-wall paintings of Shamu. Through sponsorship arrangements all the Sea World parks reduce their advertising costs; sponsors gain exclusive merchandising rights (for example, Kodak and Pepsi-Cola are "official suppliers"), cross-promotional advantages such as the ability to offer Sea World discounts along with their products, and association of their name in connection with animals and children, the environment, and family entertainment.[45]

Sea World gives the most thorough service to its parent company. The park integrates advertising, public relations, and political argument for Anheuser-Busch. For example, besides selling Anheuser-Busch's Budweiser beers and Eagle snack foods, all the Sea Worlds' "Hospitality Centers" feature a microbrewery and free beer tasting in what amounts to direct product promotion. In San Diego, the modern beer garden houses museum exhibits of brewing history and video screens that cultivate Anheuser-Busch's identity as an environmental and conservation-minded company. Pamphlets and posters exhort customers to recycle aluminum, drink sensibly, and resist increased excise taxes. Next door, in a huge stable are Anheuser-Busch's trademark Clydesdale draft horses, the registered trademark of one corporate division converted into an attraction at a wholly owned subsidiary. Anheuser-Busch-themed merchandise, from beer steins to T-shirts and baseball caps, not only generates concession sales but circulates the corporation's image, as customers pay to wear its advertising and logos. And of course, associating Anheuser-Busch and its products with animals, nature, education, and families positions the world's largest brewer as a socially concerned firm.[46]

The company uses the theme park as an environment for its messages, and this can be useful, if it is not directly related to theme park profits. Anheuser-Busch's walk-through advertising may be especially important in a time of rising anti-alcohol sentiment in the United States. Brochures promoting responsible drinking through slogans ("Know when to say when") and urging parents to talk frankly with their children about alcohol can deflect if they can't defuse widespread concern about the health and societal effects of alcoholism and alcohol abuse among children and adolescents. Similarly, by relentlessly stressing the values of recycling in its theme parks, this huge manufacturer of bottles and cans can displace the discussion of the effects of the American system of disposable packaging and stave off attempts to legislate limits on the production of waste.[47] The theme park can be turned to many public relations uses, in fact; the more diverse the conglomerate, the more issues it may need to address. In any case, at the Sea World theme parks, advertising, marketing, and public relations are so thoroughly part of the landscape that they are collapsed into entertainment and recreation, until it is very hard to tell what is publicity and what is "just fun."

In the case of Sea World, the live nature of the oceans and coasts is the heart of the successful entertainment-promotional mix. Nature—living creatures in harmonious environmental balance—exists at Sea World as a commodity for sale in its own right, in order to sell other things and to help people feel good about larger social projects and arrangements, including the high-consumption economy typified by the theme park itself. On one hand, Sea World shares this use of nature as a surface with much of the rest of American consumer culture, and in this sense, nature is just another industrial product or symbolic commodity, available today to anyone who can afford the poster, the T-shirt, or the ticket. But of course, in another sense, nature is not just another product—not only is it the basis of all human existence but culturally it carries meanings that seem special and magical. It is a world beyond the human that is invented out of inevitably human meanings and desires, an escape from the limited, the routine, and the mundane. Here the oceanic nature on display at Sea World may have special salience. There is something special about the underwater worlds the theme park constructs for viewing. They can seem especially remote, deep, and endless, free of boundaries and limits. Such nature visions promise transcendence of the polluted and conflictual social world on land, even while we realize that they are in fact terrestrial and artificial, highly processed commodities.

As a piece of industrial magic, Sea World represents an enormous contradiction. Using living animals, captive seas, and flourishing landscapes, the theme park has organized the subtle and contradictory cultural meanings of nature into a machine for mass consumption. At the same time and despite its best efforts, Sea World makes nature—one of the ideas most taken for granted in Western culture—into a problem that leads to questions. Why should nature in general and ocean life in particular be so central to the workings of this hypercommercial space? How does nature work as a commodity in the late twentieth century? In what way is what we see at Sea World "natural" or unnatural? Who wants to see it and buy it, and why?

A first way to approach these questions is, of course, to acknowledge that "nature" is not natural but social and cultural. It's not new to argue that nature is a cultural construction. Anthropologists, historians, and scholars of literature have been at pains for decades to show that every culture uses nature metaphorically and the natural world provides not only all means of material life but a common, human currency for representing ideas about that life as society and culture. Rather than a simple reflection of popular taste or fascination, nature is often deployed as part of a definition of the world, as a way to convince ourselves and others of the rightness and inevitability of the world as known. It has been used to create authority for the social arrangements of gender, for example, in ideas of woman's "nature." It is invoked to justify family structures, sexual orderings, and racial and imperial hierarchies. But how particular constellations of ideas and images of nature become current and what social relationships they represent are questions that need to be examined with an eye for social and historical specificity.

The American mass media in general and Sea World in particular give nature a seemingly universal appeal that helps obscure its specific class and ethnic connotations. In this project, mass entertainment joins a grand tradition. For at least the last two hundred years Europeans and European-Americans have made nature a transhistorical category that paradoxically contains both fundamental human qualities ("human nature") and that part of the biological universe that is intractably separate from humankind and society.[48] During the eighteenth and nineteenth centuries, European and American artists, writers, and poets increasingly treated nature as a visual, touchable, "out there" object, literally "another world," endowed with cultural and spiritual properties. As Raymond Williams has pointed out, this tradition of rendering nature opposed it to human social organization and poised it emblematically against the industrial city.[49] At the same time, art and literature emphasizing labor and the complex interactions between humans and the biological world became more marginal to the Euro-American tradition.[50] Appreciation of a separate, aesthetic version of nature suppressed awareness of class exploitation and was used to distinguish people from each other and normalize the differences between them. For example, in the eighteenth century, as Williams argues, the gentry justified their expanding property rights and dominance over the rural poor through artistic practices. Sculpting nature into country estates, celebrating it in pastoral poetry and painting, manipulating it in the form of lovingly landscaped gardens, the wealthy literally naturalized the vast social and economic power they derived from the enclosure of agricultural lands and forests, even while they consolidated their control in the laws and courts.[51]

A related and similar process of aestheticizing nature took place in the nineteenth century, as an urban, manufacturing upper class developed for itself a wide range of practices for appreciating nature. As ethnographers Jonas Frykman and Orvar Lofgren have shown in their study of the cultural self-definition of the Swedish bourgeoisie, viewing mountains, sketching trees and flowers, photographing scenery, and hiking through wilderness helped factory owners and financiers define new identities for themselves. Exposure to nature through new touristic practices and visual cultural forms helped these men become rational and sensitive, in explicit contrast to rural farm laborers and urban workers.[52] Frykman and Lofgren argue that this new conception of nature as an empty, wild place where a man could connect with his soul and his nation offered consolations for the dislocations of industrial life. Once thoroughly mastered, the conception of the wild landscape as spiritual space became a form of cultural capital that the bourgeoisie could transmit to their heirs.[53]

Much of the European tradition of nature appreciation was adapted to the American setting. At the turn of the twentieth century, Peter Schmitt shows, amateur scientists, journalists, and novelists moved a campaign for scientific knowledge out of museums and translated it into a movement for nature appreciation.[54] Turn-of-the-century nature appreciation was located in an imagined "Arcadia," a not-too-faraway wild, and was in part a project of earnest reformers, in part a comfortable town-dweller's enthusiasm. This loose movement developed curricula for classrooms, organized summer camps and bird-watching clubs, and lobbied for parks and greenbelts. While Schmitt describes nature appreciation in the Arcadian vein as having a fantastic tinge, the urge to preserve open spaces and help urban children spend time outdoors surely had many democratic and socially progressive uses.[55] But under the surface, nature appreciation could fit with "Americanization" campaigns and efforts to model a hierarchical social order. The right sort of person, as advocated by nature educators, was an English-speaking, self-controlled, property-respecting, refined middle-class citizen. Whether this "right sort of person" was actually produced is another question. But if we look at rhetorics of nature whether benign or authoritarian, we can see that for at least two centuries they have belonged to the powerful. The propertied have used nature as a material resource, a symbolic resource, and a tool of prescriptive improvement aimed down the social scale at class and racial others.

No one would mistake Sea World for a Swedish forest or a trail in the Sierra, but this theme park tries to connect with the long tradition of adventurous exposure of the sensitive self to nature, a tradition that signifies property and privilege. When Sea World's advertising constructs the park as a worthwhile recreation and a place to learn, for example, it draws on this sense of nature knowledge as cultural capital. The connections to the nineteenth-century tradition are strong and direct, while the objects of vision reveal an important difference in emphasis; Sea World allows views into coastal and marine worlds, whereas the nineteenth-century tradition of nature appreciation gazed on garden scenes and terrestrial animals and landscapes. By giving us glimpses of the landscapes underneath the oceans, Sea World asks its customers to orient themselves to the future in unexplored realms as well as to cultural capital formed in the past. A long tradition of science fiction writing and film imagines the oceans as it has treated outer space, as a future on which to work with the tools of science and technology.

While Sea World partakes of a genteel history of nature appreciation, as commercial recreation it also draws on Euro-American traditions of displaying animals. On one hand, there is a long-standing pattern of displaying scientific control by presenting animals to the public; on the other hand, animals have been caught up for centuries in less rational shows. On the scientific side, as Victorian England consolidated its global economic power, the exotic animals of the old royal menageries were relocated in the new institution of the zoological garden founded by gentlemen in the interests of research. But despite their royal and learned origins, zoos were also popular displays. For scientists and public alike, animals were interpreted in explicitly imperialist terms; as tokens of conquered peoples and metonymic extensions of the geography of empire, they were illustrations of racial inferiority and difference.[56]

In related ways, in the period from about 1800 to 1900, natural history museums popularized the global scientific worldview and integrated nature into a Euro-centered colonial map. These institutions organized nature and displayed it as the subject of Western rationality, underlining the connection between scientific knowledge and the imperial organization of the world. The classification of animals, for example, was evidence of this combined intellectual and geopolitical control. An edge of domestic social management and cultural uplift also marked the prominent institutions promoting natural history and nature education in the cities of the eastern United States. The museum's boards of directors hoped to bring rationality to a wide spectrum of the newly arrived immigrant working classes, whom they saw as having anarchic, un-American ideas. Animal dioramas and natural history exhibits, especially, were aimed to help teach immigrant workers and their children respect for law and "natural order" at home and abroad.[57]

The founders of the London zoo initially saw their institution as opposed to the city's plebeian menageries, where crowds heckled, teased, fed, and baited the animals. They restricted membership to gentlemen and issued passes only to "respectable" nonmembers. Nonetheless, the zoological society garden became enormously popular with the people of London, and as limits on visitors were worn away it became a tourist attraction. The public found their own uses for these spaces and sometimes caused concern. Crowd behavior at the zoo was hard to distinguish from that at Wombwell's Menagerie or the London Exchange. The zoo's scientific mission was revised, in part through the recognition that since the irrational recreations of the urban working class were proving difficult to suppress or control, they could in some way be made edifying. But in theory, the zoological garden was a mechanism by which scientific knowledge and the understandings of experts could be disseminated to social inferiors with, it was hoped, improving results. In the twentieth century the zoo remains a preeminent popular learning and research space as the display of animals as exotic oddities has fallen to the circus and sideshow. But perhaps the lines of demarcation between the zoo and the old menagerie sideshow, or the zoo and the theme park, are less clear-cut than they seem. For example, the modern zoo still retains some marks of its early history. It is still a geopolitical map, a display of living curiosities framed as parts of exotic worlds and foreign cultures, albeit in much less overtly racist ways than in the nineteenth century. In the twentieth century, zoos, like theme parks, are powerful tourist attractions and resoundingly popular recreations, and they have not eschewed either the themed gift shop or the trained performance.[58]

Whether or not they are aware of it (and they often seem unaware of it) the crafters of Sea World's nature stories draw on this mixed and selective tradition of representation and thought about nature, on traditions of constructing nature in order for it to be consumed, contemplated, and experienced.[59] Sea World's nature magic partakes of the uplifting tradition in which contact with nature creates or affirms a customer's identity as a caring, sensitive, and educated person, even while its origins in the amusement park and midway give it strong ties to the less rational traditions of animal display. We might think of Sea World as a braid of genres, incorporating the rational and the irrational—blending the controlled and seemingly scientific display of the perfect natural, underwater or on land, with what are often frankly circuslike decontextualizations and exaggerations. Both circus and carnival sideshow isolate animals from their wild context to individualize rather than catalogue them. In the circus animals are often humanized (and thus exquisitely dominated) in performance; in the old-fashioned sideshow they were made gigantic and threatening.[60] A visit to Sea World offers ocean visions and tamed-wild animals as rational pleasures, but, in consumer culture's revision of Carnival, it is also constructed as a cut-loose spending spree that begins with the outrageous admission prices and finishes up with throwaway souvenirs. True, there are no gut-wrenching, mind-blowing roller coasters here, but there is a crazy quilt of cultural materials, a promiscuity of the serious and the unserious. And of course, the customers too draw on and participate in this mix of museum, zoo, and carnival in a new, watery key As nature consumers, they are paying homage to one of the most complex ideas in Western industrial culture, even while they are also getting away from it all in a world of planned leisure and structured consumption.[61]

But Sea World puts nature through a further transformation. Here the nineteenth-century idea of the sensitive and rational self discovered in communion with nature persists, but it has been translated from a process of romantic national definition into an emphasis on the individual and the discovery of individual feelings in contact with nature. At Sea World, animals from another world are displayed in ways designed to bring forth positive emotions, and these emotions depend on contact, on the bridging of distances between the alien species, the faraway, and the self. Sea World specializes in and defines ways people can contact marine animals as well as see them, and this contact is offered as personally transforming in overlapping, multiple ways. Among the most popular attractions at all the parks are the pools holding dolphins, sea stars, rays, and skates that visitors can handle and feed. Similarly, the whales and dolphins perform to scripts that emphasize themes of loving, caring, and closeness between animals and people. The themes of "touching" nature and "making contact with another world" emphasized in Sea World's print, billboard, and television advertising certainly refer to the problem of crossing boundaries between terrestrial and marine environments, of creating closeness between people and animals, but they also circle around to imply that a visit to the theme park creates closeness among people, especially in families, between parents and children.[62] Sea World's spectacular nature is a medium that connects customers to nature and, in the ordered theme park world, to each other and to themselves. In this way, it both continues and revises the quasi-religious nineteenth-century tradition of nature as self-discovery and gives the domination of nature a gentle, civilized face.

Finally, Sea World's predominant language is that of reason, and the visitor to its worthwhile recreations travels a distance from the insensitive and irrational, best represented by the circus, to a more learned, forward-looking place.[63] The class messages of the long tradition of nature appreciation are reconfirmed at Sea World, as the general portrait of Sea World's audience reveals. The customers are largely white and upper-middle class. For example, the park describes its clientele as consisting heavily of "parents" who are "usually college educated and ... interested in learning about ocean life."[64] Although managers of Sea World of California, like most white Americans, are reluctant to speak in terms of social class at all or to acknowledge a racial pattern among their customers, their own market research reveals that in general the Sea World audience, drawn heavily from Southern California, is older, whiter, wealthier, and better educated than the average San Diegan.[65] In 1992, the park's market research interview data showed that only 15 percent of customers reported family annual income under $30,000; 51 percent of customers claimed more than $40,000 annual income and 33 percent stated that their family earned more than $50,000. During this same period, median income in San Diego County was about $35,000; a similar median prevails for neighboring Orange County. Even allowing for the many problems inherent in self-reporting, this is obviously an affluent audience. Fully 43 percent of those interviewed claimed a college or higher degree, while 22 percent had a high school diploma or less. Market research for the same period reports that 89 percent of customers interviewed were "Anglo" and 11 percent "non-Anglo" (only these two categories were used).[66] This figure diverges noticeably from the general ethnic makeup of San Diego County, where "whites" comprise about 75 percent of the officially counted population, and it fits with my observations of the paying audience over many years.[67] The average audience member is a "baby boomer," about thirty-eight years old, and nearly 65 percent of the audience are between the ages of twenty-five and fifty.[68]

Although other theme parks in California use dress codes and profiles to discourage the presence of "gang members," to my knowledge the people who run Sea World do not do anything active to keep ethnic minorities out of the park.[69] Indeed, the education department's programs recruit minority children via public school field trips. Considering the multiethnic demographics of San Diego and the rest of Southern California, the wealth and whiteness of Sea World's paying audience seem to indicate extreme self-selection, despite Sea World managers' claims that "we're here for everyone."

The appeal of Sea World to children and families with children gives another clue that consuming Sea World's nature spectacle is in part about social class. A large part of Sea World's marketing effort is aimed at elementary school children, and this too fits with a great tradition of defining nature. The positive association between children and animals, children and nature, is a long one,[70] In white middle-class culture, children are supposed to gain special things from contact with nature, but perhaps these special things are related as much to social ideals and cultural capital as they are to problems of growing and learning.[71] In long-standing theories of education, nature and the outdoors teach the child about the inner self, and nature confers the good childhood.[72] And, at a more mundane level, contact with nature is thought to lay the groundwork for the child's future success in biology or some other important science. It is not that any of these ideas are entirely false. But in this ideal of childhood, nature, social mobility, and the sense of self all run together. The connections between nature, children, and social class identification are expressed in the century-old, middle-class emphasis on suburban yards, summer homes, summer camps, and nature study in the classroom.[73] That many of Sea World's advertisements feature children learning underscores the theme park's claim that it helps produce the right sort of person. That the theme park is designed for children to learn in the context of the family implies that the park also helps reproduce families and their social position.

In the end, it is hard to show how or whether the general economic standing and class makeup of Sea World's audience is an artifact of the park industry's search for an affluent audience, or whether nature is a commodity with special, important meanings for white people. It seems most likely that Sea World has constructed its nature spectacles with appeal to the educated, upwardly mobile, and wealthy in mind, that is, it has increasingly styled its displays and shows according to the longstanding canons of nature appreciation in order to secure an audience with disposable income. This was not always Sea World's style. At the same time, it is very likely that price helps keep poor people and minority customers out of the park.[74] But since other theme parks in Southern California, most notably Disneyland and Six Flags-Magic Mountain, have strong followings among people of color and charge roughly the same admission prices, the cultural meaning of Sea World's product has to be considered as a force shaping its audience. It is possible that the version of nature marketed by Sea World appeals positively to white people as part of being appropriately white and middle class. Sea World draws on the tradition of thought connecting nature to self-improvement and social uplift, albeit mainly in the context of private consumption. Perhaps Sea World constructs its version of nature to appeal to consumers as much in terms of who they want to be, as in terms of who they are.

Is it possible that, conversely, Sea World's aestheticized, uplifting version of nature can seem unfriendly or irrelevant to working-class people and nonwhites? A recent study by the National Park Service at least bears out the possibility. Designed to explore why visitors to the American national parks system are so disproportionately white as compared to the larger national population, the study found that the parks were seen as unfriendly, even hostile, to nonwhites. The study took into account the costs of travel to parks and historic patterns of leisure for minorities, but found that the experience that was offered, especially the emphasis on being in the wilderness and contemplating spectacular scenery, was regarded as foreign and unappealing. Further, travel through rural areas to get to national parks and incidents of racial discrimination and hostility experienced there helped define this experience of nature as unwelcoming and even threatening for urban nonwhites.[75] It is possible that a trip to Sea World, though embedded in an urban tourism network, shares some of this meaning for minorities, for the historical reasons cited above. There is another demographic aspect to consider. Sea World has very carefully used its rhetoric of nature to pattern its attractions to appeal to "families," especially nuclear families. It has avoided adding "metal" rides and musical attractions that would bring in large groups of unsupervised teenagers—again, for white Southern Californians the presence of minority youth in groups almost automatically raises the spectral image of the "gang."[76] Despite the declarations of Sea World's marketers that "the park is for everyone," its pricing, location, mix of attractions, and the historical-cultural meanings of its nature theme have clearly marked out its audience.[77]

While the desires and identities of Sea World's customers have a long past, they are not unchanging, and the theme park reaches out to meet its customers' evolving desires. Touching Sea World's ocean magic is a way of making contact with a world of possibilities as well as affirming a social identity. All of the Sea World parks and their publicity materials, as well as the advertisements of Anheuser-Busch, appeal strongly to the environmental interests and worries of the American public. (Most recent public opinion polls show that the general public is more worried about environmental issues and in favor of stronger governmental action on environmental problems than either business or governmental leaders.) Corporations like Anheuser-Busch and multinational capital generally must deal with unprecedented environmental concern and a popular sense of local and global crisis; sponsoring spectacular nature in commercial entertainment serves corporations well.[78] Underwater visions, especially, transport the viewer to a world neither agricultural nor urban, a space teeming with colorful life that seems free of history and culture. Sea World's reconstructed marine environments seem total, unfettered, and of course beautiful.

Sea World expresses, in part, its customers' desires for nature and their worries about the future. But the job of the theme park is also to transform these longings. Customers want to see the amazing, performing killer whale and the pristine antarctic wilderness, of course, but they also hope to feel agency, that is, that however indirectly, a visit to the theme park is an act of caring. That they can do so is, in part, a result of the fact that in the late twentieth century, American business has worked hard to define consumption as a form of concern, political action, and participation. At Sea World, customers are explicitly asked to see consumption this way. As one of the killer whale show scripts puts it; "Just by being here, you're showing that you care!" In this logic, a visit to the nature theme park is a form of action on behalf of the environment.

Presenting Sea World as environmental commitment and Anheuser-Busch as an educational and philanthropic force, the theme park creates a closed circle of participatory spectatorship in which "being there" is the main form of doing. Entertainment, recreation, public relations, marketing, social mobility, and environmental concern run together to become essentially the same thing: the theme park. Certainly the circle is not closed yet, but this innovation on the traditions of showing and seeing nature is important. Untangling the Sea World versions of nature and tracking their connections to other parts of contemporary life, including American corporate culture, is the task for the rest of this book.

ENDNOTES

1. John Berger, "Why Look at Animals?" *About Looking* (New York: Pantheon Books, 1980), pp. 1–26.
2. Michael Sorkin, "See You in Disneyland," in *Variations on a Theme Park: The New American City and the End of Public Space*, ed. Michael Sorkin (New York: Hill and Wang, 1992), pp. 205–232; William F. Mangels, *The Outdoor Amusement Industry from Earliest Times to the Present* (New York: Vantage, 1952).

3. On the history of Coney Island, see John F. Kasson, *Amusing the Million: Coney Island at the Turn of the Century* (New York: Hill and Wang, 1978).

4. By 1919 the United States had between fifteen hundred and two thousand amusement parks. Every major city boasted a "trolley park" developed by street railway companies to promote and subsidize transportation. Judith Adams, *The American Amusement Park Industry: A History of Technology and Thrills* (Boston: Twayne Publishers, G. K. Hall and Co., 1991), p. 57.

5. Roy Rosenzweig, *Eight Hours for What We Will: Workers and Leisure in an Industrial City, 1870–1920* (Cambridge and New York: Cambridge University Press, 1983); Kathy Peiss, *Cheap Amusements: Working Women and Leisure in New York City, 1880 to 1920* (Philadelphia: Temple University Press, 1985); David Nasaw, *Going Out: The Rise and Fall of Public Amusements* (New York: Basic Books, 1993); Robert W. Rydell, *All the World's a Fair: Visions of Empire at America's International Expositions, 1876–1916* (Chicago: University of Chicago Press, 1984); Rydell, *World of Fairs: The Century of Progress Expositions* (Chicago: University of Chicago Press, 1993); Paul Greenhalgh, *Ephemeral Vistas: The Expositions Universelles, Great Exhibitions and World's Fairs, 1851–1939* (Manchester: Manchester University Press, 1988).

6. Adams, *American Amusement Park Industry*, p. 67.

7. Margaret D. Pacey, "For Fun and Profit: Amusement Parks Are a Hit at the Box Office and in the Boardroom," *Barron's*, July 12, 1971, 11, 20–21.

8. Bro Uttal, "The Ride Is Getting Scarier," *Fortune*, December, 1977, 167–84. The business was not without uncertainty. Bally (with interests in gaming and casinos), Taft (broadcasting), and Marriott (hotels and resorts) disengaged by the early 1980s largely because "the parks, acquired as a sideline to other, more dominant interests demanded expanding resources in the areas of capital expenditures, operating procedures, and managerial attention." Adams, *American Amusement Park Industry*, p. 122. The parks were sold and recombined into still larger leisure businesses.

9. Tim O'Brien, "North American Parks Have Banner Season," *Amusement Business*, January 2, 1994, 65, 68, 69.

10. O'Brien, "Banner Season," 68–69; in 1995, the ten largest North American theme parks accounted for more than 49 percent of attendance (or 76.4 million visitors) at the top fifty amusement and theme parks (out of a total 155,127,000 visitors). Tim O'Brien, "Attendance Climbs 7% at Top North American Parks," *Amusement Business*, December 18–31, 1995, 1, 76–78, 104.

11. Richard Schickel, *The Disney Version: The Life, Times, Art, and Commerce of Walt Disney* (New York: Avon Books, 1968), pp. 295–337. Schickel's is still the definitive account of how this was done, but see also George Lipsitz, "Discursive Space and Social Space: Television, Highways, and Cognitive Mapping in the 1950s City" (paper presented at the annual meeting of the American Studies Association, Toronto, Canada, November 4, 1989); and Sorkin, "See You in Disneyland."

12. Patricia Bates, "Disney Parks Write the Book on Corporate Sponsorship," *Amusement Business*, March 28, 1987, 4; Douglas Gomery, "Disney's Business History: A Reinterpretation," in *Disney Discourse: Producing the Magic Kingdom*, ed. Eric Smoodin (New York and London: Routledge, 1994), pp. 81–82.

13. For example, on Kraft's worldview as expressed at Disney World, see Diana Mara Henry, "Future Food?" *Southern Exposure* (November–December 1983): 22–26; Stephen M. Fjellman, *Vinyl Leaves: Wait Disney World and America* (Boulder, Colo.: Westview Press, 1992), pp. 319–347.

14. Product association and coordinated point-of-sale advertising—for example, on Carnation milk packages sold to families with children—also help theme parks deliver the correct image to the right audience segment.

15. For a planner's assessment of the possibilities, see David L. Brown, "Thinking of a Theme Park?" *Urban Land* (February 1980): 5–11. John M. Findlay, *Magic Lands: Western Cityscapes and American Culture after 1940* (Berkeley and Los Angeles: University of California Press, 1992), pp. 52–116.

16. Orlando is thought to be the most visited destination in the world. On Orlando, see Fjellman, *Vinyl Leaves,* pp. 127–149.

17. Sea World's former president Jan Schultz, interview by author, La Jolla, Calif., March 19, 1992.

18. Adams, *American Amusement Park Industry*, pp. 107–108.

19. This rhetoric of parental control over recreation was paralleled in discussions of television; see Lynn Spigel, *Make Room for TV: Television and the Family Ideal in Postwar America* (Chicago: University of Chicago Press, 1992), pp. 36–72.

20. Travel to theme parks and destination resorts is increasingly organized by corporate employers, either in the form of conventions or "incentive travel," that is, rewards or bonuses to middle management. It may be that the theme park's corporate outlook is being strengthened, or underlined, by the corporate recruitment of its clientele.

21. Amy Wallace, "Like, It's So LA.!: Not Really," *Los Angeles Times*, February 29, 1992, San Diego County edition, pp. 1, 22–23.

22. Susan G. Davis, "Theme Park: Global Industry and Cultural Form," *Media Culture and Society* 18, no. 3 (July 1996): 399–422.

23. O'Brien, "Attendance Climbs," 76–78.

24. Ibid., and O'Brien, "Banner Season."

25. O'Brien, "Attendance Climbs"; and O'Brien, "Banner Season."

26. Michael Bristol, "Acting Out Utopia: The Politics of Carnival," *Performance* 1 (May–June 1973): 13–28.

27. Derek Walker, *Animated Architecture* (London: Architectural Design, 1982), p. 20. As Walker puts it, "[D]etail is the language that makes the land of believable dreams possible."

28. Theme parks do subcontract some performances and services, but on a limited basis. Shows using outside "talent" are usually written and produced in-house.

29. Adams, *American Amusement Park Industry,* pp. 106–107.

30. Historically Disney specialized in film and animation: so did MGM (now in a park partnership with Disney), Universal, the Rank Organization (now in a partnership with MCA), Paramount, and Time-Warner. But MCA is also involved with music recording and media technologies, as is Disney; Viacom owns MTV, VH-1, and Nickelodeon; products from these channels and many others are promoted in the Paramount parks. The theme park provides a context for the renarration and enhancement of filmed commodities, because it creates a material space and place for them.

31. To take a recent example, 1994 sales of merchandise themed to the animated film *The Lion King* were projected at as much as $1 billion, while the film's box office was estimated at about $267 million for its initial run. Claudia Eller, "A Peek at *Pocahontas* When *Lion King* Returns," *Los Angeles Times,* October 20, 1994, pp. F-1, F-10; Kate Fitzgerald, "'Lion' Is New King of Licensing Jungle," *Advertising Age* 65, no. 28 (July 4,1994).

32. In 1993 Busch contracted the William Morris Agency to represent and coordinate its Hollywood interests.

33. Thomas C. Hayes "Harcourt Near Sale of Sea World," *New York Times,* August 14, 1989, pp. D-1, D-6; Thomas C. Hayes, "Anheuser Is Buying Parks from Harcourt," *New York Times,* September 29, 1989, pp. D-1, D-16. The parks were sold for $1.1 billion.

34. Recently the name was changed to Busch Gardens, Tampa Bay.

35. The *Sesame Street* theme of Sesame Place is rented, with limitations, from the Children's Television Workshop, rather than owned outright.

36. Total attendance at the Disney parks far outranks that of any other major contender.

37. In addition to the four Sea Worlds, the two Busch Gardens and Sesame Place, Busch operates two water-ride parks, also in Tampa and Williamsburg. Busch Entertainment Corporation brought $55 million in profits to the larger corporation in 1992, up 22 percent from the previous year (but still less than in 1990). Richard Melcher, "Anheuser-Busch Says *Skoal, Salud, Prosit,*" *Business Week,* September 20, 1993, 76.

38. Julia Flynn Siler, "Even August Busch Can Only Handle So Much Beer," *Business Week,* September 25, 1989, 182–187.

39. Melcher *"Skoal, Salud, Prosit,"* 76–77; on Asia, see Evelyn. Iritani, "Beer Battle Brewing in China," *Los Angeles Times,* July 25, 1995, pp. A-1, A-9.

40. Growth in the beer market in the United States has been flat for more than a decade, with numbers of young drinkers falling since the 1970s; Sea World's family image certainly extends to Busch's beers, and it may help market "light" beer to women, one of the few segments of the market that is seen to have room for expansion. Seth Lubove, "Get 'Em before They Get You," *Forbes,* July 31, 1995, 88–93. Thanks to Dan Schiller for this point. The August Busch family of St. Louis is a proponent of wildlife management efforts, such as the Ducks Unlimited organization, which urges rational management of wildfowl populations for recreational hunters.

41. Cf. Iritani, "Beer Battle Brewing." Anheuser-Busch calls attention to its recycling approach to solid waste production in its annual reports, and in its brochure, "A Pledge and a Promise" (St. Louis: Anheuser-Busch Companies, 1993).

42. A Shamu-based television show remains a possibility. In spring 1996 Busch announced a new nature- and animal-rescue-themed television show, *Second Noah,* filmed at Busch Gardens, Tampa Bay. *Second Noah* aired on the ABC network.

43. Due to a series of bad licensing and media decisions, Shamu's uses have been limited to small ventures, such as audiotapes, toys, and children's pajamas. Unknown to Busch when it purchased the Sea Worlds, all the rights to the image were held by Watson General Pictures, and Busch had to purchase them separately. Kim Kowsky, "Busch to Buy Rights to Films about Shamu," *Los Angeles Times* January 5, 1990, pp. D-1, D-2. In 1995, an animated Shamu character could be seen in "Don't Trash Where You Splash"

television public service announcements. Sea World's public relations department claims Shamu has a "Q score" (the score is a measure of the warm feelings the character evokes) equal to that of Mickey Mouse. Dan LeBlanc, interview by author, San Diego, Calif., March 3, 1992.

44. Free Willy Foundation, *Free Willy: Keiko Adoption Kit* (San Francisco: Free Willy Foundation, 1995). On Keiko, see Jane Galbraith, "A Whale of an Actor in a Killer Part," *Los Angeles Times*, May 16, 1993, Sunday Calendar, pp. 23–24; on increased interest: Sea World's director for public relations, Diane Oaks, interview by author, San Diego, Calif., September 13, 1994.

45. Stuart Elliot, "Whale of a Promotion, by Southwest Airlines Is a Killer," *USA Today*, May 25, 1988, 1-B. Sponsorship partners' names were much more visible when I began fieldwork than they would be in the middle 1990s. For example, the penguin exhibit was prominently labeled the "ARCO Penguin Encounter" when it opened; by 1995 it was designated the "Penguin Encounter," although ARCO continues to be listed as part of Sea World's "family of sponsors" on maps and brochures. Sea World may be subtly trying to make its environment seem less commercial, in pursuit of an impossible contradiction. Another explanation may be that direct sponsorships were more important when the Sea Worlds were owned by Harcourt Brace Jovanovich. Anheuser-Busch's pockets are much deeper.

46. This may be especially important in an era of public concern over advertising alcoholic beverages to youth, and over commercial connections between beer, rock music, and sports. Beer companies' extensive sponsorship of rock concerts and band tours has been criticized by health professionals and advocates of drunk driving prevention. Paul Grein, "Suds 'n' Bucks 'n' Rock 'n' Roll: Beer Companies' Rock Sponsorships Stir Controversy," *Los Angeles Times,* July 30, 1989, Sunday Calendar, pp. 8, 85, 86. Budweiser has been the major sponsor for U.S. concerts by Mick Jagger and the Rolling Stones, most recently providing millions of dollars for the 1994 "Voodoo Lounge" tour. Anheuser-Busch has come under criticism in San Diego for the promotional uses of the park; see "What's Brewing at Sea World? Baby Shamu or Shamu Light?" *Prevention File* (San Diego County Edition, summer 1992) (published by UCSD Extension, University of California at San Diego, La Jolla, Calif.), inset, pp. S.D. 4-S. D 5. A protest flier circulated in August 1993 urged raised public awareness of "the mixed messages that are sent to our communities, particularly our youth, through beer company sponsorship" of sports events. San Diego Advocates for Responsible Alcohol Advertising, "Bud Light Triathlon? Athletes Become Human Billboards for Beer Company" (San Diego Advocates for Responsible Alcohol Advertising, Solana Beach, Calif., n.d., photocopied). See also, Jennifer Loven, "Spirited Group of Nuns Takes on Big Business," *San Diego Union-Tribune,* August 27, 1995, pp. I-1, I-6, for the Adrian Dominican Sisters' criticism of Anheuser-Busch's advertising to youth.

47. Joel Bleifuss discusses the limits of recycling as environmental action in "The First Stone: Pavlov's Pack Rats," *In These Times,* November 13–26, 1995, 12–13; see also Jim Schwab, "California: Fighting for Life and Breath," in *Deeper Shades of Green: The Rise of Blue Collar and Minority Environmentalism in America* (San Francisco: Sierra Club Books, 1994), pp. 44–76 for a discussion of solid waste and toxic waste in California.

48. Raymond Williams, "Ideas of Nature," in *Problems in Materialism and Culture* (London: Verso Editions, 1980) p. 67–85.

49. Raymond Williams, *The Country and the City* (New York: Oxford University Press, 1980).

50. Williams, "Ideas of Nature."

51. Ibid.; and Williams, *The Country and the City,* pp. 87–107.

52. Jonas Frykman and Orvar Lofgren, *Culture Builders: A Historical Anthropology of Middle-Class Life,* trans. Alan Crozier (New Brunswick: Rutgers University Press, 1987), pp. 42–87.

53. Frykman and Lofgren are arguing that late nineteenth-century Sweden was both particular and typical of the rest of Europe in the general development of its bourgeois culture. They view the recasting of nature in Sweden as rather abrupt and harsh, due to the rapid pace of industrialization there. However, the intellectual and ideological developments they cite were widespread. Their study is useful for thinking about theme parks in its ethnographic, emphasis on practices and customs of everyday life, as opposed to the critical study of fine arts and literature. They are able to tell a great deal about how nature was "lived" by its appreciators, and to contrast this with the experience of the peasantry and farm laborers.

54. Peter J. Schmitt, *Back to Nature: The Arcadian Myth in Urban America* (Baltimore: Johns Hopkins University Press, 1990). Mid- and late-nineteenth-century English nature appreciators invented the small aquarium to preserve and make visible the small animals and plants they gathered at the seaside. Lynn Barber, *The Heyday of Natural History, 1820–1870* (Garden City, N.Y.: Doubleday, 1980).

55. Schmitt, *Back to Nature,* pp, 77–95. It is notable that indigenous working-class traditions of outdoor recreation have been little studied (and little appreciated by historians of environmental movements) except where they have clashed with the recreations of the propertied. See, for example, Edward D. Ives, *George Magoon and the Down East Game War: History, Folklore, and the Law* (Urbana: University of Illinois Press, 1988). See also Schwab, *Deeper Shades of Green;* and. Robert Gottlieb, *Forcing the Spring: The Transformation of the American Environmental Movement* (Washington, D.C.: Island Press, 1993), pp. 15–46.

56. Harriet Ritvo, *The Animal Estate: The English and Other Creatures in the Victorian Age* (Cambridge: Harvard University Press, 1987), pp. 205–242. The literal nature of this emblematic function is underlined when we note that humans—for example, pygmies—were displayed along with animals in menageries, parks, and zoos. See, for example, Carl Hagenbeck, *Beasts and Men* (London: Longmans and Green, 1910) and Bob Mullan and Gary Marvin, *Zoo Culture* (London: George Weidenfeld and Nicholson, 1987), pp. 85–88. Imperialist representation through animals could also leak out of the zoo. From early on, London's animal dealers supplied wealthy scientists as well as the purveyors of popular city amusements. Exotic animals became part of an urban world of cheap recreation, joining older diversions such as cockfighting and bearbaiting.

57. Mary Louise Pratt, *Imperial Eyes: Travel Writing and Transculturation* (New York and London: Routledge, 1992), pp. 15–37; John Michael Kennedy, "Philanthropy and Science in New York City: The American Museum of Natural History, 1868–1968" (Ph.D. diss., Yale University, 1968); Donna J. Haraway, *Primate Visions: Gender, Race and Nature in the World of Modern Science* (New York: Routledge, 1989), pp. 1–58.

58. Ritvo, *Animal Estate*, pp. 205–242. The social history of the popular uses of the American zoo is much less developed. See also Mullan and Marvin, *Zoo Culture*, pp. 89–137. The San Diego Zoo features more modest, more directly didactic trained animal performances than does Sea World. Although it is a nonprofit, the zoo's revenues are also heavily dependent on concession sales.

59. The term *selective tradition* is Raymond Williams's, from *Marxism and Literature* (Oxford: Oxford University Press, 1977), pp. 115–120.

60. For example, Paul Bouissac, *Circus and Culture* (Bloomington: Indiana University Press, 1976); John Culhane, *The American Circus: An Illustrated History* (New York: Henry Holt and Company, 1990). For descriptions of nineteenth-century menageries, Ritvo, *Animal Estate,* pp. 206–213; on traveling menageries, see E. H. Bostock, *Menageries, Circuses and Theatres* (London, 1927; reprint, New York: Benjamin Blom, 1972); on twentieth-century American menageries, see George W. "Slim" Lewis, *The Ape I Knew* (Caldwell, Idaho: Caxton Printers, 1961). At Sea World, the techniques of animal training derive indirectly from the circus tradition, as I show in chapter 5.

61. Dean McCannell formulates the tourist as a pilgrim to sacred ideas in *The Tourist: A New Theory of the Leisure Class* (New York: Schocken Books, 1976). For a discussion of tourist pilgrimages to nature, see John F. Sears, *Sacred Places: American Tourist Attractions in the Nineteenth Century* (New York: Oxford University Press, 1989).

62. For an examination of the theme of touch and contact in Sea World ads, see Susan G. Davis, "Touch the Magic," in *Uncommon Ground: Toward Reinventing Nature*, ed. William Cronon (New York: W. W. Norton, 1995), p. 204–217.

63. Much to Sea World management's dismay, many of its activist critics view the theme park and the contemporary circus as identical, and call for limits not only on the park's ability to obtain dolphins and whales for performances, but on the animal performance and display across the board. For example, in 1995 animal rights activists and marine mammal protectionists put forward the California Marine Mammal Protection Act (California Assembly Bill 1737), which would have banned the display of whales, dolphins, and other sea mammals that had begun their lives in the wild. On the rationality of the park's displays, representatives of Sea World debated representatives from the Humane Society of the United States and People for the Ethical Treatment of Animals on "These Days," a local radio call-in show on station KPBS, on June 12, 1995. See also "Protest Held on Mission Bay Drive," *San Diego Union-Tribune*, May 29,1995, p. B-2.

64. "Sea World Attendance," *Amusement Business,* April 4, 1987, p. 20.

65. Each of the Sea Worlds commissions extensive market and "psychographic" (lifestyle) research on its customers. Sea World of California's market research consultants interview as many as five hundred customers per month in person and the department distributes numerous take-home questionnaires to others. Sea World's senior vice president for marketing, Bill Thomas, interview by author, San Diego, Calif., March 11, 1992.

66. It is unclear whether this identification is based on observation or self-description, and whether it refers to color, historical identity, or mother tongue. Leo J. Schapiro and Associates, "Sea World of California Market Research Summary," January–May 1992, Chicago, Illinois, table 203–1. The figure for the median income for San Diego County comes from the United States Department of Commerce, Bureau of the Census, summarized in an untitled flier circulated in 1992 by the San Diego Association of Governments (SanDAG) and the Economic Research Bureau of the Greater San Diego Chamber of Commerce. (A revealing contrast may be made between the $35,000 average annual income, which would include rents and investment income, and average annual pay, which was $22,956 in San Diego County in 1992.)

67. The 1990 federal census shows that San Diego County's approximately 2.5 million population is 74.9 percent white, 6.4 percent black, 0.8 percent American Indian, 7.9 percent Asian, and 9.9 percent other. In federal statistics, the category "Hispanic origin" overlaps all others; about 20.5% of San Diego county claims Hispanic origin.

68. Schapiro and Associates, "Market Research Summary," table 203–1. The average age in San Diego County in 1992 was 31.9 years.

69. In California, "gang members" can serve as a code word for minority youth generally. See, for example, Linda Deckard, "Great America's Gang Profiles Targeted by ACLU," *Amusement Business,* July 15, 1991, 1. Deckard reports that while Great America (in Santa Clara, California) rescinded its "gang profile" screening in 1991, metal detector wands are used on "every adult and child entering the park."

70. Frykman and Lofgren, *Culture Builders,* pp. 42–87; Yi-Fu. Tuan, *Dominance and Affection: The Making of Pets* (New Haven: Yale University Press, 1984), especially pp. 115–131; Schmitt, *Back to Nature,* pp. 77–124.

71. See, for example, Richard Louv, *Childhood's Future* (Boston: Houghton Mifflin, 1990).

72. Frykman and Lofgren, *Culture Builders,* pp. 42–87. When thinking about what children "need," it is useful to distinguish contact with nature from unstructured play or autonomous activities. In the case of Sea World, there is little that is unstructured or autonomous about the "nature" children encounter there.

73. Schmitt, *Back to Nature*, pp. 77–124.

74. While Sea World managers claim that their park has a broad audience and "universal appeal," they acknowledge, at the same time, that the price of admission places it out of reach of many. The managers all said in effect, "We know there's price resistance out there, but there's only so much we can do about it."

75. Frank Clifford, "Opening Parks to All of America," *Los Angeles Times,* November 24, 1994, pp. A-1, A-34, A-35.

76. Mike Davis, "Behind the Orange Curtain: Legal Lynching in San Clemente" *Nation,* October 31, 1994, 485. Sea World's picnic areas are limited, with small tables, and perhaps discouraging to extended-family outings. On the other hand, Sea World is unusual among theme parks in that it does not prohibit people from bringing in their own food.

77. Of course, none of the cultural categories referred to by Sea World and offered to its audience are stable. For example, although defined as a family-oriented park, in 1995 Sea World inaugurated "gay night," risking, perhaps, the disapproval of customers with a very conservative definition of family but gaining some attendance and good will from affluent gays.

78. See for example, Schwab, *Deeper Shades of Green;* see also Everett C. Ladd, "What Do Americans Really Think about the Environment?" *The Public Perspective* 1, no. 4 (May–June 1990): 11–13; on business reaction to wide popular concern over pollution, toxics, and environmental degradation, see David Helvarg, "The Big Green Spin Machine; Corporations and Environmental PR," *The Amicus journal* 18, no. 2 (summer 1996): 13–21. Helvarg's examples show that Sea World is part of a much larger and very well developed corporate environmental public relations strategy.

CPSIA information can be obtained
at www.ICGtesting.com
Printed in the USA
FSOW03n1607230116
16110FS